# Public Space and the Challenges
# of Urban Transformation in Europe

European cities are changing rapidly in partial response to the processes of deindustrialization, European integration, and economic globalization. Within those cities, public spaces are the meeting place of politics and culture, social and individual territories, instrumental and expressive concerns. *Public Space and the Challenges of Urban Transformation in Europe* investigates how European city authorities understand and deal with their public spaces; how this interacts with market forces, social norms, and cultural expectations; and whether and how this relates to the needs and experiences of their citizens, exploring new strategies and innovative practices for strengthening public spaces and urban culture.

These questions are explored by looking at 13 case studies from across Europe, written by active scholars in the area of public space and organized in three parts:

1. Strategies, plans and policies
2. Multiple roles of public space
3. Everyday life in the city.

This book is essential reading for students and scholars interested in the design and development of public space. The European case studies provide interesting examples and comparisons of how cities deal with their public space and issues of space and society.

**Ali Madanipour** is Professor of Urban Design and Director of the Global Urban Research Unit at the School of Architecture, Planning and Landscape, Newcastle University. In 2010, he was the City of Vienna Senior Visiting Professor at the Interdisciplinary Centre for Urban Culture and Public Space (SKuOR), Vienna University of Technology.

**Sabine Knierbein** is Assistant Professor in the Faculty of Architecture and Planning at Vienna University of Technology. She has directed the Interdisciplinary Centre for Urban Culture and Public Space since 2008.

**Aglaée Degros** is a practising urban planner and co-founder, with Stefan Bendiks, of the office Artgineering, based in Rotterdam. Aglaée has been the City of Vienna Junior Visiting Professor at the Interdisciplinary Centre for Urban Culture and Public Space, Vienna University of Technology.

# Public Space and the Challenges of Urban Transformation in Europe

Edited by Ali Madanipour, Sabine Knierbein, and Aglaée Degros

Routledge
Taylor & Francis Group

NEW YORK AND LONDON

First published 2014
by Routledge
711 Third Avenue, New York, NY 10017

and by Routledge
2 Park Square, Milton Park, Abingdon, Oxon OX14 4RN

*Routledge is an imprint of the Taylor & Francis Group, an informa business*

*British Library Cataloguing-in-Publication Data*
A catalogue record for this book is available from the British Library

*Library of Congress Cataloging-in-Publication Data*
Public space and the challenge of urban transformation in Europe / edited by Ali
    Madanipour, Sabine Knierbein, Aglaee Degros.
        pages cm
    Includes bibliographical references and index.
    1. Public spaces—Europe.    2. Urban policy—Europe.    3. Sociology,
Urban—Europe.    4. City planning—Europe.    I. Madanipour, Ali.
II. Knierbein, Sabine, 1977–    III. Degros, Aglaée, 1972–
    HT131.P83 2014
    307.76094—dc23
    2013017739

ISBN13: 978-0-415-63834-0 (hbk)
ISBN13: 978-0-415-64055-8 (pbk)
ISBN13: 978-1-315-88049-5 (ebk)

Typeset in Baskerville
by Apex CoVantage, LLC

# Contents

# Acknowledgements

This book started in 2010 in Vienna, at the Interdisciplinary Centre for Urban Culture and Public Space (http://skuor.tuwien.ac.at), headed by Sabine Knierbein, where Ali Madanipour and Aglaée Degros were City of Vienna Visiting Professors for the annual theme 'Urban culture, public space and the state—Politics and planning'. The yearlong collaboration, which included organizing a European conference on public space, was made possible by the generous support of the City of Vienna; the Administrative Group for Urban Development, Traffic and Transport, Climate Protection, Energy and Public Participation; and Vienna Technical University, Faculty of Architecture and Planning, Department for Spatial Planning.

In Chapter 2, while the text results from a joint research, discussion and writing, the paragraphs of this text have been authored as follows: Massimo Bricocoli: 2, 3, 5; Paola Savoldi: 1, 4.

The authors of Chapter 3 wish to thank Tihomir Viderman and Johanna Aigner for their feedback on the text; Georgine Zabrana, Richard Kronberger and Hermann Papouschek—all working for the City of Vienna—provided very helpful information. All translations from German to English are by the authors.

In Chapter 8, the author wishes to thank his mentors, Alejandra Bronfman, Ella Chmielewska, Sherry McKay, and Hans-Rudolf Meier, as well as Dov Berger, Margaret Critchlow, Fiona Hanley, Hanna-Majewska-Elżanowska, Channing Rodman, Sebastian Schmidt-Tomczak, and Jennifer Young for their insightful comments and multidisciplinary perspectives. Earlier versions of this work were presented at the Social Street conference (second edition), 7th Urban and Landscape Days, Estonian Academy of Arts, Tallinn, September 22–23, 2010. This research has been funded by the Social Sciences and Humanities Research Council of Canada. All translations from Polish and German are by the author.

The first research project in Chapter 9 was financially supported by Switzerland's Commission for Technology and Innovation (CTI) and the participating cities as practice partners, and was conducted by the School of Social Work at the Lucerne University of Applied Sciences and Arts under the guidance of Emanuel Müller and with the assistance of Barbara Emmenegger, Monika Litscher, Tom Steiner, and Flavia Caviezel (2007–2009). Chapter 9's second research project was financially supported by the DORE (DO REsearch) programme at the Swiss National Science Foundation (SNSF); the participating cities (practice partners) also provided funding (2009–2011). In Monika Litscher's research team, Beat Grossrieder, Peter Mösch Payot, and Marco Schmutz contributed.

The arguments presented in Chapter 12 are developed in more detail in articles published in *Transactions of the Institute of British Geographers* and *Urban Studies*. The authors would like to thank James Kneale, Russell Hitchings, and Ann Varley for advice in helping them to develop their arguments.

The research presented in Chapter 14 has been funded by the National Research Council of Italy (CNR) within the framework of the Short Mobility Programme and of the IRAT-CNR Project 'Urban strategies'. The fieldwork for the research in Belfast was hosted by the BERI at the University of Ulster—thanks to Professor Stanley McGreal—and was developed in collaboration with the author's colleagues Claudia Trillo and Alona Martinez-Perez. The fieldwork for the research in Naples was hosted by the Department of Conservation of Architectonic and Environmental Assets, University of Naples Federico II. The text was revised by Stéphane Fournier Mateu. The editors wish to thank Dominique Peck Tihomir Viderman, Corrie-Anne Rounding and Bernadette Williams for comments, formal check and language editing.

**Image credits:** 2.1, 2.2, 2.3, 2.4, 2.5, 2.6 by Giovanni Hanninen, used by kind permission; 3.1, 3.2 by Sabine Knierbein, based on data published by the Vienna City Administration; 3.3, 3.4, 3.5 by Sabine Knierbein; 4.1, 4.2 by Katja Hackenberg; 5.1, 5.2, 5.3 by Gabó Bartha; 5.4 by Levente Polyák; 6.1 by Mila/Jakob Tigges, used by kind permission; 6.2, 6.3 by Nikolai Roskamm; 7.1 by Chloë Voisin-Bormuth; 8.1, 8.6 by Hanna Majewska-Elżanowska, used by kind permission; 8.2 by Hanna Majewska-Elżanowska, used by kind permission. Archival photograph: Bundesarchiv Wehrmacht Propaganda Unit Inventory, 101I-270-0298-14; 8.3 by Hanna Majewska-Elżanowska, used by kind permission. Archival photograph: Bundesarchiv Wehrmacht Propaganda Unit Inventory, 101I-270-0298-12; 8.4, 8.7 by Jerzy Elżanowski; 8.5 by Franciszek Mazur/Agencja Gazeta, used by licence; 9.1, 9.2, 9.3, 9.4, 9.5 by Monika Litscher; 10.1, 10.2, 10.3, 10.4, 10.5 by Maria Anita Palumbo; 11.1, 11.2, 11.4, 11.5 by Khaled Hmeid, used by kind permission; 11.3 by Penny Koutrolikou; 12.1, 12.2 by Feiona Maxwell, used by kind permission; 13.1, 13.2, 13.3, 13.4, 13.5 by Noah Billig; 14.1, 14.2, 14.3, 14.4, 14.5, 14.6 by Gabriella Esposito De Vita.

# Contributors

**Noah Billig**, Ph.D., AICP, is assistant professor of landscape architecture and planning in the Department of Landscape Architecture, Fay Jones School of Architecture at the University of Arkansas. His research interests are focused on participatory and emergent design and planning, including adapted open spaces, adaptive land-use planning, generative design and planning, informal settlements, and perceptions of environments.

**Massimo Bricocoli** is assistant professor of urban policy in the Department of Architecture and Urban Studies, Polytechnic of Milan, and 2009–2010 Alexander von Humboldt Research Fellow. His main research interests include planning practices, institutions and local governments in action, housing, safety, and urban and social policies. On these themes he has been developing several research projects, consulting local governments and agencies and publishing books and essays.

**Aglaée Degros** is, together with Stefan Bendiks, cofounder of Artgineering (2001), an office for urban planning and infrastructure based in Rotterdam. Their work has won several awards, such as the Karl Hofer award of the UdK Berlin. Aglaée currently lectures at the Academy of Architecture in Rotterdam and in the past has been a visiting professor and guest lecturer at several architecture institutions throughout Europe.

**Jerzy Elżanowski** trained as an architect at McGill University in Montréal. He is currently pursuing a Ph.D. in Urban and Interdisciplinary Studies, jointly at the Bauhaus University Weimar and the University of British Columbia. His recent projects explore the concept of the contemporary artificial ruin, the politics of commemoration in Warsaw, as well as the re-use of rubble during the city's reconstruction process.

**Gabriella Esposito De Vita** graduated *cum laude* in architecture at the University of Naples Federico II; she holds a MSc in Urban Planning from the University of Rome La Sapienza, and a Ph.D. in Territorial Sciences at the University Federico II. She has worked at the CNR as a permanent researcher since 2001 and is currently coordinating European-funded research projects. She has taught urban planning in several academic institutions. Her research field of interest is the built environment with a focus on understanding the links between social transformations and city functions and spaces.

**Katja Hackenberg** is associate professor of civil engineering at the university of Cergy-Pontoise (since September 2011). She obtained her Ph.D. from the Fridericiana Technical University in Karlsruhe, Germany, and the University of Paris VIII in the domains of architecture and social sciences. She is an architect and urban planner specialising in the sustainable development of port cities. Her primary research interests include sustainable city, urban project, globalisation, and urban governance.

**Sabine Knierbein** is assistant professor and the director of the Interdisciplinary Centre for Urban Culture and Public Space, Faculty of Architecture and Planning at the Vienna University of Technology. She holds a diploma in Landscape Architecture and a Ph.D. in European Urban Studies. She has worked on public spaces for fifteen years, and has published in English, German, French, Spanish, and Portuguese.

**Regan Koch** is a doctoral student in the Department of Geography, University College London, and works in affiliation with UCL's Urban Laboratory. His research is concerned with matters of urban public space and collective life; his thesis examines changing social practices related to food and dining trends in U.S. cities.

**Penny (Panagiota) Koutrolikou** is elected as a senior lecturer at the School of Architecture, National Technical University of Athens, Greece. She obtained her Ph.D. from the University College London in 2009, researching the factors affecting ethno-religious relations in East London, while also working as lecturer at Birkbeck College. Her current research interests focus on questions of ghettoization, marginality, and inequalities.

**Alan Latham** is a senior lecturer at the Department of Geography, University College London. His research focuses on issues around sociality, mobility and public space. He has published widely in international journals and edited collections, and is the co-author of *Key Concepts in Urban Geography*.

**Monika Litscher** is a project manager and lecturer at the School of Social Work, Lucerne University of Applied Sciences and Arts. She studied social and cultural anthropology and international law at the universities of Brussels and Zurich, where she received her Ph.D. in Popular Culture Studies about 'Urban Sceneries'. She has worked as a filmmaker the Museum of Communication in Bern and at the ETH Institute of Landscape Architecture at the Chair of Günther Vogt. Her present research focuses on public spaces, new urban ethnography, and visual anthropology.

**Ali Madanipour** is professor of urban design and the director of the Global Urban Research Unit, School of Architecture, Planning and Landscape, Newcastle University. His books on the theme of public space include *Public and Private Spaces of the City* (2003) and *Whose Public Space? International Case Studies in Urban Design and Development* (2010), both published by Routledge.

**Maria Anita Palumbo** is finalizing her Ph.D. in urban anthropology at École des Hautes Études en Sciences Sociales in Paris. She has a Master's degree in visual anthropology and a B.A. in ethnology and comparative sociology from the University of Paris X. She is a member of the Laboratoire Architecture et Anthropologie (UMR LAVUE/CNRS) of La Villette School of Architecture, where she also lectures. Maria Anita is also a teaching assistant in social and human sciences at the School of Architecture of Paris-Belleville and Versailles.

**Levente Polyák** is an urbanist, researcher, and critic. He studied architecture, urbanism, sociology, and art theory in Budapest and Paris, and he has been lecturer at the MoME and BUTE (Budapest) and TU Wien. He is a founding member of the Hungarian Contemporary Architecture Centre and a doctoral candidate at the Central European University.

**Nikolai Roskamm** studied planning and urban design in Berlin and Venice and obtained his Ph.D. in planning theory and urban studies in Bauhaus University Weimar, Germany. He is now based at the Institute of Urban and Regional Planning, Berlin University of Technology, where he is engaged in the research project "Die unbesetzte Stadt" [The Vacant City]. His latest publications include "Das Objekt der Bevölkerung" [The Object of Population], in *Raumforschung und Raumordnung* (2013, Springer).

**Paola Savoldi** is assistant professor of urban policy at the Department of Architecture and Urban Studies, Polytechnic of Milan, Italy. Her main research interests include citizen participation in urban planning processes, local development policies, urban regeneration, and large-scale urban projects. On these themes she has developed several research projects, consulted for local governments and agencies, and published books and essays. Her publications include (with Massimo Bricocoli), *Villes en Observation*, Editions du Puca, Paris, 2010.

**Chloë Voisin-Bormuth** obtained her Ph.D. in geography at the University of Lyon, UMR 5600 Espace, Villes, Sociétés, and in sociology at the Dresden University of Technology. Her dissertation was entitled: *The Building of New Public Spaces in the Centre of Dresden and Chemnitz: Which Spaces for Which Society?* Her research interests include the actual conception of European cities; the new tendencies in urban design and urban art; and the relationship between collective memory, city planning, and preservation of historical buildings.

# Chapter 1

# A Moment of Transformation

*Ali Madanipour, Sabine Knierbein, and Aglaée Degros*

European cities are changing rapidly in partial response to the processes of deindustrialization, European integration, international migration, economic globalization, and climate change. Public spaces of these cities, as essential ingredients of the urban image and experience, are increasingly playing an important part in this transition. A key question concerns the role that public spaces are expected to play in political, economic, and cultural transformation of cities, and the impact of these transformations on the nature of public space as a shared resource. How are public authorities addressing the challenges of provision and maintenance of public space, both as a catalyst for change and as a common good?

Public space is a subject with a rising significance, and it is beginning to receive the attention that it deserves in urban research and practice. There are an increasing number of academic books on public spaces, which reflects this development (e.g., Carmona, de Magalhães, & Hammond, 2008; Carmona, Heath, Oc, & Tiesdell, 2010; De Souza, Silva, & Frith, 2012; Delaney, 2011; Eckardt & Wildner, 2008; Jonker & Amiraux, 2006; Lehtovuori, 2010; Orum & Zachary, 2010; Shaftoe, 2008; Stevens, 2007; Watson, 2006). The recent civic unrest and struggles in many European cities and beyond also show the everyday political and social relevance of the topic in professional and cultural practice (Drache, 2008; Iveson, 2007; Knierbein, 2011b). Public spaces are broadly defined as crossroads, where different paths and trajectories meet, sometimes overlapping and at other times colliding; they are the meeting place of politics and culture, social and individual territories, and instrumental and expressive concerns (Madanipour, 2003b). In this book, we investigate how European urban authorities understand and deal with public spaces; how this interacts with market forces, historic legacies, social norms, and cultural expectations; and whether and how this relates to the needs and experiences of their citizens, exploring new strategies and innovative practices for strengthening public spaces and urban culture. By bringing together case studies from Antwerp, Belfast, Berlin, Budapest, Dresden, Istanbul, London, Milan, Naples, Paris, Vienna, Warsaw, and six Swiss cities of Basel, Lucerne, Schaffhausen, St. Gallen, Winterthur, and Zurich, the book aims to fill a major gap in the literature in addressing the role of the state at its intersection with the multiple roles of public space and the everyday lives of people in European cities. With different backgrounds in anthropology, sociology, geography, architecture, landscape architecture, urban planning and design, urban policy, and urban studies, the authors investigate different moments of urban transformation in European cities with a particular focus on the public space and the challenges that face cities in this process.

## Public Space and Economic Revival

The opening words of the European Union's 10-year strategy, EU 2020, hint at the magnitude of the continent's problems: 'Europe faces a moment of transformation. The crisis has wiped out years of economic and social progress and exposed structural weaknesses in Europe's economy. In the meantime, the world is moving fast and long-term challenges—globalisation, pressure on resources, ageing—intensify. The EU must now take charge of its future' (EC, 2010a, p. 5). The deep economic crisis dropped the European GDP by 4% in 2009, reverting industrial production back to the levels of the 1990s, and left 23 million people, equivalent to 10% of the European Union's active population, unemployed. As a result of the economic crisis, European public finances have severely suffered: Two years of crisis by 2009 erased 20 years of fiscal consolidation, raising deficits to 7% of GDP and debt levels to over 80% of GDP (EC, 2010a, pp. 7–8). The economic meltdown continued afterwards and the crisis of the European currency brought the economic future of a number of major countries into question. Because the majority of Europeans live in urban areas, this also signalled an urban crisis and a moment of transformation for European cities.

The EU 2020 sets out a tripartite vision to get out of the crisis. The three 'mutually reinforcing priorities' of the vision were: 'Smart growth: developing an economy based on knowledge and innovation', which was to be accompanied by 'Sustainable growth: promoting a more resource efficient, greener and more competitive economy' and 'Inclusive growth: fostering a high-employment economy delivering social and territorial cohesion' (EC, 2010a, p. 5). The vision is driven by a sense of urgency in responding to a deep economic crisis; therefore, its emphasis is explicitly economic and its keyword is *growth*. Nevertheless, it demonstrates the interconnected nature of the social, economic, and environmental challenges that face European societies at a critical point in history.

Cities are engines of economic development—places where most economic activities of production, exchange, and consumption take place. Basing the future growth of the economy on knowledge and innovation demonstrated the transition from labour-intensive to knowledge-intensive activities, from manufacturing industries to services and higher levels of added value activities (Madanipour, 2011a). The transition involved expanding the information and communication technologies, supporting the development of science and technology, enabling innovation, and encouraging the development of knowledge and skills through research and education (EC, 2010a). Cultural and creative industries are also acknowledged as the drivers of economic development, from intensive use of information and communication technologies, to encouraging consumption through the 'experience economy' and shaping or amplifying 'social and cultural trends, and—therefore—consumer demand' (EC, 2010a), and to offering services to the innovative firms (EC, 2010c, p. 17). Innovation is considered to be the beating heart of economic development and transformation; in its different forms in science and technology, as well as in creative and cultural industries, innovation draws on the encounters between different stakeholders and the meeting of minds, which is partly facilitated by the urban environment.

The European strategy on the urban environment acknowledges the economic significance of urban space. The Lisbon Strategy had aimed at making Europe 'a more attractive place to work and invest', a context in which a high-quality urban environment could play a significant role, making cities 'of key importance to the implementation of the Lisbon Agenda': 'The attractiveness of European cities will enhance their potential for growth and job creation' (EC, 2006, p. 1). Therefore, the European ministers of urban development, in their Leipzig Charter, emphasized the role of public spaces in economic change: 'As soft locational factors, [public spaces] are important for attracting knowledge industry businesses, a qualified and creative workforce and for tourism' (EC, 2007, p. 3). In addition to improving the quality of the urban environment, public spaces are a necessary ingredient of any attempt at strategic urban transformation. The examples of recent strategic planning for European cities, which are based on large-scale urban projects, show the central role that public space plays in urban regeneration. As urban regeneration projects from Genoa to Amsterdam and Glasgow have shown, a focus on public spaces has driven the changes of use and an image of an urban area with significant implications for its revitalization and regeneration (Lecroart, 2007, p. 118).

It is partly for this reason that many cities around Europe have developed policies and projects for public spaces, paying attention to their urban environment as a necessary component of urban competitiveness. It is a vision based on competition between cities, in which cities behave like private corporations in search of new investment, a new workforce, and new markets; expanding their productive capacities is a prerequisite for this competition. This entrepreneurial approach has been widely adopted by public authorities, but it has caused alarm over its social, political, and environmental consequences.

The challenge that this entrepreneurial turn has put forward is over the nature of urban transformation: an emerging orthodoxy about the necessity of market-based thinking and continuous controversy over the social and environmental consequences of this approach. Public spaces serve as a vehicle of change, and it seems highly underestimated so far that they can carry various roles and symbolize different meanings at the same time. So rather than hollowing out the need for critical reflection on public spaces that are under pressure, especially during phases of rapid transition, how can we emphasize their potentials as bearers of this change? Do they serve as interfaces between local needs (Franck & Stevens, 2007) and global pressures (Knierbein, 2010; Madanipour, 2010)? Is their potential overestimated and instrumentalized by the makers of urban political agendas, or do decision makers and implementers rather underestimate the opportunities that public spaces offer to meet very different policy goals, such as combining social inclusion and economic development, which are the joint ingredients of the European social model? Is gentrification an unavoidable outcome of economic revitalization, or can ways be found that are not necessarily dichotomous and can illustrate the challenges cities face when dealing proactively with manifold paths of transformation?

## Public Space and Social Inclusion

Recent audits of European cities show an uneven pattern of urban change in which some regions and urban areas grow, while others stagnate or decline (ECOTEC, 2007; RWI, DIFU, NEA, & PRAC, 2010). The Second State of European Cities report, which used data from 356 European cities (including 47 non-EU cities), shows a changing population pattern in which the largest metropolitan areas continue to grow rapidly, while the regional centres stay almost stable, and the smaller centres and lagging regions decline (RWI et al., 2010). It also shows that in all cities the outer urban areas have grown faster than the core areas, either through suburban expansion or through an overall loss of population in the core. Lower birth rates, smaller households, and the ageing of the population are distinguishable features in many cities.

This population trend maps onto the economic circumstances of European cities. Economic activity and wealth are concentrated in core zones in western and northern Europe, northern Italy, parts of Spain, and the capital cities of central Europe, with 'an exceptional agglomeration of wealth in the capital city' of most European countries (RWI et al., 2010, p. 14). Larger metropolitan areas are also the location of the key administrative and political functions, with some such functions performed by the regional centres. Larger cities offer favourable conditions for the development of services, which dominate the urban economy, and the growth of knowledge-intensive activities. The report argues that the agglomeration process in the European core zones has not accompanied a parallel degree of poverty and disparity within those urban areas (RWI et al., 2010, p. 17). An urban paradox, however, has been noticed since the 1990s, in that wealth and job creation have not gone hand-in-hand in European cities: Employment rates are considerably higher in some second-tier regional centres, rather than in the largest metropolitan areas (RWI et al., 2010, p. 17).

Since its beginning, the European Union has emphasized the need for social cohesion to coincide with economic development. However, research has shown a rise in income inequalities within most member states, similar to the trends elsewhere in the United States, China, and India. Indeed, for most European countries, socioeconomic inequalities were higher in 2007 than in 1980, explained by the growing imbalance between pay increases and productivity increases, resulting in a decline in labour's share of added value. The low-paid workers, therefore, have not been able to benefit from upturns in productivity (EC, 2010d, p. 18). In this period of economic growth, fuelled by economic modernisation and labour market deregulation, employment has polarised and earning inequality has widened, without being offset by social transfers and other policies (EC, 2010d, p. 44). Research, however, shows that less-unequal societies benefit from more social and economic advantages, which is why it is argued that a new model of development is required that reduces, rather than intensifies, socioeconomic inequalities. As the development of the welfare state in the period between the 1930s and the 1970s showed, socioeconomic inequalities are not inevitable and they can be addressed: 'socio-economic inequalities are not an automatic consequence of modernity, they can be reduced and kept at bay' (EC, 2010d, p. 3).

Therefore, the challenge for the larger urban centres is managing growth, and for the peripheral areas it is arresting decline and stimulating development. Managing growth in the larger metropolitan areas involves coping with high densities, traffic congestion, atmospheric pollution, high costs of living, uneven distribution of resources, and responding to the growing demands on public services. Stimulating growth in the peripheral areas, smaller centres, and lagging regions involves keeping their economically active population and attracting new people by creating attractive conditions. Urban areas, however, are not homogeneous, and there are pockets of growth and decline in all cities, reflecting their patterns of uneven development. In all cities, the challenges of addressing environmental degradation, cultural diversity, and social exclusion are paramount. The global economic crisis has also intensified the problems of economic development and regeneration, which are on the agendas of all cities.

In the context of social challenges such as ageing, inequality, and cultural diversity, what roles can be envisaged for city authorities? As European municipalities have argued, problems of social exclusion are often created at structural levels, but city authorities are expected to address them without the appropriate levels of power and resources (Madanipour, 2003a). In cities, furthermore, what roles can the public spaces play to face the urban social challenges? Would it not be naïve to expect that public spaces be part of a solution to a structural problem? One answer is that the provision and maintenance of public space is part of the delivery of public services, which in turn is one of the central ways with which social challenges can be addressed. Furthermore, it is part of the quality of the urban environment, which is a social asset for all. In particular, the quality of the urban environment in deprived neighbourhoods has been one of the priorities set by the Leipzig Charter and other European strategies and policy documents, as a necessary ingredient of sustainable development and social cohesion. Building and maintaining accessible and high-quality public spaces in all urban neighbourhoods is one of the ways of making a city fairer and more democratic, in which all parts are given equal treatment and investment in public space is not a pathway to displacement and gentrification.

## Public Space and Cultural Diversity

An Urban Audit, which was analysed in the first State of European Cities report, set out the question: 'what is characteristic about living in Europe's cities?' (ECOTEC, 2007, p. 119). In response, it outlines a picture characterised by diversity:

> Diversity appears to be the main characteristic of urban life. A growing number of people [are] living alone, particularly in the core city areas. Families tend to be coalescing in suburbs at the periphery of urban agglomerations and this group too [is] following increasingly

varied lifestyles. Although city dwellers are considerably better educated than the population at large, the benefits flowing from economic wealth generated in cities is not evenly distributed. Many urban residents face the uncertainties of unemployment, social exclusion and poverty, and these problems are strongly concentrated in particular neighbourhoods. Life expectancy is also lower in urban areas, and this can be partially blamed on pollution of the living environment. Clearly creating and maintaining prosperity while ensuring social cohesion and tackling environmental problems continues to be the central challenge facing Europe's cities today. (ECOTEC, 2007, p. 119)

Cultural diversity is a primary feature of the contemporary European urban experience, caused by the breakdown of some mass routines associated with manufacturing industries, the struggles for more freedom by different social groups, the diversification of lifestyles, the opening of national labour and education markets, migration within and between European countries, and international immigration from around the world. In this context, European cities are pulled in different directions. On the one hand, cities are the historic creations of European civilization, their buildings and public spaces symbolizing the identity of cities and nations, icons around which proud narratives are echoed down the ages. On the other hand, the cultural diversity of the modern city demands adjustment and transformation to a new social reality. How far should the urban environment change to reflect its current cultural diversity, without losing its historic character? How can the contemporary public spaces signify the increasingly diverse cultural mix?

The choice, however, is not only limited to looking to the past or the future; it also involves a selection from the different periods of the past, deciding how far back to go and which layer of the palimpsest to adopt as the more authentic. Each of these past layers, meanwhile, is loaded with historic significance, with wars and struggles that may still be alive in people's memories. The question may be formulated as a dilemma between the eclectic diversity of the present and the authentic purity of a past. As it has been repeatedly shown, however, such pure identities have been imagined and constructed at some point (Anderson, 1991; Hobsbawm, 1990), and the dilemma becomes which narrative of the past the city should embrace and embody. This is particularly significant for public monuments and public places, where collective memories may not converge into one agreed narrative, especially when they are associated with collective suffering and loss of life.

Another way that the distinction between a modern eclectic identity and an authentic historic identity may be formulated is in the distinction between the centre and periphery. The centre is taken to be the symbol of the European city, with its often magnificent and well-kept monuments and public spaces, whereas the periphery is disregarded as bland, characterless, and insignificant. In their centres, modern European cities have displayed a peaceful coexistence of the old and the new, where simple boxes of steel and glass may stand next to an elaborate medieval building, and modern means of transport give access to ancient monuments. Rather than one historic layer deleting another, they sit next to one another, or even on top of one another, creating a complex urban composition. The centre may display a seemingly easy coexistence of historic layers as part of its identity, but how can the periphery make a more positive contribution to this multilayered identity? Should the periphery not be equally taken as an integral part of the European city's identity?

These dilemmas problematize the image of the European city. Much research has been carried out to portray the (ideal type) nature of the 'European city' or the current aporia related to the European cities, and the crucial roles of public spaces in this context (Clark, 2006; Siebel, 2004). However, there is a need for systematically connecting research on public space to an investigation of particular European cities in various regions of Europe in order to ask for their differing roles as important ingredients in democracy and as local vehicles for change.

## Public Space and Environmental Care

Public space provision and maintenance is a central theme of sustainable development in the European strategic policy documents. The Aalborg Charter, signed at a meeting of European towns and cities in 1994, sets the scene for the environmental problems caused by cities:

> We understand that our present urban lifestyle, in particular our patterns of division of labour and functions, land-use, transport, industrial production, agriculture, consumption, and leisure activities, and hence our standard of living, make us essentially responsible for many environmental problems humankind is facing. This is particularly relevant as 80 per cent of Europe's population live in urban areas. (EC, 1994, p. 1)

The charter identified the lack of open space as one of the main environmental problems, alongside noise and air pollution from traffic, lack of amenities, and unhealthy housing, particularly affecting the poor neighbourhoods (EC, 1994). The Bristol Accord, which was produced at an informal meeting of EU ministers in 2005, outlined the qualities of sustainable communities in Europe: active, inclusive, and safe; well run; well connected; well served; environmentally sensitive; thriving; well designed and built; and fair for everyone (ODPM, 2006). Public spaces are mentioned as an essential ingredient of 'cleaner, safer and greener neighbourhoods' (ODPM, 2006, p. 19) as part of the vision of 'providing places for people that are considerate of the environment' (ODPM, 2006, p. 18) and contributing to healthy and safe environments that are well designed and well built (ODPM, 2006, p. 20). In the Leipzig Charter on Sustainable European Cities, signed by the EU ministers responsible for urban development, creating and ensuring high-quality public spaces is one of the key recommendations for maintaining high-quality urban environments (EC, 2007). Open areas and green spaces are, therefore, 'important building blocks for promoting quality of life in urban environments' (EC, 2010b, p. 14).

The provision of public space is directly linked to the quality of life in compact urban environments. Urban sprawl is driven by individual search for better quality of domestic space, but with adverse consequences for the society as a whole through higher rates of energy and land consumption, higher levels of traffic, air and noise pollution, and heat waves and climate change (EEA, 2009). If unregulated, urban sprawl can 'lead to dependence on private car use, increased land-use and higher demand on resources, as well as detrimental effects on the services nature delivers to us' (EC, 2010b, p. 14). To address these problems, it is essential to restrain urban expansion, which can reduce transport and energy use and protect the countryside for agriculture, recreation, and wildlife. The compact city, however, needs to offer a high-quality and healthy urban environment. The European vision of a sustainable compact urban environment is one in which city centres offer 'safe areas, green and other public spaces, as well as . . . short distances to facilities and services', making them 'sufficiently attractive to counter urban sprawl' (EEA, 2009, p. 40). Provision of public space plays a significant role in persuading the citizens to adopt a sustainable way of life inside the city, rather than leaving the city in search of open space: 'Urban areas need to provide for their citizens the foundations for choices leading towards more sustainable life styles, such as affordable housing in more compact urban areas that provide high quality public spaces and a healthy environment' (EEA, 2009, p. 102).

The environmental, social, and cultural challenges come together when dealing with the legacy of the modernist road infrastructure and mass-produced buildings and their impact on cities. Wide roads had been cut through cities to open them up to the fast movement of cars. Now, with the awareness of environmental problems, the tide is turning against the motor car, taming it rather than seeing it as the engine of urban transformation. In this context, public space plays a key role in reintegrating the fragmented pieces left by these gigantic transport projects, reshaping the city for the benefit of pedestrians and cyclists.

## Public Space and Urban Governance

In many cities in Europe and beyond, public space has been reconsidered as a cross-cutting policy field: Some cities are eager to redevelop their public spaces in order to strengthen a strong plea for environmentalism (e.g., Antwerp, see Hackenberg, this volume), while others use public spaces as a means of promoting their competitiveness (e.g., Barcelona) or to supply a new meaning to a city centre in a regional context (e.g., Lyon). Other cities use the redesign of central public spaces as a means to shape new national spaces of representation (e.g., Berlin), while others try to promote a regional culture and local values via investments in (re)designing public spaces (e.g., Glasgow). Some cities try to provoke vibrant and lively images by changing the public regulatory frameworks for public spaces (e.g., Copenhagen), others develop open spaces in order to meet EU directives against climate pollution (e.g., Lisbon). Some cities focus on the democratic role of public spaces while trying to brand themselves (e.g., Oslo as the 'Capital of Piece'). Elsewhere, public spaces are thought to provide the ground for an educational mission (e.g., Cologne). These cases illustrate that many European cities have scented the advent of a new paradigmatic shift in public urban development. Sometimes this new emphasis on public spaces is used as a model for other cities, for example, in the cases of Barcelona and New York, where certain politics of public space are shaped and then promoted as a model for application in other cities (e.g., in Buenos Aires, Lima, or Rio de Janeiro in the case of Barcelona) or in Mexico City (in the case of New York) (Fessler Vaz, Knierbein, and Welch Guerra, 2006).

Public space, as this book argues, offers the potential to make a valuable contribution in addressing the economic, social, cultural, environmental, and political challenges facing European cities. The question, however, is whether the local authorities are able and willing to use it in that capacity. Although the politics of public space have been subject to considerable analysis (Fessler Vaz et al., 2006; Low and Smith 2006; Sadeh 2010; Tonkiss 2006), there is a need explicitly to address the multifarious and partly ambivalent roles of 'the state' as a social sphere and of state actors as influential stakeholders actively shaping the processes of public space production. How do state actors deal with manifold interests of citizens and market players in order to create a balance of interests? How is public interest cast in steel and carved in stone via public policies? How do planners try to 'translate' political programmes into everyday material reality within European cities?

Studies investigating the connections between physical space and democratic processes have tackled selected international case studies (Parkinson, 2011). There is also need to ask: Does the state always contribute to shaping urban places by democratic participation (Low and Smith, 2006)? How exactly are public policies framed, envisioned, and implemented to meet differing political goals related to democratic principles in European Cities? What are the impacts of such policies and to what extent do they take into account bottom-up practices (Hou, 2010)? Does the European City concept matter at all (Giersig, 2008), or does it make more sense to grasp differences in public policies trying to shape different public places in an eclectic Europe (Watson, 2006)? In the context of European integration and globalization, might public spaces serve as a framework for theorising justice (Fraser, 2008) beyond the nation-state and the Westphalian principle of national sovereignty? What scale and scope does an analysis of public space facilitate in order to investigate theoretical concepts of justice, democracy, and solidarity?

The various challenges that cities face place a high burden of expectation on their governance. How can a city's resources be mobilized to effectively address these challenges? The processes of economic liberalisation, privatisation, and deregulation, and the recent economic crisis, have reduced the scope and the capacities of the public authorities for action. The number and range of new stakeholders in urban transformation has increased to include many non-state actors. Taking action would require coordination among these stakeholders, putting in place effective governance for urban change while protecting the common good. The public authorities, in ensuring the delivery of public services, which includes public space, and in maintaining the social and environ-mental requirements of urban living, are still playing a central role in urban development.

Beyond the different social models that have characterised Europe, from the Nordic to Anglo-Saxon, Continental, and Mediterranean models (Esping-Andersen, 1999), some have argued in favour of a new, combined European social model, which can be an asset in responding to the economic crisis. The elements of this model would include employment pacts, social dialogue, and the redistribution of the fruits of growth. In particular, social dialogue is taken to be the com-mon language across Europe that can bring the different parties together to find a way out of the problems (Barou, 2012). In this context, public space, in its various forms, would be an essential ingredient in the infrastructure that can facilitate social dialogue.

## Structure of the Book

In this chapter, we have outlined the challenges facing European cities and the significance of public space in addressing these challenges. In the case studies from around Europe that will fol-low, we analyse the way public spaces have been approached by the public authorities in their interaction with urban societies. We explore the politics of public space in three parts, each re-volving around a main subtheme: strategies, plans, and policies; multiple roles of public space; and everyday life in the city.

In Part One (Strategies, Plans, and Policies), the questions are: How do public authorities address the growing pressures on public spaces? What are the issues, strategies, and tactics of dealing with public spaces, and what do they aim to achieve? Who are the state and non-state actors involved in setting the conditions for public spaces? How are they organized and what are the relationships between different actors? How are policies initiated, formulated, implemented, and reflected, and how do people perceive and react to such policies? How do design and planning professionals con-tribute with their projects to the changing conditions of public spaces? How can socially innovative practices contribute to redefining the approaches to public spaces as a common good?

Public space is where public life unfolds: art works are displayed, commercial messages trans-mitted, political power is presented, and social norms affirmed or challenged. In Part Two (Mul-tiple Roles of Public Space), the questions are: How do these different processes take place? How do public spaces accommodate these multiple roles? How are the conflicts of interest addressed? What new phenomena of social transformation emerge in public spaces? How do contempo-rary design and planning interventions renegotiate the boundaries of public space? What is the (changing) position of arts within public space between politics and people?

Public space is the realm of sociability. In Part Three (Everyday Life and Sharing the City), the questions are: How do public spaces address people's everyday needs and expectations? How are the boundaries between public and private spheres set, and how does this affect people's daily lives? How are cultural differences and social inequalities addressed in public spaces? How is local everyday knowledge taken into account by professional disciplines of planning, developing, and designing public spaces? What latent social needs become visible in public spaces? How can a fair sharing of public spaces be arranged? How do designers deal with the involvement of people in the process of producing public spaces? How do city representatives handle the 'voices of people'?

In the concluding chapter, we will come back to the main challenges and examine the responses from these European cities, looking for identifiable trends and patterns and searching for some answers to the questions we have faced.

# Part I

# Strategies, Plans, and Policies

*Ali Madanipour, Sabine Knierbein, and Aglaée Degros*

The chapters in Part I investigate the relationship between the state and the public space, as partly mediated through the urban planning and design processes. The chapters critically engage with the different types of approaches that public authorities have adopted towards public space: market-based (Chapter 2), state-driven (Chapter 3), collaborative (Chapter 4), and transitional (Chapter 5), each set within its own context and characterised by its own specific dynamics. While the material circumstances of the case study cities and ideological orientation of their local authorities may be very different, they seem to face a similar challenge of how to relate to the market forces and civil society actors in planning, designing, developing, and maintaining the urban public spaces. In the context of growing social inequality and the ascendance of market-based solutions to urban problems, how can the provision of public space continue without losing its basic meaning, functions, and character? What is the role and nature of the public space at this intersection between the different forces that shape the city? Does it become a means of gentrification and social segregation or of democratic participation and cultural expression? To what extent do public spaces become tools for enhancing the city's image and reputation in the context of municipal competition? How can the local authorities, as the elected representatives of the public, ensure that public space is accessible and open to the public in its full diversity, enhancing the quality of life and making a positive contribution to environmental care?

The chapters in this part offer insights into very different politics of public spaces in four European Cities: Milan, Vienna, Antwerp, and Budapest. Besides the classical notions of public spaces as central public squares, plazas, promenades, and streets in historic city centres, the authors deal with a wide range of places and processes, from street markets and local parks to major regeneration projects on the waterfront and in the city centre.

Whether public spaces play a role as catalysts for change for the sake of the common good very much depends on the quality of governance and society, as Massimo Bricocoli and Paola Savoldi explore in Chapter 2, which focuses on the city of Milan. In Italy, deep changes are affecting the design and use of public spaces and the very meaning of public open space is being questioned. In a phase of reurbanisation and of so-called 'urban renaissance', the physical and symbolic features of the new open spaces being produced under the pressure of the real estate market are expressing new conditions and forms of social and spatial reorganization. On the one hand, the politics and science are still strongly focusing on the quantities of green spaces being produced as a reflection of standards. On the other hand, field research reveals that more and more, the process of urban transformation is using open space to organize separation. Bricocoli and Savoldi's interpretation is that the spatial character of urban change in Milan is endangering some fundamentals that have made the European city renown as a place of emancipation and democracy. Trends in a new aesthetics of green open spaces are discussed as exemplary devices of separation within the development of a new geometry of sociospatial arrangements, a geometry which is recognized as a diffuse trend in the new spirit of capitalism.

Chapter 3, by Sabine Knierbein, Ali Madanipour, and Aglaée Degros, investigates the current Viennese politics of public space through empirical inquiry into how public policies are reframed and how, thus, public spaces are thought to be reshaped. Alongside an explicitly formulated politics of public spaces developed in recent years, why are public spaces overemphasized in one mega-project (i.e., Aspern Lake City), while they are completely silenced out in one of the most important projects the city is currently undertaking (the redevelopment of the new central train station Vienna Europe Central)? How does the city, on the one hand, frame public policies and shape public spaces in these projects of urban extension and urban renewal? On the other hand, how does the city try to reframe public policies and reshape public spaces in the already existing urban fabric? The chapter investigates the politics of public spaces through the relations between reframing particular policies and reshaping urban public spaces. It is based on a social under-standing of space and follows the assumption that Vienna is not unique, but maybe particular in its political culture to deal with structural changes on the macro level and (latent) emerging needs at the micro level. By contextualizing the politics of public spaces in Vienna with the very different ways that public spaces are shaped and reshaped, it offers insights into the idiosyncratic nature of ongoing policies and projects and gives a nuanced evaluation of these premises embed-ded in the Viennese politics of public spaces so far.

In Chapter 4, Katja Hackenberg focuses on the mediation between public, economic, and civic interest groups within the framework of the development of the strategic plan for the port of An-twerp. In the past, port areas were not only functional spaces, but also spaces for public life where the day-to-day activities of the townspeople, sailors, and flaneurs were played out. The richly deco-rated facades of the trading posts in the Flemish port towns are testimony to the eventful epoch when European ports transformed the map of the world. The port area today appears to be a purely economic zone and the public life of the town has been largely pushed back. In Antwerp, however, the lobby work of civic interest groups is leading to the recognition of the public function of the port area in the form of cycle routes, biotopes, and quiet zones. This form of public access differs from that of the past, but nevertheless amounts to the continuation of the historic use of the port as a public area. The chapter examines the mediation process between economic and civic interest groups, which are developing a joint concept for the use of the port area within the frame-work of the development of the strategic plan for the port of Antwerp. The chapter first discusses the different points of view of the civic and economic interest groups regarding the sustainable de-velopment of the port area. In the second part, an analysis is made of the role of the public port au-thorities as mediators in this conflict of interests. The chapter then introduces the different options for the use of the port of Antwerp as developed by the public, economic, and civic interest groups.

The former deputy mayor of Budapest saw open-air markets as symbols of poverty, a view that, as Levente Polyák argues in Chapter 5, reveals Budapest's dominant policy on urban public spaces. These markets are seen as places of disorder and disadvantage, undermining the pos-sibility of economic development and keeping away the hotels, restaurants, and other businesses looking for a sterile, optimistic environment. While the city authorities close down the open-air markets or turn them into supermarkets, however, the civil society actors acknowledge the mar-kets as carriers of cultural value, local significance, and social meaning. Beyond their primary function, these markets offer meeting places for local communities, where intergenerational en-counters and the exchange of nonprimary information takes place, where jobs are found and other forms of exchange facilitated. Open-air markets may be analysed from a multiplicity of viewpoints: On the one hand, they offer affordable fresh food, central to public health, biodiver-sity, and fair trade; on the other hand, they open access to commercial activities for people with a very low profit margin, often at the peripheries of society. The chapter identifies and analyses tendencies of the transformation of open-air markets in Budapest and discusses the multifaceted importance of markets in the urban ecology and economy. By focusing on the case study of the Hunyadi Market and the emergence of civil mobilisation in order to preserve the market, it also develops a cartography of actors engaged in shaping the public space of markets.

Chapter 2

# Urban Spaces as Public Action 'Made Durable'

## Open Spaces and Urban Change in Milan

*Massimo Bricocoli and Paola Savoldi*

## Background of the Research: Urban Space as a Concretion of Public Action

This chapter presents and discusses some of the outcomes of a recent research project commissioned by the Plan Urbanisme Construction et Architecture of the French Ministry for Ecology, Sustainable Development and Planning and coordinated by us at the Department of Architecture and Urban Studies of the Politecnico di Milano. The research project aimed to answer the main theme and question raised by the call for proposals, which is the following: How are contemporary insecurities influencing and shaping contemporary policies and projects of urban development in European cities? Our research project concerned two large Italian cities, Milan and Turin, and three urban areas in each (an area of urban rejuvenation; a social housing estate; and an area of new, large-scale urban development) that could facilitate investigation of the way public action is currently exercising its power in dealing with urban and social transformations in the face of the emerging frames of social and civil insecurities. Our first approach chose to explore and analyse urban policies and projects through the material spaces they produce. Moreover, we intended to stress the consideration of *space as a concretion of public action*, and we have assumed a definition of public action as the combined result of joined—and disjoined—actions and practices developed by public and private actors (Bricocoli & Savoldi, 2010). The focus on observing the 'concrete life of places' was to identify the missing links and lack of feedback that often manifest themselves in the process of conception of urban planning and design and its outcomes, as well as to offer insight on research in this field.

On the one hand, research in urban planning and policies, as well as in architecture, has been experiencing a sort of 'social practice turn' in recent years, which has been strongly affected by a descriptive attitude of social practices which, paradoxically, underrepresent the normative power that the design and organization of space display in social settings (Czarniawska, 1997). Georg Simmel has underlined the idea that 'the significance of space for social formations lies in its capacity of fixing their contents' (Simmel, 1997, p. 146); in this respect, our research has been focused on the exploration of the extensive and relevant effects produced by urban planning tools, regulations, and standards, and consequently, the production of urban space (Ben Joseph, 2005; Ben Joseph & Szold, 2005; Lascoumes & Le Gales, 2004; Lehnerer, 2009; Palermo & Ponzini, 2010; Salamon, 2002; White, 1988).

On the other hand, in the academic domain of urban planning and urban studies, most of the relevant research developed over the last few decades regarding urban policies and projects has been strongly influenced by an approach centred on policy analysis. This has undoubtedly led to a more consistent understanding of the processes at stake when different actors interact with the design and implementation of a policy or project, and, indirectly, the focus on actors has fostered significant research on social practices and uses of space. While *governance* has become a central keyword, and it is currently utilized as a term of reference, many urban scholars have backed away from the recognition of the configuration of space as a dense and complex informative basis in itself. Even the reference to 'place making' has become somewhat distant from a close observation of the character and features of the final spatial results of urban planning and design (Healey, 2010). The risk, as we directly experienced during the discussion of initial results with planners and architects, is to be misunderstood as over 'deterministic' whenever discussing the images of the spaces under observation, we discuss the relevance and the role of urban and architectural design in defining a setting which favours or inhibits possible future uses. Moreover, we have recognized that a policy-/actor-oriented attitude in research has reinforced a traditional and antiquated tendency of many architects and urban designers, which is to disregard the observations and analysis of designed space once it is 'in-use' (Geddes, 1915; Haraway, 1991; Pressman & Wildavsky, 1973).

In the following notes, after introducing our general theoretical framework, we will: (a) introduce some reference points in comprehending the dynamics and features of urban development and change in Milan; (b) present some considerations of the relationship between open spaces and urban change, which result from two of the five case studies investigated in the field work; and (c) discuss some interpretations of what we consider to be profound changes in current urban development in Milan, and the need to reconsider critically some fundamental ideas that challenge the characterization of this European city as a place of emancipation and democracy.

## The Embedment of Practices in Places

Parallel to what has been defined as a 'communicative turn' in planning (Healey, 1997), we observe that increasing focus has been dedicated to the fine observation of the ways in which social practices develop in the context of design and planning practices. In this sense, what is referred to as a 'narrative turn' in social sciences also influences urban studies and planning (Czarniawska, 1997; Gieryn, 2000). Several studies have been observing contemporary urban change through ethnographically oriented research.

This orientation toward interpretative description has often referred to the analytical skills and tools of geographic research; yet more and more references, methods, and postures are beginning to resemble those adopted in ethnographic research. Thus, many researchers have been involved in the exploration and representation of practices in the use of space. The contribution of ethnographic research to the development of the analysis of public spaces and urban development is clearly relevant, but two emerging risks must be considered within this approach.

The first is related to an unattended convergence between ethnographic research and the objects of research itself. Most field research has focused mainly on urban spaces that feature marginality, poverty, alternative uses, and, generally speaking, distinctive features, in comparison to action models that may be considered mainstream and dominant. Furthermore, the urban researcher working on urban public spaces has often been searching for anomalies and specificities rather than for the generalized, ordinary, and diffused features of urban development. At times these orientations result in a sort of misunderstanding, as an ethnographic orientation to the description of urban space tends to underevaluate the relevance of the 'normal' city, of ordinary urban development, and of housing areas that are attractive and welcoming to the urban middle class. More generally, we intend to stress the scarcity of research projects that accurately explore the normality of urban space and the modes in which the intervention in urban space is being understood. In fact, it is within these contexts that urban planning and design are viewed as ordinary practices and, as a result, forms and modes of organizing space are taken for granted and not discussed (Coletta, Gabbi, & Sonda, 2010). An accurate observation of the connections between space and organizing processes is relevant in order to recognize the way in which spatial forms are created and in which social organization principles are embedded (Gieryn, 2000).

A second risk that we may identify and stress within investigating social practices in urban public spaces concerns the little relevance given to the material context in which those practices are displayed, as if space, in its materiality, would not be relevant to understanding not only the *setting*, but also the nature of public action itself. When the scope of the urban researcher has been observing social practices, urban spaces have often be regarded as neutral within the display of forms of social organization, and not as environments that are in fact densely permeated by prescriptions and norms. Nevertheless, this orientation of considering practices as hosted and not embedded in the materiality of space is somehow very common in most social science research. Yet the risk involves articulating a very sophisticated analysis and understanding the dynamics involved in the use of urban space, which is disjointed from an investigation of the tools and devices in use when the constructed environment is undergoing transformation. Whereas the relationship between space, power, and use has been a central issue in the major work of Michel Foucault, the research group Sui Generis developed a pertinent project on the interplay between organizational change and welfare spaces (Bifulco, 2003).

With reference to an intensive fieldwork project developed in several European cities (Bifulco & Bricocoli, 2010; Bricocoli & Breckner, 2012; Bricocoli, 2009; Bricocoli & Savoldi, 2010), we have assumed space as a representation of social order. Hence, we have observed policies and architectural initiatives 'in action'. Although frequently the assumption is that urban space is investigated as an expression of urban life and as a display of social practices, this research perspective considers urban space as a visible and material dimension of public action, of forms of government, and of policies, not only those more strictly intended as planning policies (Bricocoli & Savoldi, 2010). The city, observed with a specific focus on the organization and uses of its spaces, may shed light on the current conditions of democracy and citizenship (Fainstein, 2010; Mazza, 2007). Urban studies can surely provide empirical evidence and arguments that may be useful in discussing issues that concern forms of government that use space as a tool of government itself, and thus may reveal a societal idea that is often implicit, normative, and rarely publicly discussed. The normative power of designing and organizing the urban space in which social practices of use are displayed becomes central, as well as the influence of tools, techniques, and devices used in planning regulations and in the design and transformation of the built environment (Ben Joseph, 2005; Ben Joseph & Szold, 2005; Lehnerer, 2009; White, 1988). The spatial configuration of places may be intended, in a sense, as an expression of the ways in which public action in the domain of urban planning regulates and governs urban transformation processes. The concrete geometries of space that urban design produces may prompt researchers to carefully document the relevance of the design of places in orienting and influencing its future use. Instead of leading to a deterministic approach, this scope generates more sensitivity to the material dimensions that actually create the interplay between *place and people*.

## Urban Spaces as Public Action 'Made Durable'

'Technology is society made durable'. Following this definition of the relationship between technology and society, proposed by Bruno Latour (1991), some further ideas may be considered in order to prompt a reflection of the relationship between spaces and practices from an urban studies perspective.

If we want to understand power relations and domination, according to Latour, we shall overcome the character and the forms of social relations and scrutinize the ways they intertwine in a field, which includes 'non human actants, that is actants which offer the possibility to hold society together as a durable entity' (Latour, 1991, p. 103). The examples that Latour quotes to argue his research are varied, and the perspective in which we would consider his contribution relevant is that of translating the analytical categories that he proposes, and of applying them to a discussion of the different components in the urban space, qualifying them as 'actants': sidewalks, buildings, open spaces, gates, and so forth. Let us consider the example recalled by Latour to make his contribution more explicit: The case concerns the innovation introduced in many European hotels of attaching a cumbersome weight to room keys in order to remind customers to leave their keys at the front desk every time they leave the hotel. The weight attached to the keys designs a sort of favoured 'action programme', which tends to become prevalent and which makes the behaviour within the organization foreseeable, as most guests will avoid taking the heavy burden along with them during their city tours.

In this way the hotel manager reduces the loss of keys, and with few exceptions, the clients adhere to the notice displayed on a board at reception ('leave your key at the front desk'), but which is far more effectively obeyed through the action/weight of an object. The intertwining of key holder and client activates a translation; 'leave your keys at the front desk' has now become 'you may get rid of the weight which is attached to your key.' One main factor in this understanding is that we are not discussing the objects and social relations, but the sequences that are temporary associations of humans and of nonhumans, and that one can frequently be substituted by the other. While considering as central the dimension of the intertwining between human and nonhuman, Latour proposes that we overcome the category of 'object' and introduces that of 'actant'. In the example he proposes, the key holder is an actant. The narrower the connection between actant and action programme, the more is its reference to a technological device; the more the object is available for an unforeseeable use—an arguably dysfunctional use—the more the status of technology is debated and becomes a case of what Latour calls *quasi technology*. Actually, the object incorporates behaviour, and to openly discuss this allows for an investigation and analysis of practices and behaviours that are somewhat predicted by the asset of the objects. In this way, the contribution of Bruno Latour offers a very relevant key to the understanding of current conditions that emerge within the connection between place and people. The materiality of the urban environment and, in this sense, of its specific asset, clearly orients and predicts practices and social relations, along with an interpretation in which the physical urban spaces behave like 'actants' (as does the key holder). In many cases, this connection can be loose, while in others it can be an obvious one. If we think of the typological conformation of a building or of the character of an urban space, it is evident that they influence specific action programmes and recall (strictly or loosely) the notion of technology (which is definitely the case when typologies and urban morphologies are tied together in projects like the Unité d'habitation, designed by Le Corbusier, which is proposed as a technological way of living). In the case of technology, the relation between actant, social relations, and social practices is so strict that there is no need of consensus for its functioning, as the consensus—the adherence to a specific way of functioning—is already embedded and inscribed in the technology.

Within this interpretation, the interest for us here resides in translation. While for Latour the main focus is on technology assumed to be 'society made durable', from an urban studies perspective, it is worth considering this definition of technology with reference to urban and architectural artefacts 'in use' and therefore to interpret urban spaces as 'public action made durable' (here recalling the previously given definition of public action as the result of joint and disjointed actions promoted by private and public actors). Moreover, this appears to be a relevant interpretation and research perspective in a phase that is strongly characterized by a diffusion of forms of 'government of people through the government of space' (de Leonardis, 2011) considering places as terrains in which projects, intentions, strategies, and public action devices are inscribed. 'Putting under observation experiences of projects, action, and government from the point of view of concrete geometries of places' could be the ideal image in representing the kind of research perspective we are developing, one that values the contribution of qualitative social research and ethnographical approaches, and is able to enhance research of urban planning and the transformation of the built environment. In this perspective, places intended as concretions of public action revalue the need to consider the imprint and influence that such places exercise on practices (Bricocoli, de Leonardis & Savoldi, 2011; Bricocoli & Savoldi, 2010).

## Downtown Milan as an Emblem of the 'Return to the City': Geometries of Separation

During a public debate in the spring of 2009, the former councillor for urban planning of the city of Milan openly proposed considering the centre of Milan as the *downtown* of the vast Milanese urban region. A clear reference to a perspective of valorisation and growth of the core metropolitan area had never been so evident. Population growth and overcoming the problems of monofunctional housing areas were indicated as clear targets. The reference to a category such as *downtown* indeed clashes with the reference to an *urban region*, which has recurrently been used in the recent years in the planning and academic debate to refer to the vast urbanised area that spreads throughout northern Italy and in which Milan (a city of 1.3 million inhabitants in a metropolitan area of 4 million) is definitely the centre of gravity (Balducci, Fedeli & Pasqui, 2011). Moreover, the reference to a *downtown*, like many other terms currently being used in the Milanese planning debate, does not take into consideration the implications and imagery carried along with it in terms of city centres that either collapsed and turned into deserts, recovered at the cost of a monotonous market, or that led to the development of city centres (White, 1988).

With a population of about 1.3 million inhabitants and a dense and extended urban region, Milan is the most important economic centre in Italy. Once considered to be the core of industrial production, the industrial crisis deeply affected the economic base of the city and marked a significant turn into financial, tertiary, and service activities. The Milan region witnessed a vast process of suburbanisation and sprawled development, resulting in a significant loss of population in the central city. While the peak was reached in 1971, with a population of 1,732,000, by 2001 the population decreased by 500,000, down to 1,256,211 (Costa & Sabatinelli, 2012). In the last decade, the city regained about 70,000 inhabitants, but this is mainly due to foreign immigrants and their higher fertility rates. Back in the 1970s, the main motives of residential relocation were the search for a better environment and safer living conditions. However, in the last few decades, the significant increase of housing prices in the city resulted in an exodus of many city people to the surrounding municipalities in the urban region. Although Milan is one of the most unequal European cities in terms of income distribution among its citizens (Cucca, 2012), this city is not particularly affected by spatial segregation in comparison to other urban contexts in Europe and North America especially. However, in the past 20 years, the overall conditions of housing affordability have been severely threatened by a booming real estate market and by a laissez-faire-oriented local government. Between 1991 and 2009, the average salary rose by 18%; yet in this time of booming real estate values, market costs in the private rental market have been rising up to 105%. While the city centre is the area where the richest inhabitants are more likely to settle, in the rest of the urban context the distribution of medium- and low-income inhabitants is traditionally 'spotted' (Bricocoli & Cucca, 2012). In the last decade, the constant growth of real estate values fostered by the market and supported by the local government led to a significant valorisation of the inner core and to the redevelopment of vacant industrial sites in semi-central areas, producing a consistent offer of private housing at very high prices. During the process of producing the new general urban plan for the city, the call of the past administration for an urban renaissance in Milan resembled a desperate effort to rescue the assets of the real estate market. Given the increasingly fragile conditions of this market, many conspicuous redevelopment projects, whose destiny seems in fact quite uncertain, were a main concern in the planning agenda of the administration that came to power in spring 2011.

As a background to the Milan planning debate, we can consider that urban and population growth is assumed as a strategic aim for several European cities (Ranci, 2011). The ambition, which is often explicit, is to return to the central city those who left it for a suburban location in search of happiness, tranquillity, safety, and lower housing costs (Menzl, 2010; Minton, 2009). Some population tendencies—an aging population in search of better service provisions, the increasing number of single households and of workers whose job opportunities are strongly marked by insecurities and irregular mobility—are in fact producing some new attractive qualities for the central city as a living space (Siebel, 2010). We have therefore assumed the reference to downtown as representative of the way in which the political culture and the involved actors have defined new conditions for urban development and for housing practices, as well as fostering orientations in planning and in housing cultures in Milan. While the reference to social and functional mixing is extensively used in the argumentative register of public action, the explicit reference to downtown suggests a more selective profile that aims to relocate people and activities—those deemed without value or function in the renaissance of the central city—somewhere else. As the growing interest and development of a housing profile of the central city produces significant tension in the use of space and in land use destination, a discussion of the role and future role of public open spaces is critical.

The main question driving our research and interviewing of many inhabitants and involved actors was the following: Under what conditions, and with what expectations, do people decide to settle in the central city? What sort of city space is being designed and produced? Two of the five case studies we have been analysing will be introduced and discussed in the following pages.

## So Close, Yet so Far: The Happiness of Suburbia in the City?

Let us begin with the Pompeo Leoni area of Milan. This case is representative of a set of interventions developed in the late 1990s for the redevelopment of five vacant industrial sites (in this case, a former Fiat plant). The space, with an overall surface area of 263,938 square metres, is very close to the dense inner city, with its compact blocks developed in the late 1800s. As was done with similar sites, the local government developed a framework agreement for redevelopment that aimed to determine fixed proportions for the new development of housing, retail spaces, and offices as well as for quantities of land to be granted to public use. The design and the redevelopment of the area therefore resulted in a partnership formed by public and private negotiations. The development provides an excellent case study in which one can observe the concrete sociospatial configuration that typically results from a market-led development aimed at the quick recovery of a vacant brownfield site and at ensuring safe and fast economic returns to the investor. In the words of a developer, 'any higher degree of complexity in the composition of building and functions may result in a more uncertain timeline of sales.' From a real estate–oriented perspective, this idea may sound apparent; however, the lack of public guidance and management of its long-term impacts in Pompeo Leoni results in an overall simplified spatial structure. The design of the open spaces is threefold: a central boulevard or promenade, and two parks on the two external areas of the development. While all the housing developments basically consist of individual buildings detached from the street line, surrounded by very small yards and fences, the green spaces on the sides of the boulevard are mainly representative (Figures 2.1 and 2.2). The two parks clearly indicate the separate nature of this development from the surrounding existing urban pattern. In fact, they act as a material and visual separation of the new development from the surrounding dense urban pattern. A line of high and dense trees on the southern boundary and the track of the railway line on the northern boundary stress this separation. In the words of many, this separation is exactly what produces added value to the project. In fact, according to several of the inhabitants, the distance from the disorder and chaotic environment of the city centre was the main motivating factor for moving out of the heart of Milan. Most of the inhabitants nevertheless stress that they were not willing to move to suburban areas, and that, as much as possible, they wanted to benefit from the

*Figure 2.1* Everything that is public is green, everything that is private is built. Pru Pompeo Leoni, Milan.

*Figure 2.2* Inner-city jogger in Pru Pompeo Leoni, Milan.

resources that the city core offers. Pompeo Leoni was a perfect solution, being so close to the city centre but still offering a vision of green open spaces and large balconies or terraces for private use and gardening. Interestingly, the interviews reveal the many paradoxes of the imagined nature of suburbs transported into a semi-central part of the city. The only retail provision in Pompeo Leoni consists of a large supermarket; the agreement between the city and the developers even stated that no other commercial activity was to be allowed for a minimum of five years. The spatial organization of the buildings, which are separated from the street line, in itself prevents the development of any further commercial activity. During the interviews, it was the women who raised concerns and criticism of the existence of a single and standardised retail facility and the heavy car dependency, even though the location is thought to be central. Hence, the location lacks the basic facilities and services one would expect in a city neighbourhood.

Moreover, conflicts are arising in the area. Any sort of unplanned use of the green public areas by unauthorised individuals produces upheaval. While the inhabitants lobbied for public green areas to be designed as flat and with the least amount of vegetation as possible (in order to have maximum visibility), there have been unforeseen issues with the space, such as the settlement of groups of homeless people along the borders of the railway track on the north side of the project; the use of the green areas by youngsters; and the noise produced by students living in the student housing block and by the clients of a successful nightclub. It is on these grounds that the inhabitants have activated themselves (Figure. 2.3) and successfully initiated a lobby for more police intervention and control. In a very emblematic way, the Pompeo Leoni case raises radical questions on the extent to which the production of these public green areas responds to any criteria of public interest and common good. More questions are being raised on how the expectations of these citizens—private individuals associated in condominiums of defensive homeowners—and on what they assume to be 'their open public space' shall be dealt with. The destiny of these open spaces, which were gained from the city as a compensation of market-led development, seems to be more the valorisation of the surrounding housing than any sort of shared use. No varying idea of use of public space exists, and there is no mediation; everything that is built is, in theory, public, and everything that is open is publicly owned, but conceived by the inhabitants as private, and expected to serve as 'empty green surfaces'.

## A Planning Disaster: Separation and Its Countereffects

The Santa Giulia project is a large-scale urban project for the redevelopment of a large industrial site. With an overall surface area of 1,200,000 square meters, Santa Giulia is located on the

*Figure 2.3* Backyard in Pru Pompeo Leoni, Milan.

southern periphery of the city, though it is very well connected with a metro line and a national high-speed train station nearby. The project was conceived and promoted as a new section of the city that would provide a new way of living in the central area, as the advertisement campaign was promoting the new development claimed: 'The aim of the project is to create a new city within the city, autonomous but perfectly integrated in the urban context.' As a sort of new urban foundation, the proposal was conceived as a self-sufficient environment, offering a range of attractive urban qualities concentrated in a commercial and tertiary area, which would benefit from the activity of a congress centre and a wide range of housing units, entirely targeting homeownership. Together with the overall master plan, Norman Foster was responsible for the design of the most luxurious apartment units. His involvement was also strategic in branding the attractiveness and high value of the project. The design of the large development as a separate entity was especially evident in the introverted design of the settlement, which clearly denied any relation to the surrounding built up areas and aimed to preserve the inner areas from any sort of 'contamination' by the pre-existing elements (Figure 2.4). In Santa Giulia, the systematic use of open space as a buffer zone allows different degrees of separation. The space was allocated to public use as compensation for development. It is systematically surrounded by private housing, thus its design absolutely discourages use by nonresidents. A large park was located between the southern part of the project, which hosts middle-class housing, and the northern part of the project, which emphasizes the luxury housing (and values) of the development. However, the project has been undergoing a major crisis, resulting in a lack of attractive functions that would induce anyone to move to Santa Giulia from other neighbouring areas. In the middle of the implementation phase, the developer was affected by the real estate and financial crisis and went bankrupt. The southern portion of the project has been completed, mainly consisting of cooperative housing developed for homeownership. The new inhabitants are literally trapped in the value they have invested in their flats, which they do not dare to sell because they have dramatically lost value. Moreover, the inhabitants are now stuck in a living environment in which the separation that was meant to preserve the quality and distinguished essence of the new development has turned out to be a great distance to breach in order to reach everyday services and facilities. While the stress on separation and on 'giving up' any connection with the surrounding

*Figure 2.4* Green roundabout in Santa Giulia, Milan.

urban texture was considered to be a strategic asset and a main rationale in the development plan, the inhabitants who settled in Santa Giulia now depend on the weak connections to the public and private service provisions that exist in the area. What has been constructed, in terms of public space, is literally deserted and explicitly reveals a simple surface organized by what was positively assumed and branded by the project to be 'the distance from the city (Figure 2.5 and 2.6).'

*Figure 2.5* Courtyard in Santa Giulia, Milan.

*Figure 2.6* Facing the sidewalk in Santa Giulia, Milan.

## Urban Planning and Design on Trial

While the aim of the research was to investigate and discuss urban change and transformation processes in a time of growing insecurities, our intuition was that a closer observation of the concrete configuration of urban space could help revive the discourse on contemporary planning tools and urban design in Milan, in turn readdressing their political relevance and the process of sociospatial organization to which they lead. We felt that the consolidated approaches to case study analysis of urban projects lacked a more empirical understanding of the connections between space and spatiality for society. With reference to the work of several scholars and to their complex definitions of space, far beyond the simplified notion of space as an object or container, it is the active production of space (Lefebvre, 1974) that, during the intensive fieldwork, displayed the implementation and consolidation of social interests. The relationship between the type of urban space that is being produced and its corresponding local society is of course nonlinear and complex. While our focus has been on the materiality of urban spaces—and in this respect, Latour's work and Actor-Network Theory can be very effective references—in accordance with Mayer we certainly recognize that 'sociospatial patterns transforming in front of our very eyes are the result of specific economic and social interests, of power relations and contestations' (Mayer, 2008, p. 414). In this sense, we have critically considered the sociospatial outcomes of the planning tools and programmes implemented in the case studies and the construction of places, as intended in their different dimensions of materiality, practices, and powers (Bianchetti, 2009; Madanipour, 1999).

The outcomes of the research presented in these pages have been presented to various audiences at several public events, mainly starting with the photographic work contributed by Giovanni Hanninen (www.hanninen.it). The direct confrontation with the visible features and quality of the spaces that the photographer produces have helped us realize that a stronger focus on city materialities could qualify the debate and discussion on the emerging issues that dominate urban studies discourse. Besides the recurrent reference to urbanity, social mix, and the need to avoid the shortcomings of monofunctional housing areas, which in the public debate have often been assumed to be an accusation against social housing estates (Bricocoli & Cucca, 2012), our exploration of the two cases revealed that in Milan the urban qualities intended in terms of a complex and dense urban environment are very low (Bianchetti, 2009; Sampieri, 2011). In addition, many of the features that are supposed to be urban qualities, in the consideration of the inhabitants, have turned into negative externalities of the city. While the central city of Milan still provides services and opportunities that are considered relevant, many inhabitants relocated to the new developments with the express wish of avoiding traffic, disorder, undesired social practices, confusion, and nuisances. However, between the lines, it is evident from the interviews that there is a desire to gain distance from social changes in the city that are very often stigmatised as dangerous, and these include the presence of rowdy youth, foreigners, and the homeless.

These expectations fully correspond to the treatment of the surfaces provided by the design and management of spatial transformation in the new housing areas: Any sense of previous industrial use becomes eradicated, and when a space is dedicated to public use, the range of possible uses is clearly limited, mainly through the normative power expressed by the design of spaces itself. The possibility of the coexistence of multiple uses of public space involving various populations is without a doubt considered a risk, not a valuable opportunity. Within the aspiration of a space that is flat and smooth, any unforeseen use eventually becomes controversial, and does not have a chance for mediation, thus producing conflicts that are immediately conceived and treated as issues of public order (de Leonardis, 2011).

It is evident in all the five different case studies we observed that the main issue in spatial organization that is gaining momentum is *separation* (Bricocoli & Savoldi, 2012). This refers to the physical separation made of barriers and fences, as well as the separation produced by public green areas that go beyond the rhetoric of depicting public spaces as 'permeable and connecting surfaces' in the urban fabric, which are expected to remain void, without any sort of social practice beyond the most simple gestures. Their role mainly seems to consist of buffering, setting a distance, and separating. Hence, separation is enforced by an organization of collective housing that is mainly driven by limited investment in the innovation of typologies, one that aims to avoid taking any sort of risk in merging and combining uses and populations in the same building. For the sake of the real estate market, which relies on separation and functional simplification as ways to reduce risks and unexpected complications, what emerges is an opposition between public spaces that mainly consist of open green areas, and private development that appears to be built and fenced, though no physical or symbolical mediation develops between the two.

This concept of separation is a sort of guiding principle for the social and spatial organization in the urban transformation areas we have explored. It is along the growth of fear and insecurities that this separation gains momentum. Moreover, the development of a new geometry in which separation and segregation organize new sociospatial assets is a relevant trend that is considered diffused and coherent with the new spirit of capitalism (Boltanski & Chiappello, 1999; Brown, 2009; de Leonardis, 2011; Harvey, 2011; Sennett, 2006a). In the face of a shrinking and often despatialised public sphere, as discussed by Madanipour (1999), the role and nature of new urban public spaces indeed raises relevant questions concerning the tensions and increasing polarisation that pervade democratic societies. The conditions under which publicly owned open spaces effectively act as public spaces should be more critically considered, for they are often assumed— with little discussion on the evidence of the final outcomes—to be standards of urban quality by ordinary planning rules and elements of public interest in the negotiation with private actors.

# Chapter 3

# Vienna

## (Re)Framing Public Policies, (Re)Shaping Public Spaces?

*Sabine Knierbein, Ali Madanipour, and Aglaée Degros*

> *Public spaces must be kept public as a matter of principle.*
>
> (Vienna City Administration (VCA), 2010, p. 5)

This chapter investigates the current Viennese politics of public space through the multifaceted relations between (re)framing particular policies and (re)shaping urban public spaces during the last decade. It offers insights into the idiosyncratic nature of recent policies and projects and gives a nuanced evaluation of these processes. By public policies for public space, we mean the diverse public programmes and pamphlets, strategies and actions organized by the elected politicians and their technical staff pursuing a vision of future urban development based on the multiple roles of public spaces. Drawing on a relational understanding of space (Lefebvre, 1991), the chapter follows the assumption that Vienna is not unlike the mainstream of cities (Dangschat & Hamedinger, 2009), but—as any other city—specific in its political culture to deal with structural changes on the macro level and its (latent) emerging needs on the micro level.

Framing public policies relates to agenda setting processes in urban politics. We aim to identify which themes related to public spaces have been recently promoted, and how they become relevant for specific or general public policies. We undertook a qualitative analysis of selected programmes and pamphlets, tackling public spaces and an investigation of public spaces' relevance in strategic urban planning projects. This twofold analysis was based on the hypothesis that convergences and divergences can both be detected between political discourse and planning practice. The following research questions are guiding the investigation, first, in terms of framing general policies for public space and, second, concerning the specific importance of shaping public spaces in particular strategic planning projects: What is the role and meaning of public spaces on the urban political agenda? Which administrative sectors are particularly interested in promoting public spaces?

Finally, three questions will help to link the findings on framing urban policies to the shaping of public spaces: Which processes of (re)shaping public spaces are foreseen in selected strategic urban planning projects? Are the proceedings and expected results of these processes consistent with the (re)framed policies? Are there any (assumed) special benefits or disadvantages for the local population?

## Politics of Public Space

### Public Spaces and the Urban Political Agenda

In many cities in Europe and beyond, public space has been reconsidered as a cross-cutting policy field: Some cities are eager to redevelop their public spaces in order to fulfil multiple objectives at the same time (see Chapter 1). Vienna has only recently joined this canon with an explicit political agenda for public spaces. Apparently, the Vienna City Administration (VCA) follows a particular type of politics of public space in order to accommodate structural changes more smoothly and to pursue a political balance between quite differing political goals (e.g., 'social cohesion', 'economic competitiveness', 'ecological sustainability', etc.). Slowness and reluctance in reacting to current international trends is considered as one of the inherent features of Vienna, a conservative capital city that has been ruled by a social-democratic regime for decades, and has had a social-democratic/green city government coalition since 2010.

Public spaces can be interpreted as places where the intersection of global urban processes and local tendencies becomes manifest, both in terms of space and politics. Processes of scaling become palpable here, which is why they serve as a sphere for both analysis and action (Knierbein, 2010). While political interaction in public spaces is inseparably related to civic unrest and to the creation of counter publics, public spaces are increasingly used (again) as spheres for promoting political ideas by public authorities, too. In a transforming urban Europe, public spaces offer a vast sphere for political discourse and for political action where city administrations try to balance different political motives because it seems that they can be met here at the same time. Yet in practice they are hardly compatible with each other.

We use these ambivalent aspects to analyse the vision of public space explicitly promoted in Vienna and the reality of implementing three ambitious strategic planning projects: Aspern Lakeside Project (ALP), Main Station Project (MSP), and Schwedenplatz-Morzinplatz Project (SMP).

## Vienna

### A City of Unequal Parts

Although Vienna is a compact and spatially integrated city state comprising both the federal state and municipal administrations, a close inspection reveals significant forms of inequality, in people's minds as well as in terms of space. The city is subdivided into 23 districts, each with a socioeconomic and cultural character well known to the city's residents. The urban space is organized in a concentric pattern surrounded, as if protected, by two ring roads, the *Ringstrasse* and the *Gürtel* (Figure 3.1). The centre of the city, known as *Erster Bezirk* (1st District), is the historic core and primarily represents the city's cultural traditions and wealth. It is separated from the remaining urban fabric by the *Donaukanal* (Danube Canal) and the famous Ringstrasse. This ring road was developed in the 19th century on the wide belt that separated the historic city from its suburbs. Further comfortable districts surrounding the Ringstrasse are enveloped, in turn, by the Gürtel (belt), the outer ring road that separates them from the peripheral districts.

The passage beyond this second concentric road to an area such as *Favoriten* (10th District) is not only a physical journey into another part of the city; it is also a mental journey into what is perceived as a separate part. The metro line U1 that connects the 1st and 10th Districts in the southern direction appears to move from one world into another. This impression is reinforced when people travel from the 1st District to what is colloquially called *Transdanubien* ('on the other side of the Danube'), a suburban area comprising *Floridsdorf* (21st District) and *Donaustadt* (22nd District). To many Viennese living on the western side of the river, Transdanubia represents an unknown eastern territory rather than an integral part of their own city. Both Favoriten and Donaustadt, where two of the case studies are located, are among the largest Viennese districts, comprising together nearly one third of the urban territory. In terms of population, these two largest districts of Vienna house around 19.61% of the registered urban population (VCA Online, 2011), with further unregistered residents. In the 1st District, by comparison, less than 1% of the Viennese live on less than 1% of the urban territory (VCA Online, 2011).

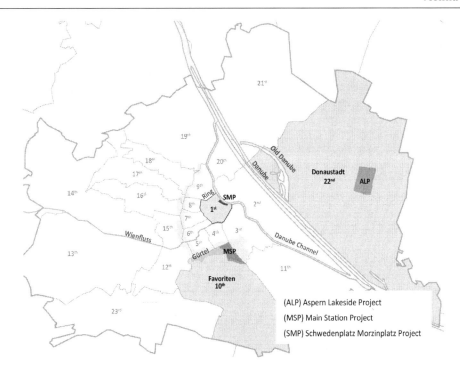

*Figure 3.1* The location of the three project areas of (a) Aspern Lakeside Project (ALP), (b) Schwedenplatz-Morzinplatz Project (SMP), and (c) Main Station Project (MSP) in Vienna.

The overall material quality of public spaces in the peripheral districts is far lower than that in the central district, despite nuances within each district. Inequality in the provision of public spaces can be generally depicted by the level of wealth invested, the diversity of population addressed, the quality of space produced, the degree of attention paid to details, and the overall redistribution of tax money invested for public spaces among the districts in relation to their inhabitants.

Before municipal elections, minor investments reshaped the most frequented areas, such as the *Favoritenstrasse* in 2005 and 2010. Yet when analysing a map of the *50 Orte Programm* (50 places programme) focusing on design interventions in selected public spaces in Vienna between 2001–2012, only two of the approximately 50 implemented projects were located in Favoriten, and none were in Donaustadt, whereas 12 projects were realized in the 1st District (Figure 3.2). Although the municipality has catered for the reshaping of 325,000 m2 of public spaces in total, and thus has provided a general quantitative improvement of public spaces, the programme results also illustrate a twisted relation in terms of quality: The bigger the districts and the larger their population, the less the reshaping of public spaces is in the focus of public policies and of public investments. This is nothing completely new, as many cities are characterised by an unequal distribution of public efforts between the city centre and the periphery (Madanipour, 2010).

Due to high rates of inward migration, urban growth in a consolidated and dense city like Vienna is likely to happen on the urban fringes or at the infrastructural conversion sites at the interfaces between centre and periphery. Central sites have come under great transformative pressure and are subject to redesign interventions in order to meet new challenges, too. That is why we focus on three projects set in three different parts of the city: the Aspern Lakeside Project (ALP; a new town in the periphery of Donaustadt), the Schwedenplatz-Morzinplatz Project

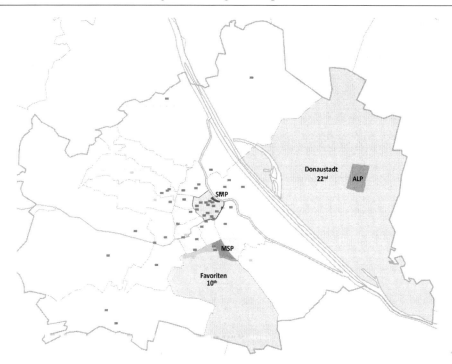

*Figure 3.2* Map of the '50 places programme' in Vienna: the unequal distribution of so far realized urban and landscape design projects in public spaces.

(SMP; a square at the borders of the Erster Bezirk), and the Main Station Project (MSP; a huge urban development project at the Gürtel on the edge of the city centre).

## A Particular Political Culture in Vienna

Vienna has been coined as a specific city as regards its socially oriented urban development paths and its relatively modest pace of change. The municipality has used the motto 'Vienna Is Different' for its marketing purposes since 1988. Dangschat and Hamedinger (2009, p. 95f) state that 'Vienna was always "unlike" the mainstream, either as a latecomer compared to other European capitals or late in its trends as the capital of Austria, very often forming general trends into specific "Austro"-styles', while depicting that the Austrian capital follows a 'third way of modernisation' by 'trying to reconcile its social-democratic orientations and values which are deeply inscribed in its political structures, with an increasingly competitive strategy'. Vienna tries to stand out by relying on a series of distinctions, which are (coincidentally) historically captured in the motto. This renders Vienna less 'unlike' than promoted, as the city reacts to growing challenges of economic globalisation and Europeanisation and steadily develops into a central European hub for different migratory flows, with public spaces being key sites for coping with these transformations (Knierbein, Aigner, & Watson, 2012).

Besides these reactions to general macro-societal tendencies, there are many specific aspects on how Vienna adapts to global and European macro dynamics beyond its conservative social-democratic attitude towards change in general: the (still) strong position of the state in (usually policy driven) urban development; the neo-corporatist tradition; the investment and assets policy of the public administration (the municipality is still one of the biggest public housing stock owners in Europe); and, finally, the strong focus on a fair redistribution of tax revenue into public services. In addition, the municipality has not yet fallen into the euphoria of vastly introducing new public management concepts and the entrepreneurial city philosophy, which structurally contribute to the hollowing out of the state.

Yet critical voices have tried to come to terms with ruptures in the social-democratic philosophy that have been happening since the early 1980s in particular (De Frantz, 2005; El Khafif, 2009; Novy, Redak, Jäger, & Hamedinger, 2001; Seiß, 2013), when the city decided to withdraw from public housing construction. This focus on public housing as *the* integral part of Vienna's urban development policies has been partly redirected to public spaces, both publicly accessible open as well as covered spaces. A first indicator for this trend can be found in the so-called *Stadtentwicklungsplan* 1994 (StEP 94; (VCA 1994), urban development plan) highlighting the 'Right to a secure life' by promoting a 'modern and action-oriented planning approach based on prevention, planning, development, design and care for public spaces and reinforcement of the development of civil society' (Pirhofer & Stimmer, 2007, p. 132).

## (Re)Framing Public Policies

### *Specific Programmes*

Vienna recently started to develop its urban development policies with a strong emphasis on public spaces. Various specific programmes show this turn explicitly: Based on understanding public space as social space, the 'Integration in Public Space' report was produced in 2006 by the municipality in collaboration with the planning studio 'kon-text' and the Centre of Sociology at Vienna University of Technology. Grounded in an analysis of existing studies on public spaces, it indicates a new tendency that has become obvious since 2002, namely that these studies have partly overcome narrow analytical frameworks and have depicted arenas for action that go beyond the traditional spatial understanding of planners (cf. VCA, 2006, p. 37). It sharpens the set of instruments required to professionalise such endeavours by introducing the so-called *Sozialraumanalyse* (social space analysis) as a tool for social urban research. It states that two 'integration machines', that is, the labour and housing markets, have lost their original strength as spheres for systemic integration. As cities can hardly steer the systemic integration because their influence on national labour market policies appears to be quite limited, and as Vienna's particularly strong role in housing markets has been (slightly) diminishing, public spaces have increasingly been rendered a core policy field for social integration and neighbourhood cohesion in Vienna (2006, p. 30f).

The report 'New Interpretation of Public Space' was produced by a local office, Schwarz Architects, which conducted empirical research on selected public spaces between 1999 and 2008 (VCA, 2008b), illustrating contemporary challenges for local public spaces that were turned into a long-term vision for political decision makers in need of tools for steering urban development. Primarily tackling districts 3 to 9, the ambitious objective of the report is to raise the awareness of all districts' political elites in understanding public space as an important topic on their local political agendas.

'Free Space Vienna Public Space', produced by the municipality, presents an interdisciplinary approach to the introduction of public space as a cross-cutting policy and action field for planning. Initiated and managed by the Municipal Department for Architecture and Urban Design (MA19), its preparations involved various experts working for the local districts and members of 25 different municipal departments. The resulting 'Mission Statement for Public Space in Vienna' contains the elaboration of quality standards for planning interventions, reflecting the process design of how these have come into being through cooperation among different people and sections. It claims to be more than just a technical directive; it explicitly 'exposes the attitude of the Urban Development Department in Vienna towards the development of public spaces' (VCA, 2009a, p. 5). It states that planning public space should combine aesthetic qualities with 'social intelligence', which means 'taking the needs of various groups into account and developing adequate design and construction measures. . . . Design can . . . be measured as the extent to which it serves the users' interests . . . : social space analysis and participating observations prior to the actual planning . . . are important requirements for turning design and planning into a learning system' (VCA, 2010, p. 8).

The 'Public Space Score' has been developed by Gehl Architects (Denmark) and tackles the public spaces of the ALP case. It was produced shortly after the ALP's master plan to pave the way for new approaches to strategic planning. Traffic planners and other disciplines now have to comply with its premises to safeguard a quantity of public spaces for the future, as public land is prioritised for offering urban development stimuli. The Viennese administrative and academic elites have appreciated the report as intent to change standard and static procedures of the formal planning system allowing for planning innovation by introducing the focus on public spaces directly after the master plan (Wien International Homepage, 2011). Yet although the report starts with a William Whyte citation on the importance of people for public spaces, its main focus is a culturally themed landscape architectural approach that does not offer clear ideas either on the social composition of the new city district or on the process design for the future community-based development of public spaces. It acknowledges that inner cities have usually grown over centuries by adapting to the changing needs of their inhabitants. However, in the ALP case, there is no time for such a smooth development, and that is why a strong focus is put on the potential that public spaces might bear for provoking a precious resource, that is, public life (cf. Gehl Architects in VCA, 2009c, p. 5). The report supports the establishment of the ALP's seemingly inclusive, albeit not less ambivalent branding strategy that is issued via a creative, arts-based approach to performative planning.

### General Pamphlets

As the sequence of these reports shows, there has been a specific endeavour by the municipality's Urban Development Department to promote an advanced understanding of public spaces over the last decade. A similar shift can be detected on the more general level of urban development policies: Whereas the urban development plan 'StEP 05' (VCA, 2005, p. 63) dealt with public spaces in an early post-Fordist fashion by highlighting the overcoming of car-oriented planning schemes, public design of street furniture, and a necessary regulation of outdoor advertisement in a quantitative manner, the new 'StEP 25' is likely to assign a new qualitative relevance to public spaces as catalysts for change and embraces public space as one of eight future transversal action fields for an advanced post-Fordist urban development policy (VCA, forthcoming 2013). The process design for developing the StEP 25 includes the establishment of four working groups, each hosting members of districts from the urban periphery, the middle-ranged districts, and the city centre, besides VCA staff, thus marking a more participatory approach to strategic cross-boundary cooperation.

Another incentive by the municipality to substantiate this paradigmatic shift towards public spaces on the overall urban political agenda in Vienna is the so-called 'Vienna Charter'. 'Based on a broad participatory process, the Viennese developed a paper defining seven core areas that are of vital importance for living together in Vienna' (Charta Wien Online, 2012b; VCA Online, 2013c; Wien International Homepage, 2012). The process was launched in 2012, comprising 12,700 hours of debates that have been (self)organized in 651 groups by approximately 8,500 people, many of whom received public funding for translation in order to foster intercultural dialogue (cf. Charta Wien Online, 2012a). One of these core fields defined is public space, to which 'the Viennese citizens attach great importance' as it 'should offer room and opportunities for different activities, e.g. meeting other people' in noncommercial places. 'Emphasis should be placed on sitting down to discuss and share things, rather than on virtual communication' (Wien International Homepage, 2012). Only recently finalised, the charter seemingly has raised international attention even before final results have been published, as it has been considered a positive example in the context of 'non-discrimination at all levels' by the UN-Habitat Study on World Cities' Prosperity (United Nations Human Settlements Programme, 2012, p. 74; VCA Online, 2013c).

Vienna has not only been facing a shift in specific policies in favour of public spaces as a transversal theme influencing current urban development policies, but the city is also understood as an unusual case where the general framing of an overall politics of public space has been informed by a particular theme intensively promoted by the technical staff of the municipal Urban Development Department for over a decade. Introducing public space was used as a strategic intent to create cross-departmental networks and establish new routines of interdistrict cooperation and transdisciplinary workflows. Nowadays, public space is not only one of the sectoral fields on the Viennese urban development agenda, but is also becoming one of the main themes of crosscutting urban policy in Vienna in general, thus marking a general shift of political premises. In order to test the robustness of such paradigmatic shifts in urban political discourses, we will now investigate three case studies of strategic urban planning.

## (Re)Shaping Public Spaces

### Controversial Perspectives

In the previous part, the 'Public Space Score' showed crucial entanglements between (re)framing public policies and (re)shaping public spaces. This section digs deeper and questions the relevance of shaping public spaces in three strategic planning projects (Figure 3.1). As all three are currently undergoing preparation and/or implementation (initial to advanced stages), a final analysis of the outcome is not yet possible. We will focus on documents and people that contribute to the realization of these projects (understood as relational processes) and direct our research towards the instruments and implementation steps that are currently scheduled for (re)shaping public spaces, and the results and impacts expected. The three areas are: Aspern Lakeside Project (ALP; strategic area 'U2 Donaustadt'), Main Station Project (MSP; strategic area 'Favoriten—Main Station—Arsenal'), and Schwedenplatz-Morzinplatz Project (SMP; strategic areas 'City' and 'Danube Canal').

*Aspern Lakeside Project (ALP)*

> *[T]oday we are striving for a city that offers more than mere functional quality. Towards this goal, public space is the central element of design, and it is the criterion that decides whether people feel at home in their city and identify with it. . . .*
>
> (Carl Fingerhuth, Chairman, Masterplan Competition, VCA, 2008a, p. 7)

Donaustadt (22nd District) represents an agglomeration of eight small villages and is usually associated with a lack of density and urbanity. In order to connect Transdanubia to the historic parts of Vienna and to create a strong link within the Vienna-Bratislava Region, the municipality decided in 2007 to develop the old airfield of Aspern (Figure 3.3) into a new urban expansion scheme based on a master plan by Tovatt Architects & Planners (Sweden). 'Our ambition has been to provide a master plan that creates public spaces that are fundamental[ly] human, lively, intimate and secure', states Johannes Tovatt (VCA, 2008a, p. 6). The master

*Figure 3.3* Students visit the former airfield of Aspern in Vienna in 2010. Only the sketchy boards offer an initial idea on the radical transition and the new public spaces to come.

plan, alluding to the Ringstraße, resembles a replica of the concentric and compact (ideal type) European city and is thought to host 8,500 dwellings, approximately 20,000 residents, and nearly 20,000 jobs (75% service sector, 25% crafts and industry). It is intended to be realized in three phases up to 2020 (Wien 3420, 2012, p. 2). Although the scheme contains a dedication to overall functional diversity and mix, a large part of the plan is functionally divided, namely into areas for dwelling (west); for research, education, and development (south); and for commercial use (east). Only the northern part (to be built last) provides functional diversity while allowing space for highest densities (4–12 storey buildings), thus crucial importance is assigned to the ground floor and its uses.

The 'Public Space Score' borrows symbolic capital from Vienna's (high cultural) music history and leaves little doubt that public spaces are understood as a programming device to create a new district for the post-Fordist service economy. It consists of four 'strings' that, 'similar to the chords of a musical instrument, generate impulses for public life' (Wien 3420, 2012, p. 5). The ring road called 'Sun Avenue' is thought to provide 'the local boulevard experience', while the 'Red Chord' shall host commercial and cultural activities, the 'Blue Chord' comprises the newly built central lake and its park and promenade, and finally, the 'Green Chord' portrays 'a sequence of locally embedded, green and open leisure zones linked to the superordinate landscape network, the "Green Belt" of Vienna' (Wien 3420, 2012, p. 5).

The importance of public spaces for this development is to provide 'outstanding green and open space quality' (VCA, 2008a, p. 10), but no idea on the social dimension of public space is projected in a qualitative sense (Knierbein, 2011a). Rather, provision of public space is associated with environmental and recreational benefits, highlighting the proximity of the Danube Floodplains National Park, and stressing the relatively high population density of the new district (approx. 7,400 inhabitants/km2, compared to Donaustadt [approx. 1,550], Favoriten [approx. 5,600], and Erste Bezirk [approx. 5,600]).

*Main Station Project (MSP)*

The huge construction site of the MSP (Figure 3.4), where 4th and 10th Districts collide at the Gürtel, covers an area previously occupied by terminus-like South and East Stations and formerly owned by the Austrian National Railway Company (OEBB) (Winter, 2011). This fillet of urban land is under development according to a master plan chosen by the OEBB, the municipality, and the Austrian Mail in 2004 (OEBB Online, 2013), and it was planned to create around 20,000 jobs (OEBB Online, 2012; VCA Online, 2013b; Hauptbahnhof-Wien, 2012). In terms of public space, the OEBB will dedicate land for streets, park, and education to be managed by the municipality. The main part of this land will be transferred to the municipality, but the subterranean parts of the main station and its vast shopping facilities—that is, the main entrance and parts of the Sonnwendplatz—will remain OEBB property. The municipality, in turn, is going to provide street infrastructure and prepare the land for adjacent constructions, and will cover maintenance and landscape development of public surfaces (Winter, 2011).

The master plan divides the area into a mall-like central station, a business district, a new residential area of mixed uses, and a public park. The residential district, *Sonnwendviertel*, will host approximately 5,000 apartments for an estimated 13,000 residents, accompanied by school and kindergartens for 1,100 pupils located at the education campus (VCA Online, 2012b, 2013b). 'The new district . . . covers around 35 hectares. . . . Situated around the new eight-hectare park, the modern and ecologically sophisticated residential buildings . . . promise . . . relaxation and an extremely high quality of life' (OEBB Online, 2010, p. 11). By focusing on the concept of 'Smart Dwellings', the municipality tries particularly to attract single households, small families, single mothers or fathers, and couples, as over one third of housing in the neighbourhood will be constructed as one to three room apartments from 40 to 70 m$^2$. A positive aspect is that

*Figure 3.4* View from Vienna's Bahnorama Exhibition Tower towards the new main entrance to the Main Station under construction. Südtiroler Platz located at the Gürtel in the 4th District is to be re-shaped in near future.

the competition guidelines for the housing projects have highlighted 'social sustainability' as a core concept for the new area, comprising low housing prices, highly flexible flat layouts, shared common rooms for different purposes, and intergenerational living (VCA Online, 2013a). Yet it remains unclear if the future public facilities will be able to cover not only the provision of the future population of the Sonnwendviertel, but also the undersupply of public institutions in the adjacent 10th District. Public spaces are thought to serve the adjacent Favoriten, yet studies on the future quality of public spaces in this area have highlighted the lack of access to the new park from the second biggest district of Vienna. The study has recommended that participation by new and adjacent residents at an early stage of planning for public spaces is needed in order to integrate the huge new part of the city into the existing ones (VCA, 2009b, 2011). Yet so far, no concepts have been publicly presented and participation is limited to the timely distribution of information during a planning process that is already in its last steps. Little hope is evoked as the municipality recently opened up a temporary urban district management office for the future residents (GB* Online, 2013).

The business area is thought to provide around 550,000 m² of office space. However, borrowing symbolic capital from the neighbouring UNESCO World Heritage Site, branding the district as 'Quartier Belvedere' has raised sharp criticism. The top-down and real estate driven urban design approach is considered to produce 'urbanistic wasteland' (Seiß, 2010). Seiß assumes that ground-floor zones and adjacent public spaces will not provide any modest public life at all if the urban design retains its projected monofunctional approach. The projected spaces marketed as 'Where Vienna Becomes World' leave little doubt that public spaces are understood as mainly privatised vehicles for consumption of goods and services for a cosmopolitan mobile workforce: Ground-floor zones are foreseen to host a food court market hall offering high-quality eating, a small museum, and spaces for (high) cultural events as well as further restaurants and bars (Erste Group Immorent Online, 2013a, 2013b). Besides the landscape design for the Helmut-Zilk-Park, there are hardly any publicly accessible plans or policies dealing with a necessary network of smaller open spaces and publicly accessible courtyards for the overall MSP area that would allow for everyday life routines, participatory actions, as well as for continuous urban transformation over time. So far, it is completely unclear how the encapsulated project will be internally and externally integrated and how it will serve the needs of the existing local population that will soon have to cope with its consequences.

*Schwedenplatz-Morzinplatz Project (SMP)*

The SMP case is a medium-scale intervention into an existing sequence of public spaces at the edge of Erste Bezirk that is frequented by approximately 150,000 people every day (VCA Online, 2013e). Two historically divided squares together cover an area of around 2.5 ha distributed along a stretch of 400 m. Besides the destruction of the separating buildings in 1945, Nazi history is present in the debates around Morzinplatz, as it is here that the Gestapo headquarters was located and approximately 50,000 people were arrested, interrogated, and tortured. Deportation to the death camps was organized from here. Today, the controversial image of the SMP is still one of the crucial bones of contention between the district government and the municipality, as the area is considered by some as 'only periphery', by others as 'backyard', or as 'post-war urban waste' in a 1st District crammed with representational public spaces (VCA Online, 2012a). Voting population in the district continuously represents a clientele for the ultraconservative ÖVP party that wants to beautify the area and to banish the marginalised groups who congregate there. This disagreement is portrayed by the question of whom to integrate into the participatory processes: the local residents or the overall users of this square of city-wide importance. Accompanied by a populist propaganda to influence the public perception of the plazas as places of risk and fear, the

*Figure 3.5* Schwedenplatz represents one of Vienna's major mobility hubs, linking long-distance buses with different metro lines and transnational ferry connections.

ÖVP has additionally put strong pressure on the municipality to act. Thus the two squares have become key sites to strategically link the 1st District to the Danube Canal that is to be transformed into a new hotspot for international tourism and related high-end leisure and consumption. Since 2005, a public debate regarding the insertion of CCTV has raised public awareness of the fact that both squares offer a particular use value for different marginalised groups that hardly find any niche space for their needs in the glossy spaces of the 1st District's propagated high culture, international tourism, and luxury consumption. The petrol station at Schwedenplatz offers 24-hour cheap-consumption facilities for the users of the public realm, and both plazas are used around the clock. The Morzinplatz, in particular, is a hotspot for local residents and workers to eat their lunch outside, for night owls, and for early birds; the Schwedenplatz provides the most relevant public transport connections (Figure 3.5), as well as a down-to-earth consumption environment where the absence of cappuccino cafés allows for spaces to host a decent and mundane public life for different groups.

The design of these public spaces is hardly remembered if at all. To contrast with this lively perception, local media reports describe the area as looking shabby and rundown and proclaim a need for regeneration. The Vice Mayor of Vienna, Maria Vassilakou (Green Party), has therefore launched an urban regeneration project: In early 2012, the municipality announced the start of participatory processes for June 2012 (VCA Online, 2013e) that comprised surveys on the future shape of SMP and gathered approximately 1,100 opinions. Kon-text planning office was contracted to produce a social space analysis for the surrounding area. In September, the intermediary results were presented for four distinguished areas in both squares with the Viennese population being able to evaluate them; 2,200 people took part at this stage, leading to the prioritisation of different goals. Final results were shown in an exhibition on site in November 2012 and will likely become the base of the expert planning process for reshaping these public spaces expected in 2013.

## Dialectics Between (Re)Framing and (Re)Shaping

### Shaping Public Spaces From Scratch?

Recent attempts to design new pieces of the city deal with conceiving abstract public spaces, since lived public spaces can only emerge where people live or work, where they stroll about or march in protest. There are traces of such spaces around the airfield, reflected in the approximately 290,000 residents of Transdanubia or in the 300,000 inhabitants of the main station's adjoining neighbourhoods. Yet these traces have so far remained socially unrecognised, a fact that points to the lost potential for understanding public spaces as connecting realms between the old and newly emerging parts of the city. Another aspect is that the practice of conceiving public spaces is based on scenarios that take current forecasts of urban growth as their starting point and might eventually come under pressure from property markets and speculation. Under these circumstances, there is an inevitable need to explore counter-scenarios that fundamentally question basic assumptions made to render such sites as 'vibrant' and 'public'. What happens if the basic assumptions of the growth scenario begin to falter? The connections these new districts are promoted to create between the new and the old will only be able to deploy their full efficacy through lived public spaces. Yet lived public spaces need a diverse range of built arrangements offering a networked and resilient space for unplanned interaction and everyday uses to eventually unfold.

What invites attention is the sharp contrast between the overexcited discourses and culturally biased practices in the ALP and the mere absence of any broad public debate regarding future public spaces in the MSP. As both projects are developed over a similar time span, the redirection of public attention to the future public spaces of the ALP contributes to a silencing of utterly necessary debates for the impacts the MSP is going to produce. This concerns both the range of everyday life practices in public spaces, as well as the future conditions of dwelling because house and rent prices are estimated to rise tremendously, and the range of distribution of the dwellings and the range of inclusion they might provide are anything but clear. So far, urban designers and planners have but little to say about the people who will not only inhabit the spaces to be built in Donaustadt and Favoriten, but also whose more or less lifestyle-oriented actions, hybrid consumption tastes, manifold spatial appropriation strategies, and differing cultural needs will decisively determine the slow and context-specific emergence of meaningful public spaces. Recent intentions to artificially produce 'meaning' by the use of (diversity) branding strategies supported by new, flexible tools of post-Fordist planning show the desperation of planners and urban designers trying to overcome positivist and Fordist planning via an inwards-oriented approach to context-specific planning in times of complexity. The awareness for the emergence of the public space paradigm in planning and for the new exigencies by a well-informed and partly empowered population is there. Yet involved planners and decision makers are only too conscious about the fact that on the ground, the speculative mechanisms and investment loops regarding urban land and urban property markets have not fundamentally changed, but rather ask for new flexible, creative, and innovative ways to increase turnover rates in the aftermath of the world financial crises in 2008. In this context, public spaces play a key, yet ambivalent, role as vehicles for post-Fordist urban transformations in Vienna.

### Reshaping Public Spaces

The challenge to reshape public spaces seemingly differs from the one to shape them 'from scratch'. The reshaping is inherently more socially and culturally saturated because people are already present and existing daily routines and everyday life patterns can be portrayed and analysed before actually deciding on the need for any planning intervention. The SMP case features a strong link to the newly framed politics of public space in Vienna, as the process design for the overall strategic intervention seemingly differs from the other two cases: The transparent use of social media and participatory techniques involved a good range of people and did not limit the relevance of public spaces to the adjacent population, but offered access to temporary users from other areas. The participatory process encouraging debate among users was accompanied by professional investigations in terms of history, social space, and mobility studies, all producing palpable ideas. The SMP has already set new standards for the reshaping of public spaces, although it could have involved more disciplines and languages (beyond German).

### (Re)Framing Public Policies?

The SMP can be considered an exceptional case where the ambitious public space agenda established over the years meets the realities of the current planning paradigm under the framing conditions of the partly outdated strategic planning policies defined by the StEP 05. In this case, the framing of public policies changed the ways in which public spaces are to be reshaped. This is strongly contrasted by the absence of an explicit policy focusing on the ambivalent roles of public spaces in new urban areas (ALP and MSP cases). Where process design has become an important step in the general municipal politics of public space when dealing with reshaping (cf. SMP), it has been replaced by staged branding processes and a biased cultural theming (cf. ALP) or by a silencing out of the relevance of public spaces (cf. MSP) while trying to shape public spaces 'from scratch'.

The ALP manual constitutes an evident attempt to draw on new urban planning instruments to cast conceived public spaces in steel and stone even before the urban design approach can gain ground. This is definitely an issue to be appreciated once it leads to the overall change of general policies for urban extensions and densifications. Here, the dialectic relation between shaping public spaces and reframing public policies might become palpable if the municipality starts to reconsider self-critically the experiences made in the ALP to reframe public policies for shaping context-sensitive public spaces that integrate the overall social and cultural context. Specific context-related instruments cannot simply be turned into general recipes in order to stimulate public life in a repetitive fashion, a pitfall that many of the actors involved in redesigning planning processes currently face. If attempts to develop new instruments are primarily directed at enhancing the symbolic value, then these promoted 'innovations' might be likely to bear their own creative destructions, as they might portray another fragmented and unstable attempt to enhance the territorial exchange value, rather than the future emergent use value that can provide robustness over decades.

The absence of any wider public debate about the future public spaces to be shaped in the MSP contrasts the ambitious attitudes that the municipality has developed for shaping public spaces in the ALP, and the continuous framing of public policies for public spaces. If the MSP is to fulfil its often promoted role as a new connector between the 3rd, the 4th, and the 10th Districts of Vienna, an overall process of engagement by citizens and public institutions mediating very distinct social, political, and cultural realities will be necessary not only for the future Sonnwendviertel, but also for the Quartier Belvedere, where public planning and related policies so far have not intervened too much, if at all.

Yet, as the current StEP 25 is in the making and a general paradigmatic shift towards an overall urban politics of public space vaguely paves its way in Vienna, there is some hope that the visionary potential of intertwined grassroots democracy and accompanying professional expertise allowing for negotiation, conflict mediation, and open results gains momentum in Vienna.

## Conclusion

With regard to the current politics of public space in Vienna, we have first been interested in how the (re)framing of public policies contributes to (re)shaping public spaces, and vice versa. The reframing of old and the framing of new policies for public spaces have induced a paradigmatic shift, as public spaces are much more relevant for the overall political agenda of Vienna now than a decade ago. The incentive launched by one municipal department found encouragement and conveyors in others, promoting public spaces to become one of the core policy fields for social integration, urban development, and environmental protection. Urban integration policies, for instance, have shifted their focus from systemic integration to social integration in specific neighbourhoods in general, and to certain settings in public spaces in particular. The municipality has pushed the topic's popularity further on the district level, leading to several small-scale processes and to a growing awareness for public spaces in local district politics.

Second, we developed an inquiry into the relation between political discourse and action of differing natures. Three case studies produced different results: In the urban periphery, public space was high on the agenda for an urban extension project, whereas there was hardly any explicit or implicit mention of public spaces in an urban densification project at the interface of the inner and peripheral urban districts. This—to some extent—has foiled our initial considerations regarding the unequal distribution of political attention towards public spaces in the centre and in the periphery. Both strategic projects are located in or close to those districts hosting big parts of the Viennese population, thus offering new stimuli for public urban life in areas that have so far been neglected.

Consecutively, we have witnessed the differences between shaping public spaces 'from scratch' and reshaping lived public spaces. Where the reshaping of public spaces links both political discourse and planning practice, there is a lack of policy for shaping public spaces in newly built areas. Where planners in the urban extension project have put their efforts into shaping future public spaces, their intentions and aims remain unclear: New instruments are shaped to overcome the positivist pitfalls of modern urbanism; however, the approaches chosen rather relate to an overstimulation of public space design for enhancing symbolic capital, and thus increasing exchange value. Meaningful public spaces cannot be artificially produced by culturally biased branding approaches that try to attract affluent service-economy urbanites. This means starting with the preconditions that frame relational public spaces as social and cultural spaces. A quantitative statement for urban density in order to enhance the genesis of future public life will fall short of its goals if it is not based on a qualitative plea for urban difference, which needs to inform the reframing of public policies and the shaping of public spaces and ask for a 'Politics of Difference' (Watson, 2006). Meaningful public spaces are based on contact with the unknown and foster learning processes for mutual tolerance in places of difference.

Providing robust public spaces for future urban growth and shrinkage does not mean decoupling the historically produced use value of public spaces from production of meaningful places, and thus, the production of meaning through everyday life experiences in the local realm. There is a potential that existing public policies can be (re)framed by learning experiences from both cases where public spaces ought to be shaped from scratch. This shows the dialectic nature of (re)framing public policies and (re)shaping public spaces. A critical review and reorganization of shaping public spaces in both the ALP and the MSP might indeed trigger the framing of public policies in order to ground new urban areas on the robust basis of lived public spaces, connecting public, social, and educational organizations that might stimulate and back up future processes of community building both inside and outside each project's realm.

The role of public spaces in the political economy of the post-Fordist city needs to be further investigated as public spaces might run the risk of being overemphasized due to the strong positive connotations and the potentials for concept stretching they evoke. Such a misuse might aim at concealing an emerging facet of flexible capitalism, causing new framing conditions for many of the current 'creative', 'explorative', and 'innovative' approaches to planning (for public spaces). This ambivalence is deeply rooted in that public spaces do not only serve as vehicles for cultural, political, and social learning, as well as tolerance and integration, but they also serve as (in)direct spheres for changed paths and new niches of territorial capital accumulation in the post-Fordist urban economy. This crucial finding partially explains why public spaces currently serve as key vehicles in processes of urban transformation in Europe and beyond.

In this context, Vienna can be considered an outstanding example on the one hand, as the municipality currently modernises and recreates vast parts of the city with public spaces promoted as catalysts for change. The municipality has developed an ambitious program that closely links to the political culture and particular context of the Danube metropolis. Public spaces also serve as connecting links for the Social-Democrats and Green Party Coalition, as it is here where particular interests for integration, environmental protection, and public participation meet already existing standards of a (relatively) fair redistribution of tax into public services and a focus on 'social sustainability' aspects of urban development. Hence, public spaces are also used as a vehicle to promote a third way of urban politics that is historically rooted in the relatively liberal Austro-Marxism of the early 20th century. That means that the municipality's underlying rationale for developing public spaces is growth, and thus, an economic and demographic precondition. As the politics of public space is characterised by the ambition to reach ambivalent or even contrary goals at the same time, future debates need to incorporate a clear balancing of these policy goals in favour of relational public spaces as social spaces of local cultural importance. That is why public spaces must be kept public (in the sense of collective) as a matter of principle.

# Chapter 4

# The Return of the Port as Public Space in Antwerp

*Katja Hackenberg*

In the past, port areas were not only industrial spaces but also spaces for public life, where the day to day activities of the townspeople, sailors, and flaneurs were played out. The richly decorated facades of the trading posts in the Flemish port towns are testimony to the eventful epoch when European ports transformed the history of the world.

Nevertheless, the port areas today appear to be purely economic zones where the public life of the city has been largely pushed back. In Antwerp, however, the lobby work of civic interest groups is leading to the reintroduction of public spaces in the port area in the form of cycle routes, biotopes, and quiet zones. This form of public access differs from that of the past, but nevertheless amounts to a continuation of the historical use of the port as a public space.

This chapter examines how these public spaces have been reintroduced in the harbour zone. It stresses the hypothesis that the introduction of public spaces in Antwerp's port is linked to a new form of governance regarding port expansion. It is an outcome of social conflicts that took place during the 2000s, which involved environmental protection organizations and economic actors, as well as public authorities. In order to support this statement, an analysis of these social conflicts is made. This analysis shows that the reintroduction of public spaces is intensely linked to the notion of sustainable development and its different semantics as used by the actors in order to carry out their interests within the political decision-making process.

In the first part, a brief overview of the historical development of Antwerp is given, concentrating on the different phases of port expansion and the relationship between port and city. The second part analyses the latest urban planning projects in Antwerp working on a new interpretation of public spaces near water. The chapter goes on to analyse the different actors involved in the governance process concerned with port expansion, suggesting distinct phases where two different forms of governance occur and identifying the Deurganckdok-Project as the tipping point in passing from one phase to another. The next part examines the Deurganckdok-Project in depth and the point of view of the environmental protection organizations involved. The last part examines how the reintroduction of public spaces within the port may be linked to the different semantics of the notion of sustainable development as used by the environmental protection organizations involved in the political decision-making process.

## Historical Overview of the Port and City Development of Antwerp

Antwerp is a port city that is rich in tradition and had its first peak during the Renaissance as a European distribution centre for products from the Far East. This was the first phase of globalization, when Antwerp was a hub for global and local cargo flows. The guild houses, with their richly adorned gables, still stand downtown today as a reminder of this period. The relationship between city and port in this period was strong to the point that city extension could not be organized without including new water channels intimately re-linking public life to the presence of water in the city. The inner circle of Antwerp in this epoch was called *Ruienstad*—Flemish for the city of the channels—indicating that the city's surface could only be increased by irrigating new channels (Van Acker, 1975, p.40). There is no aesthetic notion behind this port development. As Konvitz (1978, p.14) pointed out, it was 'pragmatic' port-city planning that followed the needs of the trader population: Increasing the contact with the water meant facilitating the transport of merchandise. In this phase, port and city were one. Port space and public space were not separated; on the contrary, public life emerged out of the trading activities near the water.

Antwerp experienced its second peak as a trading port during the industrialization process in the 20th century. It was during this time that the separation of city and port space came about. In this phase many industrial companies settled down in the port, producing and transporting raw materials for the mass production of goods for the European consumers. Monsanto, BASF, and Exxon were either chemical companies or involved in the refinery of crude oil. The separation of city space and port space was necessary in order to minimize the negative effects of these industries on public health. Consequently, the urban territory was divided into port zones and living zones following the economic needs of production, as well as the safety needs of the population. Blomme (2003, p.16) states that, 'port-related industries were located in the centre of the port area, as far as possible from urban areas for reasons of environmental effects and safety.'

This separation of city and port was first described by Bird (1963) through the Anyport model. He distinguishes three major stages in a port development process: setting, expansion, and specialisation. In the setting stage, port development is strongly dependent on geographical considerations. In the expansion stage, industrial growth impacts on port activities. This expansion mainly occurs downstream. In the specialisation stage, port development will involve the construction of specialised piers to handle freight, such as containers. Some ports will move away from their original setting to increase their handling capacities. The expansion area is usually adjacent to downtown areas.

This abstract model can be made concrete through the development of the Antwerp urban area: In the 16th century, when Antwerp experienced its first phase of globalisation, port space and urban space were not differentiated; loading and unloading ships and handling their commodities occurred in the public spaces of the city. This was also pointed out by Meyer (1999). From the industrialization of the 19th century onwards, port activities shifted downstream from the public space of the city, and the spaces that served for loading and unloading ships went their separate ways.

Antwerp is currently experiencing its second phase of globalization and serves once again as a European distribution centre for products from the Far East; however, these are placed by container ships in terminals far outside the city. The development of container activities completed the separation of city and port: Container traffic is a transportation mode that requires a lot of space even if one takes into account that containers can be stacked up to four levels. Consequently, the Antwerp port expanded further downstream and on the left bank of the Scheldt, leaving once and for all the historical centre of the city. First the Delwaidedock was built in 1982, then the Europe-Terminal and the Northsea-Terminal in 1997. This programmed expansion came to an end during the construction of the Deurganckdok-Terminal in 2005: Social conflicts with citizens' initiatives emerged. For one thing, port space expands at the cost of the natural space of the Scheldt; it leads to the destruction of the polder landscape. For another, the port expands at the cost of habitable space for people. This leads to the destruction of the polder villages and therefore of human communities. Since 2007, port planning has been involved in the construction of the last container terminal, Saeftinghedok, to achieve port expansion on the left bank. After the construction of Saeftinghedok, port expansion in Antwerp should be complete and further investment can only be made by restructuring the existing port area.

## The Development of Public Spaces Within Antwerp's Port

However, two port planning projects developed in Antwerp since the 2000s indicate that port planners tended to develop a new relationship between port and city. Two port planning projects developing public spaces near the river Scheldt are analysed in this section: the first is emblematic in the development of public space outside the harbour; the second develops public space inside the harbour zone. This analysis may help in understanding the different characters of public spaces inside and outside the harbour zone.

The conversion of the ancient harbour area of Het Eilandtje is a classic town planning project aimed at boosting the maritime character of the historical city centre. In the industrial period, port and city were considered to be separate spaces; there was no soft transition between these two spaces because the port of Antwerp was only used for the transport and the refinery of crude oil. Town planners were concerned about protecting the citizens from the negative impact of these production processes on public health.

The conversion of the ancient harbour area of Het Eilandtje created a new quarter near the city, which recalls the historical use of the area as a port but also introduces public function onto the waterfront. The docks and basins are now accessible to citizens. The ancient industrial function becomes a cultural element of public life: *Producing* near the water is transformed into *living* near the water. Similar town planning projects were also developed in Germany during the 1990s, such as the conversion of ancient coal mines in the region of the Ruhr in the Emscher Park project. Harbour space is not an economic space anymore, but a public space used by the citizens.

The urban atmosphere near the water has become an important element improving the quality of life of the citizens. The use of space is polyvalent because the former port function has become a nonmaterial element shaping the image of the city. Antwerp claims once again to be a maritime city, not in an industrial sense but in a cultural sense. On the one hand, the nonmaterial interpretation of the industrial function is recalled physically throughout by perspective views between the city centre and the existing harbour area. On the other hand, the industrial function of the port is recalled by building a cultural theme park reconnecting old and new maritime facilities within the municipal port authority, a museum of maritime history, and a museum for commerce, as well as more informal institutions like the red-light district of the city. The newly created quarter is a space of transition between the city centre and the still existing harbour area.

Yet, it is still an example of a classic town planning project in which the industrial function of the port basin ceases to exist; it is transformed into a cultural function. The project is developed within the framework of the normative town planning tools, emphasising the separation of urban space according to economic functions (working zones, living zones, leisure zones). In some countries, these functions are still very common in the development of a land use plan. The organization of urban space according to economic functions was mainly stressed by modernist architects, notably Le Corbusier. In his book *Urbanisme*, Le Corbusier (1994, p. 93) suggests the separation of production zones from business centres and living zones in order to boost the industrial development of the city. These theoretical proposals became clear later when he worked on the *Plan Voisin* (Le Corbusier, 1925), proposing the restructuring of Paris. Evidently, with the separation of production zones from living zones, the public function of the port ceased to exist.

The second infrastructure project shows the development of public space within the industrial harbour zone of Antwerp. It points to the end of the industrial space functions as they were developed by Le Corbusier. There is a polyvalent use of space (public and industrial) in the port area itself.

Due to the initiatives of the environmental protection associations, the port no longer serves the industrial use alone; ecological compensation areas have been created in the port itself in order to guarantee biological diversity of species in the port zone. This points to the end of the monofunctional use of the port as it was developed within the framework of industrialization. The industrial function continues to exist; in fact, the port of Antwerp is one of the most important ports of Europe, a 'main port'. For Loyen (2003, p. 74–75) a main port is a central port of call for intercontinental container lines; they distribute the traffic flows to hierarchically less important regional or national ports. As such, the port of Antwerp concentrates a high volume of cargo flows, container terminals, and even a small number of refineries. However, the areas near the river are transformed into ecological compensation areas (e.g., as breeding places for birds). That is the new character of the public space within the port: Compensation areas integrate education and leisure activities for the citizens, with bicycle paths or observation platforms to watch breeding birds. The integration of these leisure activities is a physical expression of the polyvalent use of port space. The port is no longer simply conceived as an industrial space, but also as an ecological space and a leisure space for the citizens. The port now unites former urban space functions previously conceived as antagonistic by town planners like Ebenezer Howard (1902), who suggested the concept of the Garden City separating leisure and living activities from productive working zones.

## The Actors Involved in Public Opinion Formation Linked to the Development of the Public Spaces Within the Port

Now, how did the city of Antwerp reintroduce public space within the port area? As my research shows, the reintroduction of public space is due to a new form of governance emerging out of social conflicts taking place between civil society, economic actors, and public authorities. The term *civil society* refers to a space and a sphere of action between the private sphere, the economy, and the state (Gosewinkel, 2004, p. 35). In the port of Antwerp, this space is represented by environmental protection organizations. Their actions may be seen as mere counterparts to those of the state and the economy. However, the reintroduction of public space in the port can be considered as a compromise between their divergent interests. An extensive analysis of these interests is made in the doctoral thesis *La communauté portuaire d'Anvers—L'identification des catégories analytiques servant à la description de son réseau informel* (Hackenberg, 2010). In fact, the rebooting of the Deurganckdok project integrated a new actor into the port planning process representing the interests of civil society—environmental protection organizations.

The distinction between these two forms of governance is laid down in two charts. The first, Figure 4.1, shows the form of governance concerning port expansion prior to the construction of the container terminal Deurganckdok. The decisions about port planning are negotiated by an informal network of public institutions and private commercial interest associations. The public institutions are represented by the Flemish region and the municipality of Antwerp. Suykens (1988, pp. 493–498) states that Antwerp is a port with a Hanseatic tradition, defining the public institutions as the owners of the 'wet' infrastructure. The term *wet infrastructure* refers to the docks, the river, and port basins, as well as the locks. For Van Hooydonk (1996b, p. 365) both parties, the city and the region, share competencies and responsibility for port planning in a unique way: 'In fact the municipal port authorities manage ports which were paid for by, and which partly still belong to, the state—now the regions'.

The private institutions are composed of a multitude of private interest associations that have organized themselves according to the different professions and tasks to be done regarding the organization of the cargo flows within the port (shippers, stevedores, logistics, distribution, production). They are united under the umbrella organization ALFAPORT (Suykens et al., 1986, p. 526). The large number of the professional associations participating and their strong networking contribute to the successful lobbying of private interests concerning port planning projects.

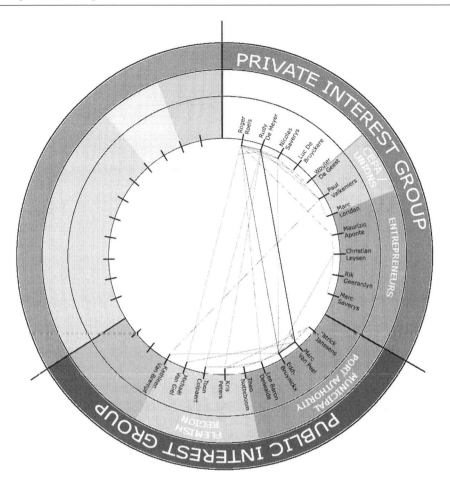

*Figure 4.1* Actors and institutions participating in port governance prior to the Deurganckdok-Project, Antwerp.

Prior to the construction of the Deurganckdok, public and private institutions developed a consensus on port planning projects. The development of this consensus was not integrated into the normative planning process, but rather happened informally. Planning of the port area was the sole responsibility of the public institutions. Civil society did not participate in port planning; its interests were supposed to be represented by the public institutions. In this phase, the governance process can be considered coherent to the Enlightenment's theory of civil society. As a historical concept, civil society derives from Aristotle's *koinonia politike:* In its original sense, it allowed no distinction between *state* and *society.* The philosophers of the Enlightenment, notably Hegel (1991), were the first to bifurcate the concept, insisting on the fact that society and institutions functioned as re-descriptions of one another.

Figure 4.2 shows the form of governance after the Deurganckdok project. Whereas in Figure 4.1 decisions about port expansion are formally and informally negotiated between the private and the public sectors, Figure 4.2 shows the rise of a third party, the environmental protection organizations, representing the interests of civil society.

Figure 4.2 shows the actors involved in port development after the Deurganckdok affair; this form of governance leads to the rise of environmental protection associations in the definition

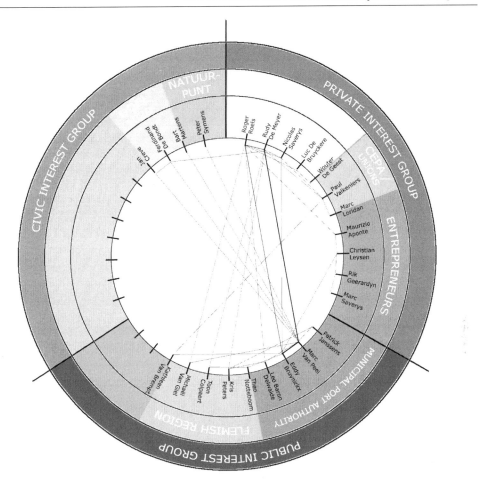

*Figure 4.2* Actors and institutions participating in port governance after to the Deurganckdok-Project, Antwerp.

and the land use of port space. In the 2000s, environmental protection organizations and citizens' initiatives have increasingly started to assert themselves on the subject of port expansion. This is no longer exclusively negotiated between the public and the private parties, but between the public, the private, and the civic. In fact, at the beginning of the process, civil society's interests were essentially represented by two environmental protection organizations—Doel 2020 and Natuurpunt—of which only the latter now survives to participate in the governance of port planning projects. This situation will be analysed in the last part of this chapter; it is notably caused by the different semantics of the notion of sustainable development put forward by each of these organizations.

Founded in 1933, the ecological association Natuurpunt is concerned with the areas that are home to flora and fauna facing the possibility of extinction. As an ecological association, Natuurpunt campaigns for environmental concerns linked to educative concerns, supposing that the preservation of nature can only by assured by enlarging the ecological awareness of the citizens. Therefore, the ecological compensation areas in the port of Antwerp are linked to platforms and bicycle paths allowing the observation of nature. In 2008, Natuurpunt managed approximately 16,600 hectares of natural land, of which it owned 11,000 hectares. Following its merger in

2001with two other ecological associations, De Wielewaal and Natuurreservaten Vzw, it now enjoys the support of a very large proportion of the population with some 65,000 members (these numbers were communicated by Peter Symens, representative of Natuurpunt, in an interview made in 2010). In the course of the process, Natuurpunt was designated as the unique spokesperson of the civil society during discussions with the entrepreneurs, the planning authorities, and the entities responsible for the future expansion of the port area.

Founded in 1997 and with far fewer members, the goal of the Doel 2020 Action Committee is to fight for the future of the polder village of Doel, threatened with destruction due to the expansion of the port. Since the beginning of the 1990s, the Action Committee emerged out of two other associations: Polders in Nood (PIN) and Boze Doelanaars. The Action Committee is supported by some 200 Flemish citizens. Even if the number of supporters of the Action Committee is minimal, its ranks nevertheless include numerous eminent personalities such as the European politician Ferdinand De Bondt, the historian Karel Van Isacker, as well as the Flemish moviemaker Frank Van Passel.

In fact, the Deurganckdok project can be considered as the tipping point for this new form of governance because in the run of this project a new planning tool concerning port expansion was developed allowing the participation of citizens' initiatives in the framework of the process: the Strategic Planning Process for the Port of Antwerp (Coeck and Tessier, 2007, pp. 168–180). Environmental protection associations are integrated into the normative course of port planning. Alongside the public institutions and the private commercial associations, they are active project participants who plan the development of the harbour facilities.

The theoretical foundation for the strategic planning process for the port of Antwerp is the stakeholder value. According to Freeman (2010, p. 2), 'a stakeholder is any group of individuals who can have a positive or negative influence' on the outcome of the planning process. In contrast to the shareholder value, which focuses on the needs and expectations of the economic shareholders alone, the stakeholder value engages a planning process in its entire social context in order to harmonise the interests of different social groups. The stakeholder value was integrated into the normative course of port planning. Through the participation of the civil, economic, and public actors in the planning process, the public function was reintroduced in the port space.

The development of a new planning instrument for the port zone in Antwerp unfolded specifically to prevent conflicts with civil society over port expansion. This is because the construction of the Deurganckdok at the turn of the millennium led to strikes and protests by the civil society, which threatened to scuttle the port's expansion project. Public institutions were confronted with the problem of integrating the interests of environmental protection organizations into the normative course of planning. This led to the development of the strategic planning process for the port of Antwerp.

This process is a matter of *bottom-up* planning, in which the goals and the content of port planning are determined in working groups. The groups are equally represented by the private commercial associations, the public institutions, and the citizens' initiatives. The working groups are organized following themes that may cause divergent interests (e.g., mobility, economics, or nature). One important task of the public institutions is mediation between the divergent interest groups. In Antwerp, this task is taken on by the municipal port authority. It is therefore no longer simply a normative planning institution and the authority responsible for port planning has instead become a moderator regarding public opinion formation about port planning. This is a new role for public institutions within the framework of the rise of civil society as a third actor in port planning. In Antwerp, an allowance was made for this new role of the municipal port authority by changing the structure of the institution (Van Hooydonk, 1996a).

The authority's Administrative Council includes not only municipal politicians and management employees, but also representatives of the private commercial associations and the environmental protection organizations. These representatives operate as bridge actors, which means that they are responsible for the flow of information between the institutions and the associations. Environmental protection organizations and private commercial associations therefore have a voice in all decisions that concern the port's long-term strategies. The informal network of the public and the private, which formed the space of public opinion formation in the port city, is now formalised, and the citizens' initiatives, as representatives of civil society, are integrated into this network.

## The Deurganckdok Affair

The preceding section identified the Deurganckdok project as the tipping point in the formation of a new governance process. In order to reboot this project, the strategic planning process was developed to include environmental protection organizations in decision making. The Deurganckdok project was to be built on the territory of the polder village of Doel, a small village located to the north of both the port and the city of Antwerp. In the face of competition from other ports along the coast, such as Rotterdam and Le Havre, the port area needed to expand quickly, with the excavation during the 1960s of docks and canals to irrigate the new industrial port areas developed on the polder. The port authorities were thus forced to encroach on the nature zone along the banks of the River Scheldt and evict the inhabitants of numerous villages on the polder. These villages, such as Kallo and Wilmarsdonk, have now disappeared. A status quo was then established until the mid-1980s, when private entrepreneurs and the port authorities wanted to develop a new container port. This change in the situation caused numerous inhabitants to sell their properties to the Flemish government and leave the villages, most of which were many centuries old. Neglected by the government, whose aim was to build the new docks on this land, these villages were abandoned and fell into ruin.

Two events cast a shadow over this programmed decline. First, at the end of the 1990s, the village of Doel became the base camp for artists and eco-militants who formed the Doel 2020 Action Committee with a view of fighting the planning policy implemented by the port authorities and private entrepreneurs. Second, the complaints filed by Natuurpunt with the European Community led to the project being put on hold in 2005. Found guilty of noncompliance with the European Natura 2000 Directive, the port's ambitions were scuppered. The public authorities did not put an end to their policy of expulsion, but offered the ecological association the chance to be involved in the decision-making process. The three players in the port community—the private entrepreneurs, the port authorities, and the newcomer Natuurpunt—then had to act as one. However, the Doel 2020 Action Committee, which participated in the action to block the extension of the port, was excluded from the new governance process implemented by the port authorities to decide the fate of the Deurganckdok, and found itself standing alone against this triumvirate.

## Environmental Concerns as a Starting Point for Reintroducing Public Spaces Within the Harbour Areas

The blockage of the Deurganckdok-Project was a veritable test of the forms of representation and action linked to the collective attitude of the citizens of Antwerp towards sustainable development. First, it radically altered the form of governance that had operated previously. While the private entrepreneurs and port authorities could ignore environmental interests in port expansions, the political decision making around the strategic planning process forced them to take ecological interests into consideration. Before the introduction of this new planning tool, the role of the players involved in this affair seemed to be founded on a distinct basis: that of industrial efficiency for private entrepreneurs; the local interest of the project for the public authorities, ensuring jobs for the population and the competitiveness of the city; and finally—after the Deur-ganckdok expansion—attention to nature for the ecological associations previously committed to the anti-nuclear cause.

In fact, the starting point for introducing public space within the port is linked to the different se-mantics of the notion of sustainable development used by the involved actors to put through their interests in the planning process. These different semantics came forth during the social conflict between the port authorities, the economic actors, and the environmental protection organizations regarding the port development project Deurganckdok. In order to compromise and to reboot the planning process of the dock, which had come to a complete standstill, the port authorities had to ally themselves with one environmental protection organization, either Natuurpunt or Doel 2020, which are emblematic for these different semantics about the sustainable expansion of the port. By choosing Natuurpunt over Doel 2020, the port authorities opted for a technical semantic sacrific-ing the cultural semantic of sustainable development represented by Doel 2020. In so doing, port authorities made possible the reintroduction of public space within the harbour zone.

On the one hand, the technical semantic of sustainable development stressed by Natuurpunt is rooted in the perception that nature is a complex biological system that can be altered by hu-mans if the latter understand how the system operates. It is within this framework that part of this environment can be destroyed and then recreated from nothing within the harbour zone in order to facilitate the expansion of the port. This systemic modelling of nature is used to justify the creation of ecological compensation areas reintroducing public spaces within the port. By allying themselves with Natuurpunt's technical semantic of sustainable development, the port authorities could justify the expansion of the port as a whole and, notably, at the expense of the existing polder villages.

On the other hand, there is the cultural semantic of the sustainable development of Doel 2020: The goal of the Doel 2020 Action Committee is to fight for the future of the polder village of Doel, which is threatened with destruction due to the extension of the port. Questioning the public utility of this extension, the activists want to protect the village and the surrounding polder landscape. Their protests are primarily founded on the recognition of an alternative way of life to industrial development, identifying culture, the arts, nature, or tourism as credible develop-ment strategies. The Action Committee has adopted the public areas of the village of Doel as the means of expressing their protest, combining public sit-ins during demolition work and messages written on the facades of the houses in the village. Founded '700 years ago' (De Vriendt, 2009, p. 1), the village is presented by the committee as an endangered species that has survived until the present day. The nature and culture of the village of Doel deserve to be protected because they are part of a broader heritage. In the opinion of the Action Committee, the village belongs not only to a broader natural heritage—the polders, which go beyond historical or architectural dimensions—but also to a 'living heritage' (Action Committee Doel 2020, 2007, p. 1), which encompasses the Flemish community and, more generally speaking, all humanity responsible for shaping the polder landscape: 'Heritage [is] a human right in Doel as well' (Action Commit-tee Doel 2020, 2007, p. 1). However, by referring to the 'living community of inhabitants' (De Vriendt, 2009, p. 3) of the village of Doel, the committee used a language similar to that favoured by environmentalist associations, but this time to shine the spotlight on protection of people. Natuurpunt defends those who have no voice: The plants and animals threatened by extinction. Doel 2020, however, includes humankind on the list of endangered species. In doing so, the Ac-tion Committee made it more difficult, from a moral standpoint, to accept the agenda promoted by Natuurpunt: that of exchanging the natural area that the port wanted to acquire for another one newly created within the port. Natuurpunt and Doel 2020 could have joined forces. Never-theless, due to these divergent interests about sustainable development, Natuurpunt preferred to stand alone in favour of the recognition of the ecological interests in port planning affairs. The

Doel 2020 Action Committee therefore had to operate on two fronts, a situation that extremely weakened its position.

While Natuurpunt considers nature a system to be preserved or recreated to rebalance ecological and economic development, Doel 2020 sees each natural component as a total social fact (Mauss, 1950, p. 147) relating to a common natural and cultural heritage. According to Natuurpunt, sustainability is negotiable. It is defined according to the consensus obtained by the different parties through discussion (economic operators, ecologists, and public authorities). The level of sustainability develops and improves insofar as the different parties are capable of finding political compromise between their individual interests. Only a balance between the economic and ecological functions of the polders is capable of ensuring their sustainability and therefore represents, in the eyes of Natuurpunt, the ultimate goal to be achieved. This was laid down in a charter between Natuurpunt and the port authority signed in 2002. This strategy enabled Natuurpunt to contribute to establishing the political compromise binding the port community and, in doing so, it also contributed to the reintroduction of public space within the port.

## Conclusion

The analysing work of this chapter gives rise to several questions concerning the strategies put forward in order to push sustainable development into town planning projects. First of all, can the notion of sustainable development be linked with the cultural heritage of the people or not? Taking into consideration the cultural heritage of the people means to recognise the uniqueness of each territory. Consequently, this semantic calls into question the creation of ecological compensation areas created out of nothing in particular.

Concerning port development, it seems undoubtedly true that the integration of compensation areas reintroduces public space in a zone formerly deprived of public life. It thus contributes to an increase in the quality of life of the citizens. However, the technical semantic referring to the ecosystem and the fauna and flora alone, excluding humankind as a threatened species, was made at the price of a biological reductionism in which humankind is deprived of its cultural dimension. The disclosure of this reductionist critique left the way clear for the entrepreneurs and port authorities to pursue their enterprise. Because the proposed industrial plans could only be harmful to the plant and animal ecosystem, these plans could give rise to compensations with regard to the reparations owed to the planet. Its naturalist expertise, which afforded Natuurpunt its sole legitimacy, gave rise to this reductionism, preventing any discussion of the validity of the decisions taken by the private entrepreneurs and port authorities in terms of the general interest or public good. It merely facilitated the negotiation of compensation based on this vision alone. In doing so, the systemic modelling characterising the environmentalist approach of Natuurpunt contributed to legitimising an institutional order. This is one of the essential reasons behind its successful integration into the governance process implemented by the port authorities. The naturalist expertise of this association—the only representative of the civil society involved—gave it legitimacy while at the same time preventing it from intervening in the process in the general interest other than in terms of environmental compensation.

Chapter 5

# Exchange in the Street
## Rethinking Open-Air Markets in Budapest

*Levente Polyák*

> *Food is a social justice issue and a public health issue; it's also an economic development issue, it's a transportation issue, it's a regional planning issue, it's an ecological issue.* (Cohen, 2010)

'Open-air markets are symbols of poverty', declared the former deputy mayor of Budapest in a recent speech (Janecskó, 2010). This statement reveals the dominant policy of the past decades on urban public markets: Open-air markets have been closed down and market halls have been turned into supermarkets because of their 'uncontrollable' nature; they serve as places for 'loiterers, the jobless and the homeless' (Janecskó, 2010). As disorderly reminders of how the 'other half' lives (Riis, 1890), they are highly intolerable from the viewpoint of economic development of a certain kind: No hotels, restaurants, or other businesses in need of a sterile, optimistic environment will move in the proximity of open-air markets, so goes the argument.

However, for actors of the civil society, as well as for progressive planners and designers, there is an increasing acknowledgement of markets as vehicles of specific values. Open-air markets are genuine public spaces of a particular kind: While functioning as meeting places for local communities, they also offer contexts for intergenerational encounters and for the exchange of information. Open-air markets may be analysed from a multiplicity of viewpoints: On the one hand, they offer affordable fresh food and they are central to public health, biodiversity, and fair trade; on the other hand, they open access to commercial activities for people with a very low profit margin, often at the peripheries of society. In the meanwhile, markets differ from each other in their format, level of formality, and social context; although one market may be a site of inclusion, others may be generators of gentrification.

In the following pages, I will examine open-air markets as public spaces, shaped by neoliberal policies of gentrification and spectacularisation, by activist interventions and campaigns, by commercial enterprises and the expectations of various publics. I will present markets in their relations to market halls, as different combinations of regulated and informal elements, a dialectic that accompanies the history of markets from the 19th to the 21st century. By focusing on the case study of the Hunyadi Market and the emergence of civil mobilisation in order to preserve the market, the chapter will also sketch a map of actors engaged in shaping the public space of markets. To frame the debate on Budapest markets, the chapter will also evoke conflicting theories of 'the public', underlining the interwoven nature of public and private interests in urban planning, as well as highlighting the social dimension and specific publics of food markets.

The juxtaposition of examples from various geographical locations and different socioeconomic contexts is not arbitrary. A New York-based NGO (Project for Public Spaces) may be invited to Budapest to organize a quasi-participatory process focusing on the redesign of an open-air market (Hunyadi tér); this illustrates that expertise on various levels and derived from various political backgrounds is transmitted through globalised circuits of information, be it a city-level policy or activist methods.

## Public Spaces Between Function and Image

In April 2010, Imre Ikvay-Szabó, then deputy mayor of Budapest, told journalists at a press conference, 'The urban landscape is negatively affected by fruit and vegetable stalls' (Janecskó, 2010). He went on with proposing to withhold permissions to sell food in public spaces in central areas of the city where tourists may be disturbed by the sight of poverty. Although Ikvay Szabó's proposal did not materialise in actual decrees effectively changing the regulation of public space, it certainly reflected a pronounced vision about public space and contributed to shaping their public perception.

The use of the word 'landscape' by Ikvay-Szabó is telling: In its reference to seeing, 'landscape' suggests a relationship to public space that is based on spectatorship, more than on agency. 'Landscape' is what is given only to the eye; instead of being a terrain of activities, the urban landscape is a set of images. While the concept of visibility has a weaker presence in planning regulations and urban policies than, say, property, the aspiration to control what one can see in the city has made its way into urban policy, from historic preservation through the protection of the skyline and to a variety of other fields.

To look at public spaces as images instead of terrains of activities is hardly an invention of the Budapest City Hall. In recent years, an increasing number of theorists have described the process in which the urban landscape gradually lost its materiality and has turned into the city's foremost visual representation. As the American sociologist Sharon Zukin wrote in 1995, 'The development of visual media in the 20th century made photography and movies the most important cultural means of framing urban space, at least until the 1970s. Since then, as the surrealism of King Kong shifted to that of Blade Runner and redevelopment came to focus on consumption activities, the material landscape itself—the buildings, parks and streets—has become the city's most important visual representation' (Zukin, 1995, p.16).

This evolution, the 'spectacularisation of urban space' (Belanger, 2000; Silk & Amis, 2006) unfolded in correspondence to the emergence of architectural postmodernism and eventually, iconic architecture. The buildings reduced to their façades, or to a city's or a region's icons, are as much deprived of activities as securitizing and sterilizing policies banalise urban streets to become postcards, embodying diverse ideals of the civic order, customised from a variety of 19th, 20th, and 21st century elements. However, inheriting an appreciation of street life and community values, urban regeneration based on beautified public spaces often looks at markets as mere aesthetic phenomena, partly ignoring their social, economic, and ecological dimensions (Zukin, 2009, p. 116). When neoliberal urban planning envisions creating public goods markets, they are circumscribed, well-targeted markets for an affluent clientele, exclusive for both vendors and customers (Zukin, 2008).

In the light of these aestheticizing tendencies, it is hardly surprising that design (outpacing other considerations) has become the predominant framework of conceiving and discussing public space, and eventually, markets. The uneasy relationship between the regulation, planning, and design of public spaces, that is, the disputed correspondence between texts, plans, and environments, is particularly apparent in the case of privately owned public spaces (POPS). Originating from New York, POPS is a hybrid construction between public and private space, allowing developers to build additional floor space in exchange for the construction and maintenance of a public plaza, owned by the developer but accessible for all. After a few decades of their existence, however, it turned out that, as the research of Németh (2009) revealed, many of the privately owned public spaces were not designed to be attractive to use—they were designed to be appealing to the eye. Benefiting from the unbridgeable gap between zoning regulation language and design drawings, many developers in New York ordered designers to create spaces that help keep their premises discrete, dispersing the crowd they are supposed to accommodate (Smithsimon, 2008).

## Public Spaces and Private Interests

Certainly, the affordances of the environment, a public space, or urban food markets do not depend uniquely on design. As is shown in many innovative design projects that seek to improve the situation of food markets and street vendors in various cities—like Aleksandra Wasilkowska's (2010) *Marketmeter* in Warsaw; *Vendor Power!* by The Center for Urban Pedagogy (2011); the *Street Vendor Project* by the Urban Justice Center (2011); and Columbia University's Spring 2011 planning studio *Street Vendors in Lower Manhattan* in New York—design works together with planning, maintenance, management, and control in creating the possibilities and limitations of public spaces. All these factors contribute to shaping the publics of a public space. To clarify the notion of the 'publics', it is useful to evoke briefly the notions of public sphere, public space, and multiple publics by posing the essential question: To whose service should public spaces be built?

Discourses of the public space often disclose a sense of loss, felt over the supposed extinction of the classical public sphere, a 'space of democracy' (Rancière, 2011), 'a forum in which the private people, come together, readied themselves to compel public authority to legitimate itself before public opinion' (Habermas, 1989, pp. 25–26). Critiques of the elimination of the public sphere often operate with a suggested dichotomy between public and private space: Private interests intervening in the public sphere with the means of privatisation or regulation, control, and surveillance are eliminating public spaces by expanding the private sphere at the expense of the public. But the traditional notions of public sphere and public space (as antonyms of private sphere and private space) came under criticism in the past decades because of their failure to acknowledge the existence of multiple publics and the blurring boundaries between private and public spaces (Zukin, 1991). As Nancy Fraser argues in her text *Rethinking the Public Sphere* (1992, pp. 65–70), because no single discursive space can represent a completely inclusive 'space of democracy', public expression is dispersed in multiple sites and is organized around multiple publics. Besides the impossibility of an all-inclusive, Habermasian public sphere for a universal public, Fraser also questions the possibility of a public sphere entirely independent from commercial and political interests (Fraser, 1992, p. 69).

An eloquent example of the ultimate interwoven nature of public and private interests is the case of the High Line Park in New York. The High Line, an aerial railway structure on the West Side of New York, had been abandoned for over a decade when, in the 1990s, discussion started about its demolition or preservation. Private owners of the adjacent lots were lobbying for its demolition, in order to clear the land for new construction. When a group of Chelsea inhabitants started organizing themselves to conserve the High Line, nobody expected that the preservation of the structure, its conversion into a public park, and the related rezoning by the city's planning department would lead to an unprecedented rise in real estate prices in the neighbourhood. The *mushrooming* of new buildings by star architects along the High Line demonstrates the extent to which the same landowners who were willing to demolish the aerial structure finally benefited from the creation of a new, high-quality public space.

Public spaces are often created to foster private advantages, as Sharon Zukin reminds us in her book *Naked City* (2009). While many of the genuine public spaces of Western cities were originally established to increase the value of neighbouring properties—Zukin evokes the examples of Union Square and Herald Square in New York—associations such as business improvement districts or local development corporations took over the maintenance and management of public spaces, implementing new means of control to exclude from the streets all undesirable uses and behaviours and to raise property values in and around public spaces (Zukin, 2009). In a more direct way, the establishment of Budapest's Millennium Center, an ensemble of public spaces and buildings hosting prestigious cultural institutions located at the Danube's riverbank, was financed by the largest Hungarian real estate developer who happens to own a major part of the land surrounding the Center—lots and industrial buildings whose value increased multifold with the arrival of the public cultural institutions. In another example, Budapest's new Corvin District was created by public–private cooperation. Because the municipality was unable to meet its obligations in designing and constructing the public plaza in-between the new residential condominiums, it gave the task over to the developer together with the right to commercialize, manage, and police the plaza for the following 99 years.

Still, with the interests of certain public and private spheres increasingly intertwined, it is no longer clear whether public space offers more freedom and diversity than privately owned or managed spaces. Authorities engaged in gentrifying the areas they govern often operate with a very exclusive idea of 'the public', addressing their services to certain publics and keeping others out of them (Angotti, 2008). While public food markets, for instance, are often seen as genuine public spaces as opposed to the closed spaces of supermarkets, they are often designated to serve a well-defined clientele whose purchasing power is stronger than the average (Zukin, 2008). A market's activity is not indifferent to a district; it radiates out in the neighbourhood through the presence of its vendors, clients, and products on the market square and in the surrounding streets. A market's clientele thus alters the image of a neighbourhood, affecting property values and encouraging or discouraging the installation of new inhabitants and merchants. This is why the regulation of markets, beyond concerns of hygiene, is also an attempt to define their publics. Through policies of rental prices and special requirements for permissions, regulators can have an influence on both vendors and buyers who frequent a market. When investigating the debate on public food markets, we have to analyse the relationship between authorities, vendors, and clients, as well as the surrounding private interests.

## Regulating Street Markets: The Emergence of Market Halls

If today's markets bother City Hall officials by their very appearance, this is by no means a newly found conflict. Markets have been seen as disturbing elements by generations of legislators, and regulating markets has regularly been on the agenda in the past 150 years. In parallel to the eastward spread of Haussmann's hygienist ideas of urban systematisation, and inspired by Napoleon's taxable market halls, concepts of reorganising food distribution also travelled significant geographical distances. The complex and chaotic food infrastructure developed by the first half of the 19th century was judged not to match the requirements of the modern metropolis: In the 1870s, city leaders agreed upon the need for restricted regulations for food markets. They estimated that there were too many markets—44 open-air markets and over 10,000 mobile vendors in the mid-1890s—in Budapest, without the necessary control, and with hygiene levels of medieval standards (Gerő, 2003, p. 39). In response to this 'public food supply crisis', a special commission was established in 1879 in order to oversee the creation of a market hall system, based on Western models (Vadas, 2005, pp. 133–139).

Market halls were not simply covert versions of the previously present open-air food markets; they were institutions in themselves, sophisticated tools in the municipality's hand to respond to the challenges of modern urbanisation. Through price control, quality assurance, and hygiene standards, market halls helped municipal institutions become mediators of urban food consumption, constituting an unsurpassable link in the food chain between farmers and consumers. Municipal control over the food infrastructure aimed at totality: Legislation following the construction of market halls proposed that in the districts where new market halls are built previous markets be prohibited.

Modern market halls consist of clear, distinguishable (and taxable) vending units, much easier to administer than irregular vending stalls in unregulated street markets in which cities see more of a loss in tax revenue than an economic opportunity. In this sense, market halls serve as architectural frames to the rational organization of the traffic of goods and bodies. The spatial arrangement of market halls—with their booths and stands organized in a grid-like 'street system'—corresponds to the disciplinary practices of the modern state, described by Michel Foucault in *Discipline and Punish:* 'Disciplinary space tends to be divided into as many sections as there are bodies or elements to be distributed' (Foucault, 1995, p. 142). Through architectural design and the management of goods, market halls exemplify the changing nature between the state and the individual that Foucault describes as *bio-politics*: where food distribution becomes an instrument to manage and shapes individual bodies and behaviour.

## Informality at the Margins of the Planned Economy: Markets in the Communist Hungary

The decades in Hungary under communist leadership had their definitive imprint not only on politics and the economy, but also on commerce, people's routines, and their use of the city. Urban public space was a pivotal arena of efforts to modernise and control everyday life from the 1950s on. The restructuring of the urban fabric by new housing estates went in tandem with the transformation of its principal public spaces: Inhabitants, discouraged from assembling in squares by the police's perpetual control, gradually withdrew into private apartments turned into semi-public meeting places. However, formalisation and control were not the only changes: Like the places of public assembly, markets also found alternative locations. In parallel to the centralised and monopolised interior spaces of food commerce, the emerging market economy of the 1980s, together with a blossoming second economy, transformed public spaces into temporary, informal markets where everybody seemed to have something to sell. Because many of the informal markets emerged next to open-air food markets, sharing their publics and often vendors as well, it is important to take a closer look at the so-called Comecon (or 'Polish') markets.

The 1980s brought about the blossoming of this peculiar type of street commerce. Comecon (an abbreviation for Council for Mutual Economic Assistance, the economic cooperation framework of the former Communist countries) markets were typical products of planned economies. They emerged in the absence of proper market mechanisms; the total regulation of the economy disconnected products from the dynamisms of demand and supply, and left many goods officially inaccessible, thus without an established price. In their article on Comecon markets, Ágnes Czakó and Endre Sík describe the way informal markets were fed by guest workers and tourists with a better access to international travel from the early 1980s: 'In planned economies of shortage, the set price of goods, which varied from country to country, along with their usually poor quality and extremely limited range, meant that those who could cross the border—and had some money as well—could buy cheaper, finer and better goods or could access things which they could not buy at home. . . . With the difficulties for shops to legally import goods, the small-scale private trader-tourists had a niche to occupy' (Czakó & Sík, 1999, p. 719). In the planned economy, informal open-air markets were well suited to exploit this niche. While a small-scale shop-based retail trade failed to fill the space that was left uncovered by the inefficient state-run commercial sector, less controlled street markets offered a more flexible, more resilient environment for small traders than established stores. This is the reason why during the Perestroika period, with the opening of borders, 'trading activities turned every conceivable space—street corners, subways, village squares—into open-air markets' (Sík & Wallace, 1999, p. 702).

The authorities could hardly stop the rapid proliferation of street commerce. While open-air markets were continuously under the threat of police raids, bribing police officers often helped markets survive (Czakó & Sík, 1999, p. 717). Besides their illegality, street markets caused disruption in public spaces. As attempts to disperse vendors mostly proved ineffective, local authorities made attempts to drive traders into designated places, farmers' markets, or second-hand markets (Czakó & Sík, 1999, p. 719). These marketplaces were more formalised, regulated environments where traders needed to obtain a licence and pay regular rent for a stall. Meanwhile, attempts at 'modernisation' also reached market halls in the 1980s. In efforts to further centralise commerce, many of the Budapest market halls were converted into supermarkets, further rationalising food distribution by imposing standards upon agricultural associations and consumers, thus eliminating the link between the latter and food producers.

## Markets After Communism

Following the fall of the Iron Curtain, the privatisation of the retail sector brought fundamental changes to commerce in Hungary as well as in the entire Eastern-Central European region. While street markets were increasingly regulated and controlled, and many traders became full-time entrepreneurs and opened shops, street markets did not lose their reason for existence. As Sík and Wallace suggest, 'open-air markets were relegated to a more residual role—supplying needs not met by the normal retail sector or at a cheaper price' (1999, p. 702). Similarly to the 1980s, the attraction of informal street markets in the 1990s was manifold. The cheaper prices of open-air markets were still possible, particularly 'trader tourism' or 'shuttle trade' (Hann, 1992). Besides this, they also offered products that were not available anywhere else, mostly goods from Turkey, Poland, or the United Arab Emirates. As Sík and Wallace (1999) underline, another important factor in the resilience of street markets is their flexibility: Due to their low infrastructural and administrative needs, these markets are capable of responding very quickly to changing demands from consumers.

In the harsh economic crisis of the early and mid-1990s, informal markets of imported goods were joined by all manners of petty trading in the streets of bigger cities in the region. These situations differed largely according to their level of formality; certain markets consisted only of a few vendors arbitrarily lining up at a street corner, others developed into stable trading locations, with a regular clientele and vendor group, and eventually, with permissions and taxes paid. The food crisis of the early 1990s was addressed by the so-called HDF markets. The Hungarian Democratic Forum, Hungary's leading political party in the beginning of the 1990s, initiated the establishment of farmers' markets bringing together the producers and consumers of agricultural goods directly, avoiding trading intermediaries and thus providing affordable vegetables and fruits to those impoverished by the recession of the transition years (Sík & Wallace, 1999, p. 707). HDF markets were organized all across the country and were coordinated by local party chapters. Vendors often operated from their cars installed in parking lots or vacant parcels of land. HDF markets began by offering only local produce, but soon imported fruits and vegetables, as well as clothes, furniture, and other kinds of goods followed. In an atmosphere where informal markets were tolerated as complementary to formal chains of food and goods distribution, improvised stalls on sidewalks and in parking lots all supported an ambiance of libertinism in the market, relatively uncontrolled, where one could barter and bargain (Szalai, 2005, p. 150) (Figure 5.1).

Some of the remaining relatively informal open-air markets give place to extraordinary economic activities. Budapest's Józsefváros market, expanding on a 12,000 square metre property owned by the Hungarian Railways, has been transformed from a Comecon market into a Chinese market in the past decades. One of the biggest open-air markets of the region, it was believed to attract 2.7 million visitors annually and to accommodate commerce worth 88 million USD in the mid-1990s (Czakó & Sík, 1999, p. 726). This turnover is seen by officials as pure loss

*Figure 5.1* Informal commerce at the Hold utca market hall entrance, Budapest.

in tax income, estimated today at 15 billion HUF. Using this estimation as an argument, together with concerns of safety and trafficking, authorities initiated the shutting down of the market in the second half of 2012.

The importance of semi-informal market arrangements persists today, as food distribution increasingly takes place in supermarkets, and market halls have virtually become the only official alternative. While some of today's market halls in Budapest are internationally known as examples of well-functioning markets, they hardly constitute the same network they did over 100 years ago. Besides the numerous market halls whose renovation was only affordable with the monopolisation of the commerce space (by introducing supermarkets dominating the halls' space), there are only a handful of market halls that are still structured around individual vendors' kiosks and stalls. But even 'market-like' market halls set important boundaries for those unable to pay the rental fee for stalls or kiosks inside the hall.

As in previous moments in the history of markets, the relationship between a market hall's inside and outside is fundamental. The traditional concept of the market is vanishing from the market halls, whose nature of spontaneity and exchange is fading (Szalai, 2005, p. 153), but spontaneity and exchange are flourishing on the pavement outside the halls, in squares, parks, and parking places, in the districts less frequented by tourists or affluent residents. Some of these 'parasite markets' are surprisingly successful. At Hunyadi Square, in Budapest's 6th district, for instance, the small park facing the market hall is filled with stalls every day.

## Between Regulations and Practices

At a recent conference about street markets, participants agreed that the key to well-functioning markets is good regulation.[1] Openness to public food markets and street vending is best manifested in tolerant regulations. Writing about the conflicts between regulations and street vending practices, Alfonso Morales underlines the fact that 'government regulation can drive potential entrepreneurs into noncompliance. . . . Planners should have [interest] in helping cities rather than harass merchants' (Morales, 2009, p. 428). Changing the regulatory framework to allow street markets to take place implies diversification of the rules and the addition of progressive measures and incentives to them. Rules need to be 'adaptable to the needs of distinct types of vendors and take into account different reasons for vending' (Morales, 2009, p. 428).

Instead of being static, Morales continues, regulations 'should be adapted to reflect the experience of merchant and government official alike, to comprehend seasonal changes, and to ensure equity and accessibility. Regulators should not expect immediate compliance; rather, the structure and enforcement should invite experimentation' (Morales, 2009, p. 438). Serving as local economic incubators, markets can be laboratories of self-employment and enterprise creation, as the Brussels-based activist group City Mine(d) demonstrated in its Micronomics project. As a result of negotiations with the City Hall, City Mine(d) arranged artist status for members of an immigrant community so that they could sell their goods tax- and permission-free at specific markets, learning vendors' skills, experiencing demand and supply, and moving on to create their own enterprises.

However, regulations are not necessarily tools of repression and control; they are also in place to protect consumers as well as inhabitants of a city or neighbourhood. Eased regulations can only be reassuring if they function in jointly with a reinforced self-control of vendors. As architect László Rajk underlined at the previously mentioned conference in Budapest, vendors must be organised and led by representatives who can guarantee the quality of food and thus exclude any undesired consequences of food consumption (Rajk, 2011).

## A Market at Hunyadi Square

Economic viability, community cohesion, and access to healthy food and to self-employment in the only remaining open-air food market of Budapest's inner districts—these were the main arguments that activists of the civil organization KAP-HT (Our Treasure, the Market—Hunyadi Square) emphasised when its members entered the fight to protect the market from demolition. KAP-HT was founded by Gabó Bartha in May 2007, when she heard the news that the district's municipal commission had voted to eliminate the open-air market at Hunyadi Square in order to create an underground parking garage serving the House of Europe, a vaguely defined cultural centre to be built in the following years and meant to replace the adjoining market hall. Linking the luxurious Andrássy Avenue to the quickly gentrifying Király Street area, the Hunyadi Square market has become an indicator of the changing demographics, value systems, and consumption patterns of the city, as well as of political attitudes towards food markets (Figure 5.2).

After long negotiations and interventions from the KAP-HT group, the local government took into account the importance of involving local residents in the decision-making process. Meanwhile, they also decided to apply jointly for EU funds for the renovation of the site. Various participatory exercises were introduced to collect views and opinions of the planned development, while the impact of the community on the final plans still remained strongly compromised. The proposed plan for the market square envisioned a 500-car parking garage under the square, which went against the agreement with the participating residents. Following an unsuccessful bid to raise EU funding for the planned car park, the local government shifted its focus to smaller interventions like renovating the park, creating a new playground, redesigning the market stalls, and turning parts of the square into a moderated traffic zone, thus allowing for more space for the Friday and Saturday markets.

Nevertheless, the conflict was renewed by the local government's plan to clear from the square a significant number of trees, considered as unsafe and endangering public use of the square. KAP-HT's call for independent expertise contributed to a deepening of the disagreement between supporters of the competing plans. Thus trees became crucial in the district's heritage preservation

*Figure 5.2* The Hunyadi tér market, Budapest.

*Figure 5.3* KAP-HT collecting signatures to save the Hunyadi tér market, Budapest.

strategy: Once the trees are removed, plans for the parking garage may gain momentum, and the existence of the farmers' market may be put into question. The civil mobilisation won the case; a local court overruled the decision to remove the trees and they remain in the square's refurbishment plan as well. However, close cooperation with the district's chief architect did not prevent the market from remaining on precarious ground. Municipal attempts to reduce its hours of activity and to increase the stall rental fee may result in a more exclusive market structure (Bartha, 2010, p. 33).

The project of KAP-HT, in the beginning, consisted of researching the municipality's files and launching campaigns to raise awareness of the plans related to the market and the hall. Later, however, the focus of the organization shifted towards less political, more community- and local economy–oriented activities: Activists of the group got involved in the life of the market, elaborating strategies for improving services and product variety (by introducing new herbs and vegetables, extending the selection of goods and foods), as well as opening up alternative channels of communication between the market traders, the wider public, visitors, and customers of the market and the local authorities. This is a strategy to deal with a diversity of potential clients—in other words, to cope with its multiple publics (Figure 5.3).

## In Praise of Markets

The polemic around the Hunyadi Square market highlights conceptual differences when it comes to food markets and the use of public space. While the KAP-HT's activities exemplify how an activist group may turn from a resistant position into a project incubator promoting more liveable and sustainable neighbourhoods and cities, the position of the district's municipal commission fell into line with the city government's repressive public space policy of recent years. If deputy mayors did not welcome the phenomenon of street commerce, community activists like Gabó Bartha, in contrast, applauded it: 'I find it senseless that municipalities want to erase a market in the name of modernisation. Let's modernise the market by renewing the stalls, to make the market cleaner, but its obliteration cannot be justified. It is enough to look at the contemporary European scene of outdoor markets to realize the importance of markets in communities, commerce and food security' (G. Bartha, personal communication).

Plans to ban open-air selling are all the more striking, as open-air markets are enjoying an increasing popularity worldwide. The proliferation of public market guides for tourists and special issues of gastronomic magazines witness the emergence of a new idea of markets. In the tourism industry's quest for authenticity, open-air markets are often appreciated par excellence as public spaces that, by being local and global at the same time, transmit a sense of familiarity and where rare encounters with local people and local products are made possible (Brand, 2005, p. 156). Food enthusiasts emphasise that the experience of food consumption is intensified at the markets. The sensory dimensions of buying food in markets transforms the practice of shopping (Siegel, 2005, pp. 105–107). In addition to this, markets may take a number of crucial roles in urban neighbourhoods. In his research about open-air markets, Morales highlights the multifold importance of markets in urban life, offering them for consideration to urban planners:

> First, markets are places, amenities attractive to neighbourhood residents because they contribute to quality of life and sociability. Second, public markets are in a tight reciprocal relationship with urban land markets and community design (markets can provide uses for underutilized and vacant sites). Third, markets play a role in addressing health, ecological, and environmental concerns. They reduce vehicle miles travelled, enhance local sustainability, and help ensure food security. Fourth, markets and street vendors contribute to economic and community development, providing a variety of benefits. (Morales, 2009, p. 426)

Certainly, Morales is not the only researcher to accredit these potentials to markets. In the scholarly and popular literature, markets are often described as genuine public spaces of encounter: 'As forums for the social interaction of inhabitants of the neighbourhood or traders coming from further away, markets often represent a meeting place of very different cultures and languages' (Czakó & Sík, 1999, p. 718). Besides this, while functioning as meeting places for local communities, they also offer contexts for intergenerational encounters and for the exchange of nonprimary information, such as jobs, sales, possibilities (Siegel, 2011). Furthermore, they can be considered as pillars of public health, by providing affordable fresh food, supporting biodiversity, promoting fair trade, and enhancing the access to commercial activities of people with a very low profit margin, often at the peripheries of society (Balkin, 1989). In another perspective, by serving multiple constituencies, from low-income city residents to gourmets, markets may enhance social and ethnic integration (Brand, 2005, p. 154). These dimensions all highlight the public interest in maintaining markets: By including schools and health centres, markets can integrate various public institutions (Tolra, 2011).

## Markets as Spectacles

Despite all the arguments that highlight the markets' social relevance and inclusive capacities, markets do not automatically embody progressive policies. As public space is often treated by neoliberal urban policies as a landscape whose foremost function is to impress and stimulate visitors, open-air markets are often thought of as spectacles of authenticity and vibrant street life, instrumental in gentrifying neighbourhoods and increasing real estate prices. In the close vicinity of Hunyadi tér, where the open market was treated as an unwelcome exhibition of poverty, open-air markets of various kinds occupy the streets every weekend.

The craft market organized in Király utca, the street leading to Hunyadi tér, will, according to the ambitions of its organizers, bring back the street's 'original fame', attracting entrepreneurs to

*Figure 5.4* Farmers' market at Szimpla Kert, Budapest.

rent the vacant shops and tourists to rent the empty apartments. In organizing the craft market, the aim of the Design Street cluster is to arrange it so that 'it becomes a cool, well-designed, entertaining, youthful place' (A. Körtvély, personal communication, January 17, 2012). In the neighbouring Gozsdu udvar, the Gouba craft market 'invites tourists and local residents to a refreshing walk in the heart of the city. . . . At the 'Portobello of Budapest', antique pieces as well as works of selected artists and artisans are displayed to the open-minded, demanding public' (Gouba Craft Market, 2012). A block further on, the internationally known bar, Szimpla kert, accommodates a weekly farmers' market, where only 'reliable' and 'authentic' vendors who are registered by the organisers can sell their produce (Szimpla, 2012) (Figure 5.4).

These descriptions make it evident that they operate with a very well-defined public, which probably excludes many of those frequenting the Hunyadi tér market. Markets are not automatically inclusive social spaces; the composition of their vendors and publics differ according to a market's priorities. Is a market organised to help its vendors make a relatively stable income, to entertain its visitors, or to help a neighbourhood develop? Markets can be tools for contradicting or even opposing planning goals. The difference, often subtle, lies in the details. This is where the task of designing, organizing, and managing a market gains its ultimate significance.

## Conclusion

In this chapter, I attempted to describe and analyse the contemporary dilemmas public food markets face; I approached them in an interdisciplinary field linking urban and architectural history, sociology, and urban policy. This chapter briefly demonstrated how the construction of covered market halls indicated an effort to control food exchange both in terms of hygiene and of taxation. Various historical periods added their own regulatory systems to markets and halls, thus further complicating the possibility of selling and buying at open-air food markets. In this history, regulations are of crucial importance: Regulations can be used as pretexts to eliminate street markets, but they can also engender market activities, thus creating thriving markets, an enhanced public health, and employment possibilities.

There is a striking difference between conflicting understandings of 'order' in public spaces. If in the Middle Ages and in early Modernity, official documents, chronicles, and descriptions used the terms *mixed-use* and *prosperity* as synonyms to express concern that 'establishing useful (physical and legal) boundaries might also provoke a diminution of "disorder" which might be interpreted as a sign of economic decline' (Calabi, 2004, p. 95).

In contrast, *disorder* and *prosperity* are seen today by many in municipal governments as mutually exclusive. If urban policymakers in many cities (including Budapest) have not acknowledged the opportunities markets offer, activists and civil organizations, as well as researchers and designers, have indeed recognized the potential of open-air markets. The success of KAP-HT exemplifies the ways in which conflicts related to markets are intertwined with dilemmas of public space design and regulations, of local economy and employment, of public health and affordable fresh food, of community cohesion and sociability, and of corruption, among others. Faithful to their tradition, markets may prove to be important tools for urban planning, and highly instrumental in creating sustainable cities. But markets alone do not guarantee even development: Depending on the policies they embody, markets can also be used as part of an apparatus of social exclusion and gentrification.

### Note

1 'A Market for Every District: Food, Consumption, Urbanism', a conference organised by the Hungarian Contemporary Architecture Centre on March 19, 2011, in Budapest. For details, see http://kek.org.hu/piac/en.

# Part II

# Multiple Roles of Public Space

*Ali Madanipour, Sabine Knierbein, and Aglaée Degros*

The chapters in Part II analyse the tensions between different stakeholders around the complex nature and the multiple roles of public space. Differences of perspective and conflicts of interest may range from the debates about the existence of public space (Chapter 6) to its role in the city's character (Chapter 7), its historical and cultural value (Chapter 8), and its management and use (Chapter 9). Public spaces are common assets; the meaning, use, and management of these assets, therefore, become the subject of divergent perspectives and interests, which are at times conflicting and controversial. The diversity of society and the multiple layers of cultural significance turn any deliberation over public space into a complex social and political process.

This is particularly the case when the meaning and use of the place are not immediate and tangible, for example, when confronting the troubled memory of a place, the fear of difference, or anxiety over an 'empty' place. They may also arise when spaces are in periods of dramatic transformation, as has been the case in deindustrialising cities and post-Socialist countries. Public space becomes the stage for symbolic reenactment of social values and preferences, and when some prevalent values or patterns of lifestyle are taken for granted, other forms of value and living models may suffer as a result. This is exemplified in the predominance of economic value in neoliberal frameworks, or suspicion of the youth in middle-aged cities, or fear of migrants in closed societies. What may be taken for granted as an ideal type of a European city and its public space, therefore, becomes challenged by the diversity and multiplicity of social actors, each with a different need and demand on the city.

The fear of emptiness and the controversies over a large empty area have been illustrated in Chapter 6 by Nikolai Roskamm. Since May 8, 2010, the former airfield of the Berlin Tempelhof airport has been open to the public by day. Since the 1990s, and especially since closing the airport operations in November 2008, there is an intensive and complex discussion about the airfield's reuse. The topics of discussions include the right to the city, the concept of open city, urban development with an implementation strategy of temporary uses, or questions about governance potentials and requirements. These debates can be clarified with a historical review of the transformations of the huge area—concerning the real use as well as the discursive implications. Furthermore, the new situation—the long-claimed and recently executed opening—and its impacts have to be regarded beyond the current development of the political debate concerning the future of the former airfield. The Tempelhofer Feld could be considered, Roskamm argues, as a colossal burning lens concerning the meaning of the term 'public space' in the different discourses where utopia seems to play a central role in order to foster people's imaginations about what the place could serve as.

In Dresden, as Chloë Voisin-Bormuth shows in Chapter 7, it is the character of the city that is at stake. Very few cities in Europe develop such a programme of redesigning their central public spaces as Dresden has done since the German Reunification; the Hauptstraße, the Postplatz, the Neumarkt, the Altmarkt or the Prager Straße, and the Wiener Platz, only to quote the major projects, are among them. This exceptional situation is due to the particular history of the city centre of Dresden. After having been destroyed by the allied bombing in 1945, the city centre has been rebuilt with a complete new plan after 1945. The GDR was convinced that urbanism can change the society. This project of a new city for the new socialist man radically breaks with the old public spaces of the conventional capitalistic European city. But it also remains unachieved. The Reunification not only puts an end to the construction of the city centre, which began during the GDR, it also brings its own transformation. The socialist public spaces are the subject of a new design that deeply transforms their shape and meanings. Another typology appears, supposed to make Dresden a European city again and its centre a new attractive urban place. A survey of the users and interviews with those responsible for core planning show an ambivalent situation: If the public places are more used than the past, this use becomes more specialized and the reception of the new projects is moderate. The question of the way to make Dresden a place of urbanity, accepted and appreciated not only by its tourists, but also by its inhabitants, is still open.

The character of the city is an open question in all cities that experience radical transition. In Chapter 8, Jerzy Elżanowski focuses on the deployment of a politics of nostalgia during the recent renovation of two key streets in Warsaw and on their transformation into (imagined) semi-pedestrian, entertainment, and cultural zones. One pivotal element of each street's refurbishment was chosen as an example of issues to be explored further. Although the material changes to each street's fabric will comprise the core analysis of the text, two main subthemes will ground the research in a historical and cultural context: the problems of place and authenticity with respect to commemorative practices in Warsaw, as well as the role of the decaying technical infrastructure of Nazi oppression in the post-catastrophic city. The trouble is, Elżanowski argues, that the recent past we long for is a particularly tragic one. In order to reconcile longing with tragedy, we sanitize the past, perhaps in self-defence, and end up with unkind reproductions—unkind to those who lived oppression, but ultimately destructive to our own capacity for change. The author uses 'we' in this text, because this is hardly a local, national, or even continental issue. How Warsaw interprets and presents its past concerns us all, because Warsaw is a central node in the Holocaust history—a history that remains at the core of the very painful memory and representation debates.

Chapter 9, by Monika Litscher, focuses on competence in the context of the performative and dynamic characteristics of public space. It presents the results of research into two applied, trans-disciplinary projects, 'Management of uses in the public space' (*'Nutzungsmanagement im öffentlichen Raum'*) and 'Expulsion from public urban spaces' (*'Wegweisung aus öffentlichen Stadträumen'*) supported by the Confederation's innovation promotion agency. From 2007 to 2009, the University of Applied Sciences and Arts in Lucerne explored with the practitioner partners from the public authorities of six Swiss cities the management of urban public spaces. A particular focus was set on youth behaviour and cultures in public spaces. The main part of the project was the empirical case studies. In this context, Monika Litscher and her colleagues analysed six public spaces in these cities. The central academic interest resided in an examination of the perception, use, and appropriation of the public space, and the interaction with the constructed space. Theoretical concepts of space, based on a dynamic, relational, and relativistic understanding of space, served as premises, according to which it is assumed that urban space is dynamically constituted by the connection of perceived, lived, and conceived space. Urban public spaces are spatiotemporal frames of action, with a certain social and cultural order, as realms of experience and of perception, and also as places of integration and diversity. The complex urban spatial structure is marked by continual material and discursive conflicts on the one hand, while on the other hand it serves as a space with multiple possibilities for many different forms of leisure activities. By means of a multimethod procedure, interpretative, comprehension-oriented approaches based on methods of qualitative social research and visual studies were applied. The results of the case studies were discussed with Swiss partners from practice. Part of this discussion and the development of strategies were, on the one hand, suggestions of application for urban development, administration, and politics. On the other hand, emphasis was placed on the importance and quality of urban public space.

# Chapter 6

# 4,000,000 m² of Public Space

## The Berlin 'Tempelhofer Feld' and a Short Walk with Lefebvre and Laclau

*Nikolai Roskamm*

'Tempelhofer Feld' is the name for an almost 400 hectare terrain of the former airport Berlin Tempelhof, centrally located inside Berlin's railway ring. The airport operations were stopped in October 2008; since May 2010, the airfield has been open to the public. The Tempelhofer Feld is a specific space, concerning its texture, quality, usage, and materiality. But it is also a specific space concerning its discursive representation in the public sphere. There has been a big and ongoing debate for a long time about the future of the terrain. That dispute became very lively after the closure of the airport, particularly during the 18 months when the huge free space was hermetically locked. In these debates—and this is already one of the particularities of the Tempelhofer Feld—some fundamental points and questions were brought into the discussion: questions about the future of the urban, about making the space public, about the conditions of the political, and about the production of space. In this chapter I would like to approach this specific space in order to explore its singularity. My thesis is that the peculiarity of the Tempelhofer Feld has something to do with its emptiness. The huge location is almost empty, without buildings (just with some small barracks), without streets and cars, without noteworthy topography, even nearly without trees. This state as an empty space is the result of a complex history which I am going to report next. And this emptiness is, too, a link to some theoretical concepts of the urban and the space. My aim is to connect both things in my report.

My contribution is structured into two parts. The first part is about the history of the place, its development, and the development of the debates about its present and future use. The second part glances at urban theory and contrasts this story with a more abstract point of view. Therefore, I suggest two short walks: Henri Lefebvre's theory about the production of space and Ernesto Laclau's reflections on the nature of the political. Lefebvre is probably the most discussed thinker in urban theory and his oeuvre affects urban studies until today; for considering a specific urban space and a specific urban discourse, a glance at Lefebvre's thinking stands to reason. Laclau is not so much represented in urban theory but his works have—in my eyes—a big potential to enhance the debates in urban theory. My thesis is that the emptiness of the area corresponds with the absence of predestination as an important point in both regarded theories. This point should bridge the history with the theory. And this is the purpose: On the one hand, the theory should help to understand the history and the present conditions of the huge public space; on the other hand, the case study of Tempelhofer Feld should facilitate the access to the abstract urban and political theories.

## History

The airport Berlin Tempelhof is a place full of historical meaning. Until the 18th century the area was used only for agriculture, but since the early 19th century the Prussian military started to use the area temporarily for field exercises. At the same time, the inhabitants of the growing Berlin city began to adopt the field and it became a popular meeting spot, particularly on weekends. Both the military and civilians used the field for aviation experiments from the beginning (Schmitz, 1997, pp. 9–10). Because of its location at the city outskirts, future development of the Tempelhofer Feld soon became an object of discussion. That means that since the mid-19th century there has been a public debate about the planning aims. The first idea was to integrate the field into the urban fabric and to build dense housing districts in the surrounding areas (and the urban planners were commissioned to draw master plans and detailed designs). The second idea was to build a so-called *Luftschiffhafen*, which means a kind of aviation centre for zeppelin and airship prototypes. The third general position was to maintain the field for recreation and leisure activities. Reinhard Baumeister, one of the first urban design theorists in Germany, cautioned in 1911 against surrendering the field for economic speculation and city expansion, because of the danger of 'sustained loss of public health, national defence power, prosperity and happiness' (Baumeister, 1911, p. 36). That statement is remarkable: Today national defence power is not anymore such a hot topic for urban development—but to oppose 'happiness' against 'economic exploitation' is 100 years later still worth reflecting on in a debate about urbanism (Dascher, 2007, pp. 59–62).

Meanwhile, the beginning of World War I interrupted the debate and the Tempelhofer Feld was used as a big sickbay. After the war, the aviation development was pushed by technological progress, and hence the airport planning was established. In 1920, the building of two runways started, the airport operations begun in 1923, and the first airport terminal was finished a few years later. The Berlin Tempelhof airport soon grew to a national and international hub and more and bigger airplanes became common. One third of the German air traffic came through Tempelhof in 1930. The planning of the project *Zentralflughafen* was started in the 1930s as well, after the Nazi takeover of the development was forced. The shell construction of the huge new airport building (planned as a symbol for Nazi Germany) was finished within 18 months. The beginning of the World War II changed the priorities again; the airport was used as production site for the arms industry and the building activities concerning the airport were stopped. During the war, more than 5,000 people worked at the airport, including a large number of forced workers (Demps & Paschke, 1998).

After the Second World War, the place was used by the U.S. Air Force. Without suffering major damages the airport could soon resume full operation, finding special importance because of the 'Berlin-Blockade' (Huschke, 1998). As reaction to the currency conversion in 1948, the Soviet occupation force blockaded all land and water routes to West Berlin, and only three air corridors remained open. Tempelhof was the most important part of the American *'Luftbrücke'* (airlift), which was for almost 11 months the only possible connection from West Germany to West Berlin, which is why it has a strong emotional meaning in the city's collective memory until today. The U.S. Air Force extended Tempelhof to an important military base but simultaneously the civil air traffic grew again. Especially the package and charter airlines led to a continual growth of passenger numbers. Meanwhile the inner-city location of the airport was becoming a problem: Pollutant emissions and aircraft noise were leading to protest from the surrounding inhabitants. Therefore, a second airport was built in Berlin-Tegel, where the complete charter air traffic moved to in 1968. Only the national airlines and the military base remained in Tempelhof. After the fall of the Berlin Wall in November 1989, the general conditions changed again. First, the U.S. Air Force base was terminated in 1993. Second, the German government decided in 1996 to close the airports in Tempelhof and Tegel and to build a new international airport in Berlin-Schönefeld. After a long discussion about these decisions (including a referendum about maintaining Tempelhof as an airport) the airline operations were terminated definitely on October 31, 2008.

Tempelhof airport—to summarise the historical account—is strongly connected to political and historical developments in Germany. On the one hand, Tempelhof became a multiple symbol: for aviation development, for the Nazi period, and for the West-Berlin location as an island

during the Cold War. On the other hand, Tempelhof's history is a result of economic development. The steady increase in airline traffic and the airline technology industry initiated its use as
an airport in the beginning of the 20th century; 100 years later the same forces led to the closure
of the airport and the construction of a new one at the fringe of the city. Therefore, closing the
airport in favour of building a new one is related to the industry's movement to the city outskirts
as a result of socioeconomic change and postindustrial urban development.

## Public Space

The closure of the airport was a milestone in the long lasting debate about Tempelhofer Feld. Already a topic of discussion, the appropriate use for the former airport became even more urgent.
To be precise, there were two different debates: the discussion about future uses, and about how
to deal with the field immediately. The future use question had a time horizon of maybe 10 or 20
years, whereas the immediate use referred to the present and to the interesting issue of what could
be done with 4,000,000 m$^2$ of free and empty space. The second dispute lasted 18 months, and after
the field's opening in 2010, the conflict seems to have been forgotten quite quickly. Meanwhile, the
city marketing machinery adopted the fascination of the people for the empty airport. Now Tempelhofer Feld is part of the last and hottest Berlin lifestyle image, not least sketched by official urban
planning and city marketing representatives. One might say urban planning is doing what it used to
do: reinterpreting urban process as a story of its own success (Kamleithner, 2008; Roskamm, 2011).
However, for exploring the particularity of an urban place, it is more fruitful to regard urban history
as a history of conflicts (rather than as history of successes). Therefore, the period in 2009 when the
battle of the field's opening was still undecided should be a strong focus of attention.

After the airport's closure in October 2008, the situation became paradoxical. In terms of
ownership, Tempelhofer Feld was a public space (with the federal government and the federal
state of Berlin as owners), but in reality the place was hermetically sealed with massive fences
preventing public access. In summer 2008, the Berlin urban planning authority proclaimed a
first temporary opening in November 2008 (promptly after closing the airport) and the rest to be
opened in spring 2009 (SenStadt, 2008). But this promise was broken. The schedule of responsi-
bilities slipped between different authorities, especially between the urban planning administration and the administration of finance. The Berliner Immobiliengesellschaft (BIM, a privatised
real estate company concerned with the city's property management) stepped in and became an
important player in the Tempelhof debate. The BIM was strictly against any opening. In January
2009, the CEO of BIM, Mr. Lemiss, declared that it would be impossible to open the field. Because of 'the risks and the costs' and due to the 'financial structure', the Tempelhofer Feld could
not be opened to the public anytime soon (Lemiss, 2009). Hence, BIM ordered the building of an
additional fence and the installation of CCTV cameras to keep observation on the free field. It
became obvious that the Tempelhofer Feld perception changed completely. Suddenly the area no
longer possessed a 'huge potential' for Berlin urban development (as it was posted in the debate
before the closure of the airport), but a place at risk of getting out of control.

Against that new edict grew resistance. A protest movement arose demanding the field's immediate opening for everyone. Tempelhofer Feld became a big topic in the media and criticism against
the lock out was raised day by day. The Green Party in particular was engaged in the discussion
and favoured opening the portals. Besides that, a couple of grassroots initiatives were founded and
they started to organise protests in the surrounding neighbourhoods. The initiative 'Tempelhof für
alle' (Tempelhof for all) initiated a big public campaign for the opening and announced an event
with the slogan 'Have you ever squatted an airport?' The climax of that campaign was the endeavour to enter the field in June 2009. A massive police force prevented the squat and the curious
image of 2,000 constables guarding a huge empty meadow was broadcast in the news.

Maybe the authorities' fear of opening Tempelhofer Feld could be explained as a kind of 'horror vacui', an ancient expression for the 'fear of emptiness'. Such a fear (that's the point beyond the term) is created from the rational man's urge to find significance in everything (Lidwell, Holden, & Butler, 2011, p. 128). An absolute emptiness (without any significance) is insufferable to the human intellect and could become a real nightmare. 'Closing the gap' is the instinctive reaction concerning urban development in general and for urban planners in particular. And if suddenly such a huge emptiness appears, the proceedings become imponderable. Locking the public space from the public with a huge security machine seems exactly to represent a strategy against such imponderability based on a 'horror vacui', a collective fear of the emptiness.

At the same time (and as a strategy against the emptiness) the debate about the future use of Tempelhofer Feld was continued at different levels. The urban planning authorities developed a so-called 'dynamic master plan' with a green park area in the centre and some buildings on the fringes of the field. The idea for an International Gardening Exhibition, IGA 2017, and an International Building Exhibition, IBA 2020, were worked out as well. In addition, the urban planning authority organised several urban design competitions, one of which was titled *Prozessuale Stadtentwicklung* (Process-Orientated Urban Development). One project of the competition attracted particular attention. The design 'The Berg' by Jakob Tigges (a Berlin-based architect) proposed building a 1,071 m high mountain in the middle of the field. The project polarised public reactions varying between enthusiasm and indignation. The point against Tigges's design was particularly an economic reason—what would be the expenses of such a project? Tigges's answer was tricky: no money at all! The design was a real imagination; the mountain should be only a theoretical construction, a mountain in the mind. The idea was just to claim the mountain, to create a collective Berlin lie. 'The Berg' is playing with the desires of the city (a city located in a rather flat landscape); the result should be a mountain of lies from where the Berliners could send postcards (The Berg, 2012a). Tigges's maximum of nothing (the phantom mountain) won many credits in Internet blogs and web-based communities (for a selection of reviews see The Berg, 2012b), but it was eliminated at the first competition level. The Berlin planning authority was not able to deal with the project (Figure 6.1).

Besides the official competitions and procedures, there was a growing independent public debate about the future of Tempelhofer Feld. During this time, there were many discussion meetings concerning the best future use of the former airport and a lively discussion evolved not only about Tempelhof but also about urban topics in general. One example is an event organised by the network Metrozones in December 2008, where some activists from academia supported the local Tempelhof actors in establishing a position grounded in urban theory (Metrozones, 2008). One point of discussion was whether the lowest common denominator of urban left wing policy in Berlin could be—or should be—advocating free and green spaces (further evidence for such a position is the debate about MediaSpreeVersenken, 2011).

Another example of the vibrant debate is the campaign 'One square meter for everyone'. This campaign was started by the critical alternative Berlin newspaper *Die tageszeitung* (taz) and had an agenda with a radical understanding of participation. The Tempelhofer Feld has almost 4,000,000 m², and the City of Berlin has almost the same number of inhabitants (Bewegung. taz, 2011). The point was to combine both numbers and to give every Berlin resident one square metre of the field. Because nobody can do something special with only one square metre, the educational impetus of the project was to bring the people (the new landowners) together to realise their ideas. The campaign initiated an interesting debate about the possibilities and borders of direct democracy and participation. However, from a more critical review, the 'one square meter for all' idea has some neoliberal flavour: Now the field is common property and the question is why it should be necessary to smash this common property into small private units for restarting a common project or, in other words, why privatise the existing public space. For this reason the initiative lost its publicity after the opening of the field.

*Figure 6.1* The Berg, Berlin.

Since May 2010, the discursive level of the Tempelhofer Feld debate was interrupted at a material level: The opening and therefore the real experience of the area. Eighteen months after airline operations closed, the fear of emptiness was overcome and finally, as a result of public pressure, the entrance doors were unlocked. The commissioning of another private company (the Adlershof Projekt GmbH, commissioned as project coordinator) contributed to making the space public (which might show that not every privatisation is automatically opposed to the public good). After opening, it was possible to explore what lay behind the fences. And it was true; most of the field was totally empty. The transformation from airport to public space was accompanied with very few small-budget measures: There is one new small facility for drinking and eating, some direction signs, and some small information desks. Otherwise the field is completely unchanged. It is not more (and not less) than an almost 400 hectare big open field, meadows with almost no trees and two runways, an airport without airplanes.

And exactly this condition seems to fascinate the people. The field is extremely well accepted. In the first year of opening (according to official statistics) around 10,000 people per good-weather day came to the field, altogether around 1.5 million visitors. The forms of occupancy are not so exceptional. People are doing what people are used to doing in public free spaces: sun bathing, promenading, barbecuing. True to the original tradition and supported by a constant blowing, wind flight experiences are very popular. The runways are especially affected: Every imaginable type of non-motorcraft movement is practised on the big asphalt routes. The wind and the asphalt, these are the main Tempelhofer Feld excitements. The third attraction is the emptiness. This emptiness is perceived as a contrast to the busy and crowded city life and is regarded as an important quality. Especially on the Internet, there are many examples where people are trying to express this quality:

> I've been here many times since the opening. What I have found has overwhelmed me. The most astonishing point was—I needed some time to realize it—that there is nothing on the place. You are going through the entrance door to the airfield and suddenly you are feeling free. There is no advertisement. No one is trying to sell anything, neither in a direct nor in an indirect way. You can stroll and unconsciously you will walk very slowly. On the other end of the field there is no purpose. And the way to the other side is long. . . . What reason could there be for walking fast? What sense could there be in reaching a place which has no quality but being on the other side? . . . In the centre of the field the city is perceived only as a calm noise of the cars. . . . You see the huge airport building and the Television tower can be clasped with two fingers. You hear the birds. Paradoxically, the vastness gives a feeling of safety. . . . There are the same activities like anywhere else. But they have a different effect. Because you can overview everything you can watch many different people, all are here because of joy and pleasure and besides they all are individual they are united. . . . All people I meet responding to my smile. Anyway there are not many reasons not to smile. On this place there is no reason at all. (Moniac, 2010)

This citation gets to the heart of the matter. The emptiness of the field is not only an emptiness of buildings, streets and cars, topography and trees; the emptiness includes the absence of economics, the absence of the imperative of valorisation. Somewhere in the middle of nowhere this absence wouldn't be of further interest; but in the middle of the city and in this huge dimension, the empty state is a real provocation—a counter-thesis to the hegemonic market ideal of neoliberalism, an opposition to the usual definition of the city as place of trade and commerce, and finally an alternative model of centrality. Being central without being commercial and without having a clearly defined urban function—this is the challenge of the Tempelhofer Feld.

What is the answer of the urban planning administration? How does urbanism deal with this challenge? The emptiness of the field remains a provocation, an unacceptable status, something to change. The official guiding principles for the recent Tempelhofer Feld planning carry the common new public management approach and are packed full with economic terms like 'valorisation', 'exploitation', 'efficiency', 'city as an enterprise', and so on (SenStadt 2010, p. 7). Of course, if a city is regarded as an enterprise, the former airport is above all a potential for making profit. And because of the inherent functionalism of urbanism and its urge to bring things into order, it couldn't take into consideration the idea of doing nothing with the field.

But in the meantime, the surprising success of the current vastness has infiltrated the discussions and plans. For instance, in the last competition, which was concerned with designing the landscape park in the centre of the field, none of the six first-round winning designs dealt with expansion or exploitation but with showing what is dominant in the present situation: the emptiness. In relation to the landscape designs that were published before the opening, the new approach respects the current atmosphere of the field. The winning design from landscape architects GrossMax, with urban planners Sutherland and Hussey (GrossMax, 2012), does not change very much. They suggest an artificial 60 metre high climbing rock (somehow in the tradition of 'The Berg') together with some new entrances and paths in concentric arrangements.

Recently, the projected International Gardening Exhibition, IGA 2017, was cancelled and displaced to the fringe of the city; the International Building Exhibition, IBA 2020, originally planned with the Tempelhofer Feld as the main building site, was dispersed in a more decentralised concept. The initiative '100% Tempelhofer Feld' is preparing a referendum on preservation of the field in its present state (THF, 2012). The calls for leaving the field untouched are growing ever louder (Figure 6.2 and 6.3).

*Figure 6.2 and 6.3* Tempelhofer Feld, Berlin, 6:30 a.m.

*Figure 6.2 and 6.3* Continued

*Figure 6.2 and 6.3* Continued

## Lefebvre: Social Space and the Urban Illusion

At this point I would like to change my perspective to reflect the case on a more abstract level. For this reason, I start a short walk with the French philosopher Henry Lefebvre. Lefebvre's definition of the urban as 'a place where conflicts are expressed' (2003, p. 175) is fundamental in critical urban theory. In my short walk, I will highlight only two aspects of Lefebvre's complex thinking: The implications of his basic assumption of space as a social product and his fundamental critique of urbanism. Both arguments are helpful in understanding the specific nature of Tempelhofer Feld.

Lefebvre's starting point is his *Critique de la vie quotidienne* (1974, 1975), in which he submits—with recourse to the early work of Marx—an affiliation to the humanistic critique of capitalism. Until the 1950s, Lefebvre was a member of the Parti Communiste Français but then he left it by the 'rarely used leftward exit'; he was at his most influential in the blazing years of the 1960s and pushed philosophy out into streets (Wark, 2011, p. 93). In this period, Lefebvre started his inquiries into the urban; *Le droit à la ville* (1968) and *La revolution urbaine* (2003) functioned as founding documents of critical urban studies. In the 1970s, Lefebvre focused on the concept of space and *La production of l'Espace* (1991) became one of the main idea generators of the 1990s 'spatial turn' in social and cultural sciences (Roskamm, 2012).

Lefebvre approaches space in a complex, multilayered, and sometimes not completely consistent way (Schmid, 2010, p. 98). He develops his concept of the perceived, conceived, and lived space respectively of spatial practice, representations of space, and representational spaces (Lefebvre, 1991, pp. 31 53). According to Lefebvre, space is a historical product and the production of space is a historical process. This production is the very object of his epistemological interest. The interleaving of the different space practices—experiences of everyday life, space appropriation, conceivability, and representation—produces space itself. Lefebvre's main point is that space is a product produced by human beings, which means that space is a social product. This thesis borders on the tautologous and in some actual contributions of the 'spatial turn' discussion this statement seems to remain without any message (Hard, 2003; Werlen, 2010); however, Lefebvre was aware of this difficulty and he delivers a profound reflection on its derivations. The first implication of his declaration (that social space is a social product) is the disappearance of the (physical) natural space (1991, p. 30). Natural space remains the common point of departure, the origin of the social process; but this space is only the background of the picture: 'Nature is now seen as merely the raw material out of which the productive forces of a variety of social systems have forged their particular spaces' (1991, p. 31). The second implication is that every society produces its own space. A study on the specific production of space becomes, in this sense, a study on the state of the present nature of the producing society. The third implication of Lefebvre's initial hypothesis is that space *is a product;* the knowledge of it must be expected to reproduce and expound the process of production, the object of interest must be expected to shift from things in space to the actual production of space (1991, p. 36). Things and discourse on space can henceforth show this productive process. Space in its totality needs not only to be subjected to analytic scrutiny, 'but also to be engendered by and within theoretical understanding'. In a very strong sense of the word—from within, not just from without (descriptively)—theory reproduces the generative process of the production of space. The historical and its consequences—all that happened at a particular spot or place and thereby changed it—becomes inscribed in space; production process and product present themselves as two inseparable aspects and not two separable ideas (1991, p. 37). In this perspective, Lefebvre first of all renders assistance on how to study a specific space (in my interpretation, a space like the Tempelhofer Feld):

> [W]e should have to look at history itself in a new light. We should have to study not only the history of space, but also the history of representations, along with that of their relationships—with each other, with practice, and with ideology. History would have to take in not

only the genesis of these spaces but also, and especially, their interconnections, distortions, displacements, mutual interactions, and their links with spatial practice of the particular society or mode of production under consideration. (1991, p. 42)

My second point is Lefebvre's elaborated and tart critique of urbanism. Urbanism in the Lefebvreian thinking is the main government instrument for programming space alongside capitalism, which means it is an instrument to establish order and to produce coherence in the messy urban reality (2003, pp. 151–164). According to Lefebvre, urbanism claims to be a system and pretends to 'embrace, enclose, process a new totality'; it wants to be the 'modern philosophy of the city, justified by (liberal) humanism while justifying a (technocratic) utopia' (2003, p. 153). Lefebvre recognises a 'fundamental void' in urbanism, because the urban illusion asserts itself to replace or supplant urban practice and because it fails to examine this practice. For urbanists, urban practice is a blind field, 'they live it, they are in it, but they don't see it, and certainly cannot grasp it as such'. With complete peace of mind, the urbanists substitute their own representations of space, of social life, of groups and their relationships for practice and they 'don't know where these representations come from or what they imply—that is, the logic and strategy that they serve' (2003, p. 153). Urbanists seem to be unaware of the fact that they themselves figure in these relationships of production as organisers and administrators. In the words of Lefebvre, urbanism is 'both antitheory and antipractice', a 'cloud on the mountain that blocks the road' (2003, p. 163).

In many cases, Lefebvre refers in his deconstruction of urbanism to the conditions and impacts of free and empty space. According to Lefebvre, urbanism is an ideology creating a space as an objective scientific and impartial sphere where its repressive logic would appear as a consistent stage (Schmid 2010, p. 264). As with any ideology, it does not stop at being simply reductive. It systematically extrapolates and concludes, as if it held and manipulated all the elements of the question, as if it had resolved the urban problematic in and through a total theory, one that was immediately applicable (Lefebvre, 2003, p. 157). Lefebvre reports that this extrapolation becomes excessive when it tends towards a kind of medical ideology. The urbanist imagines himself caring for and healing a sick society, a pathological space. He perceives spatial diseases, 'which are initially conceived abstractly as an available void, the fragmented into partial contents'. Eventually, space itself becomes a subject, it 'suffers, grows ill, must be taken care of so it can be returned to (moral) health' (2003, p. 157).

'Space is available. Why? Because it is almost empty or seems to be. . . . Free space belongs to thought, to action. Technocratic thought oscillates between the representation of empty space, nearly geometric, occupied by the results of those logics and strategies' (Lefebvre, 2003, p. 154).

Lefebvre judges in his polemic the proposals of urbanism as well. According to him, the plans of the urbanists are usually limited to 'cutting space into grids and squares'; technocrats, 'unaware of what goes on in their own mind and in their working concepts', profoundly underrate what happens (and what does not) in their blind field and end up 'minutely organizing a repressive space' (2003, p.154). Urbanism encompasses this enormous operation, dissimulating its fundamental features, meanings, and finality. Beneath its benign exterior, humanist and technological, it masks capitalist strategy: 'the control of space, the struggle against the trend toward lower profits, and so on' (2003, p. 156).

The link to my efforts in analysing the Tempelhofer Feld is obvious—all of the Lefebvre implications of defining space as a social product are part of my suggested approach: The natural (geographical, physical) space takes a back seat (but is still in place as background of the picture); space is the result of a social production and therefore a possibility for understanding social processes; and space is a product—a product of history and a product of discourse. The whole complex mixture of everyday life, urban occupancy, and space production is the space of the Tempelhofer Feld. Lefebvre's space dimensions especially could give appropriate categories for a deeper analysis according to the different levels of the Tempelhofer Feld debate; the dimensions of perceived, conceived, and lived space are here on display as if in a goldfish bowl. To find a way of understanding Lefebvre's terms 'spatial practice', 'representations of space', and 'representational space', the example Tempelhof is recommendable as well. The spatial practice consists of the perceiving processes (the debate, the discourses), the representations of space situated particularly on the master plan level, and the representational space composed of each personal adoption of the place. Finally, the role of urbanism can be illuminated within Lefebvre's attack on urbanism. As the historical account has shown, filling the gap and bringing the big emptiness into a manageable order are indeed still the main topics of the current urban planning approach. Not only the role of urbanism, but also the function of the urban can be revealed at the same moment. The urban as a place of conflicts is Lefebvre's way of thinking and the reality lies in Tempelhofer Feld, a space where the conditions and contents of such conflicts can be examined in real time.

In the centre of these conflicts is the figure of empty space. The emptiness is the object of the debate: On the one hand, urbanism (animated by its 'horror vacui') tries to fill the void with master plans, efficiency, and floor space, or at least with concepts for a designed and organised leisure area; the counter concept is to celebrate and to defend the emptiness as a place free of economic valorisation and control. The Tempelhofer Feld is—despite (or because) of its emptiness—a very central space where fundamentally different concepts collide. The aim of urbanism is to create a public space on Tempelhofer Feld, overlooking what already exists. Still more, the urbanistic approach tends to destroy the present public sphere with its attempts to bring the space back into order and normality.

## Laclau: Antagonistic Forces

My second trip into the theoretical terrain leads to the London-based Argentine thinker Ernesto Laclau and his political theory of contingency and antagonism. Laclau is popular (and contested) in political theory, especially in the so-called French theory. However, in urban studies, his exceptional thinking is less established. Laclau offers an explanation for the constitutive function of conflicts and can be regarded as supplement to Lefebvre's definition of the urban as a place of conflicts. And his theory is also a concept of space. Both aspects should expand the theoretical input so far and enhance the reflection about the Tempelhofer Feld with a sublime argument.

In *New Reflections on the Revolution of Our Time* (1990), Laclau's development of his political theory is based on the premise of a nondetermined history. According to Laclau, history is the result of contingent power relations between forces that cannot be reduced to any kind of unitary principle. Every power relation is contingent and depends on conditions that are contingent as well. Because every power relation is not determined—and this is the optimistic element in Laclau's theory—there is the possibility of changing these relations: 'If social relations are contingent, it means they can be radically transformed through struggle, instead of that transformation being conceived as a self-transformation of an objective nature' (1990, p. 35).

Laclau refers at this point to the post-foundational thesis of French philosopher Claude Lefort, who analyses the place of power in democracy (Lefort, 1990, p. 293). Intrinsically, at this place should be found the 'final reason', the deterministic fundamental for all history. The post-foundational argument is that such a final reason and such a basic fundamental do not and cannot exist because there is no final objectivity. Struggles and conflicts to occupy this place cannot be successful in an enduring way, but it's equally impossible to finish and to complete such struggles and conflicts. The essence of Lefort's thesis is that in democracy the place of power is 'essentially vacant' (Laclau, 1990, p. 293). Again, we find the figure of an empty place.

Laclau stresses the potential to transform as a condition for political thinking. And he adds an important point: He explains that history is not only based on contingent conditions, but also on antagonistic forces. In Laclau's theory, antagonism is the propellant that produces contingency, the discursive form that constitutes the borderline of objectivity and that reveals that all objectivity is partial and precarious (Laclau & Mouffe, 1991, p. 177). Antagonism is the limit of all objectivity; antagonism does not have an objective meaning, but prevents the constitution of objectivity itself (Laclau, 1990, p. 17). Laclau stresses that negativity is constitutive and foundational with the result that 'the uniqueness and rationality of history must be abandoned' (1990, p. 18). His emphasis on antagonism and negativity refutes the approaches that create the social world as an objective consensus model of free communication. In such a Habermasian understanding of politics, the assertion is that 'there is no foundational conflict' (Lefort & Gauchet, 1990, p. 111). Laclau inverts this argument. He develops a political theory where conflict becomes the crucial point. The moment of antagonism 'where the undecidable nature of the alternatives and their resolution through power relations becomes fully visible, constitutes the field of the "political"' (Laclau, 1990, p. 35).

Laclau's concept, too, is a theory of space, but a concept that is very different from space concepts in sociology and geography. At the beginning of his theory, Laclau poses the classical space question of philosophy: What is out of space? His answer is the crucial point for his whole theory: Out of space is the 'constitutive outside' (1990, p. 9) and the division between the inside and the outside is Laclau's theoretical big bang. Following Laclau, the outside constitutes every system of significance: every space—and Laclau stresses that his understanding of 'space' includes the physical space, because every space is a discursive construct at any time (1990, p. 41)—every discourse and every identity. Those systems of meaning (the inside) need the outside for their own constitution. According to Laclau's theory, all systems of signification have to try all along to become the outside. But this is not possible (because the outside is constitutive). Therefore, the outside is the cause for the permanent effort of those systems to stabilise their regime (becoming the outside) and at the same time the reason for the impossibility to comply (1990, p. 9).

According to Laclau, space is a 'system of meaning'. The crucial point in his conception is that space is—like all others systems of meaning (e.g., discourses, identities, societies)—fragile, a system that cannot be stabilised completely. Despite the fact that stabilisations are finally not possible, the feature of such a system is its permanent attempt to establish. Laclau calls the efforts for stabilisation 'spatialisation' (1990, p. 72). Spatialisation emerges in a practice of repetition with the purpose of fixing meaning or 'producing spaces', an attempt that is necessary but finally impossible to accomplish. Exactly these practices are Laclau's version of the 'production of space' and in many aspects, his concept of spatialisation seems to be compatible with Lefebvre's theory. A spatialisation cannot be successful in the last instance, but hegemonic forces can temporarily produce space in an iterative articulation. Laclau describes such a temporarily successful spatialisation as 'sedimentation'. Sedimentation is the provisional effective fixing of meaning and another word for 'objectivity'. Sedimentation is based on the 'forgetting of the origins' through routinisation (1990, p. 35; see also Butler, 1993). On the other side 'dislocation'—another key concept of Laclau—is the contrary of sedimentation and spatialisation. Dislocation stresses the uncertain, the interference, and the enduring. Equally, Laclaus's space theory explains the division between 'politics' and 'the political'. Spatialisation and sedimentation are 'politics' because they have intermittent success in the fixing of meaning.. The contradiction of politics is the binding spell of signification, the destabilisation of the systems, the fight against routines, or simply 'the political'. According to Laclau, politics and the political are controversy concepts.

In *Hegemony and Socialist Strategy*, Laclau, with Chantal Mouffe (1991), transforms his political space theory into the project of 'radical democracy'. One aim of a radical democracy project should be to preserve one's own power for 'radical imagination', which means the capability for utopia, for thinking the Other (1991, p. 190). The fundamental condition for such a project would be to institutionalise the moment of suspense and openness and to accept the antagonistic character of all the political (Marchart, 2010, pp. 13–84).

Laclaus's concept of space can be regarded as the missing element linking political theory and the urbanistic discourse about space. On the one hand, the concept distinguishes the eventful and contingent movement (dislocation) from the durable and fixed substance (sedimentation, spatialisation) on the other. And in this reading, the distinction in built and nonbuilt spaces is at least unimportant because space is at any time discursive *and* material. But with Laclau, now it is much easier to stress the specific attempts at dislocation and spatialisation and to identify these different types of antagonistic forces.

At this point we can find our way back to the Tempelhofer Feld. With Laclau's theory it becomes possible to identify the ongoing processes as antagonistic forces. The field and its emptiness is something wild, an unusual urban place symbolising the contradiction of routine. The master plans and guiding principles, the urban design competitions and the governed participation, all that activity by the local authorities are forms of spatialisation and politics. On the other side, the initiatives for obtaining the open character of the field and for resisting integration into the urban fabric are manifestations of an approach against sedimentation and references to the political. And, of course, 'The Berg' is the best example for preserving the 'radical imagination', which scrutinises the routines of urbanism and its attempts at spatialisation. Furthermore, an open question is the possibility that urbanism can change sides, from sedimentation to dislocation, from politics to the political. Can it be possible to stress the political in urban planning? Or does urbanism remain at any time on the level of politics? Maybe the Tempelhofer Feld is a good place to find it out.

## Resume

The Tempelhofer Feld is something special. The popularity of the empty place is conspicuously in need of explanation. Regarding the history, the conditions and recent processes can be illuminating. But the singularity and particularity of the 4,000,000 m$^2$ public space in Berlin needs some more explanation. The short walk with Lefebvre and Laclau has been such an effort. The theories of both thinkers are able to give some concepts and ideas for analysing the distinctive feature of the space. The huge empty place can be regarded as a symbol for different forms of absence: the absence of buildings/streets/central urban functions, the absence of regulation/order and the absence of advertisement/commercials. These forms of absence enable public action and unscheduled practice because of the undetermined nature of the emptiness. The same model—to enable public/action/practice because of the undetermined nature of the emptiness—can be found within theory. According to Lefebvre, the emptiness is, on the one hand, the link to the fundamental void in urbanism between not recognizing urban practice and its own approaches to organizing space; on the other hand, he identifies the (supposed) empty space as the proper object and cause for urbanism activities. In Laclau's theory, emptiness has a still more important function: The emptiness is the symbol for the absence of any final form of rationality/objectivity. This void is cause for the antagonistic forces that produce society and space, trying to fill the gap and unable to accomplish it. Finally, the emptiness is the cause for democracy: The place of power is vacant and the never-ceasing process of trying to occupy this place is its original mechanism.

The emptiness of the Tempelhofer Feld has many aspects and its features could be perhaps turned to a romantic (Jessop, 2003) end for my chapter. The Tempelhofer Feld has enormous utopian potential—not as a modernist technocratic and unnamed utopia of urbanism, but as 'u-topia' (Lefebvre, 2003, p. 179), as a laboratory for a 'differential space' (Lefebvre, 1991, p. 352) where the capitalistic contradictions introduce an open space of difference. Regarding the derivations of the historical analysis, of the public debate, and of the public space adoption process, the Tempelhofer Feld occurs as a transition between present and absent, between today and a projected future as a collective human project (Guelf, 2010, p. 281).

After the functional airport has disappeared, the postindustrial green field is (temporarily) dropped down from the capitalistic system of valorisation. To defend this stage, to resist a new economic colonisation, to insist on the present modus of slowness, to support an economic 'sub-optimal form of use' (Hessen Agentur GmbH & Studio UC/Klaus Overmeyer, 2008), all these points could probably connect a project of social criticism (Dörre, Lessenich, & Rosa, 2009, p. 17) with a project that is trying a different form of urban development. The Tempelhofer Feld could become a place and an object of space representation that realises—inside the practice of everyday life and outside the capitalistic organism—something like a lived space and a 'lieu du désir' (Lefebvre), or a radical imagination and an antagonistic dislocation against the forms of routinisation, sedimentation, and spatialisation (Laclau). Probably the recent history is evidence for a really different form of space production (in the place and in the discourse), a production where lived space can prevail over conceived/perceived space and where a new form of the political can appear. Understanding the different dimensions of emptiness that emerge at Tempelhofer Feld could be its first step.

# Chapter 7

# How to Build the Public Spaces of a Democracy?

## The Design of New Public Spaces in the City Centre of Dresden After Reunification

*Chloë Voisin-Bormuth*

## New Public Spaces

The current transformation of the public spaces (i.e., the public squares and public streets that are owned by the public authorities and open to everyone day and night) in the city centre of Dresden cannot be understood without knowing its recent past. Almost completely destroyed on the February 13, 1945, by the Allied Forces bombing in the course of WWII, the city centre of Dresden was partially rebuilt by the new socialist regime according to socialist principles of urban planning. The West German government did not take advantage of the destruction caused by the war to control and reorganize private property; the former owners kept their plot of land and the reconstruction of most cities in West Germany followed the old city plan, which was just to modernize according to the needs of modern life. The socialist regime, however, rejected this approach. Contrary to the Federal Republic of Germany (FRG), the German Democratic Republic (GDR) did not perceive itself as a regime succeeding the Nazi regime, but as a completely new one, and this rupture was therefore a central concept in city planning. The new principles of urban development aimed to build a new city for a new socialist society, one which should distinguish itself from the former city and from the Western capitalist one. Therefore, its city centre should be 'neither a commercial centre with plenty of shops, nor a leisure centre with elegant restaurants and cafés-concert, nor a financial centre with banks and head offices of big concerns. . . . It gathers together the political functions, the administrative and the cultural ones which give its sense to the city' (Ministerium für Aufbau der Deutschen Democratischen Republik, 1950, p. 6). It played the most important role in the city and the most important aspects of social life happened there: 'it is the place of official events, of political marches and of people's celebration' (Ministerium für Aufbau der Deutschen Democratischen Republik, 1950, p. 10). The socialists were convinced that urban, architectural, and symbolical forms could help the people understand the idea of socialism and so support the regime. That is why the design of public spaces was so crucial: By holding huge political demonstrations but also by being meeting places for the new socialist people in the course of everyday life, central public spaces had to be wide open and, moreover, to bear symbolic and political charges. Urban and landscape design, as well as public art, have been the privileged instruments because they could incarnate the new values and the norms of the regime and show them to everyone (inhabitants and visitors) directly in the public space. Durth, Gutschow, and Düwel (1998, p. 48) explain that 'the wealth of collective life and a bright future had to be shown to the new socialist people via new images' that gave public spaces a representative character, but also a joyful, beautiful, and welcoming one. The aim was to offer a better, more liveable and beautiful space to inhabitants than under capitalism, to arouse inhabitants' pride in 'their Socialism', and finally to promote their identification with the new regime (Betker, 2005; Durth et al., 1998).

The construction of the city centre was not completely achieved when the socialist regime fell in 1989–1990; some projects were unfinished (the pedestrian street of the Prager Straße) and others were under discussion (Neumarkt). Moreover, the openness of the finished socialist structure (like the one of the central square, Altmarkt, and the main avenue) offered the possibility to gain space for new buildings and to get a higher density in the city centre. Following the fall of the Wall, one question was thus shared by nearly all postsocialist cities: How to build the city centre? Which means, how to cope with the socialist heritage? And which planning model to follow in a newly born democracy and under completely new economic, cultural, and ideological paradigms (Kliems & Dmitrieva, 2007). Even if some common grounds of city transformation can be found in all postsocialist cities, the ones of the former GDR follow a particular path because of the reunification with the western part of Germany. After an initial period during which the ideas of preservation or integration of the socialist city in a new and better city were flourishing (Gerkan, 1990; Landeshauptstadt Dresden Dezernat für Stadtentwicklung, 1994), a second period followed, during which the loss of attractiveness and the crisis of the East German cities brought in its wake another urban development plan. The main planning idea was to replace the socialist city with the so-called 'European city' (Landeshauptstadt Dresden & Goller, 2000; Landeshauptstadt Dresden Dezernat für Stadtentwicklung & PP A/S Pesch Partner Architekten, 2007); among other measures, the city centre should be reopened to capitalist interests, old city buildings and public spaces should be renovated, and in destroyed cities like Dresden, the city centre should be reconstructed following simplified principles of the traditional morphology of a European city. Those measures should help East German cities to appear as 'normal' European cities, that is, like Western ones and therefore more likely to attract investments and visitors. In the context of globalisation and growing competition between cities, the image of the city becomes crucial, and it is that of the European city, bound up with the concept of urbanity and quality of life, which seduces investors and inhabitants, not the image of the socialist city (Lippert & Voisin, 2007). In this context, the redesign of central public spaces becomes a priority for the planners.

Extended interviews with planners and artists who contributed to the creation of the new public spaces in Dresden, as well as the study of their morphology and of the actual policy of public art, give a new comprehension of the new central public spaces' design (Voisin, 2013). Behind the overexposed choice of the so-called 'model of the European city', which can be seen as a memorial project as well as a successful marketing strategy (sections 1 and 2), planners and artists shared the hope of building spaces to reflect the new political and social order, which means democratic public spaces. But what does the 'building of democratic public spaces' really mean? What are the planning measures for the central public spaces (section 3) and who is really involved in their design? Can anyone directly participate (section 4)? What are the consequences of this redesign of public spaces on the uses of central streets and squares (section 5)?

## Redeveloping the Typology of Traditional Public Spaces of a European City

Redeveloping the typology of traditional public spaces of a European city is the first aim of planning new public spaces in Dresden city centre. But this does not mean reproducing the urban design of public spaces destroyed during the war, or more generally a typical historical European one (with the exception of the Neumarkt with its imitation of old buildings and its old fashioned streets lamps). It mainly meant closing the openness of the socialist city (Figure 7.1).

Figure 7.1  Dresden city centre. The socialist city was defined by its openness: City blocks had been opened up in contrast to the old dense urban structure that turned into an inferno during the bombing; it became a symbol of the new collective life without boundaries and with free spaces available for anyone. Very wide streets were built to bear the new circulation flow and the political marches. The biggest one, the *Magistrale,* was directly linked to the biggest place in the city centre, *der Aufmarschplatz,* where all the people could meet for celebrations. In Dresden, for example (see

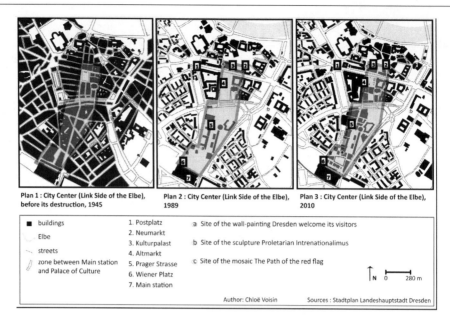

Plan 1 : City Center (Link Side of the Elbe), before its destruction, 1945     Plan 2 : City Center (Link Side of the Elbe), 1989     Plan 3 : City Center (Link Side of the Elbe), 2010

■ buildings

Elbe

streets

zone between Main station and Palace of Culture

1. Postplatz
2. Neumarkt
3. Kulturpalast
4. Altmarkt
5. Prager Strasse
6. Wiener Platz
7. Main station

a Site of the wall-painting Dresden welcome its visitors

b Site of the sculpture Proletarian Intrenationalimus

c Site of the mosaic The Path of the red flag

N    0    280 m

Author: Chloë Voisin          Sources : Stadtplan Landeshauptstadt Dresden

*Figure 7.1* Dresden city centre.

grey area on plan 3 in Figure 7.1), the space leading from the beginning of the Prager Straße on the north of the main station to the central square of the Altmarkt formed one big and fluid space without boundaries. The view was extremely open: From the main station pedestrians could see the Palace of Culture on the north side of the Altmarkt. Since the Reunification, the sites that were not built during the GDR era in the south of Altmarkt, and in the north and south of Prager Straße, have now been developed (see same grey area on plan 2 in Figure 7.1). The open view is completely closed and the Wiener Platz is clearly separated from Prager Straße. The Neumarkt on the north of Altmarkt has also been rebuilt. This new structure clearly recalls the traditional European morphology with a higher density, a hierarchical road network, narrower streets, and a clear distinction between places and streets (see plan 1 of Figure 7.1). All these characteristics are associated with the quality of life that the European city in its traditional form is supposed to guarantee, so that by choosing this typology, the planners declared the introduction of a new clarity in the city centre but also a new quality of human proportions (Landeshauptstadt Dresden & Goller, 2000; Landeshauptstadt Dresden Dezernat für Stadtentwicklung & PP A/S Pesch Partner Architekten, 2007). However, this belief is not always shared by the users; for example, most of the people interviewed on the street also regret that Prager Straße is now so narrow, because the conjunction of this narrowness and the always growing crowds of people on foot or on bicycles is a cause of stress and a reason to avoid the street on busy days.

The closing of this space has another goal as shown by the comparison between the plans 1 and 3 (Figure 7.1): to recreate the old city plan. The narrowness of Prager Straße at its northern and southern ends corresponds, for example, to the 18 metre width of the street before its transformation during the GDR era. The new shapes of the three central squares—Wiener Platz, Altmarkt, and Neumarkt—correspond to the old ones (as far as the socialist structure allows it). In Dresden, where the trauma of the loss of the old city centre during the Allied bombing is so deep and still so vivid, the reference to the disappeared city is a must in all the central projects (Margalit, 2002; Rehberg, 2002; Voisin, 2008); on every parcel where it is possible, 'old buildings' are reconstructed in a patrimonial way or in a historicist way (Neumarkt) (Voisin, 2007). Where this is not the case, there is at least an attempt to rebuild by following the simplified old plan. The parcels of the old block are reassembled and sold to investors who will build only one more or less modern building, where many stood before 1945 (the south area of the Altmarkt, and Prager Straße), so that the exterior limits of the old blocks recreate the old streets and squares (Neumarkt and Altmarkt). The choice of this morphology in Dresden is thus less an attempt to build a new qualitative structure by following the principles of the traditional European morphology than an attempt to rebuild the old plan of Dresden. It is less an invention, more a reconstitution. But is this reference to the disappeared Dresden *only* a memorial project?

## Erasing the Socialist Symbolism

The closing of the socialist openness means also the refusal of the socialist city, which is not considered a heritage that should be protected. Different opinions about the socialist Prager Straße demonstrate this clearly. The art historian Jürgen Paul declared, for example, that 'the construction [of the Prager Straße], a so important area for Dresden, is a failure as well from the point of view of city planning as from the aesthetic one because of its repulsive design. . . . The 40 years of reconstruction in Dresden did not manage to build a real town' (Paul, 1992). Ingolf Roßberg, the future mayor of Dresden, explained that 'the city centre is the horror cabinet of the urbanistic sins' (Rossberg & Tiedt, 1990). Most of the planners after the Reunification shared this opinion that the heritage of the socialist city was inadequate and unliveable. By choosing to follow the model of the city that had currency before 1945, the planners rejected this socialist heritage. But the closing of the space goes even further: It leads to the deconstruction of the socialist city. The concept of *deconstruction* can be surprising because not many buildings were destroyed after the Reunification: the Police Headquarters on the Neumarkt (2004), the 'Fresswürfel' on the Postplatz (2007), the shopping centre Konsum (2009) on Prager Straße, and a house-block on Hauptstraße (2011). The closing of the space occurs on the free and unbuilt spaces. However, these are often not uncompleted spaces but deliberately planned free space to convey a special meaning. On Prager Straße, for example, the openness was thought of as the incarnation of the welcoming wish, which was addressed to all the people—and especially to strangers—who entered this street from the main station. It was underlined through a special design that alternates, right in the middle of the street, very big fountains with spectacular water-games and green spaces with high trees and plenty of flowers. Both openness and design gave pedestrians the understanding that the outdoor space was, as a collective meeting space, the most important and valuable place in the city. The Prager Straße reflected the utopian inspiration of the city planning of the GDR in the 60s, with the hope of a prospective flourishing socialist society (Fischer, 2005). The new structure, as built after the Reunification, imposes a completely new logic on the space. The closing of both the northern and southern areas of Prager Straße tends to create a street that becomes a square in the middle, and the big fountains and the green spaces have been replaced by a tree path and a thin water band, which underline the north–south direction of the street. The new design puts the focus on the buildings, here only big shops, and encourages pedestrians to walk through and not to spend most of the time sitting and chatting with friends (Voisin, 2013). The new Prager Straße is designed as a shopping mall. In the same way, the closing of the view on the most important building in the socialist Dresden, the Palace of Culture, annihilates its political and symbolical force; with its small height, it cannot impose itself anymore on the urban landscape. Finally, the closing of the openness of the socialist public spaces aims to develop a new typology of spaces that corresponds better to the new economic and social order and creates a memorial to the disappeared old city centre. But it also diminishes the still-remaining socialist structures by emptying them of political, cultural, and symbolic force. This way of coping with socialist public art is very demonstrative from this perspective.

Another important measure of the transformation of public spaces in Dresden after the Re-unification has indeed been the removal (Voisin, 2011) of almost all the pieces of public art and other symbols that connected those spaces with the former ideology and more generally with the values of the former state (Guth, 1995). Only a few pieces of public art, the most ideological ones (statues of Karl Marx, Friedrich Engels, or Walter Ulbricht), have been spontaneously removed by the population from the public space just after the fall of the Wall. But, besides these isolated cases, almost all the decisions concerning the public art have been taken by the municipality. For example, in 1995, it convened a special commission to determine which pieces of art of the SED (*Sozialistische Einheitspartei*, Socialist Unity Party of Germany) should be removed and which pre-served. All the monuments that recalled historical facts, but only 38% of the art pieces that bore an explicit socialist message, have been kept in public spaces. Today, just three art pieces with an explicit socialist political message remain in the city centre: a mosaic, the 'Path of the Red Flag' (Gerhard Bondzin) on the west side of the Palace of Culture, a wall-painting 'Dresden welcomes its visitors' (Kurt Sillack and Rudolf Lipowski) on the south side of the former Restaurant Bastei, and the sculpture 'Proletarian Internationalismus' (Vinzenz Wanitschke) on the east side of the big city boulevard (see plans 2 and 3, Figure 7.1). But they have all been hidden as much as pos-sible: In the area where the sculpture is installed on the other side of the avenue, art pieces have been transformed into a skate park; the mosaic, which has not been renovated for years, is covered by a half transparent black net supposed to prevent stones falling on the passers-by; and in front of the wall painting, a big commercial building with an 'L' shape has been built, so that the paint-ing, which welcomed visitors from the main station during the GDR (plans 2 and 3, Figure 7.1), can no longer be seen from Prager Straße. Only the people who already know of its existence here can find it. All the other art pieces from the GDR period that have been commissioned by the city or other social organizations (not by the SED) and that are still installed in the city centre are ornamental ones. Any decision about them is taken only when a project is planned in their area; most of the time, they are removed (Hotel Bellevue, Prager Straße, Wildsruffer Straße). They can also be accidentally destroyed.

All those examples show that, in the case of the design of the public spaces, as well as the pub-lic art, the denial of their status of heritage and the hiding or even the erasing of their political, ideological, or just symbolic charge leads to the deconstruction of the socialist structure in the city centre, which appears today to be deprived of sense. It helps therefore to formalise the rupture with the former regime just as the socialists did after the war. But it is used also to set the basis for a new social, political, and cultural order.

## Neutral Space

The deconstruction of the semantics of the socialist city cannot be seen just as an iconoclastic move away from the former regime. It proceeds from a deeper change in public space planning, and more specifically from the refusal to set signs or symbols visibly into the public space. Tradi-tionally, the power structures use public spaces to stage the values with which they want to be iden-tified, the norms according to which they want to organize the society, and also the beliefs and the common mythological and folkloristic reference world. Architecture, urban design, monuments, and especially public art play therefore an important role by embodying this programme in stone.

Today, art pieces are certainly still being installed in public spaces. But all the actors I inter-viewed in Dresden between 2009 and 2010 (planners, architects, artists, public servants) agreed on this point: Those pieces should not express values or norms that would constitute the expres-sion of the public authorities' view of history, of the society's beliefs, or of moral visions of col-lective life. They should not give answers to the questions with which the society is confronted. They should, on the contrary, question the city, the structures of power, the social and economic problems, and the history, and should formulate these questions so that everyone becomes able to find their own answers. These questions should come exclusively from the artist independently of the commissioner; if a theme can be given by the Commission for Public Art, which examines all the propositions for public art in Dresden when it commissions a piece of art, neither the shape, nor the artistic formulation of the question, is laid down. Most of the time, artists decide the theme, the shape, and the place of work by themselves. For example, in their project *Info[Off]* *spring* between 2000 and 2004, Eva Hertzsch and Adam Page installed a pink container in different places in Dresden known as hot spots for urban, social, and economic problems (in the city centre, in Altmarkt, and on Prager Straße). The container served as an exhibition space for artists; as an information space about the place and urban planning in the area; as a meeting space for artists, inhabitants, and visitors; and as a pin board for everybody. Hertzsch and Page's aim was to lead people to debate about the actual situation of the neighbourhood and of the city through performances in the public space and discussions with the artists, and finally to formulate their own improvement propositions. Such critical projects are warmly welcomed by the Commission for Public Art, even if they question or criticize the policy of the city. By contrast, the ornamental ones are generally refused by the Commission with the argument that they do not meet the contemporary conception of public art. The form of the art pieces and their relation to their exhibition site therefore also changes: Instead of being obviously put on a plinth and being seen by everyone, the new art pieces are discreetly integrated into their site, sometimes so discreetly that they are almost invisible. Marion Kahnemann's project, *Hinsehen* ('to look at'), for example, has the form of a normal city bench except that the inscriptions are written on and in front of it, and it has a transparent plastic structure instead of the common one in wood. Erwin Stache's sound installation, *Klangmomente*, is hidden in common bicycle racks and can be discovered only by touching one of them. Furthermore, more and more art projects are only temporarily installed in public spaces. These examples show that the new public art does not want to impose its presence onto the passers-by, who have to play the active role by being curious and attentive to the place where they are by wanting to discover the art pieces and by giving meaning to them. That is why the memorials no longer determine one interpretation of the past; very discrete, nearly invisible as they are, they point to the historical moment with which the memorial is linked in a very neutral way. For example, the memorial for the peaceful revolution of 1989 on Prager Straße is just a date on the pavement, '8th October 1989'.

This change doubtless corresponds to a more global transformation of the conception of public art in Western countries since the 1960s with the reflection about the relation between artists and the state power, about history and official memorial projects (Christo, Mamado), about modernity and the machine (Spoerry, Tinguely), about art (Penone, Weiner) and the possibility of creating art in a capitalist and consumerist society (Fluxus, E. Hesse, Smithson) (Daval, 2010a; 2010b; 2010c). But the debate in Dresden's Commission for Art and the specific forms of the art projects found in Dresden, as well as in other German cities (most of all, the direct implication of the public in the project), shows the existence of a specificity in the German case: This revolution in public art and in urban design can be explained by the trauma of the Third Reich and of the GDR, which exploited public art to impose an ideology on society (Bushart, 1985; Guth, 1995; Kaiser & Rehberg, 1999; Loos, 2000; Münk, 1993; Rehberg, 2004; Wolf, 1999). The big challenge for planners today is to build a democratic public space (in the sense of grassroots democracy rather than representative democracy), and the answer to this challenge is not so easy. Keeping public space free of any political or symbolic sign is one such answer (Arndt, 1961). Because a democratic public space has to be directly appropriated by the citizens who are themselves giving meaning and also life to those spaces, 'more is less' was the concept for the new design of the central square Altmarkt (Landeshauptstadt Dresden, 2000; Landeshauptstadt Dresden, Friedrich, & Lerm, 2000). The landscape architect office of WES & Partner developed the project to transform the square into a 'stage' with a very big and high 'light mast' playing the same role as spotlights in a theatre. This stage is almost completely empty because the space should be filled not by the city furniture but by the events that the society has to organize itself.

Public authorities refuse to be at the origin of the semantics of public space and aim to build a democratic public space as a neutral (in the sense of 'free of symbols and signs') and empty space in order to set the society free to determine this for itself. But the deeper analysis of this public authorities' and artists' project leads to the following question: Who is and who can be really involved in public spaces? Everyone or just some (voluntarily or involuntarily) selected groups?

## Who Is Involved in the Design of Central Public Spaces?

The alleged public authorities' desire that citizens be directly involved in public spaces has limits: Citizen attempts to symbolically occupy public space or to change urban design are not frequently warmly embraced. The action of the 'protest toilet' in 2009 is one example: A toilet with flowers inside and a placard stating 'built like shit, city transformed in rubbish' has been installed on the Postplatz to protest against the new design, which was considered cold and hideous. One hour later, the toilet was removed by the police. A few days later, four new 'protest toilets' were installed on four other difficult urban planning spots, including once again in the Postplatz and the Altmarkt with its mast; its placard said in Saxon 'Ulbricht on the Altmarkt: even I wouldn't have dared it' ('Der Ulbricht auf dem Altmarkt: Nu sowas hätt'sch mor ni gedraud'). The placard on the Postplatz said 'for 60 years the interests of Dresden's citizens are always forgotten! Perfect example of an occupation's architecture' ('Seit 60 Jahren stets vergessen, die Dresdner Bürger Interessen! Besatzerarchitektur in Rheinkultur'). The placard plays with the words 'Reinkultur' and 'Rheinkultur': the first one means 'perfect example', the second one 'culture from the Rheinland region', that is, from the west of Germany. They have been removed as quickly as the first one. (The authors of this action are still unknown, but, after its removal, the actor Uwe Steimle went to the police station and paid the fee to have the protest toilet back . . . and installed it once again on the Postplatz.) Of course, the frontal critic of the installation and its placards, which distinguishes this action from the critical pieces of public art that have been approved by the city, could explain the removal of both toilets and placards. But two other examples provide further clarity: After the Reunification, many small shopkeepers set small open stalls on the Prager Straße to sell their own goods. Though they were successful, they were thorns in the planners' sides. Nowadays, small open stalls are forbidden. As compensation, three snack bars have been built instead, selling sausages, Döner, or ice cream. The keepers are clearly identified and the activity is contained within clear boundaries. In the same way, cafés, restaurants, and bartenders are not entirely free to decide how to design their terrace. For example, on the Altmarkt, a design chart has been published that imposes the position of the tables, the shape of the parasol and of the seats, and coordinates all of them on the scale of the square. Public authorities do not approve individual citizens deciding the design of the spaces with the argument that, on the one hand, public spaces belong to everyone and not just to one person, and that, on the other, they have to guarantee, as public authorities, both free access to those spaces, security, and a certain unity in the general design of the square. (The interviews I did during my Ph.D. show that the architect and landscape architect involved in the planning process share the same point of view about the necessary unity in the general design of the squares—an idea that has existed at least since the Renaissance.) The private initiatives that are most warmly welcomed are those that do not happen spontaneously and that are the result of a negotiation with the public authorities. Some of them have brought changes in the design of the public spaces; for example, public stone benches have been installed on the Neumarkt thanks to private funds collected by a private initiative of citizens who wanted to answer the renewed complaint of inhabitants and visitors about the absence of benches. But most of them are events organized by private organizations such as the Christmas market, seasonal markets, or sport contests. For public authorities, these events have many advantages: They are temporary; they don't alter the form of the space; they are institutionalised, therefore the public authorities can guarantee respect of all the rules that regulate public space usage and security during the events, and therefore they do not have to organize these events themselves and do not have to be directly involved. And finally, these events bring many people together in public spaces.

They provide an animation on the public spaces that is strongly aimed at by public authorities. The problem in Dresden is that private organizations are not very active and most organized events are small and conventional. To increase the animation through private organizations, the city has elaborated a catalogue with a description of all possible events for each square in the city centre, each of which has been given a clear profile: the Neumarkt is a place for tourists, the Altmarkt a market and events place, the Prager Straße a shopping mall (J. Walter, personal communication, 2010; former director of the urban development planning of Dresden, Stadtplanungsamt). This marketing strategy presents not only the advantage of gaining the attention of investors and private organizations, but also of attracting the inhabitants. Now that public spaces are no longer essential for cultural, political, and social life because of the virtualisation and the concentration of most activities in indoor spaces, public authorities have to develop strategies to attract people onto the public spaces in order to guarantee a minimum of animation, which is considered to be a symbol of urbanity, of good quality of life, and as typical for traditional European city centres (Fleury, 2007; Sewing, 2002). The clear profile helps people to identify the squares and thus is thought as the first step towards using them. Projects for the central public squares aim, therefore, for designs that agree perfectly with the type of events or the function, which is planned for this space. The traditional design of the Neumarkt, for example, completed the scenery of the 'old city of Dresden' that the tourists want to see, and of the traditional Christmas market that the tourists and the inhabitants love visiting because of the atmosphere. However, the planning of public spaces according to an event or to a function led to the neglect of their status as spaces for everyday life.

## New Uses of Public Spaces in the City Centre

Although all interviewed planners expressed their wish to design public spaces as meeting spaces and good places of sociability, only rarely, and never uppermost in their minds, did they really concern themselves with everyday use and comfort, which they assume to have been taken into account in the design. The carelessness about the potential users of the spaces and the absence of differentiation between them and between their different needs in public spaces is very revealing: Although a lot of old and poor people, who could use the public spaces and bring animation, are living in the city centre of Dresden (a heritage of Socialism), the planners I interviewed confessed that they have never taken into account these inhabitants as special potential users for whom a specific design could be thought out. This probably explains why almost all interviewees perceive, for example, the Altmarkt as a big empty square and do not connect with it. The consequences of this new approach to planning are therefore important for the uses of public spaces. The observation of the uses and the users interviewed both show that public spaces are used 'according to the plan', that is, according to the function that has been planned for those spaces. The Altmarkt is for most people the place of the Christmas market, and its daily use is mainly limited to passing through the square, without staying there, in order to reach another part of the city. People also clearly identify Prager Straße as a shopping mall, and they come here to shop or to look at those who are shopping, as they would do in a shopping centre (Voisin, 2013).

However, observation of the uses of public spaces and the users' interviews lead me to question the success of this planning strategy. The interviews demonstrate, without doubt, that people use public spaces today more often than they did before their transformation and show, therefore, that the new design satisfies a need. But these results can be mainly interpreted quantitatively and not qualitatively. The questions 'What does this space mean to you?' and 'Are you coming here because you have to or/and because you like to be here?' query more directly the users' bond to these spaces and sheds light on their uses of these new spaces. The first one was a very difficult question to answer for most people. To the second one, most answered 'because I have to do something here'. Only the users of the Neumarkt answered that they wanted to come there to see the place. But the Neumarkt is special in town: Its historicist reconstruction conveys the impression of a quarter with a historical and symbolic depth (Will & Schmidt, 2002), even if this new quarter is a very free interpretation of the Neumarkt as it was before 1945 and even if behind the buildings' facades modern flats and shopping centres have been built (Voisin, 2007). The interviews show that the pleasurable use of the space is to be found in other parts of the city, mostly in the older ones (in the Neustadt, the alternative quarter of the town, or on the Schillerplatz or the Körnerplatz, two small sites of former villages) or in all the natural spaces like the banks of the Elbe, parks (Grosser Garten), or forests around the city (Heide, Sächsische Schweiz). The city centre is mostly seen by the users not as a daily life space nor as a leisure one, but as a functional area. The uses correspond, therefore, so exactly to the plan that nothing happens that has not been planned. A certain lack of tension characterises those one-dimensional spaces: People come to the city centre just to do something in particular, instead of being there just to enjoy city life.

## Conclusion

The aim of the new public space planning in the city centre of Dresden was to create lively and democratic public spaces, according to the hypothesis that the old socialist city centre could not allow it because of its particular form, functions, and symbolic charge. Is the city centre today livelier than it was a few years ago? If by *lively* we understand just the number of visitors, the new planning of Dresden is without doubt a big success. If by this word we mean the development of a place of urbanity, understood as the social interaction, the success is far less evident. The public spaces of Dresden, very specialised, are not appropriated by the users, who act more like consumers than co-producers of the spaces—a phenomenon that has also been observed in other cities throughout the world (Fleury, 2007; Ghorra-Gobin, 2001; Mangin, 2004; Sewing, 2002) but which is stronger in Dresden because of the lack of historical depth of the urban structure and of the uses. In the same way, the ambition of the city was to build democratic public spaces understood as spaces whose meaning is given by the people. Public spaces are therefore free of symbols of any kind commissioned by the public authorities. But is it enough to call them 'neutral spaces'? And even if we accept this terminology, are then those public spaces still so neutral when they are designed for a specific function and when private actors set their own signs and symbols, especially through advertisements? Ambitious pieces of public art are installed in public spaces and aim to lead the people to become more aware and vigilant. But what is their reception? The interviewed passers-by could name almost none of them. And many of them are not at all perceived as 'art pieces', but only as 'things' or as 'urban furniture'. If the reception of this art is limited to a group of a happy few, and if the art piece is not recognized as art and if thus it cannot reveal its meanings, do the artists really reach their goal of creating a democratic public art?

However, the example of the protest toilet gives us another possible interpretation: If the city had rejected the action under its specific form, it had nevertheless taken into account its message of protest. A few weeks after the protest action, on the demand of the mayor Orosz, flower compartments were set on the Postplatz, resulting in great happiness for the people . . . and great unhappiness of the planners who do not consider this design as contemporary. More interesting for us, since 2010, a big visitors' and inhabitants' consultation has been organised to discover how people perceive and evaluate the central squares. A city container is therefore transported from square to square in order to inform the citizens about the planning projects and in order to collect their improvement propositions. This experiment shows another possible way to design democratic public spaces—by taking account of real users, their needs, and wishes.

# Chapter 8

# Memorials and Material Dislocation
## The Politics of Public Space in Warsaw

*Jerzy Elżanowski*

The sphere of public commemoration in post-1989 Warsaw is both typical of, and unique for, the kind of redrawing of public memory experienced in central and eastern European cities. Typical, because it followed patterns of semiotic reconfiguration seen, for different reasons and in the service of different political agendas, in cities as diverse historically, ethnically, and politically as Bucharest, Tallinn, Dresden, or Moscow. Streets were renamed; religious institutions reinvigorated; statues of communist heroes removed and replaced with national (or nationalistic) figures from the past; socialist realist urban ensembles were repurposed, sometimes seamlessly, but often awkwardly, to suit the programmes of a market economy. However, beyond these general similarities lie two phenomena specific to Warsaw. The first is a sense of tremendous dislocation resulting from the scale and method of World War II destruction in the city—what the Polish sociologist Stanisław Ossowski has called the 'dehumanisation or deculturalisation of [Warsaw's urban] matter' (Ossowski, 1967, p. 396; cf. Chmielewska, 2012). The second, its correlate, is the uncommonly dense, complex, and contested system of plaques and monuments commemorating hundreds of sites of public mass executions, attacks on Polish and Jewish civilian and insurgent groups, mass deportations, zones of racial exclusion, and other forms of wartime and post-war Nazi and Stalinist repression. Consequently, making public space in Warsaw requires close and careful attention to the *local* layers of intersecting physical and discursive spaces, which testify to the oppression of the city's Polish and Jewish populations and the mass destruction of its urban infrastructures.

In this chapter, I present several commemorative interventions as examples of the numerous discursive layers that constitute a network of remembrance on Chłodna Street in Warsaw's northwestern Wola District. Among them, I do a close reading of two separate institutional projects initiated in December 2009 at the corner of Chłodna and Żelazna Streets by the Museum of the History of Polish Jews as well as the Wola District Office. As I will argue, both institutional projects were unsuccessful because they failed to recognize the semiotic relationships between existing objects on the street, the photographic and memorial representations of those objects, and the contiguous spaces of polemic.

Before its destruction in the war, Chłodna Street was a significant east–west artery and a neighbourhood centre for manufacturing and entertainment. Its housing stock was of higher quality than in the surrounding, primarily Jewish, working-class neighbourhoods of Wola, and its population was ethnically and economically more diverse (Piotrowski, 2007, pp. 19–21). During the war, as a military transport route through German-occupied Warsaw, parts of Chłodna's roadway were walled off from the surrounding Jewish ghetto. Starting in December 1941, ghetto inhabitants could only cross the street in one of two ways—either by waiting for special gates to be opened periodically at the corner of Żelazna Street, or by a pedestrian bridge erected nearby in January 1942 (Engelking & Leociak, 2009, p. 129). This footbridge, the largest of four similar ghetto crossings in Warsaw, was most probably removed after the liquidation of the Warsaw Ghetto in the late summer of the same year (Engelking & Leociak, 2009, pp. 115, 133).

Remembering the Chłodna Street footbridge was one of the objectives of the two projects in question—an art installation titled with the punctuation mark '(. . .)' (referred to here as *Ellipsis*) as well as a complex municipal pavement restoration scheme called the *Chłodna Street Revitalisation Plan*. *Ellipsis* attempted to counteract a perceived intellectual and cultural vacuum with respect to Polish–Jewish relations and the Holocaust on the site, but did not acknowledge previous public dialogue on the matter. Similarly, the *Revitalisation Plan*, which was meant to highlight Chłodna Street's contested histories, instead privileged two simplified historical narratives over complex others and thus, paradoxically, contributed to further erasures and silences.

Since the mid-1940s, Warsaw has been saturated with memorials: first with informal plaques and wooden crosses, and later with several hundred stone tablets mounted near sites of execution. Over the last six decades, this commemorative landscape has been augmented, erased, reinscribed, and repositioned ideologically (Chmielewska, 2008; Janicka, 2011). One of Warsaw's rare symbols of Jewish heroism, Nathan Rapoport's Warsaw Ghetto Monument, was incorporated into Polish communist narratives of martyrdom and freedom-fighting immediately after its unveiling in 1948 (Bierut, 1951, pp. 202–204). Polish communists used the monument's representation of Jewish armed resistance in the 1943 Warsaw Ghetto Uprising to displace the memory of the later, primarily Polish, Warsaw Uprising of 1944, thereby silencing participants and supporters of the 1944 Uprising who were hostile to the Soviet-backed government (Young 1989, pp. 91–93). After 1989, in a forceful response by dissident groups to the persecution of former insurgents and their families, and, more recently, with the strengthening of nationalist and Christian fundamentalist political parties, monuments to the 1944 Warsaw Uprising, as well as those commemorating the victims of Soviet atrocities, have come to dominate public space and memory discourse in Poland's capital (Keff, 2011, p. 7). Bearing overtly Christian symbols with a martyrological tenor, these monuments have set a particularly nationalistic tone for commemoration in Warsaw. With a concurrent rise in interest in Jewish memory and culture, especially within Warsaw's post-Soviet left-wing groups, and with international support for projects such as the Museum of the History of Polish Jews, past and present competition between Polish and Jewish, communist and Roman Catholic, right and left wing political narratives has led to a complex and contested memorial topography.

In Warsaw, personal agendas of memory are deeply conflated with community memories as well as pre- and post-Soviet state narratives. Citizens commonly engage in historical debates and voice their ideological positions. They participate in a combination of historical reenactments, mass religious events, and commemorative state celebrations and actively support or condemn institutional actions. This was evident during the clashes between Catholic fundamentalists and Polish authorities over the planned removal by the government of a wooden cross spontaneously installed in front of the Presidential Palace in Warsaw to commemorate the sudden death of President Lech Kaczynski in April 2010. This participatory context often stands in opposition to pluralistic and local forms of remembrance because, as Bożena Keff warns (2011, pp. 9–10), ideological rivalries over imagined and desired national pasts have dominated Warsaw's social life.

However, within smaller groups such as historical societies, housing cooperatives, nonprofits, or citizen-journalist collectives, this exceptional engagement with political history can have positive consequences for a nonschematic remembering that privileges lived memory in the local space of the neighbourhood over municipal or national political and religious ideologies. In the following sections, I present the numerous forms of, mainly online, citizen-initiated information, polemic, pressure, and protest that have accompanied both the *Chłodna Street Revitalisation Plan* and the *Ellipsis* project. I suggest that there is a place for a kind of pluralistic public memory in Warsaw where enacting *difference* has the potential to productively destabilise rather than reinforce nationalist narratives (Bhabha, 2004, p. 221). Using the example of the Wola District, I unpack the relationships between personal viewing and remembering, and municipal ideology and rhetoric—what

Christine Boyer (2012, p. 326) characterises as the spaces between 'the eye of the spectator and the logic of governmentality'.

## Viewing

In a contemporary photograph of Chłodna Street an elderly man peers into a brass box attached to a vertical structure before him (Figure 8.1). It is late afternoon on an autumn day; the sunset casts him in shadow as it lights the newly paved sidewalk on which he stands. The object is a new

*Figure 8.1* Corner of Chłodna and Żelazna streets with the *Footbridge of Memory* designed by Tomasz de Tusch-Lec. Warsaw, 2011.

Text on image: "Kładka nad ulicą Chłodną, łącząca obszar dużego i małego getta    1942    Footbridge over **Chłodna St.** connecting the small and the large ghetto"

*Figure 8.2* Contemporary photograph of an archival image of Chłodna Street in 1942, taken through one lens of a stereoscopic viewing device mounted on the *Footbridge of Memory*. Warsaw, 2011.

memorial entitled *Footbridge of Memory*—part of the recently completed *Chłodna Street Revitalisation Plan,* encompassing Chłodna and Elektoralna Streets from Aleja Jana Pawła II to Żelazna Street. The memorial consists of four painted steel posts, which recall the spatial configuration of the footbridge that spanned the street in 1942 and connected two sections of the Nazi-constructed Jewish ghetto. The pavement is an integral part of the memorial—patterns made with granite, brick, concrete, and cast iron represent pre-war, wartime, and early post-war cartographies. Coloured pavers trace the outlines of 19th century buildings demolished both during and after the war, indicate areas once occupied by these buildings and mark the approximate locations of Nazi objects of oppression: bunkers, ghetto walls, and the footbridge itself.

Inside the box, through a set of sturdy brass binoculars, the man sees a stereoscopic image of the site as it appeared in 1942 (Figure 8.2). Automobiles, trams, wagons, and pedestrians squeeze past two sets of brick walls and under the wooden footbridge. The walls flank the street along almost its entire length. As a primary military transport route for German armies, the cobblestone roadway of Chłodna remained open during the war, but the sidewalks and the buildings along the street belonged to the ghetto. A 1930s apartment building, visible in the background beyond the intersection that temporarily marked the ghetto perimeter, served as an inanimate witness to imprisonment and humiliation. From its windows, the Gestapo could survey the footbridge and the adjacent vehicular crossing. The building still exists today, and structures the composition in the present-day photograph of the man and the monument. Directly behind the man a steel and concrete inlay in the pavement follows the line of one of the ghetto walls.

The brass box instructs tourists (in English) to 'TURN THE KNOB UNDERNEATH UNTIL YOU SEE ALL 4 SLIDES IN 3D'. Each consecutive ghetto scene (Figure 8.3) is meant to be viewed stereoscopically, but photographing it for this chapter flattens the experience to two dimensions. At the same time, it captures information beyond the scene at the centre: layered

*Figure 8.3* Contemporary photograph of an archival image of the Chłodna Street footbridge in 1942 taken through one lens of a stereoscopic viewing device mounted on the *Footbridge of Memory*. Warsaw, 2011.

apertures obscure the image of the footbridge grabbed quickly through the eyepiece. The English language descriptions, '1942' and 'Chlodna St., [*sic*] footbridge . . .' fade into the lower margin. The footbridge is truncated, and the descending crowd squeezed between the tectonically brutal raw brick wall, the refined details of the architecture of the city, and the apertures of contemporary viewing. From the archival fragment at the centre, faces stare through uncountable layers of representation. They stare at 'Amthor', identified in the Wehrmacht Propaganda Inventory as the photographer of the 1942 scene, stare at the elderly man standing in the shadow of the *Footbridge of Memory* in October 2011, stare obliquely at the photographer of the image under discussion, and stare at the reader of this text.

## Layering

Since 2004, Grzegorz Lewandowski, co-founder of Chłodna 25, a trendy café and performance venue located in the 1930s apartment building visible in Figures 8.1 and 8.2, has been working with local residents deliberately at the point where culture and trauma intersect: Intellectually, by consistently hosting politically contentious discussions that address the place of the Warsaw Ghetto in Polish society, but also physically, by choosing Chłodna as the location for the club. Lewandowski's mission has been to encourage civil society in an area that has remained on the social and economic margins since the end of the war. Events organized at the café address topics from feminism and racism to public space and neighbourhood design. The results, as varied as the different groups of people who attend the events, have helped both to animate and silence the corner of Chłodna and Żelazna Streets. While most of the initiatives considered at Chłodna 25 have been extremely nuanced, others represent a troubling conflation of Holocaust and military history with tourism and urban regeneration.

In February 2005, neighbourhood residents met at café Chłodna 25 to discuss the future of their street. A group of community members recommended that the Wola District attract tourists by looking for ways to engage groups walking the street on their way back from the Warsaw Rising Museum (the institution uses a variation on the accepted term 'uprising') recently opened nearby. Among other requests, they asked that a horse-drawn tram be run on weekends along Chłodna (presumably to transport tourists to and from the museum), that the ghetto footbridge be 'recreated', and that a historical reenactment present battles fought on the street during the Warsaw Uprising (Zyśk, 2005).

In April 2007, Chłodna 25 hosted a much more focused intervention. In cooperation with the District Council, the café held a public dialogue with Marek Edelman, one of the few surviving leaders of the 1943 Warsaw Ghetto Uprising. After the event, directly across from the café windows, local graffiti artist Adam Jastrzębski (pseud. Adam X) unveiled the first commissioned monument to the footbridge titled simply *The Footbridge Was There* (Figure 8.4). The title was painted in three languages: Polish, Hebrew, and Yiddish—originally with basic errors in the Yiddish, later corrected with an additional text—an unplanned sign of both the disappearance and the trace survival of the Yiddish language in Polish culture. The mural takes advantage of the

*Figure 8.4* Adam Jastrzębski, *The Footbridge Was There* (2007). Chłodna Street, Warsaw, 2009.

triptych-like quality of the three existing concrete panels used as its base—fragments of an abandoned billboard from the 1970s, the height and positioning of which roughly correspond to those of the former ghetto wall. The mural includes a simple map of the site indicating the location of the footbridge as well as a stylised perspectival view of Chłodna Street modelled after an archival photograph from 1942.

Over a year later, in the fall of 2008, the City of Warsaw formally acknowledged the footbridge site with a compact memorial situated across the street from Jastrzębski's mural. The memorial, designed by architect and sculptor Tomasz de Tusch-Lec (the same artist who would be commissioned to design the *Footbridge of Memory* only a few months later), is part of a larger network of commemorative plaques, pavement inlays, and information pylons placed at key points along the path of the former ghetto wall. At the corner of Chłodna and Żelazna Streets, the installation consists of a standard patterned concrete pylon, reminiscent of a wall fragment, and a tactile brass map of the ghetto with a small knob marking the visitor's location in the city. The map is accompanied by a reproduction of the same archival photograph used by Adam X and a text, this time only in Polish and English, describing the wartime history of the site. A few metres away from the pylon, iron, and concrete panels, with the words 'Ghetto Wall 1940–1943' set in low relief, fragmentarily mark the approximate locations of the wall on either side of Chłodna.

The mural, the pylon, and the pavement inlays join a host of older memorials surrounding the neoclassical Roman Catholic Church of Saint Charles Borromeo. Plaques, stones, crosses, and sculptures commemorate events related to the wartime and post-war persecution of primarily non-Jewish Poles, including Polish soldiers sent to Soviet gulags in 1944, and the murder of the Solidarity martyr Father Jerzy Popiełuszko by Polish internal security services (*Służba Bezpieczeństwa*) in 1984. This kind of density of, and variation in, commemorative activity is ubiquitous in Warsaw, but, until recently, it was less common to see new monuments to the Warsaw Ghetto alongside Christian markers. The proximity of these markers may suggest a newfound interest in Jewish memory in Warsaw and the potential for a productive layering of Polish and Jewish memory in public space. However, as Ewa Malgorzata Tatar writes (2008; cf. Meng, 2011, p. 250), this proximity may also represent 'Polish-Polish rather than Polish-Jewish questions about the memory of the Holocaust . . . in the [local] space of culture'. Tatar is referring to a desire for the cultural reappropriation of Jewish wartime memory, observable in Polish politics since the erection of Rapoport's Warsaw Ghetto Monument, and its inscription into accepted and often ethnically homogenous Polish nationalist narratives.

## Abbreviation

On December 29, 2009, just days after the Wola District announced the *Chłodna Street Revitalisation Plan*, but several months before construction started, Anna Baumgart and Agnieszka Kurant, working in cooperation with the Museum of the History of Polish Jews, stretched enormous silver Mylar balloons across Chłodna Street at the approximate wartime location of the ghetto footbridge (Figure 8.5). The installation consisted of three inflated spheres bracketed by two crescents intended as a three-dimensional representation of the punctuation mark '(. . .)'. According to the artists, *Ellipsis*—titled in promotional texts with the punctuation mark only—would 'instigate new and unpredictable social situations . . . in Warsaw's urban space, so saturated with traumatic past and so taboo-ridden.' The object was to travel the world and appear 'wherever there are unsolvable problems and near-inexpressible subjects'. At Chłodna, its test site, it was to signal to Varsovians that 'the mass murder of Jews happened before their very eyes.' The museum hoped that for local residents it 'may be the first collective experience . . . with their street's Jewish past' (Museum of the History of Polish Jews, 2011).

*Figure 8.5* Anna Baumgart and Agnieszka Kurant, *Ellipsis* (2009), with one crescent shaped Mylar balloon missing, probably pierced by a firecracker set off during New Year's Eve celebrations. The corner of Chlodna and Zelazna Streets is visible directly behind the art installation, Warsaw, January 2010.

According to the most popular Polish daily newspaper, *Gazeta Wyborcza*, project curator Ewa Toniak saw *Ellipsis* as a revolutionary act: 'For many people the installation may be shocking. But it is an artistic revolt against the emptiness on the site of the footbridge. Until now, nothing has been done here to remember that trauma. We hope *Ellipsis* will incite . . . dialogue about our memory' (Urzykowski, 2009; some sources attribute these words to Agnieszka Kurant, see Sienkiewicz, 2010). By assuming that the local population knew nothing about the street's Jewish past, by omitting existing interventions on the site, and by taking for granted that Chłodna's residents would somehow find new meaning solely through *Ellipsis*, the project highlighted the artists' and the Museum's own omission of both institutional and community-based attempts to interact with the site's traumatic past. Citing a pamphlet, printed to publicize the project, which included Baumgart and Kurant's names in large type angled inside two brackets of a stylised ellipsis, Sebastian Schmidt-Tomczak (2010) argues that the installation was unsuccessful because the artists believed that they could speak an omission. In the end, *Ellipsis* was no omission at all, but a heavily narrated promotional campaign, with pamphlets, photographic materials, staged discussions, and an invited lecture by the art critic and editor of *Frieze* magazine, Jörg Heiser (2009), who then promoted the project in a blog post published on *Frieze*'s website.

Apart from criticism of the project's technical failures in *Gazeta Wyborcza*, and two insightful articles by Ewa Malgorzata Tatar (2008) and Thomas Urban (2010), both the local and international press followed *Frieze*'s lead and simply summarized the artists' prescriptive project brief, as if it were their own interpretation of the object *in situ*. There was no recognition of the fact that narratives created around the artwork are not necessarily synonymous with the meanings of the work in urban space. Just because *Ellipsis* was *intended* to provoke neighbourhood discussion and highlight taboos does not mean it actually did so.

*Ellipsis* was supposed to be, simultaneously, a universal symbol of memorial omission, and an expression of extremely detailed curatorial content. But these notions were contradictory. If *Ellipsis* was to promote dialogue on a subject that the artists assumed was foreign to the public, how could it do so through an ambiguous installation, which said nothing about the discursive spaces it intended to address? This volley of assumptions about the project's meaning and reach was symptomatic of a recent tendency in Warsaw to universalise the topography of mass murder through ambiguous performances of memory, negating the specificity of both marked and still unmarked discreet sites of execution, deportation, murder, and burial. After all, the corner of Chłodna and Żelazna represents tragic and humiliating events, but, as opposed to hundreds of other marked and unmarked locations in Warsaw, it was not, to my knowledge, a site of mass murder.

In the interview quoted above, Toniak (or Kurant) failed to mention all the projects, discussions, and events, both progressive and reactionary, that had been initiated over the years at Chłodna 25 and by the City of Warsaw to commemorate the site of the footbridge and 'incite dialogue' about Chłodna's wartime and Holocaust histories (Urzykowski, 2009; Sienkiewicz, 2010). Even a cursory glance at press material on the subject reveals that Chłodna's residents were not only well-informed about the location of the footbridge but had even voiced their intentions to install a representation of this object of Nazi oppression into the street's tourist landscape. If anything, *Ellipsis*, through its ambiguity and its pop art references, has only reinforced a disturbing combination of spectacle and Holocaust commemoration on the site.

## Dislocation

In 2008, over one year before the installation of *Ellipsis*, but three years after residents had first gathered at café Chłodna 25 to discuss strategies for urban regeneration, the Wola District produced a feasibility study for the restoration of Chłodna Street. The plan took into account some of the residents' suggestions, including the idea for a horse-drawn tram, but also proposed to reorganise vehicular and pedestrian traffic on the street and to strip its 19th century cobblestone pavement (Kraj & Szczepaniuk, 2008). In response, 750 petitioners, headed by Maria Dąbrowska from the Zmiana [Change] Foundation (a nonprofit organization dedicated to educational initiatives as well the preservation of cultural heritage) reacted with a nuanced reading of the site. Petitioners demanded that the street's cobblestones be left in place, arguing that the 'planned changes to the street will result in the destruction of its historic layout to the point that it will no longer be possible to identify the space with archival photographs' (Fundacja Zmiana, 2009). Petitioners recognized that, in a topographically disturbed city, a valuable relationship had been preserved between photographic representations of the street, especially those dating from the war, and objects in the city.

By late December 2009, just days before the installation of *Ellipsis* on the same site, the District published the completely revised *Chłodna Street Revitalisation Plan* online, together with detailed drawings of all the project elements, including de Tusch-Lec's *Footbridge of Memory* discussed earlier. This time it seemed that the 19th century pavement was not only to be taken into account, but that it was to form the conceptual backbone for a restoration strategy, which included the permanent display of archival photographs on the site. The online brief outlined the project thus:

> The idea to revitalize Chłodna is based on a conscious decision to search for and highlight traces that testify to the street's former grandeur . . . the search for traces is limited to the ground plane where a large number of authentic historic elements have been preserved such as the cobblestone pavement with tram tracks, kerbstones with drainage grills cut into the sidewalk, and characteristic profiled granite carriageway entrances . . . [T]he purpose . . . is to create an uncommon composition in the pavement of Chłodna Street (with a background educational role) to be . . . an inspiration and guideline for future projects. (Urząd Dzielnicy Wola, 2010)

The District's 'search for traces' was tantamount to the destruction of the very 'authentic historic elements' that it aimed to preserve. Paradoxically, this also meant that, despite the project's focus on the photograph as a mode of commemoration, the relationship between the photograph and the city, so dear to Zmiana Foundation's petitioners, would soon be extinguished. The pavement would be stripped, cleaned, cut, sorted, and then, according to a promotional pamphlet published by the District Office, 'painstakingly . . . arranged just as [it was] before the war' (Urząd Dzielnicy Wola, 2011c, p. 35). This statement, of course, contradicts itself. *Arrangement* implies discretion on the part of the arranger, which negates the authenticity claim, itself a spurious one. The 'historic elements' could in fact only be 'arranged' as they were in 2010 at the outset of the project and not as they were in 1939, while those newly added manufactured elements meant to recall objects missing from an imagined and incomplete pre-war past (lampposts, benches, ornamental drainage grills, manicured trees, horse-drawn trams, etc.) are, of course, not historic.

According to the Haitian historian Michel-Rolph Trouillot (1995, p. 26), 'silences enter the process of historical production at four crucial moments: the moment of fact creation (the making of *sources*); the moment of fact assembly (the making of *archives);* the moment of fact retrieval (the making of *narratives*); and the moment of retrospective significance (the making of *history* in the final instance)'. Silences, which accompany all stages of historical production, can be read through objects in the city—something that the architectural theorist Mark Jarzombek (2001, p. 65) has called (in relation to post-Soviet Dresden) 'object-lessons'—things in places 'intended to construct if not actually reconstruct the citizens' temporal and historical understanding of the city'. Jarzombek sees Dresden's object-lessons in two ways: controlled by layers of bureaucracy, but also as opportunities for citizens to read past intended meanings and take advantage of the 'democratic' nature of public space where no 'letter of introduction' is necessary to engage with urban objects. I use Trouillot's description of the process of historical production and Jarzombek's term 'object-lessons' because both ideas help to highlight the conceptual failures of the *Revitalisation Plan*. *Chłodna's* old/new object-lessons—repositioned older artefacts arranged alongside newly fabricated ones—are the result of the simultaneous production of sources, archives, and narratives, where the *creation, assembly,* and *retrieval* of facts, as well as the final retrospective historical interpretation, have been collapsed into one public works project (see Figure 8.6).

By shifting around old stones and attempting to redetermine what *is* and *is not* the street's 'authentic' history, the District administration's design and construction teams helped establish bureaucratic control over the *future* narration of these objects. As a consequence, they undermined the petitioners' strong voice—their understanding of the importance of stones *in situ*, of proximities in space. For the community represented by the petitioners, the cobblestones were points of temporal and spatial reference, facts assembled and available for retrieval at any time. They were the means by which the information in abstract historical documents, such as archival photographs, could be reified and invested with retrospective significance. This group saw the street as a different sort of archive than the highly curated District model. For them, it was an assemblage of *in situ* artefacts, the significance of which was determined not by perceived didactic opportunities, but by existing semiotic relationships.

With this analysis in mind, viewing the street can be understood as the *emplotment* (Ricoeur, 1984) of ever-changing proximities between objects. Although a single opening in an old wall or a single cobblestone—not yet *emplotted* sources—can partly inform the viewing of a street, only the reading of proximate relationships between objects, complemented by surrounding cultural discourses that acknowledge (or dismiss) the shifting of these proximities, can generate layered historical narratives. For example, two bricks removed from an existing fragment of the ghetto wall in Warsaw and sent to the U.S. Holocaust Memorial Museum in Washington, DC, on their own

*Figure 8.6* Pavement detail with reused 19th century cobblestones. Concrete and iron inlays in the foreground and background show the locations of ghetto walls at different times. Between the inlays, parallel strips of small dark pavers symbolize the wooden steps of the Chłodna Street footbridge, which existed on the site in 1942. Warsaw, 2011.

convey little, if any, information. But the empty spaces and the descriptive plaque left behind on the wall fragment, as well as a billboard announcing the EU-funded 'revitalisation of areas surrounding the Warsaw Ghetto wall' (Janicka, 2011, p. 37), speak strongly about the competition between local and international Holocaust narratives and the commodification of the Holocaust in general.

Material dislocations can produce violent silences, or project meaning onto object-lessons that were never *intended* to carry that meaning. On the other hand, dislocation is also a necessary part of city building. The quality of the emergent public space is dependent on how material dislocations are managed and narrated. In the case of Chłodna Street, in an effort to settle a particular representation of the past into a desired narrative, local authorities have literally set in stone a representation of that narrative. Chłodna's 'revitalised' pavement is a mosaic of reused original cobblestones interspersed with newly cut, multicoloured granite, brick, and concrete pavers of various sizes (see Figure 8.7). 'It was painstaking work,' said the project architect Krzysztof Pasternak in an interview for *Gazeta Wyborcza*, 'we overlaid the pre-war parcellation plan from cadastral maps and aerial photographs onto contemporary plans, which allowed us to "weave" the composition of the new pavement.' The new patterns trace the exterior walls of destroyed pre-war buildings or their lot lines, emphasize unused carriage entrances, inform of pre-war addresses, and commemorate German wartime infrastructures—the ghetto walls, the footbridge over Chłodna Street, and two bunkers. All this implies an experiment in geometry rather than a careful historical reflection. 'I like this kind of "busyness" in the sidewalks,' confesses Pasternak, 'why invent curlicues,' if the historical information about the street can 'render intriguing patterns?' (Bartoszewicz, 2011). Placed alongside commemorative structures such as the ghetto

*Figure 8.7*  Two courses of red brick (parallel to ghetto wall inlay) outline the perimeters of buildings destroyed during the war or dismantled after 1945; shorter pavers, darker in hue, placed between the brick perimeters and the vegetation in the background, show areas once occupied by these buildings. A broad strip of lighter pavers marks a former carriageway entrance (diagonally across the frame in front of the pedestrians). Chłodna Street, Warsaw, 2011.

perimeter monument, but without any explanatory texts, these patterns are confusing rather than intriguing. Pasternak's passive voice with respect to history reveals an implicit problem with responsibility; after all, rather than the autonomous force of 'history', it was the architect who rendered the patterns.

The dislocated original fabric and the new cadastral puzzle are impossible to read because the distinctions between cartography and archaeology, between what once existed and what exists still as detritus, have been blurred. With the recent addition of inlays that mark the location of the ghetto wall on Chłodna Street between January and August 1942 *only*, the ensemble has become a topography of limits with serious implications, which go far beyond the appeal of geometric motifs. All these red lines, borders, patches, and symbols are not just, as Pasternak says, intriguing patterns. Given that building walls often doubled as ghetto perimeter walls, and in the presence of contemporary anti-Semitism, they map onto the city, and potentially reinforce, Nazi-imposed racial boundaries.

## Staging

The local press keenly followed the technical developments of the *Chłodna Street Revitalisation Plan*, but failed to notice the inconsistencies between the District's rhetoric, which promised to bring back the street's 'former grandeur', and the accompanying physical shifts of the pavement, street furniture, and commemorative markers. Official municipal documents popularised an image of pre-war Chłodna as an exciting metropolitan thoroughfare with numerous cinemas, cafés, and restaurants—in short, an extraordinary nightlife. Accurate or exaggerated, these descriptions have shaped the now-disappointed public's expectations for the 'revitalised' street.

The District promised to bring vibrant cosmopolitan life to Chłodna, but from a planning or zoning perspective, apart from designating parts of the street for pedestrian use, nothing was done to densify the street or bring services to its ground floors. Instead, the *Revitalisation Plan* has focused on commemorating the street's destruction and its traumatic Holocaust past. This inconsistency has resulted in an uneasy combination of local entertainment and cultural tourism on the one hand, and commemoration and Holocaust tourism on the other. 'Former grandeur', the catch phrase for the entire project, is tightly bound up with a desire for a Polish–Jewish multiethnic past. At Chłodna, representations of ghetto history have eclipsed other historical narratives, producing heritage caricatures. Chłodna's revitalisation was pitched as an enjoyable reconstructed cosmopolitan throwback to an interwar period filled with Polish and Jewish culture, but materially the project focuses on the commemoration of objects of the later Nazi oppression of both Jews and Poles.

A colourful map, published by the District and sponsored by museums and media organisations, shows the length of Chłodna Street populated by pictograms of key buildings and numbers inside splashes of colour, which index monuments, restaurants, and nightclubs (Urząd Dzielnicy Wola, 2011b). The black background and neon colour scheme hint that Chłodna is to be enjoyed at night. The map quotes from one nightclub's pamphlet: 'Our tradition is rock'n'roll and we *are* our tradition' (my emphasis). Directly below the pink box advertising the club, there is a cartoon of a horse-drawn tram, which, until it was cancelled for financial reasons, was to ferry tourists a few hundred metres from one end of the pedestrian section of the street to the other and back again. The tram is not just an anachronism, but a deeply disturbing reenactment of events that took place in the Warsaw Ghetto. Because the ghetto interrupted main tramlines through the city and because Jews and non-Jews were not allowed to share trams after 1940, horse-drawn buses and trams partly served the Jewish population inside the ghetto walls (Engelking & Leociak, 2009, p. 110). More importantly, horse-drawn vehicles were used to transport Jews, bound for Treblinka, to deportation points (Engelking & Leociak, 2009, p. 134). During the war, a horse-drawn tram or bus would not have travelled regularly down Chłodna Street, which was, for the most part, excluded from the ghetto.

The District's justification that the tram represents the public's nostalgia for 19th century Chłodna is problematic in light of the project's focus on Holocaust history. On the map, the tram is placed among several graphically equivalent yellow pictograms, including an elevation sketch of the footbridge slung awkwardly across a broad blue line indicating Chłodna Street. Because the memorial to the footbridge is missing from the map and because all other pictograms show elevations or perspectives of existing buildings, the map implies that the destroyed footbridge exists in its original location and form. This is of course inaccurate and indicative of what appears to be the municipality's tendency to confuse real objects with their representations. It might be necessary to indicate the *location* of the footbridge as a key element of the street's ghetto history, but it is problematic not to make graphically clear that what is being shown no longer exists. Placing an image of the footbridge on an entertainment and tourist map of Chłodna raises questions about Holocaust tourism and the motivations behind having the memorial to the footbridge function as the beacon for the whole revitalisation project.

The Wola District enticed Warsovians to join the official opening ceremonies for 'new' Chłodna Street, promising that it will be 'filled with pre-war automobiles and rickshaws, and "Warsaw's tricksters" will entertain pedestrians' (Bartoszewicz, 2010; Urząd Dzielnicy Wola, 2011a). The theme for the festivities was the pre-war marketplace with local businesses and craftspeople advertising their wares. At the end of the street party, in the dark and in keeping with the promotion of its nightlife, the district chose ceremonially to illuminate the footbridge monument—a final act of staging aimed to present Holocaust memory and contemporary longings and desires in one palatable package.

In the end, *Ellipsis* and the *Revitalisation Plan* attempted both to *take place at* and *take the place of* the memory of the footbridge, silencing Chłodna Street by bracketing out the residents' capability to remember. This hijacking of the discursive space extends to the street. Both projects attempted to override the existing material absences on Chłodna—missing cobblestones, bricks, lanterns, and, perhaps most importantly, the missing footbridge itself—by labelling as absent the very discursive spaces that guaranteed the presence of these absences. Assumed absence allowed for the space to be filled with objects, in this case, specifically didactic 'object-lessons' intended to carry memory in finite directions, which precluded absence as productive to remembering. Because of their pretentions to fill rather than acknowledge the value of absence and discontinuity on Chłodna, both *Ellipsis* and the *Revitalisation Plan* dominated, or at least dulled, certain citizen groups' more complex and disputative readings and performances of the street's history. The projects *occupied* the physical and the discursive spaces of Chłodna, but failed to engage with the street as a complete historical source, any of the existing commemorative objects, or the residents' voices.

This occupation could be felt viscerally in the autumn of 2010. Instead of delicate restoration, one could see an urban dissection: The pavement was stripped; its torn elements lay in piles reminiscent of rubble. Workers with rotary saws cut old kerbstones and created a heady fog that enveloped the area (see Figure 8.8). Cobblestones were piled high and the ground was broken. Archaeologists hovered nervously and watched bulldozers push around shapeless mounds of clay. Old iron tram tracks sat in heaps waiting to be cleaned, straightened, and reused. Those still in place led directly to the construction site and abruptly stopped at a set of gates almost as wide as the road. Past the open gates and the edge of the deconstructed pavement, tightly bound cobblestones gave way to looser patterns and then single granite blocks dispersed in the beige clay that defined the construction area. All this took place behind a tall fence, blue on the outside and white inside, which ran on either side of the street almost exactly along the same lines as the former ghetto walls.

*Figure 8.8* Chłodna Street under construction. Warsaw, 2010.

I do not argue here that the answer for Warsaw is to attempt to preserve everything unchanged. Dislocation is not only necessary to a vital city, but it is also essential to remembering—something that humans can only do through a recognition of difference. It is nonetheless important to embrace the process, rather than the product, of change. When Ossowski wrote in 1945 of the 'dehumanisation' of Warsaw, he referred to the city's 'matter', its transformation into something resembling its 'raw' or 'deculturalised' state. He saw this rawness as antithetical to the existence of an urban condition because matter in the city is almost always cultural. This means, impractically for rapid post-socialist urban development, that the entire city—its material manifestations together with the discursive spaces that modify and mediate them—must be questioned as a historical source and read for what has been excluded from schematised memory (Gross, 2000, pp. 136, 141). To adapt a controversial idea from Jochen Gerz's *2,146 Stones Against Racism* in Saarbrücken (Young, 2000, pp.140–144), if Chłodna's residents were to remove the street's cobblestones by hand, pile them up, and then relocate them one by one, this kind of interaction with the city as a primary source—this making of *difference*—could unearth silences and reinforce local, lived memory.

# Chapter 9

# Urban Public Spaces in Switzerland
## 'Betwixt and Between'[1] Performance and Competence

*Monika Litscher*

For several years, public spaces have been experiencing an upswing, in political debates and in debates in the media, as well as in the intrinsically transdisciplinary contexts of urban research and development. In these scientific and practice-oriented domains, the manifold challenges of this complex and dynamic construct are, for the most part, being acknowledged and discussed from diverse perspectives, with different epistemological interests. Here, the establishment of transdisciplinary scientific initiatives and strategies of governance which, with various biases and desires, accept the specific public spaces, or that deal with social, architectural, economic, political, aesthetic, artistic, and cultural dimensions and interrelations at a theoretical and practical level, can also be seen to an increasing extent. Debates and processes of this very nature are then often situated at interfaces between fields of responsibility that were previously more clearly marked out.

With an intrinsically application-oriented focus, academic research needs to bridge the gap between practice and science, and to bring about a transfer to teaching. Although this balancing act is fruitful, at the same time it also always requires a challenging change of perspectives and appropriate language. This act is probably one of the most frequently voiced demands, for which we make a case on the basis of (among other things) the results of two research projects on the subject of public spaces. In many aspects, among the involved parties in their everyday practice and among professionals in planning, urban development, and social occupations, there is a need for more knowledge and thus more competence regarding public spaces.

This chapter is to look into what this keyword 'competence' (which indeed is now also a buzzword in the context of public spaces) is all about, and into the extent to which (and whether) competence is compatible with the complex characteristics of public spaces, which are of an intrinsically performative and dynamic nature.

First, though, I would very briefly like to look at the notions of competence and performance, then to go into the subject of public spaces before presenting the realised studies that are taken as a starting point, that is, the selected results of relevance in this context from the two application-oriented and transdisciplinary research projects: 'Management of uses in the public space—Strategies and instruments for dealing with usage conflicts in public space' ('Nutzungsmanagement im öffentlichen Raum—Strategien und Instrumente für den Umgang mit Nutzungskonflikten im öffentlichen Raum', e.g., Emmenegger & Litscher, 2011[2]) and 'Expulsion from public urban spaces' ('Wegweisung aus öffentlichen Stadträumen', e.g., Litscher 2011a, 2011b; or the final report, Litscher, Grossrieder, Mösch Payot, & Schmutz, 2012).

## Of Competence and Performance

The notion of competence has different meanings. First, it leads back to the 1960s on communicative competences of 'how to say things' (e.g., Chomsky, 1965). Later on, in the 1990s, the subject of the 'entrepreneur of the self' (Boltanski & Chiapello, 2005) in the context of Michel Foucault's *Biopolitics,* ethics, and the governmental studies (e.g., 2004, 2008) provides a shift and wider meaning of competence in discussion. With the reconfiguration of quotidian practices in our neoliberal system, the human capital and every kind of private and professional activity functions more and more as a personal investment; all consumption is now understood as a kind of production and that renders every actor as an entrepreneur of the self. This transformation in an economic figure involves also 'the city'. It turns it to an activating company and leads to a management of the urban public spaces, though today the spotlight on the notion of competence is wider and means always 'to know how to say things' and 'to know how to do things'. This practice furthermore includes the real performance 'to know what to do, how to do, and in which complex situation to do'.

This change of practice to a certain governmental way of private and professional life, the economical optimising of everyday practice, is also part of the hype of the performative turn (Bachmann-Medick, 2010, pp. 104–143). It finds its expression in urban public spaces. Performing (saying and doing at the same time, e.g., Judith Butler, 1997) means to conduct and to act simultaneously. The perception of this performance and its products is an equivalent part of that performative play. However, the outcomes of action and the acts are likewise the focus of certain moral judgments through individuals (citizens), society, and organizations. The reception of the competence and performance is quite often linked with a qualification as good or bad practice. What kind of quality or improvement of the competences is sufficient can be taken as a part of the personal and professional competence of human activity, although as an act and an outcome of action at the same time, and education, training, and communication make it possible (Figure 9.1).

*Figure 9.1* Kleine Schanze close to the National Parliament, Bern.

## Dimensions of Public Spaces: Between Regulations and Management of Uses

At a heuristic level, the relativistic, relational, and dynamic spatial concepts and terminology that have found their way into many domains in recent years (particularly cultural and sociological research)—such as Johanna Rolshoven's 'space triad' (2003, 2010), Martina Löw's sociology of space (2001), or Henri Lefebvre's production of space (2000), which has recently been rediscovered in architectural and political domains—offer figures of thought that make it possible to operationalise issues in spatial contexts. Their lowest common denominator is the inherently consistent consideration of a kind of space as a socially produced space, that is, lived space, perceived space, and constructed space, function equally as constituents within a complex, dynamic, and procedural fabric and are to be thought of together, in theory and practice.

In this chapter, the attribute 'public' is to be seen primarily in terms of its legal, political scope, which enables an understanding of free access for all, every day, every night, around the clock. The fact that in public spaces dynamic and complex interrelationships take effect and overlapping, sometimes contradictory flows of different actors at the same time, nonstop circulations of people, goods, and knowledge, tempos and coexistence, manifest and operate in a performative way, is already a clear indication of the incalculable human factor, and of the urgent need to always give equal consideration to the parties involved and the social components in connection with the subject matter and the specific societal spaces. In these societal spaces, 'various simultaneous "publics" overlay each other, layers of utilisation, of perspectives and meanings, which are assigned to the space by the cultural production of its occupants' (Reiners, Malli, & Reckinger, 2006, p. 26). Particularly, in connection with this point and in the attempt to do the phenomenon of public spaces justice, urban researchers such as Louis Wirth (1938), Georg Simmel (1984), and Henri Lefebvre (1972) have always made a case (each with different perspectives and contexts, and always a dash of idealism) for, among other things, the essential urban qualities such as diversity, events, and encounters, which are associated with incalculable and unexpected occurrence, as well as vital flows, which are to be maintained, tolerated, and lived in the specific urban space. This opens up options for societal participation, possibilities for the construction of meaning, and the negotiation of significance, or even the discovery of, and encounters with, splendid facets, colourful borderline phenomena, and bizarre circumstances within our society.

Within these theoretical frames the two transdisciplinary research projects also pick up on these urban qualities. The results regarding the topic of urban public space were only one part of the project. 'Management of uses in the public space—Strategies and instruments for dealing with usage conflicts in the public space' involved a wider research into how public spaces are dealt with in six Swiss cities. In a multistage, multidimensional process, this project considered institutional, structurally analytical, and action-oriented aspects, at times taking different perspectives on the societal entanglement of power and hierarchy. This project focused on the cities' practice in the management of public spaces; here, the relevant urban players were given an opportunity to enter into an exchange regarding their practice and knowledge (in a technical and democratic way), to gain insights into the working methods of others, and to discuss approaches beyond urban boundaries and beyond the internal boundaries within administrations (Steiner, 2009).

## Six Case Studies

The actual happenings on site and the interplay of the perception, usage, and structure of space in specific urban spaces were looked at in case studies with an empirical and qualitative orientation. With an ethnographic perspective, the locations (selected in cooperation with the politicians, administration, and experts from the city partners of Basel, Lucerne, Schaffhausen, St. Gallen, Winterthur, Zurich), most of which were close to the city centre and characterised by intensive usage, were observed in a participatory manner; the local players in the specific societal spaces were tracked down and interviewed, photographs were taken, films were made, and structural design aspects were recorded. The settings of the six case studies gave a certain contrast, which simultaneously made it possible to make comparisons and to single out site-specific and city-specific aspects, as well as themes, trends, action patterns, and patterns of meaning that the cases had in common. The findings showed that the cases shared three main threads, corresponding to the subject areas 'use and functions', 'interaction and communication', and 'atmospheres'. Moreover, in a third and final step, the results were given as feedback to the administrations, incorporating experts from various departments (e.g., social welfare, planning/design, waste disposal, security) in the participating cities . In this process, by means of tailored knowledge transfer, it was possible to initiate a discourse in these six cities, and to take the specific local challenges into account in each case. This final, concluding step was based on 11 recommendations for action, which were developed from the results of the project, particularly those of the case studies, and include fundamental premises (e.g., the aforementioned urban qualities to be taken into account in connection with the subject of public spaces), methods, and codes of practice for possible and necessary cooperation beyond the boundaries between disciplines and departments.

In summary, the basic positions and premises target the following: (a) appreciation of the good supply of public spaces; (b) being aware of the fragile balances and complexities in public urban spaces; (c) acceptance of contradictions and diversity in public spaces; (d) respect for the most prominent users of public spaces: youths; (e) recognition of the significance of social aspects in public urban spaces; and (f) consideration of specific logics: every location is distinct. In connection with methodology and practice, the following points can be cursorily included: (a) incorporation of local knowledge into the planning of concepts for usage and design; (b) the call for transdisciplinary, cooperative, and participatory planning; (c) taking notice of tensions and usage conflicts in public spaces at an early stage; (d) advancement of competencies for public urban spaces; and (e) adaptation of upkeep to suit the 24-hour day.[3]

On the one hand, alongside the appeal for urban qualities, such as an acknowledgement of diversity, which highlights contradictions, unpredictability, and dynamism as characteristics of the urban public space and of urban everyday life, and is thus also geared towards opportunities to participate in society, the obtained findings led to fruitful input regarding the challenges of political and administrative management of public spaces in increasingly complex settings. On the other hand, among other things, the empirical and theoretical findings also showed that in public spaces, formal checklist-based control falls short and is impossible (regarding the planning of uses, for example, such control can hardly be effective in addressing social challenges, sometimes only limited to superficial, aesthetic treatment). Here, against the backdrop of increasing societal differentiation, there is a constant need for new competencies in dealing with public spaces, on the part of space users and space managers—in interdepartmental and transdisciplinary discussions, cooperative and participatory processes, or in dealing with foreigners, with the different, with the contradictory, and with complexities and dynamics. The increasing regulation in public spaces must include an examination of the complexities and dynamics of spaces and encourage autonomous action in a creative and pleasurable way. In short, the results of this comparative research—without focusing on the specific local context and dynamics in this chapter—show that with regard to public spaces, everyone involved needs more knowledge, more practice in dealing with the spaces, and more competencies, whether for their everyday practices or for their professional practices (Figure 9.2).

In the research project 'Public order against incivilities in public places of the city—Expulsion from public urban spaces', the main interest was in exactly this kind of increasingly introduced

*Figure 9.2* Heiliggeist Kirche close to the railway station, Bern.

regulation in public spaces, particularly the effects and mechanisms of expulsion measures in the three Swiss cities of Bern, St. Gallen, and Lucerne. Here, the focus was on the subjective perspectives and experiences with the people directly affected by the expulsion, with incorporation of the applicable legal standards. In addition, the people who still remain in the public space and the police who issue the expulsions, as well as contextual material from political and parliamentary debates on the expulsion standard and the juristic standards, were also taken into account. This study was methodologically oriented towards ethnographic lifeworld analysis, i.e., focused on everyday practices and concerned with comprehension-oriented description of small social lifeworlds. In a multimethod approach, narrative interviews, guideline interviews, expert interviews, participatory observation, and qualitative content analysis were realised on four levels. The standards laid down in police law, which act as disciplinary and control measures and are applied in most Swiss cities, are diametrically opposed to the aforementioned urban qualities, as well as to basic rights and civil liberties (which, among other things, should also guarantee the mode of integration), and have a decidedly inclusive and exclusive effect. Accordingly, social work and policy are, for example, primarily concerned with taking preventive measures to forestall marginalisation and exclusion. Second, they deal with multiple, and often rigidified, forms of exclusion from the welfare state (Baecker, 1994; Fuchs, 2000). The mechanism of contradictions and paradoxes resulting therefrom and referred to the dynamic dialectics of exclusion and inclusion are widely discussed; the mechanism of inclusion works always with exclusion (e.g., being inclusively part of it without the excluded people).

## Mechanisms of Inclusion and Exclusion

Hereby, measures were discussed that aim especially at integration, but in themselves forward exclusion, as well as the mechanisms of inclusion and exclusion in an activating welfare state, especially with reference to the relationship between the measures taken by post-welfare-state institutions and social norms (see, e.g., Foucault, 2004, 2008). These can be added to the long list of various security policing measures, sociopolitical measures, and structural design interventions with specific architectural, functional, and social impetus and representative effectiveness. On the one hand, these include, for example, the five very contradictory discussed concepts of 'broken windows', 'defensible space', 'CPTED—crime prevention through environmental design', 'DOC—designing out crime' and 'community oriented policing' (see, e.g., Schreiber, 2005, pp. 74–79). All these concepts lead to the buzzword 'zero tolerance' with the strong purpose of 'governing through crime' (see, e.g., Belina, 2006, p. 20). They are manifesting, on the other hand, for instance, various forms of management, governmental practices, regulatory mechanisms, and control mechanisms that, in most cities shaped by Western influences, have been gradually phased out during the last 30 years, or are currently being phased out (Wehrheim, 2006). With regard to expulsion as a regulatory measure and phenomenon in an international context, comparisons can be made with, for example, the term *Platzverweis* (a kind of sending-off) in the German-speaking world. Discourses and debates in the French-speaking world revolve around terms like *incivilités* or in similar fashion to the debates in the United States about *incivility*, while in Great Britain, the so-called *anti-social behaviour orders* (ASBOs) primarily aimed at 14- to 16-year-olds, come to mind and are woven in the discussion about the reception of actions as socially deviant behaviour. Particularly, these more recent urban methods of government, in cities which, in a transformed sense, act in a similar way to commercial companies (entrepreneurial city concept), are increasingly also giving rise to new social configurations that involve more privatisation and denationalisation of public spheres, and that also effect societal interrelations (see, e.g., Michel, 2005; Rose, 2008). In parallel to this, in keeping with a neoliberal style in a weak state, the risks of life are privatised, while in contrast, when it comes to surveillance and penalties, a stronger state emerges and takes drastic measures. Indeed, the expulsion standard is also part of the strong state dimension.

## Swiss Law and the Practice of Expulsion from Public Spaces

According to this standard, people or groups perceived as 'disruptive' or 'dangerous' can be expelled from certain public spaces for certain amounts of time in each case. The laws and measures are formulated differently from canton to canton. An example from the cantonal legal norm of Bern, written in 1998, is: 'The police can send people away or prohibit a return to a certain place or area for a certain time . . . if there's a founded suspicion that the respondent or his group are a danger or harm to the public order and security'.[4] The practice of expulsion can (e.g., in St. Gallen) be applied if, for instance, 'proper usage' of the public space is hindered. Lucerne goes a step further and enables restrictions of rights to spaces if the feeling of piety experienced by third parties is infringed upon (e.g., a group of young people is drinking alcohol, the level of conversation increases and this kind of presence is infringing on the wishes of certain other people). With such entrenchments, which make an expulsion dependent on the disturbance of third parties in the public space, the law enforcement agency is granted vastly increased spatial 'competencies' in the sense introduced before, and these are accompanied by a simultaneously increased sensitivity to social norms and an ever-lower threshold which, if breached, can lead to an expulsion.

At the same time, it becomes clear that the longer expulsion is practised, the more determinate dedications of public spaces are instrumentally realised. This means that certain uses, which equate to restricted usage of urban spaces, are considered common practice and prevail to the benefit of what is in principle a freer and more tolerant concept of common use of public spaces. These inclusive and exclusive mechanisms are generally to be understood as a response to the divergence in uses of public spaces. The expulsion measures and standards are one possible way of dealing with the socially-different is applied, which aims at the centre of society. This reveals structural interrelations between the different holders of power (e.g., local policemen or owners of restaurants or retails stores), the authorities, and various values and attitudes, particularly regarding security, order, cleanliness, and consumption.

As a theoretical frame for the study, we adopted a relational and interactive understanding of inclusive and exclusive processes (Mäder, 2009, pp. 35–52; Wehrheim, 2006), paying equal attention to the social, legal, and economic dimensions. Here, in the economic isolation of the labour market and consumption, two of the most important elements of identity building in Swiss society play a role and indicate that (economically speaking) poor people neither count as producers nor consumers; thus, in two ways, they are defined as superficial according to market logic. Increasingly, the legal dimension of inclusion and exclusion appears to play a more significant role, and is thus also becoming the subject of increased interest. If the social dimension is also taken into account, there is evidence to the effect that isolation occurs, due to social norms, behaviour patterns, and lifestyles that are not seen as common, and thus the possibility of living according to certain values and life goals is denied. This type of societal exclusion mostly affects people or groups as a result of unwelcome behaviour and presence, as well as the 'failure' to comply with the social status, or nonconformity with the ideology, of public spaces, as a kind of status charges inherent in the conceptions of public spaces. If the possibilities of access to public spaces are restricted, it must also be taken into consideration that 'social actions are spatially and temporally bound and exclusion from spaces also means exclusion from the social, economic and political life in these spaces' (Wehrheim, 2006, p. 36). In this regard, these dimensions of inclusion and exclusion mostly appear along with spatially oriented disciplinary and control measures, such as the practice of expulsion, and are to be discussed together with urban consumption landscapes and the subject of security *and* insecurity (Wehrheim, 2006, p. 36). Expulsions are mostly issued because of the uneasiness and discomfort of city residents and city visitors due to noise and dirt, so in the broadest sense, it is because of an aesthetic dimension and by no means a response to any real threat or criminal act (see Gasser, 2004; Litscher et al., 2012).

One of the study's findings is that the expelled belong to different milieus and strata of our society, and that their ages and origins vary. A noticeably high number of young people are among them, often (particularly in the media and in politics) mentioned on a discursive level in the same breath as so-called 'marginals' (drug addicts, punks, the homeless) and also in performative practice as 'being marginal'. They are assigned the across-the-board label 'youths', along with structural attributes and practices ascribed to the ideal-type, and a positioning in the specific urban space occurs. Thus, being sent away from public spaces is one of the regularly recurring experiences of young people in public spaces. The interviewees were often young people, who overcame hurdles regarding work, body, institution, and family (see, e.g., Bude & Willisch, 2006, whose study about young adults and the power of jobs and trainings, healthy conditions of the body, education in institutions and family-networks regarding success, and inclusion and exclusion on different scale of society). Nevertheless, due to their life stylisation and their affiliation to a certain societal group, they regularly experience exclusion from public spaces. Those affected see these informal expulsions (usually issued without explanation) as unjustified, arbitrary, and demoralising, yet they routinely accept them and see them as part of normality. Thus, despite the ostensibly spatial and temporary dimension of the expulsion, which is then also played down, it is seen as tragic and illegitimate. The stigmatisation and imposition of discipline (perceived as arbitrary) on the basis of age, gender, group membership, and lifestyle is thus pervasive and to be interpreted as multidimensional exclusion. This is the case, even though after an expulsion the young people concerned seek, if possible, other places and options within the urban jungle that can (still) be used for an appropriation and for the purposes of their own consumption. However, such seemingly self-reliant reaction and awareness always depends on the individual dispositions, competencies, and positions of power (see Reiners et al., 2006, pp. 182–190) (Figure 9.3).

*Figure 9.3* Roter Platz in the inner city, courtyard of Raiffeisen Bank, St. Gallen.

## Young People and Urban Public Spaces

The young people spoken to in the expulsion study appear to have capital and resources, in the sense described by Bourdieu (1983, pp. 183–198) with differences between economic, cultural, and social capital (Bourdieu, 1987), which enable them to deal with the curtailments in public space, the stigmatisation and the imposition of discipline (e.g., usage restrictions, expulsions), as well as their own needs. However, at this point it should already be noted that applying regulations informally, which is indeed also how the practice of expulsion is handled, appears highly problematic. Those affected find it difficult to understand, because there is usually no criminal act involved, nor any intention to commit one. The across-the-board labelling as possible offenders and the message of being unwelcome, which imply dismissal and expulsion, are also seen as arbitrary interpretation, as contrary to the structural conditions, and as abuse of the position of power. This is also made clear by the following two quotes from interviewed young men in Bern who have experienced expulsion many times, over a number of years:

> I didn't break anything, I was just there. . . . And it wasn't anything illegal. If they just don't want people to consume alcohol, then they just shouldn't sell any alcohol . . . instead of selling at the same time, and later saying you're then not allowed to consume it here.

> They just send away the people who don't fit the frame. If a couple's there talking to each other, they say nothing. If a bigger group's there, then it no longer even matters what they look like. Youths who could damage property, or could do graffiti or make a mess, that's who they go for. As soon as they notice them, they go for them. That's how I see it.

In this regard, it is ironic that for young people in particular, public spaces are known to serve as practice fields in the process of growing up, in the transition phase and, not least, to the effect that they count as people who will come of age in the future and who can (and want to) take part in democratic processes. For the most part, the young people who have been experiencing such expulsions for several years balk at the idea of resistance or protest. It seems remarkable that they do not know about their rights, nor about the thresholds that can lead to a formal expulsion, and that despite experiencing being unwelcome, experiencing across-the-board labelling as potential offenders, and experiencing the sense of injustice triggered by being sent awayby the police, there is currently hardly any evident resistance to curtailments of rights to spaces, even among young people. Instead, somewhat demoralised and with gritted teeth, they usually choose an evasive strategy which nevertheless, due to high mobility and new media, the young adults, who usually have resources at their disposal, seem to find relatively easy. In particular, the statements regarding routine intervention and acceptance of expulsion experiences among young people, and the lack of any perception of such measures among the people who remain in the spaces, show that the practice of expulsion (Litscher, 2011a) in contemporary urban spaces in Switzerland is implemented almost invisibly, and discipline is regularly imposed on public spaces in this way.

Despite the lack of reaction, an expulsion is a realisation of multidimensional exclusion, the long-term effects of which are difficult to foresee. What can be deduced is that it seems to be increasingly the case that neither public negotiation processes about the definition of public spaces, nor direct points of contact with the societally different are occurring any longer, nor do they appear to be desired anymore. With the broad approval of the respective cantonal[5] introductions of expulsion legislation, as voiced in the public referendums, a lack of curiosity and of urban competence also becomes apparent, the public spaces are weakened rather than strengthened, and the feeling of a very slight looming risk upon frequent visits to public spaces noticeably disappears. To no small extent, this is because with the seizure of space and the power of control on the part of the (security) police in conjunction with the imposition of (among other things) expulsion measures and the symbolic enactment of security, a more fragmented urban space is created. Thus, urban space is increasingly subdivided into monitored spaces, into which clear indications of inclusion *and* exclusion of certain behaviour patterns and people have been (or are being) written; at the same time, it is suggested that these spaces are dangerous, and last but not least, fragmented transition zones and intermediate spaces within the city are being created, where there are also calls for surveillance and enacted security. In this regard, various studies (e.g., Beckett & Herbert, 2008, based in various European cities) clearly show that neither security enactments, nor political enactments, nor the real and symbolic separation between (for instance) the included consumers and rich residents on the one hand, and the excluded, allegedly disruptive nonconsumers on the other hand, increases the subjective feeling of insecurity in the urban space (Figure 9.4).

## On the Search for Lacking Competencies

These findings from theory and empirical evidence enable various conclusions to be drawn. Particularly in the project 'Public order against incivilities in public places of the city—Expulsion from public urban spaces', it is very clearly shown that the ability to allow the unexpected, to encounter the foreign and the different, to arrange negotiations, or to act in the supposed and popularly accepted squishy declared public interest in public spaces (not in the sense of Richard Sennett's 'public man', 2008) largely appears to be stunted. Here, the appeal for more competence in everyday actions and in professional practice again comes across considerably more clearly than in the project 'Management of uses in the public space'. At the same time, however, both projects tangibly demonstrate the performative and dynamic dimension of the respective public spaces which, despite regulations, can hardly be controlled or completely eliminated. This is despite the (mostly) parallel introduction of structural design interventions, control measures, and disciplinary approaches which, above all, primarily occur in the inner-city consumption landscapes and at the public transport companies' semi-private sites. These are realised by

*Figure 9.4* Public space close to the railway station next to the KKL (Kultur- und Kongresszentrum Luzern), Lucerne.

means of inclusion and exclusion measures and are intended to maintain the aesthetic surface of the (urban) spaces, but which, as already mentioned above, aim at the heart of society. Thus, regarding alcohol consumption and revelry among young adults, for instance, practices can be observed which are to be read in the context of the transition phase from youth to adulthood, but which, from a societal point of view and as public behaviour, are indeed also frowned upon or forbidden.

One thing that the two projects have in common is that a deficiency is identified, albeit from different perspectives, which wants to be, or should be, addressed. At the same time, it is repeatedly asserted that certain practices must be curbed and controlled. Taking this shortcoming as a basis, first and foremost, it is necessary to ask where this need for control comes from, why the sensitivities are increasing, why the rise in the feeling of disturbance is gradually diminishing, and what behaviour leads to this feeling of being disturbed, or even threatened, as well as how it does so? Here, two aspects from the deliberations of Robert Pfaller on *The Filthy Sacred and Pure Reason* (2008) could perhaps provide helpful inspiration and deliver a possible answer. In connection with his temporally diagnostic observations on pleasure prevention and asceticism in contemporary neoliberal societies, and also with part of the results of the two studies we conducted, Pfaller detects, among other things, a drop in the subjects' ability to attend to and enjoy their interests. Thus, the 'filthy sacred' (which is not seen in a religious conceptualisation, but instead as the extraordinary, unpredictable, and unreasonable, which comes across as colourful and fascinating, yet at the same time dangerous and anomalous, e.g., young people in urban public spaces) is degraded. Particularly due to the latter attributes, this so-called 'filthy sacred' (smoking is a recent example or young people drinking in public space as seen in the empirical results of the two studies) is considered dubious; it is suppressed, forbidden, and, in the name of pure reason, abandoned. Pfaller explains: 'Even the moderation that regulates our mundane life can become immoderation. This is exactly the situation we live in at present. We are moderating ourselves immoderately. Thus, if the moderation is not doubled, i.e. if it is not (as would be consistent) also applied to the moderation itself, such that it moderates itself moderately, one ends up in an obscene excess of moderation' (2011, pp. 26–27). In repression, according to Pfaller, this leads to a lot of things that are reasonably nice and standardised, yet boring, mundane, and flat.

All these attributes hardly seem to be qualities worth striving towards for concepts of urban public spaces. In particular, when making a detour through the subject of public spaces, Pfaller speaks of a freedom, which is increasingly understood to mean that nobody feels disturbed anymore, and of a culture of total self-legislation which, also in public spaces, only continues to tolerate what appears reasonable in private spaces (2008, pp. 105–109). Also along these lines, the philosopher, psychoanalyst, and cultural scientist then explains why humorous, playful behaviour in public spaces is in the public interest (certainly in a kind of ideal typical manner, but also including the hard-fought and now long-established rights to freedom such as freedom of assembly, freedom of expression, and freedom of movement) rather than in the private interest. Thus, it is precisely the prioritisation of what one is familiar with, and of what one finds reasonable, that entails an arrogant abstinence, and which opposes pleasurable play and enjoyment. Pfaller cites various illustrative examples, for instance, that everyone knows that donning a red nose at a carnival is a bit silly, but that the decision can then be made either to playfully get involved, in the knowledge that it is a game and silly, or indeed to abstain and to be reasonable, also in precisely this knowledge that it is a game and silly. Pfaller thus exposes the supposedly tolerant and pleasure-seeking late modern age as dictatorial and ascetic, devoid of the courage to take life's risks, and thus ultimately devoid of the good life, which includes the ability to enjoy properly (2011, pp. 15–47) (Figure 9.5).

*Figure 9.5* Inseli close to the university, the KKL, the railway station, and the lake of Lucerne.

## Conclusion

In my view, Pfaller's diagnostics and his appeal for enjoyment are also to be read as an appeal for the so-called 'good' and 'attractive' public spaces. It appears difficult to assess the extent to which the parties involved can (and want to) obtain the competencies that this calls for in their everyday practice in public spaces, and that form the professional practice of administrators, urban developers, urban planners, and professionals in social and cultural domains. All the while, it is becoming apparent that it is hardly possible to ever reconcile the questions about (and the calls for) competence in this regard with control management and the current regulations. Above all, due to the incalculable human factor, it is hardly likely that the spatial settings can ever be made calculable. At the same time, it is also the case that the contradictory dimensions and inter-relations (entanglement) of public spaces, and thus also their complexity, dynamics, and perfor-mance, cannot be entirely freed from the unexpected; therefore, by means of the mechanisms and dynamics of public spaces, and on the basis of precisely these genuine characteristics, they still resist complete taming, although their performative capacity and the unexpected (and at the same time, the competence in dealing with the unexpected) are on the decline. Thus, the real challenge is in fact to tolerate and reproduce the public spaces with public modes of behaviour and practices, and to appropriate and use them as public practice fields for forms of play that are worthy of existence—also those of the 'filthy sacred'.

### Notes

1  In reference to Victor Turner's concept of liminality, which addresses the transitional phases in rituals (1964).
2  For the results, see also the research reports at http://www.hslu.ch/s-nutzungsmanagement (accessed 1/10/2012).
3  See the report at http://www.hslu.ch/s-schlussfolgerungen_zu_den_fallstudien_und_handlungsemp-fehlungen.pdf.pdf (accessed 1/10/2012).
4  Berner Polizeigesetz Art, 29b. See at: www.sta.be.ch/belex/d/default.asp (accessed 20/01/2013).
5  *Cantonal* means on the level of a canton, which is a corner or district. In the Swiss context there are 26 cantons. They are all member states of the federal state of Switzerland.

# Part III

# Everyday Life and Sharing the City

*Ali Madanipour, Sabine Knierbein, and Aglaée Degros*

The chapters in Part III evaluate social diversity as experienced in public spaces and the analytical and policy approaches adopted towards public space and challenges of sharing space in large and complex cities. The authors argue that in large cities, concentration of diversity in some areas offers a new yardstick with which to measure the rest of society (Chapter 10); that much of social life unfolds outside public spaces (Chapter 11); that overemphasis on social criticism may mask the positive face of public places (Chapter 12); that public spaces can be an integral part of people's lives even if they live in unfavourable conditions (Chapter 13); and that public spaces can be part of the necessary measures for social integration in divided societies (Chapter 14).

In Chapter 10, Maria Anita Palumbo aims to redress the essential role that public spaces play in redefining political, economic, and cultural transformation of Paris and French society in general. Barbés is a historical migrants' neighbourhood of Paris with a specific everyday life, characterised by a combination of density and diversity, a place where 'foreigners'/stranger's practises take place in the streets of this northeast Parisian area: (il)legal trade of exotic goods, Muslim prayers, religious celebrations, as much as banal interaction and mutual visibility, make the visitors and the inhabitants feel they are elsewhere. Barbés is, in fact, a North and sub-Saharan African concentration in Europe. Recently, this neighbourhood has been brought to the national media and political scene because of different aspects provoking debates at multiple levels: The process of social changes started by the city of Paris, determined to change the 'commercial landscape' of the neighbourhood and addressing the 'Islamisation' of public space (street prayers), in reaction to which a 'French aperitif' with pork sausages and wine (forbidden for Muslims) was organized by a Facebook community on the day of the prayer. These recent events show how this diverse and heterogenic urban area is involved in the French contemporary identities debates, especially on the matters of religious visibility. Barbés, as a heterotopia (Foucault) or a 'carnival' space (Michel Agier), is functioning as the inversed mirror of Paris, constituting a counterexample of potential and spontaneous use of public area. Barbés is a cosmopolitan public space that works as a worldwide crossroad since the end of the 19th century, in which juridical law, as much as urban designs policies, is changing the public space and simultaneously revealing current social change issues and the arena of actors that participate in this process (from inhabitants to political figures) reclaiming multiple uses—and norms of use—of public space.

In Chapter 11, Penny Koutrolikou focuses on issues regarding ethno-religious diversity in London, which have been strongly associated with the city via discourses of social cohesion, immigration, integration, security, and everyday life. At the same time, these associations are spatially expressed through concerns about segregation (even ghettoization) and addressed through discourses and practices referring to social mix, neighbourhood regeneration, and public spaces. Yet, from another perspective, ethno-religious diversity is explored on the basis of intergroup relations or conflict studies that tend to place limited attention on spatial processes. Nevertheless, interpretations of 'contact hypothesis' become more and more the foundations of recommendations concerning urban ethno-religious relations. This chapter explores the spatialities of 'governing urban diversity' and the dominant discourses of social mix and 'fleeting interactions' as the primary vehicles for ethno-religious conviviality, and discusses the possibilities and limitations of these discourses. In doing so, it discusses notions of private and public and their differentiated significance for ethno-religious relations, while also highlighting the notion of the 'in-between'. Through the examples of inner London boroughs of high ethno-religious diversity, it discusses the spatialities of ethno-religious relations, the way they are affected by policies, and the questions that everyday practices and perceptions raise.

In Chapter 12, Regan Koch and Alan Latham argue against how critical urban scholarship typically frames discussion and research on public spaces to focus on exclusion, encroachment, and claim-making. Important though these issues are, the authors argue, they can end up restricting our analytical vocabulary. By researching different public spaces in London, the authors suggest a number of possibilities for expanding how urban scholars might attend to the collective life of cities. They argue that attending carefully to how people come to inhabit public spaces—how they in a sense domesticate them—and how these modes of inhabitation change, offers a fruitful way of opening up how we understand public space and its ongoing transformation. They draw upon recent changes in London to illustrate these ideas, aiming to highlight the extent to which public life is constantly being remade in ways both ordinary and surprising.

Chapter 13 evaluates the resident-defined open spaces in Istanbul's informal housing settlements (squatter settlements, *gecekondu*). Noah Billig analyses three Istanbul squatter settlements in terms of how everyday public spaces on and near the street are formed, adapted, used, and valued. For this chapter, previous studies evaluating urban open space typologies and their use in Istanbul informal settlements are analysed. Observations and a survey of residents (i.e., their thoughts about their open spaces) are also conducted in the settlements. The overlapping boundaries of the private and public realms are examined. Additionally, this study evaluates how the public spaces on and near the street become dynamic spaces of social, cultural, and economic interaction and sharing. It is found that these flexible public spaces host heterogeneous gatherings in terms of age, sex, and activity types. Finally, the way these public spaces are adapted and used is related to overlapping social constructs: the prevalent social neighbourhoods ties and their historical roots in Anatolian village culture, and the modern community representation in Istanbul's city government through the neighbourhood delegate (*Muhtar*). It is found that the everyday shared spaces in these neighbourhoods are inextricably linked to the social structures and cultural practices prevalent in Istanbul squatter neighbourhoods.

For Gabriella Esposito de Vita in Chapter 14, the city is a social event developed by a combined action of plans and free-will activities, political wishes and human needs, radicalisms and intercultural fusions. Public spaces of the built city are the typical expression of a historical stratification and, today, are under the pressure of social transformations that have occurred, in particular, as a result of globalisation processes and migratory flows. The main topic of this chapter is to develop a methodological approach to community planning that targets enhancement of multiple roles of public places in order to favour the overcoming of religious borders and boundaries in order to transfer these experiences for communities where organized crime works as a driving force for spatial segregation and exclusion. This chapter focuses on the contradictions between the loss of the role of public places in encouraging sociability in everyday life and the rediscovery of these places, as well as the way cultural differences and social inequality are addressed in public spaces and places. The interpretation of latent multicultural social needs is aimed—with the involvement of people from different parts of society—to define community planning strategies in order to improve processes for producing inclusive public spaces.

In Chapter 15, which concludes the book, the editors bring the main themes of the chapters from the three parts together and revisit the challenges that face European cities and the possible role of public places in meeting those challenges.

# Chapter 10

# Urban Transformation, Social Transition

## Barbès, Paris, Where 'Otherness' Takes (Public) Place

*Maria Anita Palumbo*

Moving from ethnographical field results to anthropological analysis of contemporary urban transformations, this chapter aims to investigate how public spaces participate in political, economic, and cultural transformations as objects, instruments, and mirrors of social changes in a historical working class and migrant neighbourhood of Paris.

If many scholars have addressed the need for an 'open' public space in the contemporary metropolis, showing the articulation between spatial and social transformations (de Biase & Coralli, 2009; Jacobs, 1961; Madanipour, 1996; Sennett, 2006b), the tendency we observe in urban public policies is the opposite: the production of a homogeneous and increasingly standardised and controlled public space. This process does not take place without fractures, without selection between forms of being in public and inhabiting public space that are valorised, and others that are on the way to being erased or excluded. In the context of urban transformation of European cities, what position do we intend to reserve for neighbourhoods, zones, and streets where a different urbanity is manifesting itself within the public space? This chapter intends to develop an answer to this question by observing Barbès-La Goutte d'Or, a Parisian multicultural neighbourhood that has worked as a worldwide crossroads since the end of the 19th century, and which has a very dynamic public life. The past, present, and future of this area constitute an excellent case study of the relations between urban transformation, diversity within cities, and public space. But first let's have a closer look at this place.

## Barbès Patchwork

'It is not like when you arrive at La Motte-Picquet, or anywhere else in Paris. When you arrive at Barbès, you can feel that things are happening here, that things are going on, that people have stories to tell, it's alive, it's rich!' (Julien, student frequenting the neighbourhood). This is one thing people could agree on: Barbès is definitely, for better or worse, an *exceptional* place. Public religious celebrations take place regularly following different calendars, and different selling habits are juxtaposed on market days: Exotic fruits are sold in boutique stands, while fake Christian Dior glasses and Louis Vuitton bags are sold by street sellers holding their merchandise or exposing it on the roofs of parked cars. From the way of dressing, to the odours coming out of restaurants, and the rhythms of music played in shops, on the streets of Barbès there is a high mutual visibility of people belonging to different cultural worlds that together contribute to a different atmosphere.

One of its characteristics is its *density*: 'I remember the first time I arrived in the neighbourhood: I got off at Chateau-Rouge; there were people everywhere, it was crazy, everybody standing and talking around the metro exit. In that moment I asked to myself "where am I?"' (Gérôme, architect, living in the neighbourhood for the past 20 years). The density you perceive on arriving at the metro stations of Barbès or Chateau Rouge, the two 'entrances' to the area, is highly disorienting especially when combined with the *diversity* people get in contact with: 'Here the population is very different from the rest of Paris: lots of Arabs, lots of Black people. It is true that the first time I came to visit the apartment [where he lives now] I was astonished and preoccupied passing by the northern part of the neighbourhood. It is true that you feel in another universe. But all these peoples don't bother me, this folkloric touch doesn't bother me at all!' (David, dance teacher, recently moved in). This universe is definitely 'strange' for new inhabitants like David, a young white man that suddenly experienced what it feels like to be part of a visually perceived minority.

For others like Malik, for example, a student from Senegal now attending La Sorbonne University, Barbès is, by contrast, the place to be in order to feel 'at home': 'When I used to come to the neighbourhood before moving here, it was because of an atmosphere that reminded me of the neighbourhood life in Senegal. There is something there that you will never find here [in Paris]: in the evening people get out of their houses, they sit in front of their doors, they talk, they drink some tea. Life is not like here [in France]. [In Barbès] you cross somebody on the street, you speak with him, you ask him some questions, you say hello, you laugh together, and then he goes off. And it's not only the Senegalese that do that, they are just people from here. Sometimes they are French or of other nationalities, not only Africans. So I had to ask myself: is it because the people that come to this neighbourhood decide to do the contrary [of what they normally do], they get rid of what they really are to join the atmosphere of this neighbourhood during their stay here, afterwards to go back to another atmosphere?' For Malik, if this area plays the role of a surrogate home, its definition is stretched beyond the description of an African environment because he doesn't build it on an ethnic definition when he recognizes that everybody is participating in, and therefore somehow producing, this 'way of life'.

In fact, Malik is talking about an *urbanity* (a public sociability) in which he feels comfortable but which he doesn't describe as being exclusive to African users. This would suggest that it is not the fact of being an African neighbourhood that evokes in him a sense of belonging, but rather the particular openness of the neighbourhood's public space to 'incoming cultures'. The complexity of the neighbourhood, with respect to the dynamics of identification, is confirmed when other African interviewees state that for them, by contrast, this place doesn't work at all as a surrogate home: 'Barbès??? It's dirty! I would never go to live there. Too many people, it is dirty!' said a woman from Congo, Zaire, who I met in Belgium, and who regularly goes 'down to Chateau Rouge' from her home in Charleroi to buy African provisions. The exceptional dirtiness and density of the area are here pointed out as characteristics that prevent her identification with the place that she nonetheless uses as a consumer. If the role of Barbès as an 'African commercial centrality' in Europe is a matter of fact, although not valorised by institutions, its identification as an African neighbourhood is rather problematic.

Other characteristics of the public space of the neighbourhood are central to the experience of other inhabitants: 'The first time I was here I found myself pointing out that I was the only woman on the street and the only white one. Sometimes it is strange especially if you came from the province, because you are not used to that. The crowd, the very diverse neighbourhood' (Corinne, resident in Barbès since 2001). It looks like this area works as a space revealing people's identities. Suddenly they discover that we are white, female or male, that we are African, French, or both, and a very subtle game of self and external identity attribution or identification starts on the streets of Barbès. This 'identifying' and 'othering' process takes place also at the level of social class: 'At the beginning, it was hard for me to do my shopping at Franprix, I would hesitate to buy this or that product 'cause I would run into the guys that had in their basket 3 litres of milk, one baguette and some sugar, every night, every night the same thing' (Valerie has worked and lived in the neighbourhood since 1992). What Valerie and other inhabitants experience every day is the 'otherness' in terms of social class, which reveals her own sense of belonging to a different economic class.

Informal street selling, very common in the neighbourhood, is another visible sign of *precarious-ness*. In fact, this daily use of public space to buy and sell is one of the most peculiar aspects of Barbès. The informal market, which occupies a few streets of the neighbourhood and attracts thousands of people, especially during the weekend, contributes significantly to the characterisation of the area, provoking the sympathy of some and a negative reaction from others. 'You cannot even imagine how organised they are, and how much money they do per day. They go weekly to Dubai buying stuff and they sell it here . . . there is not such a place in Paris, this is why it is so famous. Is a very complex network, and we still think they are poor' (Philip, Ph.D. student living in the neighbourhood).

'What is not allowable and what is most disturbing in the neighbourhood is the dereliction and I really do not agree with that. We cannot allow the informal market; ok, it is contributing to the folkloric atmosphere, ok, we can say that they don't have anything else to live on but you cannot allow that. Because if you have '*liberté, fraternité, égalité*', a law is a law! I think this is bothering more than everything here' (Gérôme, architect, living in the area for 20 years). In this conversation with Gérôme, Barbès emerges as a 'place out of order', where the law doesn't seem to be effective, an exception on French territory for not respecting the principles of the French republican spirit. This impression of a place beyond the law is confirmed by other practices visible in the public space, like drug addicts and prostitution centred on the Boulevard Barbès.

Yet the neighbourhood is not an *immobile setting*. On the contrary, for at least 40 years it has been a permanent work in progress. 'The neighbourhood has changed and the way I look at it as well. Since I live here now I have my habits, I feel at home here. At the beginning I didn't feel at home, it was not my environment, I was not used to that' (Corinne). It is interesting to track the evolution of the area through the biography of the inhabitants who can measure a change in their own feelings or who can talk about their lives through the life of the neighbourhood. 'I don't know, all I knew no longer exists, there is not that much left, everything has changed, the neighbourhood I knew is gone. And it is still changing, but what do you want, we must do something against insalubrity' (Baptiste, employed by the health service centre, has worked and lived in Barbès since 1975).

This evolution provokes *ambiguous feelings* between structural problem solving and social change, and it can increase or decrease a feeling of being at home. 'The area is evolving well, for instance the area around the Saint Bernard Church where they renovated the square, is amazing! I think it's going to evolve in a certain way that we are going to like more, more conformed to our way of life and that the neighbourhood will look in 10/15 years more like what we imagine, like what we are used to, maybe with more shops like in the 20th District that was once like this. But at the same time you also ask yourself how is it going to be for these people because it's their area at the moment and in relation with Parisian life, how Paris is gonna evolve you ask yourself, and afterwards will I still pay only 400€ rent? Is it gonna be like this for us as well? (David). While recognizing that the *future face of the neighbourhood* is for David more known than the present one, he also doubts that he will be able to live there in terms of economic costs. That is to say, a higher identification with the neighbourhood does not automatically go hand in hand with a projection of the self in its future. On the contrary, some people can feel that the place is changing its identity and anticipate that they might not feel at home anymore: 'Slowly they are renovating. . . . People feel very well that the neighbourhood is changing, that it is increasingly less of a working class neighbourhood and that what we knew before is gone' (Alain, working as a butcher in Barbès).

By contrast with the other neighbourhood typologies very common in our contemporary urban world, and characterised by a high 'protection' from the external world or by a blinding homogeneity, in Barbès we are constantly rubbing up against the world. We could almost say that the 'The Weight of the World' (Handke, 1977) is stronger here. Barbès's public space puts in crisis a 'common' experience of the city, common in the sense of 'shared' and in the sense of 'usual'. Barbès is a space of intersection of very different individual and collective stories, networks and perspectives, and its public space is the scene where all these mix, adjust, and cohabit. In urban public spaces of equal complexity, we can ask from what this diversity results and what it produces. Which roles of 'living together' allow cohabitation within these spaces and what 'idea' of public space emerges from this co-presence game? What is the future of such a controversial place within the urban transformation process and how do public authorities address its ongoing transformation?

Arguing that public space is produced by different practices situated at different levels and scenes of society, I have been conducting ethnographic fieldwork in the area from 2006 to 2011, combining participatory observation and recorded interviews questioning the nature of this public space, where proximity and diversity adjust and constant negotiations take place between the heritage of the past, the problems of the present, and the projects of the future. In the following pages I will articulate the genesis, the everyday life, and the transformations of Barbès in order to explore the tension between a marginal space and its global users, a 'problematic' public space and its social efficiency.

## Genesis of a Borderline Public Space

Similarly to its famous neighbour, Montmartre, Barbès-La Goutte d'Or was initially developed as an agricultural area then situated outside Paris. From 1837, the area was quickly urbanised by private promoters, all the streets were traced, and modest buildings and 'hotel meublé' (furnished rooms hotels) were built to welcome migrant families or single male workers who had come from the French provinces to compensate for the shortage of manpower during the construction of the Nord Railway. At the same time, it worked as a shooting spot for the population that Haussmann's renovation of Paris excluded from the city centre. The miserable conditions and alcoholism in this working-class district have been portrayed by the French writer Emile Zola in his master piece *L'Assomoire* (published in 1877). This area was finally integrated into the core of Paris at the end of the 19th century, when the frontier of the capital was displaced a few kilometres further out under Haussmann's urban plan of 1860. This first Parisian urban plan, following military and hygienic principles, completely reshaped the French capital. It gave Barbès its actual borders by constructing the most important Parisian train line in the east and two big boulevards in the south and west. Somehow Barbès resulted from what was 'left over' from Haussmann's intervention. With the decline of the colonial empire around 1950, this portion of the city asserted itself as a reception place for migrants. Inhabitants came from colonial or ex-colonial regions. Later on, significant migrant waves arrived from North Africa. Other arrivals from West Africa, Yugoslavia, and Asia contributed to the neighbourhood's melting pot ambience. By then, Barbès had already been working for a century as an 'Immigrants Centrality' (Toubon & Messamah, 1990) and became progressively an open-air trading spot, an icon for popular trade (Lallemant, 2010). More precisely, the subsection Château Rouge started to work as an 'African centrality' (Bouly de Lesdain, 1999), well known in a national and international scale.

Parallel to this migrant and commercial history, a public urban policy (named *la politique de la ville*) started to 'work on' this area in the 1980s to provide basic infrastructures and socioeconomic development. This moment marked the starting point of an official process of urban change defined by sociologist Donzelot as a process of 'urban inclusion' (Donzelot & Estebe, 1994; Donzelot et al., 2003) that was to last throughout the 1990s. This process was vigorously followed up by the strong local associations network, which often reacted against radical projects proposed by the Municipality of Paris, reorienting the kind of interventions proposed within the neighbourhood towards more basic infrastructures and socioeconomic development interventions. Meanwhile, despite the endurance of a dominant image of Barbès as an insecure zone (Palumbo, 2009a;

Toubon & Messamah, 1990) in the last 10 years, a new population of inhabitants has shown that Barbès, with other former working-class and immigrant areas of Paris, is going through a process of gentrification. However, this is proceeding very slowly and the outcome seems to be uncertain in this specific neighbourhood (Bacqué & Fijalkow, 2006). The economic crisis of 2008 reinforced the uses of public space as a place for the informal economy, where the visibility of generalised precariousness seems to slow down the efforts of normalisation carried on by the public authorities. Although the lack of ethnic statistics in France has always made it difficult to precisely picture the type of population actually living in the area, constant changes of population and the consequent visibility of diversity became an element of continuity in the social history of this area. The presence of people from diverse cultural and social horizons determines a stratification and sedimentation of its urban and social landscape that makes it an exceptional multicultural and multisocial area. In 2010, the French state, municipalities, and social landlords confirmed their partnership in the project called *Contrat Urbain de Cohésion Sociale* (Urban Contract of Social Cohesion). Barbès, with 10 other neighbourhoods, is again a priority territory for political and economic interventions aiming to rebalance inequalities in urban areas.

## Barbès Every Day, Figures of Inhabitants and Production of Public Space

Who lives and how, daily, in Barbès's public space? How is it to inhabit and be inhabited everyday by this complex public space? Observing and interviewing dwellers and also workers and habitués of Barbès' public space, I have pointed out four 'figures of inhabitants' (Palumbo, 2009b)—four different ways of perceiving, practicing, and therefore producing public space, corresponding to different ways of being in public and of feeling at home in public space (Figure 10.1 and 10.2).

*Figure 10.1* Marché Rue Dejean, one of the densest streets of the Barbès neighbourhood, Paris.

*Figure 10.2* A group of people gather to observe an intervention of firemen, rue Richomme, Paris.

## Barbès as a Surrogate Public Space

> The first time I arrived in the neighbourhood, it was like breathing fresh air. I came here because a friend wanted to meet up with me here. Ever since I come here every day. There is a strong Senegalese community here, but also some Guineans, Malians, Ivoirians, Algerians. Since I belong to two different cultures, Senegalese originally from Guinea, I have a lot of family here! (Tibo)

This area constitutes for some users a place of return to cultural roots, of mental replenishment. Whether as an everyday meeting place or a spot for rituals during particular celebrations, the public space of this neighbourhood offers the space for different ways of gathering, consuming, selling, and buying, following the rhythm and codes of interaction that allow a connection with a cultural universe situated elsewhere (Amselle, 2001). This specific way of practising the urban space as a place of cultural resource produces in a way a surrogate African public space. Especially during the weekends, the Goutte d'or and Château Rouge transform into open air commercial and cultural spaces. They are very popular spots for socialisation, for people find here not only material goods, but also a way of being together, a way to belong: circulation of pedestrians is dense, shops are full, benches on the boulevard Barbès welcome the tired bodies of passers-by, their hands full of shopping bags. On this occasion, frequented mainly by African or French clients of African origin, the neighbourhood gets overwhelmed by an ambience that remains latent during the week. What is pushing people to frequent this place is a relational modality, suddenly shared by a majority of people and becoming dominant in public space.

### The Place of 'Others' or the Art of 'Make Do With'

> At the beginning you ask yourself some questions: is it dangerous? And going back home in the night? It's anyway a neighbourhood with a special energy. Some drug addicts, people selling cigarettes, there are a lot of them on the Boulevard Barbès and around the metro station. I got used to do my stuff without feeling in danger cause I know that they won't come and attack me or ask for my money. There is not that kind of energy. At the beginning you feel unsecure and then I got used to the fact that they are there, they do their business you like it or not, you do your life with that! But at the beginning you ask yourself if they are going to be aggressive with the white guy that is there. (Daniel)

For some inhabitants, the practice of the space is defined by a localisation of others' culture embodied by others' way of being in public space in Barbès. Space is therefore qualified and shared in different ethnic or gendered atmospheres and this geography of diversity is a way to justify choices in public space use and habits. This description and distribution of *ethnic atmospheres* reveals an understanding of public space as a place of coexistence of different degrees of otherness, unequally accepted and connected to different self-definitions, also unequally admitted. This way of perceiving and acting in public space is constructed around the principle of reacting to the proximity of others with the rules of distance. This 'make do with' attitude seems to be constructed around a focused avoidance to ensure the necessary disengagement in order to 'pass through' without getting involved. The register of weak ties gains on socialisation and at the same time neighbourhood relations in their most basic form of salutations and mutual recognition are presented as 'normalizer' elements of the relations with the neighbourhood, giving the right to be there, limited to the right of 'passing by'. Future transformations are expected and lived as a chance of higher identification with the public life of Barbès.

### Territory of Serendipity

> I could not live in the 16th district for example. It is completely dead over there! Before, I was living in Porte de la Chapelle. I have being renting a flat there for 6 years but after a while it deteriorated. Before it was good, there was some prostitution on the sidewalk, there was some life; since Sarko is in charge, this part of the 18th district became squalid! Prostitutes went somewhere else, and I thought it was good to dialogue with that population, this women that were there, I found it was good to say good morning. The building I was living in got deteriorated as well. I mean that they put everything on security. The building lost its soul! So this is why I bought a flat here.

> Chateau Rouge sounds dangerous for some people but to me not at all. I love when I get off the
> metro, always things moving, always things happening around. (Mathias)

The public space of Barbès can also be lived as a territory of different 'spectacles' available
for a form of consumption of and in the public space. The valorisation of a cosmopolitan neighbourhood goes with an attitude of discovery that recalls the figure of the *flaneur* of the big city.
The neighbourhood is then perceived and produced as a place of exception at different levels.
In contrast to the securitarian dispositions that appear to define public space in Paris, Barbès
became the place of possibilities, real or imagined, for a different social life, a place that can still
surprise. Frequenting of neighbourhood life goes with a particular disposition and availability to
encounter other inhabitants and users of the public space who embody any kind of diversity. As
has been observed by other scholars, this attitude to using public space is the fruit of a rejection
of uniformity and an attempt to escape proximity with those of a similar social status, but who
carry a very different social conception (Simon, 1998) (Figure 10.3).

### Place of Engagement

> It is not aggressive what I do. Also on Richomme street, the urinal of the neighbourhood, even
> to the crack smokers, taking the risk of getting punched, I tell them 'pissing there is forbidden!'
> (Gérôme)

For some individuals, the experience of public life in Barbès is of a place of growing conscious-
ness of inequalities and social diversity among the neighbourhood inhabitants. The constant
'rubbing along in public spaces' (Watson, 2006) can manifest itself as a transfer of behaviour

*Figure 10.3* Self-made poster on the entrance of a building in rue de Panama, Paris, reclaiming silence and
remembering interdiction of pissing in public space.

particular to the private and public sphere. Having an active role in local schools and participation in political party life and in local democratic decision processes are different paths taken to 'find a place' in the neighbourhood by choosing different 'contexts of mobilization' (Bacqué & Fijalkow, 2006). Public space is not perceived as place of return to one's roots, of consumption, of avoidance, but of confrontation and debate. Political or associative engagement is a way to react to the paradox that arises from spatial proximity and social distance. They become actors of an active citizenship as a way to construct a common world. It's a form of militancy on a daily scale by talking in public and reacting to others' behaviour—a strong interaction with and in public. They react to a social world that they perceive as imperfect and problematic but also lived as a resource, a positive exception to be preserved, provided that it maintains this aspect of openness to change (Figure 10.4).

## 'Otherness' as an Urban Condition . . . Changes as a Horizon

The experience of Barbès's public space is without discussion the access to a multitude of different people where everybody experiments with the density and diversity of urban population and gets involved in proximity with foreigners/strangers and practices.

The parallel analysis of these different ways of perceiving and producing public space in Barbès shows how in this neighbourhood not only do diverse persons live together, but they also carry, produce, and defend different perspectives with regard to a normative use of common space. Each practice and discourse seems to affirm the prevalence of one particular quality of public space: a transitory space, a place of freedom, a space for temporary appropriation, or a scene of political discussion. These qualities refer to different modalities of relational engagement

*Figure 10.4* A recently constructed building with a new florist shop in the ground floor, rue Doudeauville, Paris.

*Figure 10.4* (Continued)

taking place in public space. Barbès is a territory of production of interactional rituals guided and justified by different interpretations of public space as space of co-presence, accessibility, replenishment, and cooperation. Moreover, the daily experience of Barbès produces an idea of what public space should be. What creates the complexity of Barbès is not only the presence of different 'others', but also the sense that each person gives to shared places and common spaces. The complexity of public space we observe in Barbès does not result from the fact of socially and culturally different people inhabiting the same space, but from the coexistence and interaction of different forms of relations to diversity and the acknowledgment that all these forms actually compose a common world. This is why Barbès's public space provokes a deep experience of the self and forces a renewal of the perception of being a stranger or feeling at home. Moreover, the ongoing transformation of Barbès and its public space intervenes as a horizon of inhabitability. Constant urban and social transformations seem to play a role in 'feeling or not feeling at home' in this plural environment (Figure 10.5). In the future Barbès, will I feel more or less at home? Will I be able to stay, or will I be forced to go? And in case I can stay, is my own idea and practice of public space the right one?

## Future Barbès, Reducing 'Otherness'

After observing how public space is experienced, understood, and produced by individuals in everyday life, I will now address the question of how the public space of Barbès is 'under debate'. I selected three field examples that illustrate, at different social and political levels, the ongoing attempts to transform the area. In the following examples, public space is not addressed directly as the object of a particular policy. What is at stake is the actual transformation of the urban context that contains the public space and participates in creating such a specific public life.

*Figure 10.5* An exemple of the very common beauty shops in Barbès, Paris.

### *Commercial Landscape, or 'Where Do I Buy My Baguette?'*

According to the data of the Municipality of Paris, of the 490 shops existing in Barbès, 395 sell African goods. This 'homogeneity', normally referred to as 'monoactivity', is now under discussion. Communication papers of the municipality, as much as the local newspaper, express the necessity of reinserting a certain *mixité* into the commercial life in Barbès, and in local neighbourhood assemblies the debates frequently raise the issue of the lack of 'proximity shops' (*commerce de proximité*). In the context of this commercial urbanism programme, the municipality publicly defends the strategy to refuse planning permission to 'ethnic' or 'exotic' sellers. The mayor of the district himself argued in a monthly public administration meeting of the 18th municipality during a discourse about the new commercial plan for the area: 'The situation is complex but it is true that I personally don't know myself where to buy my baguette'. Visible changes in the neighbourhood are the empty ground floor spaces waiting to be attributed to new commercial offers and a few new small supermarkets. For the past year we can, at least in my *boulanger*, buy a French baguette branded as 'French tradition, nobility of territory'.

### Inside/Outside: A Market of the Five Continents

The local municipality of the 18th district, together with the Municipality of Paris, has been working for more than five years on a project to create a market of the five continents, concentrating exotic trade in one place in order to free Barbès from the traffic created by all the small sellers displaced within the neighbourhood. It is not by chance that the place chosen to host this new commercial project is an ex-industrial area outside the actual Parisian border, in the northern suburban area. The project has slowly gained critics among inhabitants, shop owners, and local associations.

On the one hand, the project is accused of being a strategy to accelerate the gentrification process; on the other, it is considered as a necessary step to solve traffic problems in the area.

### Pork, Wine, and Prayer

On June 18th last year a 'Frenchy aperitif' was organised via Facebook by a presumed female young inhabitant of Barbès, Sylvie Françoise, to protest against the 'Islamisation' of public space. The meeting was arranged on a Friday during the Muslim prayer, on the street usually used by the exuberant numbers of attendants who normally pray on carpets placed on the street during the 15-minute service. Pork sausages and wine (forbidden food for Muslims) were the instruments used by the organisers; these were brought into the public space in order to celebrate 'good French traditions'. Of course only a few hours passed before a counter-aperitif was organised by others, calling participants to bring mint tea and sweet honey cakes. The police, alerted by the escalation of media attention and public debate on the question, forbade any demonstration that day on the public space of Barbès, which did not prevent the mysterious woman and her 7,000 adherents from changing the location of their rendezvous online, redirecting people to the Champs Elysée, a place where the initiative of consuming sausages and wine seemed to take on a completely different meaning. Despite the cancellation of the event, the media kept discussing this news over the following weeks. The Facebook profile of Sylvie Françoise disappeared two days later.

## Urban Planning and the Place of Otherness

Without discussing the different value and scale of these three examples, all of them show, in different ways, how this diverse and heterogenic urban area is involved in contemporary identity debates in France, which is a direct transposition in the tension between territory and identity (de Biase and Rossi, 2006). These debates focus especially on the visibility of diversity, from the commercial sector to the religious one, and are calling for political and urban intervention. It is interesting to see that in all these cases the material world, from space to food, seems to be a euphemistic way to talk about society, culture, and otherness. Beyond the different configuration of actors and different levels of discussion and action involved, the aim is to 'domesticate' the public life of the neighbourhood by transforming its landscape, displacing the object of urban change from what is necessary for living in good conditions to an almost aesthetic and identitarian design. Beyond narrative differences, the debate is driven by two opposite poles. From inhabitants to local community organisations, from the voluntary sector to policymaking institutions and local political figures, the wish for 'normality' and the desire to retain the specificity of this neighbourhood are both narratives that orient action, participation, and local media production. In the debate concerning this specific territory of Paris and its 'normal' or 'not normal' public life, which idea of society emerges? Urban public space as the most accessible and visible part of social life seems to be the object of debate between the rules of hospitality and the needs for identity reconfiguration, between cosmopolitanism and national identity. It must not be forgotten that this implied debate is taking place while an equally implicit discussion about French national identity swings between an idealistic affirmation of a republican society and a realistic description of a multicultural one. Migrants and their historical implantation in a specific area seem to be the object and the space where this debate takes a specific place.

Which identity will Paris chose to conserve? And which public space is to be constructed in order to design the next face of Barbès? The tendency drawn from the example presented above and the public debate accompanying it, describe a public space that is becoming the scene of urban conflicts between the 'rules' of dwellers and the habits of 'users', between a normal neighbourhood life and an 'unplanned' urban centrality. Despite their specific aims, urban policies nowadays tend to privilege dwellers and their needs as the legitimate actors of public space against the traders and their clients, producing a form of diffuse residentialisation of the area and raising questions such as: For whom is the space of a neighbourhood public? Are the dwellers of an area the only legitimate 'users' of its public space? Awaiting a decision, Barbès, from its public space to its commercial space and usage, is standing still as an 'interferential ambience' (Sansot, 2009) within the Parisian landscape. Urban transformations of this area aim to find an unbalanced equilibrium between an exotic territory and a Parisian place. Meanwhile, Barbès, as the place where 'otherness' uses public space to escape 'local' rules, is likely to be the most 'global' place in Paris rather than the most 'peripheral' one.

## Conclusions

### Rethinking Public Space: The Importance of Distances and the Lessons of 'Otherness'

I would like to conclude this chapter with a remark: For a few years we have been facing a slow and silent process of smoothing and polishing of public space in European cities, which takes place via public policies and juridical laws (by defining what is allowed or not in public space, for example) and also via urban planning choices. In fact, both these disciplines are part of the process of constructing and organising spaces in our society from a social and spatial point of view.

The tendency is to homogenise and standardise legitimate uses and users, reducing spaces for uncertainty. This hyperorganisation of places involves a reduction of fortuitousness/casualness and an increase of a certain 'entry selection'. Places where we run the 'risk' of finding ourselves next to an unknown person (socially and culturally) who is radically different from us are decreasing. We could summarise this by saying that there is a progressive reduction of the social distance that lies between people who find themselves in the same place; the reduction of this distance means that we live, without noticing, within worlds that are smaller and smaller, where the impression that the world we live in 'is a small world', is nothing but the result and the measure of the effectiveness of contemporary segregational forces. In fact, it is not that the world is small, it is that we have developed more and more techniques to direct ourselves into affinity networks that make us evolve in a very homogeneous environment, less and less able to interact with the great diversity that is waiting for us outside our network, and more and more able to develop sophisticated techniques of avoidance. At the opposite side of this protective tendency of contemporary urban worlds, Barbès stands as an exception. In this neighbourhood, people keep rubbing against and taking on 'others' and the 'world' daily, and therefore continually question the self. A. Germain (1997) wrote in her analysis of multicultural Montreal, 'the more ethno cultural diversity is the object of everyday experience, the less it is source of inhibition and malaise'. Accordingly, we should recognize and defend the 'socialisation function of public space' such as in Barbès, a formative space that involves a displacement, an identity reconsideration, and adjustment for inhabitants as well as for visitors. Within this *place of otherness*, there is a distance between people, and this distance might be the basis of a 'political' public space in its primordial sense. As H. Arendt says: 'The political arises in the space that is between humans, therefore in something fundamentally outside exterior-to-humans. That is to say that the political does not exist as a real substance. The political arises in the intermediate space and it is constituted as a relationship' (1995). Politics result from what is separating people (in what people are parted from) and therefore requires from people a relational effort 'in order to treat the problem of space between them' (Lussault, 2007). This would confirm the efficiency of distance in social relations as against the over-valorisation of proximity and intermixing, as we have shown here. This tendency to polish public space seems dangerous, for it erases the possibility of a distance, limiting occasions for experimenting otherness within the space and between people. And yet, it is indeed this otherness that plays a heuristic role, in terms of knowledge and politics, for it is involved in the construction of commonness. According to what Isabelle Stengers (2005) defined as 'cosmopolitical proposal', public space in global cities must be reconsidered not through a normative definition, closely connected with a western conception of civic space, but through a descriptive approach ready to recognize what a common space is, and the fact that the existence of 'others' is not making our life complex, but is pushing us to understand the 'complexity of life'.

In his text 'Of Other Spaces: Heterotopias', Foucault talks about a desire for 'a science that would, in a given society, take as its object the study, analysis, description, and "reading" (as some like to say nowadays) of these different spaces, of these other places. As a sort of simultaneously mythic and real contestation of the space in which we live, this description could be called heterotopology'. He adds, 'But among all these sites, I am interested in certain ones that have the curious property of being in relation with all the other sites, but in such a way as to suspect, neutralize, or invert the set of relations that they happen to designate, mirror, or reflect' (1967, p. 25). Piero Zanini, an Italian geographer, in his book about 'border areas', extended the quoted passage of Foucault and defined heterotopias as 'places of objectivity' (1997). Taking the example of frontier places, he argues that these are places where a certain objectivity can emerge (taking the shape of relativism, cosmopolitism, pluralism, citizenship) bringing out a larger idea of community beyond differences and belonging, or radicalised identities under the forms of localism and communitarianism. Heterotopy either relativises or radicalises identities. I would rather define these kinds of public space as *places of objectification* that allow a detour revealing the 'self' and the structure in which we evolve. Public spaces of such a kind are places where the 'identity-otherness' game is played at all scales (from individual to politics and media) unlike that which we observe in our new global urban context of 'affinity urbanism' (Donzelot, 1999). In Paris, Barbès is the exception that proves the rule, a laboratory for the empiricism of the norm. The uncanny public space, considered as a heterotopias, works as a 'carnival' space (Agier, 2000), an inversed mirror of the city (i.e., system), constituting a counterexample in terms of the potential and spontaneous use of public areas.

Somehow, like the classical sociological figure of the stranger, with his outsider perspective and his different way of being, as Simmel (1990) pointed out more than 100 years ago, public space in migrant centralities reminds us of the constructed and therefore arbitrary essence of our world and its conventions.

# Chapter 11

# Public, Private, and Other Spaces in Multicultural Hackney, London

## Spatial Aspects of Local Ethnic-Religious Relations

*Penny (Panagiota) Koutrolikou*

## Approaches to Governing Diversity in the Beginning of the 21st Century

In the 1990s, prominent scholars, such as Alain Touraine and Stuart Hall, commented on the significance that 'living together' would have in the 21st century (Hall, 1993; Touraine, 2000). While in the 1990s diversity gained recognition and became something to be 'celebrated', the 2000s started to be concerned—albeit not for the first time—with the relation of diversity and social cohesion (CIC, 2007; Demireva, 2011; Hooghe, Reeskens, & Stolle, 2007; Hudson, Phillips, Ray, & Barnes, 2007). By the end of the 21st century's first decade, it had become clear that diversity has become a 'hot' point of discussion, with Council of Europe (CoE, 2011) phrasing these concerns in its report by the 'Group of Eminent Persons': 'Living together: Combining diversity and freedom in 21st century Europe'. Thus, whilst diversity has been associated with multicultural richness and has ensured a level of recognition and rights for different groups, it has also been perceived as a possible threat to societal cohesion due to 'irreconcilable' differences.

Debates about the 'best' model of governing diversity are not new, and they were often shaped by concerns about national identities, (in)equalities and recognition, conflicts and social cohesion, while also reflecting national preferences and histories. In Europe, such debates involved mainly national variations of multiculturalism and assimilation and their respective perceived pros and cons. More recently, interculturalism was promoted as an alternative approach that would ameliorate the problems of the above-mentioned models whilst retaining some of their respective benefits.

While up until the 2000s diversity and different ethno-religious groups were generally viewed as beneficial for local societies (or were at least tolerated) in the 2000s the general approach towards diversity started to change. In conjunction to violent events both internationally and locally, diversity started to be associated with revamped fears of Others, fears regarding security and the collapse of social order; fears that in many occasions became part of the mainstream (Putnam, 2007). As a result, ethnocultural diversity came to be perceived also as a potential threat to social cohesion (or even national unity) (Kalra and Kapoor, 2008). Particularly in countries that have followed a model of governing diversity closer to that of multiculturalism, the dominant public discourse became concerned with the assumed fragmentation of the society due to significance given to distinct ethno-religious groups. In the British context, this resulted in a concern about cohesion (community cohesion in particular), which was mainstreamed as a target to be achieved in a range of policies. More broadly, it contributed to the growing 'backlash against multiculuralism' (Grillo, 2005; Meer & Modood, 2011; Rath, 2011; Vertovec & Wessendorf, 2010) leading to more recent statements about the failure of integration and the death of multiculturalism (as for example from British Prime Minister D. Cameron, at his speech at the Munich Security conference in 2011, and the German Chancellor A. Merkel, at a meeting of young members of the CDU in 2010) or to renewed concerns about a coherent and strong national identity. Although theories of multiculturalism involve diverse perspectives about what multiculturalism is and how it is supposed to be implemented, strong critiques were voiced concerning this backlash against multiculturalism, concerning the prominent role that community and/or social cohesion ended up having in policy and discourse, as well as concerning the actual or perceived fragmentation that was caused by previously adopted policies (Rath, 2011; Vertovec & Wessendorf, 2010.

Whilst multiculturalism came under fire, another model gained popularity: interculturalism. Although interculturalism is associated mostly with localised or sectoral policies and initiatives (such as education or dialogue-based initiatives), intercultural approaches came to be presented as a prominent model in managing—particularly urban—diversity. Interculturalism, in this context, was presented as a bridge; as a combination of successful features of other models (such as of multiculturalism or assimilation) without their perceived problems and with a strong emphasis on social cohesion (and national identity) and citizenship (Emerson, 2011; Wood, 2009). Communication and intercultural dialogue are advocated as the main elements of intercultural policies and initiatives, while as stated, interculturalism is (or would like to be) closer to a two way process of mutual integration. An array of local projects and policies (CLIP Network, 2010; Herve, 2010; Wood, 2009) as well as large scale projects and recommendations (such as CoE/EU Intercultural cities project and Eurocities Intercultural cities project) are characteristic of the relatively recent popularity of interculturalism as an approach, although their success remains to be seen and there are already significant questions and critiques about them (Meer and Modood, 2011).

Nevertheless, the main concern of this chapter is not to contribute to the debate among multiculturalism, assimilation, and interculturalism, but rather to examine the spatial dimensions of governing diversity and in particular those relating to public spaces. All these models of governing urban diversity are reflected—to a bigger or lesser extent—on local policies that affect a broad range of sectors, as well as everyday life. In his research about local policies concerning migrants and/or minorities, Alexander (2003) distinguishes local policies in five models: non-policy, transient or guestworker, assimilationist, pluralist, and interculturalist. From his analysis on different European cities, it becomes evident that the chosen national or regional model of governing diversity is directly reflected on local policies, with some divergences according to the local context. Among others, space and space-related issues acquire particular significance in the analysed policies. For example, access to social housing differs in different models; while the 'symbolic use of space' is opposed in the assimilationist model, it is accepted as a recognition of Others in the multicultural model, while the intercultural model promotes the functional rather than the symbolic use of space (Alexander, 2003).

There is a wealth of research and literature on how different sectoral policies have been developed in a given context and how they relate to immigrant or minority populations. However, policies (national or local) might be able to influence (to lesser or greater extent) places, services, and institutions, but they represent some of the parameters to be considered in regards to the complexities of local relations among diverse groups. Everyday life, cultural or historical trajectories, local injustices, and intergroup competition (especially when resources are scarce) or cooperation are also significant factors for local relations; local relations that do not exist in abstract spaces but in places.

## Spatial Dimensions of Urban Diversity and Its Governance

Space becomes a more and more significant terrain for assessing the impact of policies concerned with governing diversity. In most spatial manifestations of the models of governing diversity there are some pivotal issues that always come up in the debates: (a) ethno-religious segregation, which also involves issues of housing; (b) urban regeneration or renewal programmes that target particular neighbourhoods and often involve elements of social and/or community development; and (c) public spaces and, more recently, intercultural and/or neighbourhood spaces.

Ethno-religious segregation has been primarily considered as a problem through the establishment of separate or 'parallel worlds' that may threaten society's cohesion. There have been numerous studies and reports regarding urban segregation, the particular reasons that contribute to increasing segregation in given contexts, comparisons among cities, as well as evaluations of the impact of ethno-religious segregation on people and places (Arbaci, 2007; Gans, 2008; Ireland, 2008; Marcuse, 2005; Massey & Denton, 1993; Musterd, 2003; Peach, 1996, 2007; Schönwälder, 2007). Those supporting the problematic perception of urban ethno-religious segregation argue that increased segregation facilitates the establishment of monocultural deprived areas (or even ghettos) reduces opportunities for intergroup contact and social mobility, limits the possibilities of integration (or even of assimilation) to the host society, and as such, it poses a threat to the cohesive social fabric. Characteristic of the 'attention' that segregation has recently gained in public discourse are the German Chancellor's (Siebolt, 2010) statements regarding the failure of integration and the existence of 'parallel societies' in German cities. Of course, she has not been the only one; particular attention regarding the establishment of parallel worlds has also been given by the British Prime Minister (Cameron, 2011) with particular focus on areas with a significant percentage of Muslim residents.

However, this is only one side of the story. There are scholars that challenge the solely problematic view of urban segregation and argue that segregation may also provide support and socialisation opportunities for vulnerable populations, as well as create niche markets for local economic development (Peach, 2007). Ethno-religious segregation becomes a concern when it is associated with minorities and poverty; otherwise, when it concerns wealthier or more accepted social groups it remains omitted, while nonsegregated areas do not necessarily have greater interaction among their residents (Musterd & Ostendorf, 2007). From yet another perspective, other writers comment on the structural rather than the cultural factors that may increase segregation, such as discrimination, limited access to the housing market, and poverty—a view that is often sidelined in public discourses.

Yet, in terms of policy, ethno-religious segregation continues to be perceived mainly as a problem (CIC, 2007), and a number of policies and programmes are put in place for countering it—programmes that, spatially, tend to promote social mixing as oppositional to segregation and, socially, to promote complementary activities that, as they state, enhance social interaction and mobility while often incorporating context-specific approaches to integration.

Most European cities have in place urban programmes that aim to address—at least as they state—urban deprivation (Jacquier, Bienvenue & Schlappa, 2007) ranging from the EU initiatives (such as the now completed URBAN programme) to nationally or regionally funded programmes (such as the Big City policy in the Netherlands, the Stadt Soziale in Germany, the now-terminated Neighbourhood Renewal programme in England, the Politique de la ville in France, or the Llei de Barris in Catalonia, Spain) to city-specific initiatives. These integrated urban programmes involve social, spatial, and economic approaches, often combined with local political arrangements (such as neighbourhood councils) and targeted community development funds. In most of these programmes, statements or initiatives that promote sociospatial mixing are evident (deFonseca-Feitosa & Wissman, 2006; Koutrolikou, 2012; Manley, van Ham, & Doherty, 2011; Uitermark, 2003). This is primarily achieved through making the targeted areas more 'attractive' to newcomers, either through housing incentives or through social housing and area redevelopment. However, as argued (Lees, 2008), these approaches often involve obscured gentrification processes and may lead to displacements of particular groups, while the anticipated mixing often remains a statistic rather than a reality since newcomers often establish their own networks and systems parallel to the existing ones (Butler, 2003) and mixing may remain superficial.

As already mentioned, these integrated urban programmes also involve governance arrangements and funds dedicated to local- or group-specific activities and services. While neighbourhood management programmes seem widespread in several European cities and follow a similar organisational structure (such as neighbourhood councils, local partnerships, etc.), community development and funding that is aimed at local organisations and projects often reflects local or national approaches towards integration and urban diversity. Commonly, approaches closer to assimilation tend to have (local and/or national) funds for available to groups on a project or need basis, while multiculturalism tends to have (local and/or national) funds available for particular ethno-religious groups and their development, and on a project basis. The latter approach, at least in the case of Britain, has been questioned with regard to possibly fracturing rather than enhancing social cohesion (CIC, 2007), while for some (Amin, 2002; Jackson, 1980) it has been associated with competitions and, at times, with local tensions. On the other hand, assimilationist approaches concerning group funding were also criticised as disempowering and for potentially ignoring the needs of particular groups.

In the varied approaches of governing diversity, housing and local social mix are not the sole spatially associated elements. In particular, local urban policies concerning minority integration and social/community cohesion have another crucial spatial aspect: public space (Belmessous & Tapada-Berteli, 2011; Raco, 2003). Public space holds a prominent position in theoretical approaches regarding cities and urban life. It has been considered as the ultimate political space, the place of democracy, as spaces for everyone and as places where citizenship is experienced and enacted (Crawford, 1999; Young, 1990). In social terms, public spaces have been considered as essential elements of urban life, as spaces for socialisation and as 'places of encounters' (Dines, Cattell, Gesler, & Curtis, 2006; Holland, Clark, Katz, & Peace, 2007), or, on other occasions, a marketable feature for the specific neighbourhood that enacts forms of 'consumer citizenship' (Fyfe, Bannister, & Kearns, 2006).

Of course, the prominent role given to public space in the discussions concerning urban diversity does not remain within the field of theoretical or political discourse. Rather, the significance of public spaces is reflected in the number of policies directly or indirectly concerning public spaces—policies stating the environmental and health benefits of public spaces, their significance in neighbourhood life, their potential as city/neighbourhood marketing tools, their relations to safety and (in)security, as well as their potential for promoting interactions and strengthening social cohesion.

This view of public spaces as 'places of encounters' and interaction is significant with regards to governing diversity and how it is spatially expressed, particularly in terms of policies and expectations from programmes and projects. Mostly, in terms of policy but also echoing certain writers, increased contact and interaction among groups are viewed as processes that can improve community relations, reduce isolation, and strengthen social cohesion.

For example, the European network of Cities for Local Integration Policies for Migrants (CLIP), in its analysis of 'Intercultural policies in European cities' (CLIP, 2010a) and its 'Good practice guide', considers public spaces as 'important locations for meeting and interacting with others' (CLIP, 2010b, p. 6), and also as spaces where conflicts might arise and they emphasise on 'initiatives promoting peaceful use of public spaces' (CLIP, 2010b). Also, the Intercultural Cities joint action (EU and Council of Europe) views public spaces and places that are open to all as one of the 10 elements of an Intercultural City Strategy (Wood, 2009). Similarly, for the British Commission on Integration and Cohesion (CIC) in its final report and recommendations (CIC, 2007), as well as in its background documents (Comedia 2007), space has a prominent position in enhancing (community) cohesion (albeit community cohesion remains a contested notion).

Public spaces retain their significance as places that encourage interaction, emphasising the necessity of their management and safety.

In these reports and policy recommendations (but also in other relevant documents that consider 'living together') the idea of public space includes parks, squares, and streets; libraries, playgrounds, and sports fields; as well as markets and occasionally local centres—places that as will be discussed further on, can also be considered as 'in-between': neither exactly public nor private. Nevertheless, the prevalent policy perceptions consider public spaces as prominent places of contact and interaction among different people and groups, and as such it turns them into prominent places in terms of governing urban diversity.

Both the perception of public spaces as prominent places for social cohesion and the view that events and shared activities can enhance interactions and community cohesion are primarily rooted to Allport's (1954) 'contact hypothesis' that argues that contact may potentially reduce prejudices and negative stereotypes. However, Allport places his hypothesis on certain parameters that need to be fulfilled, while others have highlighted the limitations of contact and commented on the role of sustained interactions (Dixon, 2006; Pettigrew, 1998; Tajfel, 1982; Vertovec, 2007a). From these perspectives, contact might be useful, might lead to 'familiar strangers' (Milgram, 2010) or to fleeting interactions, but it is not necessarily enough for relationship building. Thus, in these conditions, the same consideration applies to public spaces and temporary events.

Critiques regarding the potential of public spaces to inspire 'meaningful interactions' and to challenge stereotypes have also been voiced by geographers such as Amin (2002, 2008) and Valentine (2008). At the same time, other approaches towards place and interaction are emerging. In the last decade, there is an observable increased interest not only in public spaces but also in other places that can be considered as somewhere in-between public and private and can potentially enhance interactions among people and groups (see for example Amin, 2002, 2008; Oldenburg, 1989; Vaiou & Kalandides, 2009). Watson (2006) discusses 'city publics' and encounters in places that are not only public; Fincher and Iveson (2008) discuss spaces where common interests and activities can take place; and Dimitriou and Koutrolikou (2011) talk about places shaped by 'collectivities' and 'commons'. Moreover, markets receive particular attention as 'spaces of encounter' (Watson & Studdert, 2006).

As mentioned earlier, this interest on in-between spaces is also reflected in policies and their recommendations. In its concept of public spaces, CLIP network (2010a) includes also libraries and other meeting places, while within the framework of the Intercultural Cities action, particular attention is given to intercultural spaces and centres (Bloomfield & Wood, 2011) that are inclusive, make people feeling safe, encourage different perspectives, and facilitate public dialogue. Lownsbrough and Beunderman also discuss 'spaces of potential' to 'foster positive interactions' (2007, p. 19), a view that is also echoed in the then-governmental guidance on meaningful interaction (DCLG, 2008). These 'spaces of potential', that can be public, but they also include exchange spaces, productive spaces, spaces of services provision, activity spaces, democratic/participative spaces, staged spaces, in-between spaces, and virtual spaces (Lownsbrough & Beunderman, 2007). In addition, CIC also notes the potential of shared spaces for all that can act 'as the locus for shared activities' (CIC, 2007, p. 55).

This discussion concerns a rich diversity of spaces that can be defined as 'in-between', with different characteristics, functions, and users. As with public spaces, when thinking about the influence of such 'in-between' spaces on intergroup relations, they cannot be taken solely for generic spatial elements but need to be considered within their social and everyday life context. Moreover, as the discussion about public spaces has already explored, the 'for all' concept that is commonly employed for in-between spaces as well, is not neutral, might entail its own internal conflicts, and it does not necessarily mean that intergroup relations will be improved only by its existence. Despite this 'spatial turn' and interest about the interconnections of space, cohesion, and intergroup relations, local relations among groups are affected by several complementary factors that also need consideration—factors such as competitions, discriminations and inequalities, and past histories, among others.

## Hackney, East London: Exploring the Terrain

Hackney has been in the forefront of news and lifestyle magazines for more than 15 years now, embodying both famous and infamous identities. Located in the East of London, it has been shaped by processes of industrialisation and deindustrialisation, in- and out-migration, as well as by political struggles. Dalston's redevelopment ex-industrial and manufacturing buildings and its significant population and reputation change in the past years is one example of the transformations of Hackney's neighbourhoods (see Figure 11.1).

Hackney's residents represent a very diverse mosaic of races, cultures, ethnicities, and religions. Ethnicity, as well as religion, are important for several groups in Hackney, both in terms of group identity and in terms of socialisation and occasionally in terms of civil society organisations (CSOs) and their funding. Throughout Hackney there are numerous religious spaces (Christian churches including a number of Evangelical and Pentecostal churches, mosques, synagogues), some catering for the whole of their local congregations and others paying greater attention to particular ethnic or racial groups.

At a micro scale, Hackney is a collage of different worlds living next to and within each other, something that is also reflected in the number and diversity of local community organisations. Ethnic segregation in Hackney is not high, and most ethnocultural groups are quite dispersed (Plachta, 2003) with the exception of the Charedi community, which is more concentrated at the north of the borough. This ethnocultural mix is primarily experienced in the landscapes of everyday life through the existence of diverse local shops (especially food stores and newsagents) and relevant landmarks (such as religious buildings and cultural centres next to each other), as well as through street visibility and housing. Nevertheless, one might identify micro concentrations of ethnic groups (for example, of the Vietnamese around London Fields

*Figure 11.1* Redevelopment of ex-industrial and manufacturing buildings overlooking the canal at Dalston, London.

or of the Turkish between Dalston and Stoke Newington), which are particularly expressed through businesses and community centres, although it is not clear if this is replicated in housing.

Hackney, characterised with a decades-long multiple deprivation Index of Multiple Deprivation, is the most deprived borough of London. However, a closer look reveals a more complex spatial reality since the borough has pockets of wealth along with areas of poverty. For example, Broadway market (Figure 11.2) is one of the most gentrified neighbourhoods of Hackney, London, as well as a terrain of local struggles against the loss of local shops (as well as a key feature of a number of documentaries).

Hackney in general, and specific neighbourhoods in particular, have undergone processes of intense gentrification, becoming some of the trendier neighbourhoods of London. At the same time, Hackney is and has been a fertile ground for alternative political and community initiatives, from squats to collective actions. As Sutcliffe (2001) vividly describes the transformations of Shoreditch:

> Inside ten years, Shoreditch has morphed from post-industrial desert to social Mecca. Disused warehouses, where marchers bedded down before neo-Nazi rallies in the 70's, have become havens of sand blasted minimalism. Fun seekers pour down the Old St. wind tunnel and spill out of bars on to Charlotte Road. Chuck a stone over your shoulder in Hoxton Market and you'll probably hit a film crew. . . . However did desolation get so hectic?!

While segregation in Hackney is not a prominent feature, economic polarisation is more evident (Hackney, 2003), which is reflected in local lifestyles. In conjunction with gentrification, housing enclaves also generate leisure and shopping enclaves that the rest of the neighbourhood would find difficult to use. This economically polarised coexistence, whilst facilitating an economically mixed environment, is also assumed to contribute to resentments towards new residents and developments, to high crime rates in specific areas, and to tensions associated with groups

*Figure 11.2* Broadway market is one of the most gentrified neighbourhoods of Hackney, London, as well as a terrain of local struggles against the loss of local shops (as well as a key feature of a number of documentaries).

of young people (albeit not necessarily formed along ethnic or racial lines). Chatsworth Road at Homerton (see Figure 11.3) can be considered as one of the latest cases in a long list of polarised urban transformations, where gentrification is starting to become evident alongside a number of deprived council estates in a neighbourhood that has also suffered from high crime reputation.

Hackney has a reputation of a borough where different people get along well, something that was reflected even in the indicators regarding community cohesion and in opinions expressed by several of the interviewees. Wessendorf also observes that diversity in Hackney 'is not being seen as something unusual' (2011, p. 4); rather it is 'commonplace', as she defines it. Maybe this is the reason why the local authority tends not to be so concerned with issues of multiculturalism and diversity (besides the conventional 'celebrations' of local diversity), but mostly with issues of inequality and community cohesion (with a particular focus on crime reduction and youth).

This everyday conviviality is primarily attributed by many local residents to the extensive social housing of the borough and to the rich diversity of local groups and, secondly, to the fact that local residents had to face and resolve various personal and local problems. As commented by a local resident:

> In general, relations are not bad. . . . Although cultures and lifestyles are different, there are many areas where we encounter, contact and talk to each other (especially in an area such as Hackney) such as residential areas (living in close proximity and shopping from same places), in work, in health and other services. (Personal communication, 2004)

Yet, behind this rosy image, there are also various prejudices and occasional tensions and conflicts among the different groups—conflicts that reflect competition for resources (such as funding, representation, or even housing), cultural differentiations, or forms of territoriality (Koutrolikou,

*Figure 11.3* Chatsworth Road at Homerton is one of the latest gentrified neighbourhoods of Hackney, London, also a deprived neighbourhood with a high crime reputation in the past.

2012). In addition, throughout its trajectory of gentrification, there have been overt or covert resentments and tensions towards the gentrifying newcomers—resentments that were based on exclusion of local residents from the new activities, on taking over and changing local everyday places (such as shops, cafes, or even festivals), or on wealth disparities (something more prominent in the younger generations).

## Exploring Interactions in Hackney's Public Spaces

Despite abundant guidance and numerous recommendations regarding the design and manage-ment of public spaces, the dominant form of public space in most neighbourhoods in London (and elsewhere in Britain) is that of the park or the communal garden and, of course, the street. This is also true for Hackney, which besides its Town Hall square and two other smaller 'civic' squares that relate to redevelopment projects, the main public spaces are parks. For example, London Fields park (see Figure 11.4), just around the Town Hall, despite its modest appearance is a very popular destination for both local residents and visitors.

When the weather is good, parks become a major feature of public life in the borough—some more than others—and they tend to reflect Hackney's rich diversity of people and groups. One might encounter families or friends having barbeques, children playing at the playgrounds or at the park, people playing cricket, individuals lying on the grass enjoying the sun, people having fun, and, of course, meeting and chatting to others. There are park spots that are more or less 'reserved' by a specific group, spots that attract most people, and spots that are avoided (even at daytime). The way and frequency of their use is tightly related to their location (and their sur-rounding neighbourhood), as well as to the activities that take place there or around them. Since some of them are particular local landmarks, they are used by more than local residents.

As it has been observed by other research concerning public spaces, not all groups use such spaces in the same way, while sentiments of anxiety, fear, or discomfort are often expressed in regards to the use of public space by different groups. Similar sentiments were expressed by local Hackney residents concerning parks. Some groups—particularly the more religious ones, as it was mentioned in interviews—felt uncomfortable with certain park behaviours. Moreover,

*Figure 11.4* Despite its modest appearance, London Fields park is a very popular destination for both local residents and visitors.

considering Hackney's infamous reputation regarding crime, the liveliness that local parks may have changes significantly when the night comes and parks often become a place to avoid or a place of fear.

Of course, another crucial form of public space is the street. Hackney has a vibrant everyday life and, as such, particular local streets become very significant public spaces. Such local streets (for example Broadway Market (see Figure 11.5), Hoxton Market, Bell Lane, or Stoke Newington High Street) tend to be former markets or high streets and instead of being passing-by places, they actually become places of socialisation, primarily due to the leisure shops they have (cafés, pubs, restaurants) or their market activities. These streets often become a point of reference and of everyday activity for locals (and others), meeting places for people, and—at times—of the local community. Yet, streets as such tend to be dominated by one or few of the local groups, while the rest rarely socialise there. Gentrification has also been a defining factor for many of these streets, turning them to hotspots of 'urban village' life and displacing older activities, shops, and people.

One of the most characteristic examples of such a change has been the case of Broadway market, with the obscure and well-publicised evictions of local shopkeepers and the local struggles to counter the evictions (see, among others, Kunzru, 2006, for the story of Tony's café). As is often the case, the displacement of older local associational places is accompanied by the disappearance of the local groups that frequented them from the street life.

Another aspect relating both to public spaces and to approaches towards ethno-religious diversity concerns the activities that take place there, and in particular, local festivals and events. For many, such local festivals and events were very significant for the neighbourhood and for the groups themselves, since they offer an opportunity for celebrating and illustrating aspects of a group's culture. Moreover, there were seen as a great opportunity for social mixing and learning about other cultures. However, in other cases, new festivals were created for 'branding' a neighbourhood or local festivals were rebranded along the lines of the new gentrifiers, thus creating resentments to those involved with the festival in the past. As commented by a local resident:

Some years ago we had a multi-ethnic festival at Hackney Downs . . . where many cultures and groups were coming together. Then the Church St. [Stoke Newington] festival took

*Figure 11.5* Broadway market, London.

over the multi-ethnic one and now all the money go [sic] there and smaller events can't get anything. . . . Broadway Market had a festival when they first got the regeneration money, in order to become more attractive.

During at least the last decade, local ethno-religious or multicultural festivals have become a significant feature of many neighbourhoods, particularly of those neighbourhoods with a diverse resident population. Both ethno-religious and intercultural festivals and events were considered as crucial actions for intercultural policies (CLIP, 2010a). Ethno-religious festivals were considered important for celebrating, legitimising, and publicly accepting different cultures, becoming thus significant for the identity of the specific groups. Multicultural festivals have been a prevalent way of celebrating and legitimising local multicultural life. Both kinds of festivals also contribute to income generation for the host communities and increase the liveliness of the area. In terms of local relations, both kinds of festivals are seen as events that open up opportunities for socialisation, for meeting people from diverse backgrounds, and for facilitating interactions. On the other hand, it can be argued that in terms of intergroup relations, the impact of such activities may remain unclear, since more often than not encounters and interactions remain fleeting. Moreover, while such festivals may provide a terrain for familiarising oneself with difference, there is also the danger of strengthening perceptions of otherness through the promotion of 'exotic' aspects of cultural identities. All of these arguments are also true about Hackney's local festivals, which were numerous and usually well attended, although in the last decade most of the (financial) support of the local authority was withdrawn. Public life in Hackney includes a range of ethno-religious and multicultural celebrations, some bigger than others and some more outward-looking than others. As mentioned before, a cause of resentment that was voiced concerning festivals was related to gentrification and to festivals being 'reshaped', minimising the involvement of previous groups.

In the discussion about facilitating 'living together' and cross-cultural contact, public spaces and the celebrations that take place at them emerge as significant elements. Hackney's squares, parks, streets, and festivals express the area's diversity, bring different people and cultures together at the same place and potentially in contact with each other, while removing fear of 'otherness'. At the same time, they occasionally express the economic polarisation of its neighbourhoods, with some public spaces of the gentrified neighbourhoods being dominated by better-off or trendy residents. Moreover, this side-by-side coexistence in space doesn't necessarily mean greater contact or interaction among different groups. Despite their potential for familiarity and contact, the interactions that take place there are mostly fleeting. Sustained interactions are mostly observed in public places that are part of the local routine everyday life (as is the case with the streets described previously or with playgrounds). In understanding such local relations, considering the local mix of residents, shops, associational places, and services becomes critical.

## Hackney's Private and In-Between Spaces and Their Potential for Ethno-Religious Relations

Commonly, the notion of private space is associated with that of the home. Yet, when discussing groups, one can observe group-specific places that can be described as group 'private'. Such places include group-specific community centres or religious centres. Some consider these places as essential for the group since they provide support, opportunities for social life, and legitimisation of the group's identity. Yet others see them as places that promote separation and tensions (especially when they have to compete for local funding), or even as oppressive to group members. Both views were expressed regarding group-specific places in Hackney, but such views often entailed overt or covert biases according to the group in question.

As discussed before, besides public and private spaces, there is an array of places that do not conform to established notions of either public or private. These 'Other' or 'in-between' places have degrees of 'publicness' and 'privacy' and take many forms.

Community or local neighbourhood centres, as well as spaces of multigroup local associations that are not group-specific, can be considered as in-between places. In a way, they are public since they are open to a broad range of people, but at the same time they are private since they usually refer to particular groups or communities. Hackney has several of them, mostly in the form of community centres in housing estates and few multigroup centres (including the space that hosts the local civil society umbrella organisation). Despite difficulties and potential tensions of managing such spaces, they do provide a terrain for sustained interaction either due to their local embeddedness or due to the activities they host. Even community centres that are mainly run by one group often run projects and programmes that target a broader population, occasionally aiming at sharing experiences, increasing understanding, or reducing tensions (characteristic examples are art-based projects that target different youth groups). In specific cases, places as such are established through the cooperation of specific groups, forming alliances among them. However, these latter forms of spaces are not just shared or common, and neither are most of the activities that they host; rather, they are the outcome of particular groups or associations.

Similarly, the open spaces within social housing estates can be defined as in-between places;— places that may include parking spaces, playing fields, and playgrounds, or green spaces and gardens. Yet, the way that such places are used differs significantly from the multigroup community centres and depends greatly on local factors. Often, they become places of fear and avoidance since they are dominated by particular groups or activities, which in the case of many Hackney housing estates, usually means the youth (which has been associated with criminality and fear and was greatly demonised). Equally often, they are just empty or become contested spaces over their use (which usually means turning them into parking spaces). However, there are occasions when such spaces become places of interaction among different people and groups. For example, playing fields and playgrounds can become places of sustained interaction, and gardens (or allotments) may end up bringing together several people from the estates (PAL, 2005).

As other writers have observed (Lownsbrough & Beunderman, 2007; Watson & Studdert, 2006), street markets represent a particular kind of place. This is also true for Hackney, where street markets (temporary or permanent) are a significant feature of everyday life in particular neighbourhoods. The mundaneness and everydayness of food, as well as the stable presence of markets, create a terrain where discussions can be initiated and where more than fleeting relations can be developed.

On the other hand, neighbourhood changes, such as gentrification or population changes, may also inspire resentments to those that are losing their established 'territory' (see also Watson & Studdert, 2006), something that was more evident in the case of Dalston market or Broadway market.

In this brief trajectory of Hackney, space can simultaneously be a contested terrain and a place of interactions. Public spaces are significant, but in regards to ethno-religious relations, so are other, in-between places—even private ones. However, it is not only space that affects local ethno-religious relations. Other factors, such as intergroup competition, actual or perceived inequalities, and local histories (group-related or borough-related) are also significant.

## Conclusion

In the past decade, space has acquired particular attention not only regarding design, well-being, and quality of life, but mostly about its relation to social cohesion and social relations in multicultural urban settings. In this discussion, and particularly in terms of policies, public spaces hold a prominent position and are viewed as places of encounter and contact and, as a result, as places where 'living together' could be enhanced. However, this perception is also challenged since interactions in public spaces can remain fleeting and do not necessarily result in deeper intergroup relations. In addition, other approaches are also emerging that challenge this prominence of public spaces and argue about the potential of other, not only public spaces for local relations. The presented case of Hackney illustrated the diversity of places where interactions (fleeting or sustained) among ethno-religious groups occur, the potential and limitations of these places, and some external factors that impact on people and places, without being exhaustive. While for some people or groups public spaces might be a fertile ground for relationship building, for others such ground is found in other, less public places and activities.

However, space is only one parameter in the complexities of local social relations; social relations that are also context- and group-specific and influenced by several other factors also need to be considered.

Chapter 12

# Inhabiting Cities, Domesticating Public Space

## Making Sense of the Changing Public Life of Contemporary London

*Regan Koch and Alan Latham*

A city's public life is constantly changing. Take our home city of London. A visitor from the city's past, even as recently as a decade ago, would notice lots of subtle shifts. They would spot people navigating the city not with *London A–Zs* but with smartphones in their hands and headphones in their ears. They would see Londoners queuing up for oversized coffees to go, or topping up their Oyster cards to travel on the tube. They would notice people riding electric-hybrid Routemaster buses, blue public Barclay's Bikes, and jogging to work with a change of clothes on their back. They might find corner stores stocked with Nigerian SIM cards, Polish beer—*Żywiec, Tyskie, Lech*—and Romanian sausages sold next to Turkish cheeses. On weekends, they would encounter a city populated by farmers' markets, museums open free of charge, and festivals of all different kinds. It is easy to overlook these sorts of gradual changes to a city's public life when thinking in terms of bigger trends that are often the focus of urban scholarship. Contemporary London, in particular, is often described within the context of sweeping transformations. A long time world city, it has now emerged as a global city, a post-industrial control and command centre for transnational flows of information, capital, and labour (Sassen, 1991). The city's political landscape has been altered by a new mayoral system and by national policies of neoliberal governance that have reshaped relations of state responsibility and private enterprise (Massey, 2007). Socially, London has become a super-diverse cosmopolitan hub defined by a tremendous influx of immigrants (Vertovec, 2007a) and the formation of new hybrid cultures. But it is also a city marked by widening income inequalities (Hamnett, 2003) and gentrification (Butler & Robson, 2003).

For many urban scholars, public space is an important concept because it provides a way of assessing the impacts of large transformations on cities. By focusing on new developments—buildings and built areas, as well as shifts in the ownership, management, and financing of urban space—it is possible to describe and interpret the collective effects of broader processes of urbanisation. The idea of public space also presents a set of criteria—norms, ideals, and historical precedents—against which issues of democratic access and 'the right to the city' can be evaluated. These analytic framings have led to critiques of powerful forces manipulating urban space to serve narrow interests, and to accounts that detail moments of resistance and claim-making by the less powerful (Iveson, 2007; Mitchell, 2003; Watson, 2006). Yet there is a tendency in urban scholarship and commentary to narrate concerns for public spaces in overarching terms. The dominant, almost taken-for-granted stories are that public space are being continuously encroached upon, struggled over, retreated from, or in some cases colonised by the middle classes (Low & Smith, 2006; Zukin, 2009).Public spaces are becoming increasingly exclusionary, commercialised, securitised, and depoliticised (Flusty, 2001; Kohn, 2004; Madden, 2010; Minton, 2009; Sorkin, 1992). Although these claims are often based on case studies in U.S. cities, they frequently come to frame the accounts of transformation in European cities and public spaces too (see Akkar, 2005; Allen, 2006; Atkinson, 2003; Belina & Helms, 2003; Jackson, 1998; McInroy, 2000; Munoz, 2003).

These narratives are seductive. But they can also be misleading or exaggerated. They can divert attention away from a whole range of ways in which the life of public spaces in European cities is constantly being reinvented—sometimes for the worse, sometimes for better. In this chapter, we want to argue for the importance of attending to the routine activities, mundane objects, and everyday events through which this reinvention emerges. We think much urban scholarship has become proficient in critiquing what is wrong with contemporary public spaces, but is limited in its ability to register what goes on within them (Koch & Latham, 2013a, 2013b). This undermines the capacity to develop imaginative and effective solutions to problems cities face when seeking to enhance the qualities of their public spaces. In what follows, our arguments are organised in three parts. First, we outline how critical urban scholarship typically frames discussion and research on public spaces. It tends to focus on exclusion, encroachment, and claim-making. Important though these issues are, they can end up restricting our analytical horizons. Second, we suggest a number of possibilities for expanding how urban scholarship might approach the collective life of our cities. We argue that attending carefully to the materialities and atmospheres involved in how people come to inhabit public spaces—how they in a sense domesticate them—offers a fruitful way of opening up how we understand public space and its ongoing transformation. Third, we draw upon three examples of recent change in London to illustrate these ideas. Our aim is to highlight the extent to which public life is constantly being remade in ways both ordinary and surprising.

## A Brief Contemporary History of Thinking About Public Space

If critical urban studies as an academic field can trace a lineage back to the 1960s and early 1970s, a sustained focus on public space only really emerged in the 1990s. Influential work from writers like Davis (1992), Sorkin (1992), Smith (1996), and Mitchell (1995) applied ideas from democratic political theory to case studies in the privatisation and redevelopment of urban environments. Along with a lament for the ways in which traditional spaces of the city no longer met their historical functions of sociability and encounter came critiques of new places of social gathering such as shopping malls, water front plazas, and master-planned neighbourhoods (see Crawford, 1992; Goss, 1999; Gottdiener, 1997; Harvey, 1990; Zukin, 1995). Promoting the general idea of a decline in authentic forms of public life, some texts went so far as to signal 'The End!' of public space (Mitchell, 1995; Sorkin, 1992). In response, a range of counter-arguments stressed the danger of appealing to an idealised, romantic version of the public realm. Feminist and postcolonial theorists, in particular, demonstrated the various ways in which social space is inherently conflictual (see Deutsche, 1996; Fraser, 1990; Massey, 1994; Wilson, 1992). They also questioned the value of upholding the past as a lost era of egalitarian possibility. Running alongside these debates, scholars reconnected with established traditions that championed the emancipatory potentials of urbanisation. Cities were valorised for the particular affordances they offered for forging connection and encountering difference (see Fincher & Jacobs, 1998; Young, 1990). Cultural and identity theorists articulated new visions of cosmopolitanism whereby plural and accommodating subject positions could be fostered amidst the tolerance and diversity of urban life (see Keith & Pile, 1993; Sandercock, 1998).

In hindsight, what is notable about these debates is how they contributed to a rather peculiar yet resilient set of propositions about public space. From the first two strands of engagement a bleak picture emerges: Neither an ideal public realm, nor true public space ever really existed, and those few democratic urban spaces that can be found are under threat. On the other hand, the assertion of cities as having emancipatory potential valorised the ideal qualities of publicness and generated demands for further investigations into the changing nature of public space. These somewhat awkward pairings fixed engagements with the topic of urban public space so that the concept has come to function in three overlapping registers. First, public space references an ideal—an aspiration for democratic civil society. Second, it defines a set of normative criteria, more or less explicitly spelled out, against which actual sites and conflicts can be evaluated. Third, public space is understood as an arena of contestation and negotiation whereby different groups assert their rights to the city.

This lineage of thinking about public space has been influential in how the concept has been put to work in recent years. Most generally, it is deployed to evoke and address a set of concerns about contemporary cities that are typically framed in one of three ways. First, there are issues around equality of access. The term *public space* implies democratic inclusiveness, yet scholars have drawn attention to the range of ways that marginalised groups are often excluded. These exclusions can stem from proscriptive rules and regulations, prohibitions on certain activities, symbolic and aesthetic codes, and through appeals to order and safety (Herbert, 2008; Minton, 2009; Rogers & Coaffee, 2005). Most often affected are the poor and homeless, but tactics of exclusion are also enacted upon young people, minority groups, and those with disabilities or outward signs of mental illness. People involved in political activities such as protests and leafleting, as well as those trying to earn a living through things like busking or vending, are also frequently targets of prohibitions and tactics of dispersal. Second, there are concerns about encroachment of public space by powerful interests. These relate to changes in the way public spaces are owned, financed, and governed, with a major issue being the extent to which liberties can be safeguarded in the absence of democratic forms of control. Neoliberal governing strategies and entrepreneurial models of urban regeneration, coupled with new forms of social regulation and punitive styles of policing, have only accelerated these fears (Chronopoulous, 2011; Fyfe et al., 2006; Helms, Atkinson, & MacLeod, 2007). Third, there is a concern with public space as a site of claim-making. A wide range of work has highlighted important moments of conflict and struggle, whereby rights to the city have been secured through appeals to the concept of public space (Iveson, 2007; Mitchell, 2003). Other scholars have examined more subtle processes through which the boundaries of public space are constituted (Lees, 2003; Miller, 2007; Watson, 2006), or where urban inhabitants transgress norms and appropriate public spaces through activities such as play (Stevens, 2007), mourning (Franck & Paxson, 2007), street vending (Jimenez-Dominguez, 2007), and congregating socially on streets, sidewalks, and squares (Domosh, 1998; Law, 2002).

These concerns largely stem from a desire among critical scholars to highlight inequalities and promote more socially just forms of living together within cities. Curiously, however, these enduring views of what public space is about seem to be restricting our sense of what matters in much of everyday life. While urban scholarship generally prefers to focus on moments of big political transitions—and there certainly are many empirical cases from the last decade of transformation in Europe—what largely goes on within public spaces is most often not about overt conflicts or struggles, and sites of politics and political formation are distributed far beyond spaces of urban co-presence (Amin, 2008; Barnett, 2008). Public space is mostly defined by routines and emergent patterns of use (Berman, 2006; Degen, DeSilvey, & Rose, 2008). It is about people working, shopping, observing, getting from point A to B, relaxing, flirting, meeting up with friends and family, and so on. The public qualities of these activities arise out of the degree to which they involve some sort of orientation towards, trust in, perhaps even responsibility for, the diversity of people with whom one collectively inhabits a particular space. When public spaces work well. these relationships are inclusive, convivial, and democratic. They are shared. Yet held to historical standards and political expectations, the public spaces that make up our cities often fall short of the ideals, norms, and hopes placed upon them in political theory. For some time, predominant frameworks in urban studies have concentrated almost exclusively on evidencing these failures. As Hubbard has recently commented, 'Caught in a theoretical impasse, debates about public space circle endlessly, becoming ever more self-referential and less relevant to cities where the Internet now rivals the streets as a space of dialogue and sociality' (2008, p. 524).

## Thinking Differently: The Everyday Domestication of Public Space

To attend more carefully to how public life in cities is put together, we think that urban scholarship needs to be more expansive in how it thinks about publicness. With this in mind, we would like to offer some alternatives to the usual framings of exclusion, encroachment, and claim-making. We want to explore how certain kinds of spaces come to afford a home in the city. In focusing on this notion of home making, we want to link into a diverse tradition of urban scholarship concerned with the practical possibilities of public space—how they can foster mutually beneficial ways of living together in cities. These include the progressive tradition with its notion of 'civic housekeeping' (Jackson, 2001), the activist-scholarship of writers such as Jane Jacobs (1961) and William H. Whyte (1980, 1988) concerned with the micro-orderings of public life, and urban designers like Hans Monderman (Vanderbilt, 2008) and Jan Gehl (1987, 2010) who attend to the role that objects of different kinds play in the fostering of everyday urban life. It is also to connect with the more recent scholarship of urbanists such as Richard Sennett (1994, 2010), Gary Bridge (2005), and Ash Amin (2006, 2008, 2012) who, in various different ways, theorise public life as a collective grammar of social interaction. We also want to argue that thinking about the necessarily domestic qualities of public spaces makes it imperative to think carefully about how such spaces—and the social action that occurs within them—come to be *domesticated*.

Within critical urban studies, domestication has primarily been used pejoratively. It is synonymous with words like *taming* and *pacification* as a way of critiquing changes seen to corrode public life (see Atkinson, 2003; Jackson, 1998; Munoz, 2003; Zukin, 1995, 2009). In other disciplines, however, domestication is viewed in a more pragmatic light. Studies in anthropology (Cassidy & Mullin, 2007; Ingold, 2000; Vitebsky, 2006), media and technology (Berker, Hartmann, Punie, & Ward, 2006; Silverstone & Hirsch, 1992), social history (Kasson, 1978; Thomas de la Pena, 2003), and post-socialism (Creed, 1998; Stenning, Smith, Rochovská, & Świecek, 2010), for example, share a common conceptualisation of domestication as a process through which certain kinds of (variably) beneficial relationships between humans and other things—be they objects, sets of ideas, or other forms of life—take shape. In this sense, domestication is not a normative concept, but an analytical one. It provides insights into how relationships that might at first be alien or novel evolve in various indeterminate ways to become familiar, ordinary, routine, and useful. We think the concept of domestication can usefully be extended to scholarship on urban public space precisely because it draws attention to this kind of becoming mundane. It frames the analysis in terms of the social practices that populate public space and how these practices are enmeshed with particular objects, materials, and material configurations. Thus, domestication might equally be deployed to inform understandings of broad social transformations across cities, or as a practical conceptual aid in matters of urban design or management.

So, how exactly might the concept of domestication help to make sense of public spaces? We would like to suggest three heuristics—inhabitation, materiality, atmosphere—that are helpful in organising our understandings of how processes of domestication are enfolded into the everyday public life of cities (Figure 12.1).

The first heuristic, inhabitation, refers to corporeal (and corporeally extended) forms of action and routine activity that populate urban public space. It speaks to the fact that as publics we are embodied beings-in-action. Our regular movements through the city, our day-to-day activities,

*Figure 12.1* Much of everyday life in the city is about mundane, practical uses of public space: people queuing up, resting, and people watching, or getting to where they are going (to name a few examples). London.

our relatively unthinking habits of interaction are largely what urban public spaces are taken up with. As Amin notes:

> The movement of humans and non-humans in public spaces is not random but guided by habit, purposeful orientation, and the instructions of objects and signs. The repetition of these rhythms results in the conversion of public space into a patterned ground that proves essential for actors to make sense of the space, their place within it and their way through it. Such patterning is the way in which a public space is domesticated, not only as a social map of the possible and the permissible, but also as an experience of freedom. (2008, p. 12)

Spaces become public not only because laws or discourses recognise them as such, but through all sorts of corporeal, largely routinized practices. In public space, we are walking, working, driving, sitting, cycling, resting, and riding transport. Some of us are at work, others at leisure. And in a whole range of ways our gestures, actions, use of objects, spacing, and movement amongst one another have collective effects (Bridge, 2005; Laurier & Philo, 2006). Our analyses of urban public space can be strengthened by attending more carefully to how forms of inhabitation are woven together, and how the presence of certain practices offer affordances for some people and activities and not for others (Thrift, 2005; Whyte, 1980).

Second, we can think about the domestication of public spaces in terms of their materiality. The concept of materiality focuses attention on how the materials that comprise public spaces—the objects, surfaces, architectures, hard and soft technologies, amenities, and provisions—act into the life of a space. To think about materiality is to recognise that materials are not mere substances, but rather 'transductive field[s] in which physical, technical and affective realities precipitate' (MacKenzie, 2002, p. 35). The matter that surrounds us thus 'matters' depending not just on how it is arranged, but how we encounter or relate to it, how it works through or upon us, and how it generates feelings, moods, behaviours, problems, and responses.

Materialities are constitutive of the types of public action and address, as well as the collective actors (publics) that come to form relationships within a space (Degen et al., 2008; cf. Iveson, 2007), and often in ways that are unanticipated. We can better understand public space in a multidimensional sense by thinking through how different materialities act together, are accounted for or overlooked, to generate particular material ecologies and affordances for domestication.

Third, we need to consider that public spaces swirl with a whole range of relational intensities or atmospheres. Thinking in terms of atmosphere is a way of trying to attend to the prevailing moods, feelings, emotions, and meanings that collectively shape the experiences within a given site. It is about recognising that many aspects of domestication—how forms of exchange take place, the way rules of acceptable behaviour are established, how feelings of inclusion or exclusion are produced—are in large part constituted through forms of expression independent of or beyond individual human subjectivity (Bissell, 2010; Dewsbury, Harrison, Rose, & Wylie, 2002; Latham & McCormack, 2004; Massumi, 2002). They are about the ways in which public spaces can be experienced as crowded, empty, festive, mundane, dangerous, inviting, and so on. The relationships people come to develop with public spaces take place within these atmospheric contexts. They shape the extent to which spaces and practices are made routine and familiar. They can also help to prefigure expressions of the common good, of a baseline sense of democracy, and of the pleasures and potentials of cosmopolitan urban life (Amin, 2012).

We recognise that as so far presented these ideas may appear rather abstract. So, let us turn to some specific examples to illustrate how the heuristics of inhabitation, materiality, and atmosphere can orient our readings of the changing shape of some of contemporary London's public spaces.

## Reinventing and Reimagining London's Public Life: Three Examples

This chapter began by contemplating some of the numerous changes London has undergone in recent decades. Some have been large scale, others more prosaic. Certainly, many feed into prevailing concerns about public space: the privatised mega-development of Canary Wharf; the self-contained Westfield shopping centres in east and west London; restrictions on the right to protest in Westminster and the City of London; to say nothing of the contentious matter of the 2012 Olympic Games and its associated developments. At the same time, other stories can be told about London's public life being transformed in more welcoming and surprising directions. In this final section we want to examine three such examples: the adoption of 'shared space' street designs, the revival of cycling, and the emergence of new street markets. Our intention is not to merely celebrate these trends, or to suggest that public space in London has simply become better. Like all big cities, London has too many geographies and trajectories to allow for such neat conclusions. Our aim is to demonstrate the utility of thinking about public space as enfolded in an ongoing process of domestication, and how the three heuristics of inhabitation, materiality, and atmosphere can help attune analysis in this way (Figure 12.2).

*Figure 12.2*  Top row: Shared space schemes reconfigure the norms of interactions between cars and pedestrians by organising materials to facilitate negotiation of multiple uses. Bottom row: Street markets offer a range of opportunities for social interaction. The expansion of cycling has altered the patterns of inhabitation in use on many streets in London.

## *Shared Space Street Designs: New Foundations for Street Life*

Some of London's newest streets are missing many taken-for-granted forms of demarcation—street markings, traffic signs, stop lights, guardrails, and even kerbs. These omissions are a deliberate design strategy, part of a set of 'shared space' principles first developed in Holland by traffic engineer Hans Monderman (Hamilton-Baillie, 2008; Vanderbilt, 2008). The most high-profile example in London is Exhibition Road in South Kensington. Aside from the street's tremendous width, Exhibition Road's most striking feature is its paving. Clad in a checkerboard of granite slabs, there is little delineation between what is meant to be the domain of motorised traffic and what might be used by pedestrians or cyclists. The design concept echoes classical notions of public space as the site of face-to-face interaction: The very point is to force drivers to interact with and therefore show responsibility towards nonmotorised users of the street. This approach is a radical shift in how traffic safety has been typically framed by London's planners. Much of the city is currently defined by a chaos of traffic engineering, the product of decades of incremental interventions to the streetscape: signs, lights, rails, bumps, and bollards all jostling to direct drivers and pedestrians through the city. These thickets of engineering clutter are the product of two parallel ideas. First, that to keep pedestrians safe from vehicular traffic they must be kept separate from it; and second, that the orderly flow of traffic should be not be disrupted by the presence of pedestrians. In these respects, London's streets are generally effective, but they are also frequently inhospitable to pedestrians. Navigating the city on foot—nevermind by wheelchair or stroller—is often about getting through an unpleasant, noisy, crowded maze of narrow footpaths, pelican crossings, and guardrails.

Shared space schemes like Exhibition Road, or Seven Dials in Covent Garden, thus involve an innovative reordering of the materiality of streets as the domain of automobile traffic. They are not about removing cars, vans, or buses from streets, but about reorienting their relationship with pedestrians. They force drivers to view pedestrians as having an equal claim to street space, and they prompt an ongoing awareness of the risks generated through the presence of motorised traffic. They are also the most visible examples of a whole series of new developments and experiments across London aimed at engineering streets and junctions to better accommodate a plurality of demands. Trafalgar Square has been pedestrianized; Oxford Circus has been redesigned with an enhanced Shibuya-style diagonal crossing; High Street Kensington has been substantially decluttered. In examples such as these, transport planners and designers are thinking very seriously and in novel ways about material objects and their arrangement to shape interactions in public space. Importantly, these interactions are consciously reconfigured as *personal* interactions between morally responsible agents. As experiments in domestication, they are about allowing the multiple publics that travel the city's spaces to negotiate how they do so situationally rather than letting traffic engineers or the brute force of vehicular transportation predetermine this in advance. They are about trying to produce more pleasant, accessible, and democratic ways of configuring London's public spaces.

These changes have been controversial. Many people find shared space principles disconcerting and dangerous. Exhibition Road's redevelopment took nearly a decade and involved extensive consultations and debates about safety. There was a lawsuit demanding concessions for persons with visual impairments, which along with demands for resident parking, compromised a pure application of the shared space philosophy. Conflicts such as these are a reminder that the politics of public space are often about rather mundane details, competing demands, and decision-making processes that take place away from more obvious sites of public life. Importantly, they also highlight that laying foundations for better public spaces are about more than the material. In terms of street configuration, for example, they are also about the legal and the regulatory—about things like road codes, liability law, vehicle licensing and registration, and speed limits.

They are also about atmospheres and feelings that shape perceptions about risk, trust, and appropriate behaviour. Sometimes they are about making the unimaginable something that can be experienced or experimented with. Efforts to redesign London's streets illustrate how altering the configuration of public space is far from a straightforward process. It is often about small, incremental changes that can sometimes raise rather profound questions. In this case, the question is about what and whom streets are for, and how best to organise them.

### Street Markets: New Invitations to Inhabit Old Public Spaces

London has had street markets for as long as it has been a city. Some, like Borough and Smithfield, have run continuously since the Middle Ages. Sadly, many traditional markets have been in gradual decline (NABMA, 2005) and some, such as Covent Garden and Billingsgate, have been moved to the edges of the city. Other markets, such as Camden and Portobello Road, seem to be suffering from their own success, at risk of becoming tourist traps, losing much of their cultural relevance. At the same time, there has been an emergence of a range of new street markets across London: temporary pop-up markets, craft markets, food truck markets, German Christmas markets, and especially farmers' markets, which have increased in number by 250% since the late 1990s ('Choice cuts', 2003). Drawing on this enthusiasm and inspired by policy innovations popularised by institutions like New York's Project for Public Spaces, many of London's boroughs have come to view markets as strategic tools for enlivening public spaces, often with the broader aim of generating economic activity. It is possible to read these changes as the continuous commercialisation of the urban landscape. However, markets can play a vital role in providing invitations for public life to come together (Watson, 2009; Watson & Studdert, 2006), for publics to cohere through collective routines of inhabitation.

Take the example of The Prince of Wales Junction in West London. Long a notorious crime hotspot, the Junction was redeveloped through a local partnership which placed the new Maida Hill Market at the centre of broader changes in how the space was designed, managed, and policed. Prior to its redevelopment, the Junction had possessed a public life, albeit one primarily focused on street drinking, drug dealing, and prostitution. The introduction of the market offered a range of new ways for people to inhabit the Junction. It involved setting up new patterns of use: the thrice weekly running of the market, the routines of people breakfasting or lunching, of residents reading the morning paper over a cup of tea, doing the Saturday grocery shopping, and so on. The materials and objects assembled to facilitate these desired changes also acted in some surprising ways to bring new publics together. The moveable chairs and tables at the centre of the market, for example, were not just available for market customers. They were also used by residents from a nearby care home, by the families of traders, and by men reading *The Racing Times* before heading across the street to the bookmaker. Atmospheres previously marked by the presence of illicit activity were altered by new patterns of foot traffic, routines of traders setting up and taking down stalls, of residents browsing, buying, eating, socialising, or just people watching. In short, we could say that the Junction became domesticated—became useful, familiar, trustworthy—as a better kind of public space for most people.

Of course not all of London's new markets have been unambiguously beneficial. Hackney's Broadway Market has been criticised for its role in the gentrification of the surrounding neighbourhood (Bradley, 2010). There have been similar controversies around recent changes to Hackney's Chatsworth Road Market and Brixton Market. Many new markets seem oriented towards attracting tourists or meeting the needs of the middle classes, rather than providing regular conveniences or amenities for a range of local residents. Our point is not that new street markets are inherently good or bad. Rather, we think that they are interesting for the new arrays of practical activities and furnishings and they bring to public spaces. They can help to reimagine even the most struggling of neighbourhoods as potentially hosting a richer variety of offerings, and they provide a smaller-scale, locally based alternative to the seemingly insatiable growth of large supermarkets and shopping malls. As possibilities for configuring the consumption needs of urban inhabitants, they are entangled—as we have seen from the Maida Hill example—in the continuous invention and reinvention of a city's public life in ways that allow for experimentations, innovations, and improvements in how people live together in cities.

### Cycling in London: New Forms of Mobile Publicness

London is not an easy place to be a cyclist. In common perception and everyday practice, the city's streets were long given over to motorised traffic. Yet in the past decade, cycling has seen a remarkable renaissance, and not because of some substantial shift in public policy. The re-emergence of cycling is in large part a solution to the difficulty of moving around a city that has become remarkably congested. Public transport may have improved over the past decade, but in many parts of the city it is still slow and unreliable, not to mention expensive. The growth of biking as a form of everyday mobility has occurred as a broad range of people have discovered it to be a practical, environmentally friendly, inexpensive, and enjoyable way to get around. The widespread and visible growth of cycling not only gives the practice a greater material presence, it acts as a kind of invitation for others to cycle. Fold-up bikes can be seen under the arms of suited city workers as they board the Tube; fixed-gear bikes have become a must-have accessory for east London hipsters; bike shops and 'cycle cafes' have been popping up around the city; and the London Cycle Campaign has more than 11,000 members. The Barclays Cycle Hire scheme has seen 8,000 public bikes added to the city, making cycling available to those without bikes. Through much of central London, rush hour is no longer defined by a crush of cars, buses, and pedestrians, but also by swarms of cyclists weaving in and out of traffic.

London's streets were hardly welcoming to this expansion. Cycling in London remains far more dangerous per kilometre travelled than more cycle-friendly cities like Copenhagen, Münster, or Amsterdam (Morgan, Dale, Le, & Edwards, 2010). Navigating the city by bike involves being marginalised to the edge of narrow streets often lined with guardrails, sharing lanes with buses and taxis, cycle lanes that end abruptly, and multilane gyratory systems designed exclusively with motor vehicles in mind. But as cyclists become a larger proportion of London's vehicular street traffic, car, truck, and van drivers are forced (not often willingly and not always quietly) to accommodate the distinctive rhythms of bicycle propulsion.

What we want to highlight that is not simply that bicycles have been added to the mix of London's traffic, but that cyclists have become involved in domesticating the city in two distinct ways: first, by way of practice, and second, by way of politics. In terms of practice, the material presence and routine habits of cyclists means that bikes have become understood as an ordinary, useful, and routine (if not controversial) part of the everyday urban fabric of London. They are objects that planners, architects, developers, property managers, business owners, and landlords have to reckon with, or face pressure to do so. Cyclists are people with whom automobile drivers can expect to share the road. In terms of politics, what is notable is the clear emergence of a cycling public, a diverse body politic asserting its presence in London's public sphere in various ways. Following John Dewey, we can understand this cycling public in a processual sense, as constituted through 'all those who are affected by the indirect consequences of transactions such to the extent that it is deemed necessary to have those consequences systematically cared for (1927, p. 15–16). Publics thus come together as a relatively spontaneous form of collective action that attempt to meet particular needs or assert particular demands, and not necessarily in coordination with the state (Davidson & Entrikin, 2005). We can see this in the small, loosely organised, and sometimes ephemeral collectives London cyclists have been engaged in: the rise of cycling clubs and coalitions, cycling cafes, cycling fashion shows, critical mass bike rides, bike repair workshops, and online discussion forums. We can also see cycling moving into more formal channels of municipal politics. Debates about the public provision for cyclists were central to both the recent London mayoral elections of 2008 and 2012. Strikingly, the debates did not centre on whether candidates were pro- or anti-cycling. All candidates professed an enthusiasm for cycling and vigorously courted the 'cycling vote'.

The policies of the conservative Mayor Boris Johnson, who was re-elected to a second four-year term in 2012, highlight the ambiguities around these politics. Johnson is himself a cyclist, and stated that his administration would continue the bike-friendly policies of the previous mayor, Ken Livingstone. He thus introduced the widely used cycle hire scheme and began constructing a system of cycle 'super highways' aimed at facilitating the flow of commuter cyclists into central London. Both schemes, it should be noted, were initiated by his predecessor, but were used by Johnson to promote his administration as pro-cycling. At the same time, Johnson has also made significant concessions to motor vehicle lobby groups. He has rolled back the central London congestion charge, allowed motorcyclists to share bus lanes with cyclists, and has consistently shown a bias towards motorised traffic. In the case of the cycle super highways, he was reluctant to extend them into large roundabouts for fear of impeding automobile traffic. The death of two cyclists at the Bow roundabout near the Olympic Park have spurred a range of protests by cycling groups and forced Transport for London to review the implementation of the programme. Similarly, the high profile redevelopment of the approach to Blackfriars Bridge in central London ignored the needs of the high volume of cyclists using the area. This prompted a series of mass protests at the bridge demanding that Transport for London and the mayor reconsider the design and lower the speed limit on the bridge in the interests of cycle safety.

## Conclusion

We have written about three examples of London's public spaces being reinvented and reimagined, but it is possible to think of a whole range of similar cases. None is without certain contradictions or ambivalences, but all present certain possibilities for making the city more inhabitable and mutually beneficial. We might also think of new ways publics are coming together: through innovative forms of political organising such as UK Uncut or London Citizens; through renewed enthusiasm for traditional activities like community gardens and debating societies; or in relatively new activities like charity walks and fun runs, urban gaming, or location-based social networking. There are also new forms of public or quasi-public resource provision: shared car schemes, public bikes, wifi, neighbourhood tool sheds, and Freecycle. And, of course, there are a wide range of electronic forums—some London-specific, some global—for meeting up, sharing ideas and information, mobilising action, debating the rules of public life, and for shaming those who violate them. We can also think of all sorts of new activities that have repopulated London's public spaces. From a rediscovered enthusiasm for picnicking or using the 'beaches' along the River Thames, to new forms of exercising, to name just a couple of instances. The examples of shared space street design, the rise of cycling, and new street markets are interesting not because they present unproblematic responses to challenges associated with urban transformations, for indeed these trends have generated conflict in many ways. Rather, they are interesting for how they illustrate the ongoing alterations, innovations, experimentations, and negotiations that are constantly bubbling up within a city's public spaces. In some cases—as with the recent popularity of cycling—changes emerge as popular responses to new or unmet demands. In others—such as shared space street designs—they are about efforts by urban authorities to intervene upon or engineer the practical, conflicting demands of public space and to enhance what they have to offer.

Positioned against grand narratives of urban transformation, new and shifting forms of inhabiting public life might seem quite mundane. Yet considered in the aggregate, they are important. In thinking about what are apparently smaller stories and practical changes, the grand narratives about the transformations happening in our cites often start to reveal themselves as less coherent, unified, or stable as they are sometimes made out to be. A great deal of the time, cities like London possess a remarkable continuity of form; changes in their public life are often subtle and easy to overlook. For all the attention that sweeping transformations and big mega-projects get, cities and public life are primarily defined by small adaptations, reinventions, and reinterpretations. We have been arguing for the usefulness of domestication as a concept for interpreting urban public space because it provides an expansive set of analytics through which we might attend to subtle processes of change and gradual transformation. To think in terms of inhabitation is to attend more closely to how, exactly, people populate public spaces. The concept of materiality focuses attention on how particular materials and relations between them provide affordances for some kinds of inhabitation and not others. Atmosphere helps in thinking about intensities of feeling and emotion that swirl through cities; they can imbue public spaces with a sense of collective well-being, but also with a sense of unease or even outrage. As an alternative approach to framing analyses of public space in terms of normative concerns for exclusion, encroachment, and claim-making, the concept of domestication offers a set of heuristics that can be put to use in attending to these matters. It can help us make sense of many of the practical problems and potentials right in front of us as we go about urban life.

# Chapter 13

# Everyday Life and Sharing of Open Space in Istanbul's Informal Settlements

*Noah Billig*

Istanbul is unique among European cities: It is a mega-city with a population of 10 to 15 million, 50% of its residents live in informal housing (Leitmann & Baharoglu, 1999), and it is located in both Europe and Asia. These converging factors provide an interesting milieu for studying urbanism and open space. In particular, Istanbul's informal settlements provide a distinctive glimpse into emergent urban social spaces that are at once part of rural tradition (i.e., Anatolian village culture) and urban culture (i.e., modern Istanbul). These informal settlements contain user-built open spaces that host flexible and active sharing and interacting.

This study analyses three Istanbul informal settlements in terms of how their everyday public and private spaces on and near the street are formed, adapted, used, and valued. For this chapter, previous studies evaluating urban open space typologies and their use in Istanbul's informal settlements are evaluated and summarized. Based on these studies, observations are also conducted in the settlements and a pattern language is developed for these settlements. The overlapping boundaries of the private and public spheres are examined. In addition, this study evaluates how the spaces on and near the street become flexible spaces of social, cultural, and economic interaction and sharing.

For this study, public spaces are defined as 'those areas of a neighbourhood to which persons have legal access and can visually observe—its streets and sidewalks, its parks, its places of public accommodation, its public buildings, and the public sectors of its private buildings' (Lofland, 1973, p. 19). Also for this study, *public space* refers to outdoor open spaces.

Because of this complexity of informal settlements, three main aspects of informal settlements/*squatterisation* are proposed as definitions:

1 A transition process reflected in form: 'A transition process from rural to urban life, a transitional life style and its reflection to space' (Turgut, 2001, p. 19).
2 A phenomenon defined in terms of distribution of wealth, social structure, social security, and socioeconomic impacts (Arslan, 1989; Hacihasanoglu & Hacihasanoglu, 2006). Examples in informal neighbourhoods include residents' access to internal social networks and economic opportunities (e.g., jobs or the speculation process of renting self-built apartments). This definition looks past informal settlements as simply a built form.
3 Defined in terms of ownership, legislation, and construction processes. This phenomenon is defined as 'casual buildings which have been built on lands or plots without having any ownership and the right to build on it in terms of building legislation and laws' (Turgut, 2001, p. 19).

## Turkish Informal Settlements

Many studies analyse the planning, development processes, and conditions of the Turkish squatter settlements. Some of these studies also evaluate the architectural spatial elements of the squatter communities, mostly focusing on interior spaces. Other researchers have studied open spaces in Turkish housing settlements, but they have primarily focused on the planned/formal sector (Ozsoy, Altas, Ok, & Pulat, 1996; Turgut-Yildiz & Inalhan, 2007). Also, the particular areas of this study—Pinar, Karanfilkoy, and Fatih Sultan Mehmet neighbourhoods—have been studied by multiple researchers (Alkan, 2006; Arefi, 2011; Ergenoglu, Türkyelmaz, Baytin, & Aytug, 2005; Ertaş, 2010; Gonul & Corut, 2007; Gulersoy, 1999; Keyder, 2005). This study seeks to offer an additional analysis of Istanbul's informal settlements through examination of their open spaces. In particular, the street and areas near the street are studied in three informal settlements as the places where everyday sharing takes place.

Istanbul informal settlements are often viewed as some of the world's most liveable informal communities. This is partly because they often have a great amount of infrastructure in place, higher levels of sanitation, more open space, and municipal government representation (Mahmud & Duyar-Kienast, 2001; Neuwirth, 2005; Neuwirth, 2007). These attributes have led some to see Turkish squatter settlements as an example for informal neighbourhoods in other countries (Tibaijuka, 2005).

Turkey's informal housing initially occurred simultaneously with the country's rural to urban migrations for industrial jobs (Baharoglu & Leitmann, 1998; Egercioğlu & Özdemir, 2007; Ergun, 1991; Keyder, 2005; Metz, 1995). This informal development began to emerge in the 1950s, as housing demands for these new urban workers outpaced housing supply. Istanbul has experienced this phenomenon, with 50% of its current population living in informal settlements (Leitmann & Baharoglu, 1999). Senyapli provides a summary of the policies and history of Turkish informal housing (see Table 13.1).

Turkey's informal housing has often been analysed as a problematic phenomenon in need of change (Dündar, 2001; Tas & Lightfoot, 2005; Türker-Devecigil, 2005; Türkoglu, 1997; Yalcintan & Erbas, 2003). For example, Turker-Devecigil (2005) examines it normatively as places in need of urban transformation. Also, studies have consistently labelled Turkey's squatter residents as an 'inferior other' (Erman, 2001).

There is also a call for an understanding of Turkish informal settlements that goes beyond such normative transformations:

> Such an urbanization starting with migration to towns from rural agricultural-traditional areas and ending in an urban, industrial-modern society can be analysed for its values of culture-space interactions according to different scales, leading to a better understanding of *squatterisation* as a fact, not only as a problem area. (Turgut, 2001, p. 19)

There have been studies and articles that have focused on Turkish informal settlements as innovative environmental adaptations:

> The result is no mass slum. Even the most basic of these settlements—a hillside of one-storey brick of wood huts with two or three narrow rooms apiece—has the feel of a settled community. The place is dusty, but not dirty; it has schools and mosques; there is space, sometimes a small garden, around each home; the children's clothes are clean; people are poor, but not desperately. . . . This shows that Turks are self-reliant, ingenious and, as citizens or city authorities, admirably practical about bending rules. ('Cities of', 1991, pp. 15–17)

Cultural, social, and psychological components in traditional Turkish houses are analysed, including organization rules, the effects of the basic social components, and the presence of these principles within Turkish informal housing before and after 1980 (Ozdemir & Gencosmanoglu, 2007).

Table 13.1 Framework of transformations of squatter housing in Turkey.

| | 1950–1960 | 1960–1970 | 1970–1980 | Post-1980 |
|---|---|---|---|---|
| Government Model | Nation state, welfare state | Nation state | Nation state questioned, rise of the local | Nation state narrows down, increasing dominancy of the local governance concept |
| Economic Policy | Liberal development model, Keynesian policy, rapid development, government intervention for full employment and stability, industry led growth, foreign aid, eradication of poverty, and equity in distribution of income to be achieved in time in development, growth poles, spill over effect | Planned development, import substitution model, internal market protected by customs, quotas, only factors of production imported, neoclassic economic approach | Impact of oil crisis, urban problems hinder national development, solution of these will lead to general development, World Bank enters the poverty agenda, collaboration with IMF, criticisms of import substitution models, reorganization of production towards flexibility | Foreign debt crisis and transition to neoliberal, export-oriented, privatization model, flexibilisation of markets, social policies structured by market forces |
| World Bank Policy | Conducts research especially in Latin America and Asia to clarify the squatter problem | Research continues, culture of poverty, poverty is fate, therefore it is the problem of the poor | Restructuring of policy after Turner approach, financial support to project-based site and services | Restructuring of policy, enabling general urban policy, housing and urbanization finance organizations |
| Type of Urban Planning | Comprehensive | Comprehensive | Incremental, project-level approaches, strategic planning, infrastructure development | Structure planning, strategic planning |
| Dominant Urban Land Supply Model | Illegal invasion | Shared ownership | Housing cooperatives | Mass housing, cooperatives, transformation of squatter housing |

(Continued)

*Table 13.1* Continued

| | 1950–1960 | 1960–1970 | 1970–1980 | Post-1980 |
|---|---|---|---|---|
| Public Approach to Squatter Housing Problem | Squatting is an illegal and dilapidated housing problem, elementary measures to stop or to redirect migrant flow, the problem is temporary; public housing, multiparty system starts political patronage | Housing sector is unproductive, squatting is a housing problem, central government intervenes through Law 775, legalizing and classifying existing stock, prohibiting new stock, political patronage expands, worker migration to Europe eases migration pressure on cities | Populist subsidies to rural area, credit flow and subsidy to prices of agricultural products slows down rate of migration flow, politisation of squatter housing areas between nationalist and radical left groups cooperative organization in housing sector; squatter problem more and more identified with poverty, starts to lose its housing connotation | The problem is now poverty, rent allocation provided through Law 2981, commercialization of squatter areas, transformation, forced migration from the east, increased migration to especially coastal cities, internal fragmentation and rising conflicts in squatter communities due to decreasing opportunities |

*Source:* Senyapili (2004)

The laws governing Istanbul's informal housing changed to allow higher buildings in 1983–84: 'In Turkey, in 1984, each squatter was given permission to build 4 floors and many squatter areas rapidly transformed and turned into high density areas' (Terzi & Fulin, 2005, p. 1). This higher-density pattern is found in Pinar and Fatih Sultan Mehmet. Typical physical differences in the old and newer squatter neighbourhoods include: 'Traditional squatter areas' . . . characteristics are 1–2 storey single family buildings, 100–250 persons/ha neighbourhood density. New squatter areas . . . characteristics are 3–5 stories attached or detached apartments, relatively new buildings, 250–500 persons/ha neighbourhood density' (Türkoglu, 1997, p. 58).

The physical progression of tradition squatter housing—from a temporary one-room building to a semi-permanent multiroom building to a larger, multistorey permanent building has been analysed (Turgut, 2001). Turgut, Aksoy, Paker, Inceoglu, and Saglamer also take this analysis to the relationship between homes and streets in squatter communities (Turgut et al., 1995). These morphological studies provide examples of the Turkish squatter settlement as a physical manifestation. Senyapili analyses Turkish informal settlements as places of social and architectural flexibility (1978). Cagdas also evaluates the spatial, morphological, and functional aspects of Turkish informal settlements, but stays at the scale of the house (Cagdas, 1995).

The culture of the Anatolian village remains strong in the Istanbul squatter communities (N. Ergun, personal communication, 2008). This can be seen when one traces the origins of squatter residents:

> One finds, among the realities of *gecekondus*, that they are dynamic social environments whose residents maintain implicit and explicit links to rural areas, extended families, and village groups even as they are economically integrated into the employment offered within the city. It can be shown that when building *gecekondus*, immigrants were guided by knowledge they learned while living as rural people or village residents.
>
> To better understand *gecekondus*, architects . . . must also understand the housing communities as positive adaptations by rural masses to the urban situation in ways that are fundamentally sensitive to nature and open to change. (Cavender, 2006, p. 1)

Many within a given squatter community are from the same or neighbouring towns in Anatolian Turkey. For instance, Pinar Mahalle's residents primarily come from the Sivas, Kars, Ordu, Amasya, Zonguldak, and Kastamonu areas of Anatolia (N. Ergun, personal communication, 2008), while Karanfilköy's residents are mostly from central Anatolia and the Black Sea area (Alkan, 2006). The common heritage and geographical roots of the residents do seem to explain some of the strong social ties and activities. The rich social interactions that get played out in the streets and the spaces near the streets within these informal communities are directly linked to neighbours knowing each other. Indeed, Ergenoglu et al.'s (2005) study of Fatih Sultan Mehmet points out that the sense of community and social support is linked to a common background:

> Close social relationships and collaboration between the resident are important characteristics of these settlements. Residents try to support each other and act respectfully to each other. One of the reasons for the people belonging to the same ethnic group to live together is this characteristic; because, they know they will get support when faced with a problem. (p. 9)

Every Istanbul neighbourhood has representation with the municipal government through a delegate called a *muhtar*. *Muhtars* and district mayors play the most important role in conveying demands from citizens to service providers. These part-time representatives to the State are found in every neighbourhood of Turkish cities. They channel demand for infrastructure and services to utilities in either an *ad hoc* manner or in a structured way (Baharoglu & Leitmann, 1998).

With regard to the public open spaces of a given settlement, the *muhtar's* representation can be a key for receiving services and infrastructure, which is crucial for how open spaces are formed. For instance, the street paving, water connections, and other utility upgrades are often linked to neighbourhood lobbying through their *muhtar.* Also, land use and development issues are often voiced through the *muhtar.* Thus, many physical factors pertaining to the creation, adaptation and use of open spaces are related to the *muhtar* (e.g., infrastructure allocation that alters roads).

### Introduction to the Study's Settlements

Pinar, Karanfilkoy, and Fatih Sultan Mehmet informal neighbourhoods are all located in European Istanbul, approximately one kilometre from the Bosphorus Strait. Karinfilkoy and Fatih Sultan Mehmet settlements were originally connected along part of their settlement. The construction of the Trans European Motorway (TEM) (which leads to the Fatih Sultan Mehmet Bridge [completed in 1988] crossing the Bosphorus Straight) divided the neighbourhood into two distinctly separate settlements (N. Ergun, personal communication, 2008). This division caused by the TEM also coincided with changes in Istanbul's squatter settlement laws—some neighbourhoods were allowed to build at higher densities, such as Pinar and Fatih Sultan Mehmet.

During the 1980s, along with all the other shantytown dwellers, residents in Armutlu (Fatih Sultan Mehmet) were also given the right to obtain papers that allowed them to regularize their possession rights so as to be able to construct four- or five-storey apartment buildings on their lots, which until then had contained picturesque single-family dwellings surrounded by rudimentary gardens (Keyder, 2005).

A few neighbourhoods, such as Karanfilkoy, were not allowed to increase densities due to preservation development rules associated with their proximity to the Bosphorus Straight (Alkan, 2006). Since these two events in the early 1980s, the neighbourhoods have developed separate urban design patterns and attributes. Fatih Sultan Mehmet has a main square near the TEM, a denser settlement pattern, and high-rise apartment buildings. In contrast, Karanfilkoy is removed from the freeway and has maintained mostly one- and two-storey detached housing with gardens and yards. As such, Karanfilkoy is understood to have many of the physical and spatial attributes that were found in the original Turkish informal settlements (2006).

In summary, the mix of development patterns in Pinar, Fatih Sultan Mehmet, and Karanfilkoy provides an interesting and varied spatial cross-section of Istanbul's informal neighbourhoods. However, all three neighbourhoods share a similar history in terms of general cultural antecedents. That is, Pinar, Karanfilkoy, and Fatih Sultan Mehmet residents typically have come from the Anatolia region of Turkey (Asia) after 1950 (Alkan, 2006; N. Ergun, personal communication, 2008). Most residents work nearby as physical labourers, civil servants, and/or are self-employed. These neighbourhoods share a similar culture, but also have unique social, cultural, and spatial identities.

### Previous Pilot Studies

Previous pilot studies have used observation analysis to evaluate open spaces types and uses in the informal settlements of Pinar, Karanfilkoy, and Fatih Sultan Mehmet (Billig, 2009a, 2009b, 2010). These studies found that the street and areas near the street are the most used spaces in the settlements. These spaces also contained interesting and innovative user-defined adaptations. One study evaluated different open space types and their use patterns in a settlement (Billig, 2009a). It found that the main street, side streets, and the areas immediately adjacent to the side streets were the most used and heterogeneous spaces in the settlement. Another study found street use—particularly residential streets and the spaces near them—much greater in an informal settlement than a planned settlement in Istanbul (Billig, 2009b). A third study evaluated differences and similarities in the settlements in regard to their adaptations of infrastructure

(Billig, 2010). Again, the street and spaces near the street were open-ended and flexible spaces. The infrastructure of the road was co-opted by residents for many uses other than driving cars, including informal and formal economic activity, play, sitting, conversations, eating, and so forth (Billig, 2010). Although the constructs from each study varied (i.e., open space types and use, street use in formal verses informal settlements, and open space/infrastructure relationships), they all found the street and areas near the street to be vital as adaptable spaces that can accommodate a multitude of users and uses.

## Observations

The three settlements were observed for open space use and type, with particular emphasis on identifying a pattern language (Alexander, 2002; Alexander, Ishikawa & Silverstein, 1977). The open spaces typologies observed were informed by the aforementioned pilot studies in the settlements. Thus, main streets, side streets, and the spaces near the streets were observed. Also, parks, mosque gardens, and other undefined green spaces were observed. Photographs and field notes were taken for each settlement, recording the various ways the open spaces were used. The notes were primarily qualitative descriptions. The observations were the basis for defining a pattern language for the settlements.

Alexander defines patterns as 'a rule for making or partly making some important type of centre, necessary to the life of a living human environment' (2002, pp. 344–345) and also gives 11 essential ideas that make pattern languages. Observing and recording recurring patterns, using Alexander's 11 features as an operationalizing guide, results in a 'pattern language' for the settlements. It should be noted that this study uses Alexander's features numbered 1 through 9, as 10 and 11 are more about applying a pattern language to planning, design, and development projects, whereas this project is concerned with observation. Alexander summarizes the observation technique for discovering a pattern language as follows:

> The essential technique in the observations of centres, in any social situation, and in any culture, is to allow the feelings to generate themselves, inside *you*. You have to say, "What would I do if I were one of the people living here, what would it be like for me?" thus inserting yourself into the situation, and using your own common sense and feelings as a measuring instrument. (2002, p. 352)

The patterns identified and described in Karanfilköy and Fatih Sultan Mehmet are successful examples of people and a culture creating living centres that follow the *generic* patterns that Alexander advocates. Importantly, these patterns are successful in both the context of each neighbourhood, and the context of the modern, urbanizing Istanbul of the last 50 or so years. As Alexander points out, such examples are rare:

> The crux of the whole thing is that we seek patterns which are *good*, patterns which will generate life when we create them in a building built in the context we are facing…In our modern world, where societies are often in flux, the stability and coherence of such a traditional society is rarely found. Instead, people are usually struggling to create for themselves a system of coherent environmental objects and spaces, in which they can live well, be comfortable, and feel at ease. (2002, p. 346)

Some of the patterns found in the settlements are patterns found in *A Pattern Language* and *The Nature of Order—Book Two* (Alexander, 2002; Alexander et al., 1977). As Alexander mentions, there are patterns unique to each place, as well as patterns that are successful across various cultures and places but are manifested distinctively in each place (Alexander, 2002). This study identifies both.

Table 13.2 identifies and sometimes briefly describes patterns found in Pinar, Fatih Sultan Mehmet, and Karanfilköy that contribute to greater wholeness and often stronger sharing. The list is divided into categories of spatial, structural, and/or social characteristics.

*Table 13.2* Patterns in Pinar, Fatih Sultan Mehmet, and Karanfilköy, Istanbul

*House, garden and street relationships*

1. Gardens near the street
2. Houses and stoops form the street (in Pinar and Fatih Sultan Mehmet only)
3. Narrow gathering stoops between house and street (in Pinar and Fatih Sultan Mehmet only)
4. Windows on the street (in Pinar and Fatih Sultan Mehmet only)
5. Patios between house and street (found more in Karanfilkoy)
6. Degrees of publicness/intimacy gradient. In Karanfilkoy, there is an intimacy gradient in residences that goes from more public on the street, to semi-public in the patios and gardens, to more private in the homes. Pinar and Fatih Sultan Mehmet have two main types of intimacy gradients. One is with homes that have a yard, patio or stoop to form semi-public space. The other is where an apartment building has a zero lot line with the street or sidewalk, but still has some elevation to give privacy to some quarters, such as the higher floors. In the latter case, the intimacy gradient is weaker.
7. Interplay between interior private house and public street (conversations, etc.)
8. Gardens/patios/yards interlock with street (found more in Karanfilkoy)

*Gardens and vegetation*

9. Green near the streets
10. Private yards/gardens (found more in Karanfilkoy)
11. Half-hidden gardens. In Karanfilkoy, many gardens are half hidden by low gates, low walls, and vegetation. This half-hidden quality provides a simultaneous intimacy and openness; privacy and welcome. Some yards in Pinar and Fatih Sultan Mehmet are half hidden by gates, walls, and vegetation. Here the hidden yards feel more private and less open to the street than in Karanfilköy.
12. Walled gardens and yards (found more in Karanfilkoy)

13. Living courtyards and patios
14. Living walls. Many shrubs, trees, and walls or fences with vines growing on them form walls between the street and yards and between yards.
15. Gardening (as an activity). Many residents are active in gardening, including growing vegetables and flowers and caring for trees and shrubs.
16. Extensive pruning and maintenance of plants; Respect and care for trees
17. Gardens and patios interlock (found more in Karanfilkoy). Gardens and patios flow into each other, helping to form distinct boundaries and spaces. Also, the boundaries where they interlock often become spaces in themselves.
18. Structures modified to accommodate trees
19. Green space and fences form the street (found more in Karanfilkoy)
20. Green streets
21. Connection to the earth
22. Fruit trees
23. Gardens growing wild
24. Garden seats
25. Vegetable garden
26. Climbing plants
27. Gardens in buckets and/or pots
28. Two- to three-storey buildings (Pinar and Fatih Sultan Mehmet)
29. One- to two-storey houses (Karanfilkoy)
30. House clusters/groups (found more in Karanfilkoy)
31. Entrance transitions and thresholds
32. Gates
33. Archways
34. Decorative window safety bars
35. Roof seats
36. Lean-tos
37. Outdoor rooms
38. Common areas at the heart
39. Roughness
40. Warm and rich colours for (some) houses

41. Outdoor sitting circles/seat spots
42. ArchwaysArches, quite often decorative with various wrought iron designs and growing vines, are common in Fatih Sultan Mehmet. They most often signal a threshold.
43. Front door seats
44. Street seats (particularly in Pinar and Fatih Sultan Mehmet)
45. Different chairs
46. Sitting wall
47. Things from your life

*Networks and infrastructure*

48. Loose, informal paths to outside of neighbourhood
49. Taxi stands
50. Dolmus (mini-buses)
51. Busline
52. Hierarchy of streets
53. Organic street patterns with undulating edges
54. Network of paths, streets, and cars
55. Distinct, yet permeable border/identifiable neighbourhood
56. Main gateways (kind of)

*Social activities and relationships*

57. Activity nodes
58. Household chores in gardens, patios, and/or yards
59. Eyes on the street
60. Conversations with passers-by
61. Cats
62. Dogs
63. Mosque-sacred space forms a centre
64. Calm streets
65. Quiet yards
66. Car-pedestrian symbiosis (on the side/small streets, not on the main roads through the settlement)
67. Streetball (soccer/football, basketball)
68. Bicycles in the street
69. Connected play (to other children, visitors, adults, nature, the physical neighbourhood, etc.)
70. Children in street, public spaces, and private spaces (with and without adult supervision)
71. Multiple generations (life cycle)
72. Men and women
73. Household mix
74. House for a small family/for one person/for a couple
75. Housing clusters for extended family
76. Old people throughout neighbourhood
77. Teenage society
78. Family
79. Friends
80. Web of shopping. The main commercial street provides multiple small businesses.
81. Work community and socioeconomic relationships and networking
82. Physical work and adaptations
83. Self-governing workshops and offices
84. Small services without red tape. The residents often provide direct services, such as repairs and building, by dealing directly with each other.
85. Street cafes and/or food stands on or near the street
86. Restaurants
87. Teahouses for gathering of men
88. Small grocery stores
89. Produce stores
90. Produce sold on streets and from trucks

The people of Pinar, Karanfilköy, and Fatih Sultan Mehmet have been largely successful in creating and repeating patterns that are *good* and generate life. As Alexander points out, the patterns and centres found in these neighbourhoods get to the heart of the matter of the residents' experiences and functions (Alexander, 2002, pp. 357–360). The patterns listed in this study are less concerned, for the most part, with stylistic concerns, and instead concerned with the important essentials and life of the place and spaces in the neighbourhoods.

Most patterns are found in all three settlements—Pinar, Fatih Sultan Mehmet, and Karanfilköy. The distinctions between the three settlements in terms of pattern languages most often emerge from differences in building height, size and type, and what those characteristics do to form the spatial and social relationships to people and their environment. For example, the street in Pinar and Fatih Sultan Mehmet is often more distinct as a social place in areas where there is a zero lot line (Figures 13.1–13.3), compared to the looser use of the street in Karanfilköy (Figure 13.4) where it borders a garden and/or garden wall.

*Figure 13.1* A cantilevered, user-built car park adapted for tea, Istanbul.

*Figure 13.2* Daily chores on and near the street, Istanbul.

*Figure 13.3* Seasonal fruit for sale on main commercial street, Istanbul.

*Figure 13.4* Residential gardens near the street, Istanbul.

Related to building size and placement, other differences in patterns between the three settlements involve the relationship with the street. Pinar and Fatih Sultan Mehmet's buildings and open spaces front the street—and in some cases the open spaces are in the street (Figures 13.1– 13.3). Karanfilköy, in contrast, more often has a buffer of gardens and/or yards between the buildings and street (Figure 13.4). This has the effect of making the recurring patterns more often happen in private or semi-private spaces.

The patterns that involve connections to plants and earth are found in both settlements. However, Karanfilköy has more connections to the plants and earth, and these connections are more often found immediately adjacent to people's homes in the form of gardens and yards (Figure 13.4). Pinar and Fatih Sultan Mehmet have these features, but the connections to the plants and earth are more often juxtaposed with hardscape surfaces, such as concrete paving and planters. This confirms Alkan's (2006) intensive study of Karanfilköy. Alkan identifies the residents' attitudes towards plants, nature and 'greenness':

> These features, being a green and low storey settlement, are also used as very strong arguments in the identity construction of the neighbourhood. In most of the declarations by the neighbourhood, it is always mentioned that Karanfilköy is quite different from the other *gecekondu* areas as well as close settlements like Sarı Konaklar, Bahçeşehir etc. in terms of being green and sensitive to the environment. "Since the inhabitants prevented massive concrete development, attached importance to green and they are careful about air pollution with their cultural and environmental consciousness, Karanfilköy became the 'lungs' of the region," states one of the declarations. They claim that they are not "gecekondu" but "green-kondu" in Istanbul. In short, green characteristic of Karanfilköy appears as a very important feature to defend the neighbourhood against the possible attacks, although it has a very physical attachment to the place. (2006, pp. 64–65)

This observation is important in terms of shared spaces. The residents of all three settlements, but particularly Karanfilköy, share their spaces via the context of green infrastructure. That is, the garden and the shared activities that go along with that space become the vehicle for social interaction, physical exertion, and open-ended activities. For example, the gardens in Karanfilköy often host gardening (planting, pruning, weeding, fertilizing, harvesting, etc.), eating, household chores, play, and so on. These activities take place in—and extend the spatial extent of—the crucial area of semi-public/semi-private activities. The flexibility and relaxed atmosphere of these gardens near the street act as open-ended spaces that are able to host practical, social, playful, private, and public activities. They might be thought of as the spaces that tie the neighbourhood together in Karanfilköy. It must be noted that their close proximity to the street is crucial for their success. A wholly private garden space could ostensibly be open-ended for the private users, but it would lack the socially cohesive and impromptu elements that are found next to the public streets. Thus, the interplay of the street and the gardens near the street is a crucial aspect in their success.

The pattern languages in each settlement reflect both step-by-step, on the ground adaptations *and* repeated elements used by many of the residents. These patterns thus reflect both individual adjustments and neighbourly/community cohesion of physical parts. The observations and subsequent pattern identification confirm findings from the aforementioned pilot studies in regard to peoples' use of open spaces and the types of spaces used. That is, people use the street and the spaces near the street much more than other open spaces (Figures 13.1–13.5). Also, people gather in heterogeneous groups in these spaces (i.e., in groups with both sexes and multiple ages) (Figure 13.1 and Figure 13.5).

Sharing on and near the streets is widely practised and experienced by the residents of each informal settlement. Economic activities, gardening with neighbours, playing, household chores,

*Figure 13.5.* Seasonal garden near the street, Istanbul.

conversations, and eating can all be seen, smelled, heard, tasted, and felt on the streets. These flexible spaces for shared activities push boundaries between public and private spaces. Windows, patios, steps, and walls all become conduits for interactions between public and private. For example, boys play football in the street and summon a friend at the window. This boy's living room becomes a shared semi-public space for a few moments, while the street becomes an extension of his family's space. Moments later, that spatial relationship changes and the living room once again becomes more private as the boy's friends bike away. Delineations are there, but they become adapted and blurry. These findings confirm Alkan's observations regarding Karanfilköy:

> There are not definite borders between public and private in the neighbourhood itself, since the neighbourhood is treated as a common public space, because of strong sense of belonging to the place. The borders blurred in Karanfilköy because of the uncertainness of the property rights and habit of using the space by the locals. Since there are very strong social relations between the locals, the streets and the semi-open places of the houses become public places used by the inhabitants. The streets in Karanfilköy are also places for their social interaction. (2006, p. 69)

Another example of sharing in the settlements is in the economic activities—both formal and informal (Figure 13.3). Formal retail restaurants and services line the main streets, often spilling out onto the sidewalk. Also, they often accommodate informal or temporary economic activities, such as selling seasonal fruits and vegetables on front steps and out of trucks (Figure 13.3). Informal economic activities also exist on the sidestreets. These activities often share time and space with neighbours, family, and friends, as well as with other activities.

The small public parks host few activities. However, those that were observed included sharing food, conversations, play, and so forth. The parks held spaces that were open-minded in terms of activities. In contrast, the mosque garden saw activity, but it was all men and included less sharing of conversations, food, and so on. This study is not qualifying these spaces (in the parks and mosque gardens) and their activities as either good or bad. However, it is clear that the street and spaces near the street are where the strongest mix of activities occurs. That is, these spaces are more open-minded and heterogeneous, hosting multiple activities and people at once and/or in the same day.

The observations for this study also included the literal sharing of space, food, conversation, play, and goods with the author. Residents repeatedly offered tea, shared in impromptu football games, and so on. One family gave goods—a coffee cup and some socks. This sharing all took place either on the public spaces of the street or at the intersection of the public and private near the street. Although interactions and observations occurred in other spaces (e.g., parks and mosque gardens), the aforementioned street spaces and spaces near the street were the only places of sharing with the author. It might be inferred that the novelty of having a foreigner in the neighbourhood elicited such sharing actions. This may be true. It also may be true that this same sharing would occur in other Turkish neighbourhoods as a result of cultural and social norms which encourage sharing. However, a pilot study shows that planned neighbourhoods use their open spaces on and near the street differently from informal settlement residents' use of space (Billig, 2009b). Within this study's neighbourhoods, some types of open spaces (i.e., the street and spaces near the street) saw sharing and some did not. Thus, these neighbourhoods' shared spaces are associated with the public and semi-public spaces of the street.

The spaces near and on the street in Pinar, Karanfilköy, and Fatih Sultan Mehmet can also be thought of in terms of openness and social tolerance. The aforementioned observations, pilot studies, and survey bear this out, as does research on the settlements (Alkan, 2006; Ergenoglu et al., 2005). Ergenoglu et al. point out the residents' perceptions of freedom in their open spaces in Fatih Sultan Mehmet:

> [T]he people [who] reside in squatter settlements see these areas as "toleranced" living spaces [where] the residents can act freely. These people also think that the living spaces in the planned areas are "pressuring/restraining" that one has to be more cautious. (2005, p. 9)

## Conclusion

Using data triangulation and convergence of evidence (Yin, 2003, pp. 97–100) through multiple modes of inquiry, this study confirms that the public open spaces most valued and used in Pinar, Karanfilköy, and Fatih Sultan Mehmet are the spaces on and near the street. These are the spaces for everyday life, interaction, and sharing. They are a result of decades-long government self-help housing policies and the Turkish informal culture. That is, government policies and socioeconomic conditions encouraged the Turkish informal housing phenomenon, and the culture of the Turkish residents—originally based in Anatolia—provided the milieu for the street as an active public space. These everyday spaces are heterogeneous in terms of age, sex, and activity type. They also accommodate a variety of spatial and functional changes through the seasons, the week, and the day. The spaces can be seen as successful adaptations by the residents. Hopefully these adapted spaces for sharing everyday life can be an inspiration to other cities and neighbourhoods.

Chapter 14

# Segregative Power of Violence in Belfast and Naples

## Exploring the Role of Public Spaces Reconnecting Divided Societies

*Gabriella Esposito De Vita*

## Rationale for this Research

Some preliminary remarks should be made before entering into the body of this chapter. The investigation presented here focuses on the built environment as an expression of a multicultural and multifactor urban demand by a transforming society (Sassen, 1991). 'Population groups, differentiated by criteria of ability, age, gender, class, ethnicity, sexual preference and religion, have different claims on the city for a full life and, in particular, on the built environment. How can planners contrive to make positive responses to these claims?' (Sandercock, 2000).

In order to give a response to this wider claim in terms of planning and design for diversities, this research started by focusing—according to the seminal notion by Lefebvre (1968) of the 'right to the city'—on a specific sector of the built environment that includes places for encounter, exchange, playfulness, and civic gathering: that is, public spaces. Public spaces are expressions of a changing society (Carmona et al., 2010) and their role as places open to dialogue between diverse components of society needs to be preserved, in order to facilitate intercultural relationships and non-conflicting contacts.

As will be demonstrated through the development of the following case studies, urban spaces that are formed either diachronically through subsequent cultural cross-pollinations, or synchronically through the action of different communities, are more welcoming and recognizable for anyone who accesses them when compared to urban areas that are poor in multicultural influences and anonymously discourage the use of public spaces for relational activities (Clemente & Esposito De Vita, 2008). In contexts of positive quality of life and where public spaces are well connected and recognizable, high levels of conviviality and density of human relationships can be developed (Gehl, 1987). 'Public space, if organized properly, offers the potential for social communion by allowing us to lift our gaze from the daily grid, and as a result, increase our disposition towards the other' (Amin, 2008, p. 6). Shared spaces have played, on the one hand, the role of symbols of collective well-being and formation of civic culture and, on the other hand, of competitive struggle and social conflicts (Beguinot, 2009). The contemporary public space is the urban place that, more than others, has been influenced by recent transformations of production-related activities and acceleration of dynamics of the urban system (Crang, 2000). The 'city of stones', the built environment, has changed through the centuries, adapting itself to the transformations of the 'experienced city', that is, the way people are 'living' urban public spaces (Beguinot & Cardarelli, 1992). 'In an age of urban sprawl, multiple usage of public space and proliferation of the sites of political and cultural expression, it seems odd to expect public spaces to fulfil their traditional role as spaces of civic inculcation and political participation' (Amin, 2008, p. 5). It obviously cannot be affirmed that the design or redesign of public spaces is the unique condition for solving social tensions and inequalities (Marcuse, 2009). Nevertheless, the different cultures that coexist in contemporary cities impact upon architecture and *forma urbis* and, more specifically, on the form of public places, in the same way that lifestyles and conflicting habits impact upon change in the use and perception of such spaces (Choay & Merlin, 2000). Conflicts, risks, and insecurity appear exaggerated in the perception of urban inhabitants due to mistrust and incommunicability among the diverse components of society, and generate impacts on the physical city; gated communities, video surveillance, and abandonment of public spaces are some of the emerging phenomena changing the face of large areas of cities (Madanipour, 2004; Shaftoe, 2008).

As a result of the research in progress and that of previous phases of studies on the intercultural city, this chapter focuses on urban public spaces as well as facilities and services for public use. This field of research is useful for pursuing a common framework to connect the diverse issues that follow:

• Activities for encounters
• Sites for public gathering and/or for conflicting expressions
• Urban identities that can be renewed or dissipated
• Networks of civic practices and public culture
• Demands for recognizable and secure spaces for everyday life.

Cities are losing elements that make their own public spaces recognizable and that facilitate urban populations in orienting themselves (Mazzoleni, 1990); in addition, there is a proliferation of paternalistic policies aimed at stimulating the melting pot through codified normalized 'units' of ethnicity that are reproducing the 'dialectal' character of the original *forma urbis*. The inadequacy of both approaches is made evident by the failure to construct a new inclusive and shared identity (Harvey, 2000). This scenario cannot be isolated and analysed *in vitro* using laboratory techniques; since the city is a complex system, it escapes rigid classification. It is therefore necessary to pursue a systematization that does not produce standardization and uniformity (Merleau-Ponty, 1945), but should instead be a source of inspiration for building strategies for public spaces that combine different cultural needs. In this way, public spaces and public-use spaces (that is, on private property) can be identified as strategic places to be designed according to the need for new relationships between local identities in order to collaborate in preventing conflicts (Whyte, 1980). Public spaces represent successful experiences only when these places appear as a complete representation of identitarian values of their respective urban communities (Madanipour, 2003b). All peoples show a strong tendency to live in recognizable places (Mazzoleni, 1990). Therefore, a clear need exists to provide for the creation or adaptation of public spaces through participatory processes shared by different social components in order to meet the needs of a multicultural society, enhancing the symbolic value of public space already evident in the historical and consolidated city (Jacobs, 1961). Although, according to Amin, 'it is too heroic a leap to assume that making a city's public spaces more vibrant and inclusive will improve urban democracy' (2008, p. 7), we need to investigate the grey area between an optimistic determination to improve the quality of public spaces in a consistent way and a fuzzy renunciation thereof (Clemente & Esposito De Vita, 2008).

The work in progress here presented is aimed at exploring the possibility of directing urban development towards solving long-standing and renewed social and cultural conflicts—strongly influenced by the suitability of spaces for promoting primary relationships, including those of a transient and unstable dimension—and for offering inhabitants the opportunity to have their increasingly complex needs met (Bonnes, Bonaiuto, Nenci, & Carrus, 2011). In accordance with Habermas's observation that 'public spaces become the object of practices of cultural representation, with which the public sphere is arguably more and more concerned' (1989), this research considers the holistic idea of public spaces as an expression of the cultural gaps within a conflicting society and, at the same time, as place for improving conflict-solving practices by favouring public gathering (Fraser, 1992).

Through a case study approach, this research deals with the role that the design of existing or new public spaces can play in meeting these complex needs, fostering intercultural encounters, and mitigating conflict between the different social groups. The factors taken into consideration—with the aim of grasping the complexity and avoiding reductive simplification and crude determinism—are as follows:

- Profiles of public space uses with their characteristics and changes due to the placement of new habits and lifestyles in the 'society of flows' (Castells, 1983)
- Risk perception and the sense of insecurity related to the organization and use of public spaces in areas beset by sectarian conflicts or criminal uses (Low, 2006)
- Enrichment arising from the coexistence of different identities in public spaces (Madanipour, 2003b), improving possible conflict-solving practices.

Based on these reflections, the main focus of this ongoing research is to develop a methodological approach for integrating urban design and community planning in order to provide operative guidelines for producing places for an inclusive urban life. 'Social exclusion is a multi-dimensional process and it needs multi-dimensional responses, which include the provision of public spaces' (Madanipour, 2004, p. 284). Among the different forms of public spaces, such as streets, squares, plazas, market places, playgrounds, and parks, as well as their multiple roles—classified as physical, ecological, psychological, social, political, economic, symbolic, and aesthetic (Akkar Ercan, 2007)—a paramount role can be recognized: A public space can be a place for free expression of activities, rhythms, and perceptions, providing a venue for expression of diversity—of diverse ways of being and living.

The theoretical approach has been tested by pilot fieldwork in Belfast (UK) and Naples (Italy). Belfast was chosen due to its interreligious conflicts and Naples for its widespread criminal influences, both of which have produced a visible and profound multifaceted crisis involving the transformation of public spaces. The case studies refer to the extreme expression of the 'interfaces' between Protestant and Catholic communities divided by the so-called 'peace walls' in Belfast, as well as the abandoned parks and playgrounds in Neapolitan peripheries oriented to criminal activities. The case study of Naples focuses on an extreme case of abandonment and informal transformation of public spaces due to the management of criminal activities by the so-called 'Camorra'. On the one hand, the urban pattern of some areas in Belfast offers the opportunity to identify the impact of social conflict on the forms and uses of public spaces and on the 'securitization' of the urban grid. On the other hand, the northern fringe of Naples—characterized by a high crime rate and pervasive illegal activities such as drug trafficking and prostitution—represents a significant expression of informal transformations that occur to community facilities and public spaces as a result of fear factors and conflicts among criminal organizations. Both of these experiences—although they are not readily comparable—offer an opportunity to reflect on the design and management of borderline public spaces in producing and/or dealing with the above-mentioned conflicts. In these selected contexts, communities are troubled and public spaces play a contradictory role, losing almost every possibility of being used as intended, as well as increasing marginality and associated risks. Therefore, the research focuses on these extreme contexts as case studies for building a base to verify and validate this approach and generalize to other urban contexts.

## Public Spaces in Conflicting Areas: The Segregative Power of Violence

The organization of public spaces—as a response to social conflicts or illegal behaviours, whether produced spontaneously or by design—needs to be studied in order to identify the way people adapt their own spaces for everyday life. In order to interpret the relationships between public spaces, on the one hand, and religious, political, and cultural urban conflicts, on the other, the research in progress is focused on public spaces in marginal neighbourhoods that have been 'privatized' or abandoned due to conflicts, risks, or decay.

Many cities, not only in Europe, 'have promoted public spaces as a vehicle of social integration, such as in Berlin's Potsdamer Platz, which is meant to heal the wounds of the dividing line that was imposed on the city for decades' (Madanipour, 2004, p. 268). Public places' forms and uses reflect the way divided societies have struggled with conflicts due to a systemic combination of different factors: immigration, increasing poverty, and social marginality, as well as cultural and ethnic divergences, political divisions, and criminal permeability, and lack of participation in decision making.

The ideal of favouring socialization, in opposition to the tendency to segregate and fight, needs to be pursued through the creation of public spaces for encounter and dialogue (Sandercock, 2000). This approach is related to the ways people meet each other in contemporary cities, transforming the forms and functions of public spaces (Gaus, 2002). It is possible to affirm that the creation of adequate social life spaces could favour encounters between diversities: Mutual influences encourage progress among all the parties involved, reducing the sense of insecurity and conflict (Davis, 1992). In multicultural societies, the increase of a sense of insecurity has been associated with complex explanations that include factors ranging from segregation to marginalization and social distress and, more recently, to religious fundamentalism. Communication gaps and absence of dialogue increase when this process is associated with choices of spatial self-segregation in specialized areas based on social class, religion, and ethnicity; in this case, gated communities have been developed that physically separate the different social milieux more or less rigidly by means of walls and fences. Scholars in the field as such as Sassen (1991), Beguinot (2009), and Madanipour (2011c) have covered these findings: Cultural, ethnic, religious, and social diversity creates forms of conflict that can hardly be attributed to a single matrix. Focusing on the unwritten codes of self-organization and the sense of community attributable to the traditional idea of the neighbourhood unit, Jane Jacobs (1961) carried out fundamental research on the relations between form and uses of public spaces, as well as the building of new forms of social networking, beyond religion, ethnicity, and general mistrust.

Starting from this idea, the research process described in this chapter is oriented to identifying a possible expression of urban planning and architecture *of* dialogue and *for* dialogue (Beguinot, 2009), starting from two case studies that can be considered ultimate expressions of physical and social division. Fieldwork has been focused on deprived and abandoned neighbourhoods that should be considered of particular interest for addressing the topic of improving the number and quality of places for socialization that are accessible, shared, and equal. Public spaces 'cannot be genuinely public as long as they are planned, produced, and controlled under the hegemony of a specific group or groups. Real public spaces can only emerge if they are planned, designed, developed, and used through the involvement of as many and varied groups as possible' (Akkar Ercan, 2007). Therefore, as the research focuses on areas struggling with tangible forms of violence due to religious conflicts and the influences of organized crime, specific tools for community engagement that can be used to collect instances of accessible public spaces are needed (Fyfe, 1998). Public spaces need to be interpreted as possible 'participatory landscapes' (Francis, 1989)—places of cohesion and integration where high degrees of social conviviality have been guaranteed.

This purpose needs to be tested where conflicts generate extreme consequences: In those areas in which deprivation indices are only the emerging aspect of religious–political conflicts (such as in Belfast), as well as in those in which there are conflicts or fear due to organized crime (such as in Naples).

## Public Spaces as a Vehicle of Integration: The Definition of a Methodology

The research methodology is based on a particular case study approach (Yin, 2003) by developing a qualitative analysis of direct observations and visual interpretation, perceptive mapping (Lynch, 1960), and interviews with key actors, to be overlapped with selected statistical data. The overview is articulated in:

- A visual representation of the paths through photos and sketches (Gaber & Gaber, 2007)
- A Lynch-style interpretation of key elements of the territory (Lynch, 1960)
- Mapping of the borderline public spaces as transformed by conflicts, insecurity, and incommunicability.

The fieldwork sessions were carried out during the autumn-winter of 2010 on workdays and weekends, in daytime and evening. The first cluster of active observations were developed without the filter of prerecognitions, in order to identify edge areas between the different communities, conflicting spaces, interfaces, abandoned buildings and open spaces, neutral areas, and other key elements that are typically recognizable in conflicting neighbourhoods. The first extemporaneous mapping was contrasted with a review of the literature on the specific urban contexts, as well as a first group of informal interviews with local stakeholders, scholars in the field, and activists. This phase of the research project was oriented to selecting representative areas to be submitted to a second session of active observations which were carried out while walking, driving (guided by local activists), and while moving on different means of public transport. The results of this working session have been mapped using the Lynchian syntax of urban elements: the *legend* of the maps has been constructed based on the perceptive taxonomy produced and tested by Kevin Lynch in *The Image of the City* (1960). The reason for this choice is basically due to the necessity to share with local people the interpretation of forms, functions, *vincula*, permanent items, and transitory uses or abandonments, in order to discuss possible transformations of public places oriented to enhancing the relational potential of interface areas. According to Nasar (1998), this taxonomy has been adapted to the character of those open spaces that play a specific role of interface between conflicting neighbourhoods (Table 14.1). The design of the 'Lynch style' perceptive map has become the foundation of the ongoing discussion among decision makers, grassroots movements, and end users of urban spaces.

The principal objective is to define generalized procedures for identifying and sharing with local communities the key elements of their borderline areas in order to involve them in the redesign of public spaces through their retrofitting and reconnection to the urban grid—long interrupted because of defensive behaviours or illegal uses. The innovative character of this methodology is based not on the definition of the taxonomy nor on the interpretation methodology, but on the way this approach has been adapted and refined by highlighting the physical transformations that have occurred as consequence of the segregative effect of violence and by mapping them in order to discuss meanings, consequences, and perceptions with neighbours. Moreover, in order to engage people from the diverse and/or conflictive communities, this incremental process provides a preassessment of the prominent urban elements to be submitted to the people involved for discussion on proper strategies for the redesign of their public spaces. Each one of them recognizes, as an individual or as part of a social group, the meaning of the key elements of their open spaces

*Table 14.1* The proposed taxonomy

| Lynch-style taxonomy | Conflicting legend | Urban retrofitting |
|---|---|---|
| PATHS: 'channels along which the observer customarily, occasionally or potentially moves' | BROKEN PATHS | Line-of-desire rebuilding |
| EDGES: 'linear elements not used or considered as paths by the observer' | BARRIERS | Linear interfaces |
| DISTRICTS: 'medium-to-large sections of the city' | ENCLAVES | Cul-de-sac removal |
| NODES: 'strategic points into which an observer can enter' or to and from which the observer is travelling' | ACCESS CONTROL POINTS | Accessible public places |
| LANDMARKS: places external to the observer seen from many angles and distances and used as references | IDENTITARIAN FOCI | Multicultural landmarks |

and the roles they play in defining the public realm. The overlapping of this synthetic imaging has led us to carry out a multiple-layer mapping to be submitted to a sample of key stakeholders and community activists through semi-structured interviews, role-plays, and in-the-field campaigns. In this empirical phase, the multiactor spiral process of consultation and implementation has allowed us to develop a qualitative and quantitative complex of needs, obstacles, and resources.

## Open Spaces in Conflicting Areas: The Case of Belfast

The urban pattern of Belfast can be interpreted by emphasizing how the conflict has severely interfered with the urban morphology, and with the way public spaces are experienced in the interface areas between conflicting communities. The roots of the conflict in Northern Ireland have been extensively investigated and have given rise to interdisciplinary debates during the period of fighting and during the peace process. This urban context has been a place of struggle and violence for decades, irreversibly changing the way open spaces and paths are experienced. This chapter proposes a spatial and morphological interpretation of the phenomenon, leaving the sociological and political perspectives to the copious literature available on the complex issue of the 'troubles' of 1969 and other related events (Boal & Royle, 2006).

The complex relationships between the loyalist and the nationalist communities have created sociopolitical processes that have led urban transformations toward segregation. From the perspective of urban organization, various features can be readily recognized: an armoured city centre, militarized and protected with checkpoints, surrounded by the Catholic and Protestant districts whose boundaries have been places of violence.

These boundaries: streets, parks, open spaces, strings of buildings, and retail areas have been transformed in order to mitigate risks by producing residential gated communities with internal distribution provided by cul-de-sacs (Figure 14.1), as well as visual control of the territory and regulation of access by physical separations (walled industrial areas, militarized police stations, and buffer-area infrastructure resulting from government initiative).

The prominent defensive typology consists of the so-called *peace lines* (Morrisey & Gaffikin, 2006)—fences built over decades to protect communities or to increase their perception of

*Figure 14.1* Some urban elements resulting from the conflict in Belfast: walled row houses with identity symbols.

security. This is the key node to be discussed: Even if the peace lines and the related interface areas are linked with an extreme and unique conflict event, Belfast offers a well-defined and recognizable way of transforming public spaces in response to a conflict and sense of insecurity (Table 14.2).

The complexity of the relationships between the communities and of the profiles of public spaces in these borderline areas mirror the sensitivity of the interface matter and emphasize the importance of an in-depth study centred on a 'soft' participatory approach to the problem (Gaffikin, McEldowney, & Sterrett, 2010). In this scenario, the development of the case study allows us to identify possible nontraumatic processes for redesigning the interface areas, to accompany a gradual rediscovery of those public spaces as places for self-expression, dialogue, and intercommunication. This process could accompany the next generation in building a new shared awareness of being two interdependent expressions of the same culture.

The fieldwork has led us to focus on the connective tissue between the city centre—Cathedral Quarter, home to the University of Ulster and catalyst for cultural and recreational activities—and the residential areas north of the Crown that have a strong majority of either Protestant or Catholic populations: The Shankill, Falls, and New Lodge (Boal, 2008).

In this context, a significant number of each typology of physical transformation of the territory has been found, for reasons that have been recorded in the defensive urban environment (Somma, 1991). This context is significant because it expresses an extreme transformation of the built environment and of open spaces in response to conflicts.

This strongly defined urban grid, with its ruptures and defensive elements—and the sharp division between conflicting social groups—could be an ideal laboratory for the interpretation of the role of public spaces in dividing or supporting interrelations between people in challenged areas (Figure 14.2). The situation of a cross-community public space—the Alexandra Park—needs to

*Table 14.2* Physical expression of defensive transformations of public and quasi-public areas in Belfast

| Morphological and functional transformations | Conflicting taxonomy | Urban retrofitting |
|---|---|---|
| Peace lines: concrete or brick walls, fences, chevaux-de-frise, protected gates, public places abandoned or divided by walls | BARRIERS, BROKEN PATHS, ACCESS CONTROL POINTS | Line-of-desire rebuilding |
| Buffer zones: fenced industrial areas, abandoned and walled retail areas, abandoned and bolted row houses, empty spaces, mobility infrastructure such as highways, CCTV surveillance, police stations | ACCESS CONTROL POINTS, BARRIERS | Accessible public places |
| Gated communities: residential areas served by cul-de-sacs, fenced playgrounds and schools, row houses transformed into barriers by eliminating all the minor interconnections between buildings and urban grid | ENCLAVES, ACCESS CONTROL POINTS | Cul-de-sac removal, accessible public places |
| Interface areas: public and quasi-public areas divided by the above defensive transformations | IDENTITARIAN FOCI, BROKEN PATHS | Linear interfaces, shared-and-recognizable landmarks |

*Figure 14.2* Fenced public spaces in Belfast: a peace line.

be highlighted: It could be an opportunity to promote contact and dialogue; however, it is crossed by a continuous wall of steel that separates the Catholic and Protestant play areas for children. Moreover, the main commercial streets such as Falls Road and Shankill Road, which appear vital and busy during the day, are attended only by members of their communities or neutral visitors. The gradual reconstruction of the physical and functional relations between the divided parts of the city—considering the strong emotional impact of the barriers on the individual and collective imagery—could start from the creation of inclusive public spaces. No open or public space has been designed in contested areas of Belfast with the daily habits of the diverse communities as project guide. As well, secondary roads that were stopped or diverted as a result of the construction of barriers have not been reconnected to provide pedestrian paths. These planning choices, coupled with other changes dictated by fear and mistrust, have strongly influenced the built environment by reducing accessibility and connectivity and discouraging the development of shared public spaces.

The peace process, which started with the Belfast Agreement in 1998, has been oriented to favour dialogue between communities, but the absence of welcoming open spaces for sharing experiences and problems can be seen as a strong obstacle. Reciprocal mistrust and diffidence continue to hinder the work of many activists from both sides of the larger community, due to the lack of spaces suitable for dialogue in everyday life.

Assuming the retrofitting process in urban design as the primary way for improving urban connectivity in order to favour pedestrian uses (Boarnet, Joh, Siembab, Fulton, & Nguyen, 2011), the concept could be adapted to interpret and design possible transformation of the interface areas in order to create (or recreate) the interconnection grid between shared public spaces and places for public services (Figure 14.3) to be accessed by the different components of a complex and multifaceted society (Fincher & Jacobs, 1998). This process of urban retrofitting in border areas

*Figure 14.3* Signals of new trends: a pre-fab shop on a corner between divided communities in Belfast.

is here defined as the system of integrated actions oriented to improve the forms and function of those public spaces challenged by conflicts, in order to favour a multiple perception of the sense of places and a shared use of open spaces and paths for pedestrian use.

One of the key elements of this idea of retrofitting is the identification of the *lines of desire*, ideal type paths expressed by local communities that need to be implemented in the organization of open spaces. This consolidated definition of mobility planning based on the spontaneous demand for accessibility (Boaga, 1972) has been applied in the case study in order to recognize the hidden shared lines of desire along the borders, which are completely or partially broken by the defensive barriers that have been constructed. Once the multilayer map that forms the basis for discussion with community workers and stakeholders has been created, the web of *lines of desire* of the individual and collective memory of the divided communities can then be detected—symbolic elements from which the process of rebuilding lost physical and mental connections can begin (McNeill, 2011). This result would not be considered as a point of arrival, but as a simplified way of representing a complex hidden demand of physical and mental interconnections in order to share every single step of the redesign process of those public spaces affected by loss of meanings and uses.

## Public Places and Organized Criminality: The Case of Naples

The findings of the fieldwork developed in Belfast have been the starting point for the testing phase developed in Naples. Briefly, Naples can be considered one of the prominent ancient settlements in Europe and part of the Mediterranean basin. Its historic centre is a unique example of architectural stratification through the centuries and is still a vibrant catalyst of mixed activities without any 'museumification' phenomena. Along with these positive aspects there are many problems, such as the high population density; the low education indices; the severe status of the labour market linked to the lack of private activities and job creation initiatives; the presence of criminal organizations; and the strong rehabilitation needs of the built environment, including the cultural heritage.

The complexity of this local scenario of resources and challenges is the humus for nourishing the development of this case study. The first step was the definition of the case study domain in terms of location, size, functional organization, and general characteristics. Through dialogue with the Urban Planning Department of the City of Naples; active observations at different daytime hours, weekdays, and seasons; as well as discussion with local stakeholders and scholars in charge, a specific area has been chosen in order to address the topics of the research.

The selected area, the Scampia-Secondigliano district, presents several functional, morphological, and social elements that can be compared and contrasted with the case study from Northern Ireland. The area is characterized by social housing settlements built in the 1960s in the former rural settlement of the northwest area on the administrative border of the City of Naples. This area is internationally well-known due to Roberto Saviano's book titled *Gomorra* (Saviano, 2006), in which he chronicles the power and control exercised by the criminal organizations that are collectively called the Camorra. His factual accounts mainly take place in the so-called 'Vele' neighbourhood (Figure 14.4)—seven housing blocks built between 1962 and 1975, and partially demolished in 1997—which in the space of a few years became the symbol of criminal power in that area (Barbagallo, 1988). This criminal organization, which emerged as a secret society in Naples in the 17th century, became in the 1800s a sort of *'massoneria della plebe'*, a hidden freemasonry of the common folk that was a parallel power to the official government (Monnier, 1863, p. 62). Its web of connections and influence on social organization decreased during the first half of the 20th century and its current structure as a system of

*Figure 14.4* The so-called 'Vele' of Scampia with a symbolic sentence on the wall, Naples.

organized crime began to take form after the Second World War, when links were established with the American mafia (Allum, 2006). The extensive on-the-field literature provides a wide definition of this criminal system that has evolved in different forms over the centuries and has developed different relationships with the other components of the social system (Allum, 2011). The contemporary manifestation of this phenomenon has been studied in depth and in an interdisciplinary manner in order to understand social implications, economic context, political connections, and territorial distribution, as well as the organization's illegal paramilitary structure (Sales & Ravveduto, 2006). This organization generates over 12 billion euros in illegal revenue each year (Eurispes, 2008), engages people in deprived areas by offering opportunities for illegal or informal job creation (*affiliati*), and directly or indirectly involves different social classes and different urban areas.

According to the literature in the field, the zones of influence of the different criminal groups that make up the Camorra can be recognized in the metropolitan area of Naples (Amaturo, 2004). In particular, copious literature illustrates the complex scenario of the case-study district, in which different social groups coexist with the presence of 'families' of criminal organizations (Barbagallo, 1988). These complex aspects call out for specific study and reflection: The deprivation indices (including an unemployment rate of over 60%), the high crime rate, and frequent press reports on drug trafficking and other illegal activities are only part of this multifaceted context. With regard to the main topic of this study—the development of a methodological approach that targets enhancement of multiple roles of public spaces in order to favour social inclusion and cultural interactions—some significant social, morphological, and functional aspects of the public space situation have been identified. Applying the methodology developed in the Belfast case study, which includes visual analysis, Lynch-style mapping, and interviewing key actors, it is evident that there is a high density of nonprofit organizations, NGOs, and other activist organizations involved in social and cultural issues in the area despite the remarkable crime rate.

*Figure 14.5* Public spaces challenged by the presence of social deprivation and criminal activities in Scampia, Naples.

Indeed, a first interpretation of the role of public spaces in the everyday life of the residents is taking form (Figure 14.5).

As in the Belfast interface areas, morphological and functional transformations of public spaces that have been specifically caused by criminal activities can be identified in Scampia: Ground floors of buildings have been blinded to create physical and visual barriers; through streets have been transformed into cul-de-sacs; public spaces such as parks, playgrounds, and gardens have lost their original functions and have been fenced in order to host illegal activities; buffer areas between blocks have been created by diverse groups for defensive purposes; and front street commercial activities have been strongly discouraged. The militarized organization of parts of this deprived territory has determined the rupture of the urban grid, the building of gated communities, the lack of social services and facilities, the decay and abandonment of public spaces, as well as the transformation of architectural typologies and the creation of access control points, walls, and fences (Figure 14.6). The result of these wide transformations is a controlled space where pedestrian uses and open-space activities are discouraged and the idea of public spaces for public uses of everyday life is ignored (Table 14.3).

These physical transformations are the visible expression not only of fear and mistrust but also of the breakup of social networks and a sense of community, all of which are produced by the pervasive presence of groups of criminal organizations in these areas (Amaturo, 2004).

Activists and community workers, as well as volunteers and local administrations, are involved in a process of urban regeneration oriented towards progressively reducing the influence of criminal organizations on the everyday life of the local communities by supporting the refurbishment, retrofitting, and reuse of the web of public spaces. Open spaces and places for the delivery of public services need to be given back to local communities to facilitate encounter and dialogue between people and to contribute to the isolation of criminal groups.

*Figure 14.6* Defensive transformations of buildings in Scampia, Naples.

*Table 14.3* Physical expression of defensive transformations of public and quasi-public areas in Naples

| Morphological and functional transformations | Conflicting taxonomy | Urban retrofitting |
|---|---|---|
| Security lines ('peace lines'): concrete or brick walls, fences, chevaux-de-frise, protected gates, public places abandoned or divided by walls | BARRIERS, BROKEN PATHS, ACCESS CONTROL POINTS | Line-of-desire rebuilding |
| Buffer zones: abandoned and walled retail areas, abandoned and bolted houses, abandoned ground floors and empty spaces | ACCESS CONTROL POINTS, BARRIERS | Accessible public places |
| Gated communities: residential areas served by cul-de-sacs, fenced playgrounds and schools, houses transformed into barriers by eliminating all the minor interconnections between buildings and the urban grid | ENCLAVES, ACCESS CONTROL POINTS | Cul-de-sac removal, accessible public places |
| Interface areas: public and quasi-public areas divided by the above-listed defensive transformations | IDENTITARIAN FOCI, BROKEN PATHS | Linear interfaces, shared and recognizable landmarks |

The mapping of conflicting elements through the taxonomy here described has been discussed with local stakeholders and is now in the process of being implemented in order to identify priorities and to involve local people in decision-making processes. This process could be a way to accompany divided communities as they accept a gradual removal of existing barriers, as they reach new awareness of their own needs and perceptions, and as they define the pivotal elements for the enhancement of their daily quality of life.

## Conclusions and Takeaway for Practice

This research in progress, presented in accordance with Healey's definition of planning as 'managing our co-existence in shared space' (Healey, 1997, p. 3), identifies some critical points of the role of public spaces in encouraging social life and cultural interaction by focusing on the specific context of extreme social segregation, as well as the sense of community erosion due to religious conflicts and the pervasive power of criminal organizations.

Community engagement and debate on inclusive ideas for urban transformation can be the key to making possible effective decision making and successful and shared plans of actions, avoiding the risk of tokenism and delays (Arnstein, 1969). The identity of the city is a dynamic expression of cultural cross-pollinations manifested in the public spaces that are now suffering from privatization, uniformity, and various expressions of exclusion of diversities. Therefore, we need to discuss the way in which the design of public spaces can play a multifaceted and complex role as community catalysts (Simpson, 2011). Applying the taxonomy of perceptive interpretation on the transformation of public spaces—an unhealthy transformation that has occurred as a consequence of the pressure of different forms of violence and threats—a procedure for starting this participatory process has been developed, integrated by active observations and mapping, and validated through formal and informal interviews with key actors.

A shared range of needs would be the desired result of drawing up shared project guidelines oriented to redevelopment, transformation, and reconnection of public spaces in marginal neighbourhoods through a retrofitting process. To do this, a case-study research method has been adopted in order to capture the multifaceted issues related to the interfaces between conflicting neighbourhoods in Belfast and Naples, allowing us to identify and test a possible urban design approach to promote dialogue between divided communities through reconnecting the urban grid that has been interrupted due to defensive issues. The in-the-field survey, accompanied by interviews and discussions, has made it possible to identify the impact of episodes of violence, as well as the outcome of continuous threat in terms of urban form, and in particular in terms of connectivity and accessibility of public spaces: Morphological barriers mirror the interrupted social network. This process has been oriented to understanding priorities in the process of retrofitting and gradual removal of existing barriers that impede the shared use of public spaces in 'cross-border' areas.

Further implementations of the findings of the Naples case study will be carried out in cooperation with local stakeholders in order to test and support the planning process in this challenged area, and to strengthen the efficacy and transferability of this methodology.

# Chapter 15

# Public Space and the Challenges of Urban Transformation in Europe

*Ali Madanipour, Sabine Knierbein, and Aglaée Degros*

Our aim in this book has been investigating the politics of public space at a moment of crucial transformation for European cities, analysing the public space as a crossroad in which different stakeholders interact within the context of economic, political, social, environmental, and cultural challenges. What can we learn from our case studies about the role of the public authorities, the interplay between these different challenges, and the experiences of European urban societies? The European national and municipal policy documents and programmes place much emphasis on the need for public space and on its potential towards addressing these challenges. Are these policies implemented in practice, and if so, how, to what extent, and with what impact? Can the provision, improvement, and management of public space equally and simultaneously facilitate social inclusion, economic development, environmental sustainability, and cultural diversity, or are these incompatible demands on the urban environment that cannot be reconciled at all?

Our case studies are by no means inclusive and representative of the very wide range of circumstances in European cities, and how each city is affected by, and responds to, the range of challenges we have identified. As the case studies show, different public authorities have adopted different approaches towards public space, reflecting the political orientation of the current administrations as much as the city's historic specificities. However, it is possible to identify some common trends among these cases. At least in their rhetoric, public authorities show awareness of the challenges they face in a changing world, and they tend to place democratic governance, economic development, environmental care, social inclusion, and cultural enrichment on their agendas, especially when dealing with public space provision and improvement. In practice, however, some of these claims tend to be favoured at the expense of others. What our cases have explicitly demonstrated is that, while public spaces have found a central role in responding to the challenges of urban transformation, social inclusion, cultural diversity, and environmental care have occupied a lower part of the agenda, which is dominated by the challenges of economic development and efficient governance, especially in the context of current economic crisis. Social, cultural, and environmental concerns tend to become a subject of attention when represented by strong voices and vigorous protests from civil society groups, or when they have been instrumentally used in the economic and political agendas.

In what follows, we present three discussions that cut across the social, economic, cultural, environmental, and political challenges, identified in Chapter 1, and link them with the structure of action and response that we identified in our three-part structure of the book, in plans, roles, and experiences of public space. As places where history unfolds, where diversity is explored, and where power is negotiated, the politics of public space are played out in ever more significant ways. The ideal type image of well-ordered and beautiful historic cities is faced with highly unstable economic conditions and a highly diverse social reality, in which the processes of governance may look for a stable settlement, but one in which high prices may be paid by the more vulnerable parties.

## Where History Unfolds

An important finding from these case studies is the significant role that an ideal type image of the European city plays in discourses and practices of urban transformation. This ideal image combines a number of potential contradictions: It is a well-ordered city but with a picturesque appearance; it is a modern competitive economy but with a historical atmosphere; it is rooted in an ancient high culture but is open to new ideas and emerging cultures. The European city image is expected to provide a strong instrument in economic development, used in branding and city marketing, making cities more competitive and welcoming to visitors and investors. The cities in economic transition show anxiety about (re)establishing this image, as a way of joining the ranks of other European cities, as the cases of Dresden and Budapest show. The more stable cities, nevertheless, use it as a way of managing the intensified speed of change and maintaining an already established image, as in Paris and Vienna. Politics of public space in European cities are, therefore, largely entangled with the portrayal of the image of a picturesque and historic but well-ordered and competitive modern city. Many tensions, however, are associated with this image.

The first tension is with the historicity of the city, especially when it has had a troubled past. The questions revolve around which narratives of which periods in the past should be preferred, and which symbols should be kept or discarded. In Dresden, after the fall of the GDR and reunification with the rest of Germany, the intention was to move away from the image of a socialist city and return to what was thought to be the image of a normal European city, simultaneously dealing with the deep historical trauma of the Second World War that devastated the city while laying the foundations of a new urban image. By enclosing the openness of the socialist city, removing public art, reinstating the previous map of the city, removing the palimpsest back so as to erase the socialist city from the city's collective memory, a symbolic gesture was adopted for transforming the identity of the city, a complete break from the past and setting the scene for a new economic and political order. In part, it is similar to some other European cities dealing the legacies of modernism, which had left deep traces in the urban landscape, but here it had found extra political and symbolic meaning, and their removal was seen to be a complete change of direction.

As the case of Warsaw shows, the remembrance of this past is constructed through various narratives. The meaning on display in public space may be contested when present cultural difference overlaps with a troubled history. Which traces of the past are remembered and displayed, and which layers are forgotten or ignored, and how do these representations of the past relate to the experiences of the populations (then and now), the official narratives, or marketing imperatives, can all cause fresh controversy in a place such as Warsaw Ghetto, which has witnessed the horrors of the Second World War. The juxtaposition of the references to the 19th century grandeur, the interwar vibrant night life, and the wartime Holocaust, all along the streets of Warsaw, creates an uneasy coexistence. Who tells which story, through what system of signs, and for what purpose, becomes the question. What role does the designing of public space play in these uneasy contexts?

In both cases of Dresden and Warsaw, we are witnessing the creation of the future city through a reinvention of the past, selecting some elements of the history to tell a particular story about the present and shape the direction of the future. The search for authenticity, and linking it to memory, is always a process of social recreation, depending on where to place the historical indicator from which the supposedly authentic state started. In cities with long histories, this is a futile task, as these cities are palimpsests of many layers. Constructing an authentic image out of this multilayered reality would become no more than a fiction that would conform to a particular imagined standard. Rather than authenticity, would eclecticism or neutrality offer a solution?

Dresden has attempted to respond to the historical ruptures that the city has experienced, going through Nazi, socialist, and capitalist changes in a relatively short period of time, each attempting to leave their mark on the city. Now the artists and designers wish to create a neutral space that does not represent the authorities' perspective but questions those perspectives and allows individual citizens to decide on the meaning of public space and public art, which take subtle rather than overbearing appearances. As personal expressions, it may be difficult to reach this state of neutrality, but it is obvious that the old idea of the public spaces being explicitly an expression of the powerful institutions and elite aesthetics has given way to a more dispersed symbolism, in which the values of consumerist culture may be on display side by side with those of the cultural groups and historical narratives. Subtlety of expression, attempting to keep neutrality and emptiness, and offering the possibility of multiple interpretations and democratic use may be a way forward. However, as Berlin shows, when the size of emptiness increases, or as Dresden shows, the expressions are not approved by the professionals and authorities, maintaining this neutrality becomes a difficult task. Furthermore, as Dresden shows, subtle interventions may be lost to the people who consider them as street furniture rather than an invitation to a democratic creation of meaning in public space. As Warsaw shows, silence and absence can be potentially more powerful than the objects that are used for the recreation of meaning.

## Where Diversity Is Explored

Addressing the multiplicity of historical layers is made more complex by social diversity. In addition to deciding which historical layer to bring to the fore, another challenge is to decide which cultural and social group to include, and in what capacity, in the narratives of the city. As we saw in Chapter 1, the central feature of European cities today is thought to be their social and cultural diversity, so the questions revolve around how public spaces should be designed and transformed that would cater to the needs of a diverse population. As our case studies have shown, this diversity is simultaneously embraced and feared, as a spectacle with aesthetic and economic value, as well as a phenomenon with far-reaching social and cultural impacts on the city.

This is evident in Barbés, Paris, which is a place of heightened diversity and urbanity, with a multiethnic population from around the world; its public spaces are not just places of co-presence, but also of initiating different forms of relating to this diversity. The neighbourhood offers a cultural resource, a way of being with others that would help the locals and the visitors, particularly those with African heritage, make connections with their memories and cultural roots. Some who do not identify with this character, nevertheless, may not feel threatened or alienated, but are disengaged and tolerant, just getting used to being in and passing through the public space, treating it as a place of avoidance. Others, however, may positively enjoy the diversity as an aesthetic and social experience, viewing it as a spectacle, a place of possibility and surprise, a place of consumption. For another group, public spaces of the neighbourhood are places of active engagement and debate, participation in, and challenging others over, local affairs. Yet another group, who see this diversity as undesirable and alien, do their best to displace and dismantle it. The case of Barbés shows how these groups operate, from the paradoxical efforts of the planners that prevent the further expansion of diversity in the name of *mixité*, to the idea of relocating the market activities to outside Paris, as a reminder of previous experiences in the city for ordering what seems to be disordered and undesirable. Otherness, however, lies at the heart of the urban experience, as observed by the early sociologists, and the co-presence of strangers an unavoidable condition, whatever the efforts of planners and designers to create what may end up being homogeneous and increasingly standardized and controlled public spaces. The resulting homogeneity and controlled character of the urban environment, however, is in sharp contrast with the ideal type image of the European city and with the inherent diversity of urban life, continually reproducing an unresolved tension.

The two accounts of London offer two very different readings of the same city: one celebrating the differences that the city has witnessed in recent years and questioning the usefulness of critical accounts, the other registering the process of gentrification that replaces one form of diversity with another. These differences show how the analysis of public space, and more broadly the urban analysis, is located in particular perspectives, seeing the world and its transformation from a particular angle, often reflecting the personal experiences of the researchers and their disposition and position in social space.

Cultural diversity and social inequality are two different, though related, phenomena. Differences in age, gender, lifestyle, and religion are present in all large cities. In some cities, such as London, ethnic and cultural diversity has already become a fact of life, as the white British population is now in the minority (BBC, 2012). At the same time, there is a widening socioeconomic inequality, which has been a primary feature of life in many countries for a generation (OECD, 2008). Cultural diversity may become a source of spectacle and pleasure for the prosperous citizens, but a source of intensified deprivation for the socioeconomically disadvantaged groups. Therefore, diversity should not be reduced to a single category of Others, which may cover a very wide range of circumstances. Furthermore, diversity should not be reduced to its visual manifestations, as reliance on appearances may be misleading and remain on the surface of deep differences or substantial similarities between individuals and groups. The discourse about diversity, nevertheless, tends to be shaped by a generalized concept of diversity, which is about Otherness, and is in danger of being taken over by intolerant voices that may point a finger at the Other as the source of most social ills.

One way of treating social and cultural difference, as the Swiss cases show, has been through expulsion from public space, which is often applied to the young people who may appear to threaten the sense of normalcy by behaving differently. Ruling out the unexpected through expulsion and exclusion, however, is an 'easy way' out of addressing social complexity and difference, reducing the possibility of contact and of developing the competencies that are necessary for dealing with otherness, ruling out the possibility of playfulness in the name of orderliness and comfort. It resorts to security measures to organize social behaviour into acceptable and unacceptable forms, and accordingly social space into included and excluded parts by means of discriminatory selection. It aims at portraying an image of peace and tranquillity by resorting to violent means against those who may not deserve it, but are only singled out for being different.

Exclusion may also be exerted through spatial planning and design. As the Milan cases show, public space can become a vehicle of separation, rather than a place of integration, which is against what the policy documents and the academic literature suggest. This spatial separation is accompanied by discriminatory selection mediated via symbolic design codes and socioeconomic limitation of access to housing. When society is fragmented and differentiated along cultural and socioeconomic lines, it seems the possibility and desirability of social encounters between different groups loses out in competition with the feelings of insecurity and risk, which are fuelled by some media and politicians. Public space, as part of the overall socio-spatial organization, is used to help separate the fragments from one another, acting as a buffer zone that would support a process of social sorting.

The separation may also be at the scale of the whole city, creating centres and peripheries with widely different features. While the city centres continue to be associated with the idealized image of European cities, their peripheries may be treated as epiphenomenal rather than an integral part of these cities and their images. To find a more accurate understanding of the city, however, it is necessary to go beyond the tourist-friendly image as a coherent historic entity endowed with accessible and beautiful public spaces. This image, which is often associated with the city centre, breaks down when, as we have learned from the example of Milan, suburbanization and the decline of the centre happen alongside economic restructuring and social stratification and differentiation. Attempts at maintaining the ideal type image of the city centre may lead to an uneven urban landscape through real estate booms, high land prices, and gentrification. Meanwhile, rather than recreating an urban character in which public space is accessible and open, these attempts may suburbanize the urban, using public space for recreating an out-of-town feel for the urban environment, masking the complexity of the social scene behind a green screen.

When, in contrast, the suburb is urbanized, as the Aspern case from Vienna shows, the result may not succeed in avoiding uneasy socio-spatial juxtapositions. It redirects attention to the underrepresented parts of the city, bringing infrastructure and investment to a peripheral and often neglected area of the city. The strategies and outcomes, however, may be ambivalent, both in the way the area is developed and how it is received by the existing local population. Meanwhile, the Vienna city centre determines the local, national, and international image of the city, attracting most investment, showing a discrepancy between the policies of public space and the practices of selective and unequal attention and implementation in different parts of the city.

The intensification of diversity has been historically approached in a variety of ways, from a presumed need for assimilation to the acceptance of cultural difference, and the realization that these different cultures are part of the same society in need of intercultural relations. This has added different colours and nuances to a long-established debate about whether different cultural groups should be living together or apart (Madanipour, 2011c). The question of whether ghettoization should be taken for granted as a support mechanism for the vulnerable or it should be seen as a process of stigmatization and social exclusion has been hotly debated (Madanipour, 2011b; 2012). The meaning and character of public space in any of these scenarios would be different, from one in which public space is a more 'neutral' place for a presumably coherent culture, to one in which public spaces reflect particular communal characters and identities that keep others out, and to one where different groups are all present and recognize each other as such.

In this context, co-presence of difference may be seen as a superficial treatment of diversity. Co-presence, however, should not be dismissed as irrelevant. In the highly segregated cities, the possibility of different socioeconomic groups even becoming aware of one another is undermined, as the rich and poor often live and work in different parts of the urban environment, and their only contact may be through hierarchical structures of work. This combination tends to dehumanize the poor as people who are rendered inferior in the workplace and invisible in the urban space. The next step would tend to be the erection of physical barriers against the poor, such as walls and gates, and the threat of violence to keep them away. The possibility of co-presence, even if superficial and fleeting, therefore, must be seen as a contest to this arrangement.

The widening social divide, in its socioeconomic and cultural forms, needs to be addressed in many ways, and inclusive public spaces may be one among the many such measures that are needed. This is particularly evident in the case study of Belfast, where a religiously divided society that searches for reintegration is in need of support from the availability of public space. In Belfast and Naples, social and cultural divide has led to conflict and violence, which in turn erects physical barriers and creates blind spots, segregated places, turning the open ground into a social and cultural void, a battle zone, or a place to be avoided at all cost. Public spaces, however, are needed to support the process of healing the wounds of divided societies, where difference has slipped into open conflict. Public space can play an important role in reintegrating a divided and conflicting society, when there are enough social measures to make peace possible but the legacy of the past conflicts has solidified conflict and segregation in stone, which now needs to be unwound for sowing the seeds of peace. By making places and processes accessible, opening up blocked pathways and establishing desired patterns of movement, using plurality and variety in landmarks, public spaces have a role to play in supporting the peace process.

## Where Power Is Negotiated

How can the image of a well-ordered historical modernity be created and managed in the context of social and historical change, where many stories may be told about the same place? Public spaces are common and collective places, which are viewed and valued differently by different stakeholders. As such, public spaces are simultaneously places of potential conflict as well as positive encounter.

Associated with the ideal image of a historic city is a certain idea of order in the urban space, which is upheld by the public authorities and professional experts. Activities and symbols that comply with this explicit or implicit system of ordering can find expression, and all the others may be viewed with suspicion or rejected out of hand. Informality crops up in public spaces wherever the presence and exertion of order is transformed; from informal markets in Paris to informal spaces and settlements in Istanbul, informality challenges the image of a well-ordered city that the public authorities have in mind. As Budapest exemplifies, economic transition out of the socialist regime was softened by the creation of informal street markets; as Istanbul shows, the development of informal settlements has created lively public spaces and stable neighbourhoods; as Paris shows, informal street markets have catered for the needs of many Parisians. However, these informal activities tend to unsettle a presentable image and an ordered organization of the city, which the municipalities aim to achieve by suppressing the informal economy, closing down the street markets and redeveloping the informal neighbourhoods.

As the Budapest case shows, public spaces can have economic as well as symbolic values. After the demise of communism in Hungary, many public spaces were turned into informal marketplaces, facilitating the exchange of goods and earning a living for a population in economic transition. Open-air markets show the different meanings that a type of public place can have, at once seen to be a place of informality, disadvantage, and poverty that is condemned to disappearance, to be replaced by places of spectacle and gentrification. The widening gap between different socioeconomic groups is reflected in the uses of public space, as a place of sociability and survival for some and a place of pleasure and prosperity for others. The public authority, which collaborates with the private sector in urban transformation, sides with the affluent vision of space, which may be limited in practice, and distances itself from the vision of informality and poverty, which may be a more accurate reflection of the reality. The informal use of space takes over when the public authority has lost some of its control over the urban space, and the formal economy is unable to provide employment and exchange opportunities for people, which can be found in many cities around the world. The public authorities, however, refuse to accept this loss of control, doing their best to bring public space, and hence the urban life, under control. Maintenance of a genteel and well-ordered urban atmosphere may thus depend on the hidden harshness of the instruments that make it happen, as the two sides of the same coin.

Order and disorder, meanwhile, have to be placed in a particular cultural and urban context. The practices of ordering social space are not the same in different European countries and regions, where the attitude towards order, and the material and institutional capacities for ordering phenomena, vary widely. Order, therefore, may not be reduced to an abstraction with a universal character, but should be seen as an exercise of power by some over others, and, as shown by this book, played out through the production, management, and use of public spaces in very different ways.

Analysing the political and economic processes would help understand spatial transformation as an integral part of the larger global urban processes, in which the cultural and everyday significance of the urban space plays a crucial role. Ignoring the political nature of public space may open our eyes to new aspects of public space, which must be a welcome expansion of our senses and analytical tools, but it may not remove the fact that society is made of different groups with different levels of power and access to resources. Simultaneously, it invites us to forget about the pain of inequality and the injustice of exclusion, located in places and processes that may not work in favour of the more vulnerable populations; it brackets out the political, embracing and accepting a situation without asking questions. A critical assessment, instead, helps see the world from the perspective of those who are in a less favourable position in social space, disadvantaged and marginalized in the existing arrangements, and therefore questioning their fairness.

As the cases of Milan, Antwerp, and Budapest show, public authorities have worked closely with the private sector developers and investors in the process of urban transformation. Such collaboration may be interpreted as a pragmatic move by the local authorities to access the resources and productive capacities of the private sector. Rather than the tyranny of aloof bureaucracies, a collaborative approach has been introduced, which would open up the process to new voices and visions. The problem with this economically driven partnership arrangement, however, is the absence of social and environmental concerns, and a depoliticization of the public realm. The involvement of the private investors would inevitably redirect the joint enterprise towards higher returns for private interests, which may compromise the protection of the environment and the provision of public goods for all. Such cases show a politics of public space that could be interpreted as exclusive and technocratic, rather than inclusive and democratic. In a consumption-driven economy marked by desires and needs of an affluent service-sector workforce, public spaces have been sanitized for the sake of enhancing the mood for consumption. With temporarily rising levels of prosperity, public spaces are polished up to filter and redirect streams of potential consumers into the worlds of sales. In the long run, this tendency contributes to wiping away the simple places of popular consumption, thus reducing the offers and access for satisfying basic needs of provision relevant for a considerable part of the local urban population.

As the case of Antwerp shows, public authorities have tended to go along with the market forces, as they have hoped that this alliance would lead to economic revival for their constituencies. Such a public–private alliance, however, could ignore social and environmental considerations in the name of economic regeneration. In Antwerp, however, the process was forcefully halted by civil society actors who protested against the port expansion. As a result, the port planning process opened up to the inclusion of civil society actors, albeit with a technical rather than cultural orientation, resulting in the reintroduction of public spaces in the port area. Unlike the cases that remain entirely within the control of the public and private organizations, Antwerp shows the significance of the civil society actors and what they can achieve by their presence in the planning process. This is why the inclusive governance of space in the context of the new challenges is increasingly significant. The environmental imperative may thus find a place on the table, offering a technical solution that can legitimize the public-private arrangements in urban development. But the cultural and social dimensions may still be absent, resulting in the development of areas that are only sensitive to some ecological processes and inclusive only to some parts of the population, with ambiguous or destructive impacts on the historical heritage and the weaker inhabitants of the city.

The differences between the two campaigning stakeholders in Antwerp reveals the nature of the civil society as a collection of various ways of thinking and acting, rather than a homogeneous entity with a single concept and interest. The civil society networks can be beneficial for those who are involved, but can attempt to keep others out so as to maintain the benefits of the stakeholders. The mere involvement of some non-state actors, therefore, may not guarantee a democratic outcome and an inclusive public space. This is equally applied in the way the public is envisaged: While the word seems to apply to a universal concept that includes everyone, in practice it is formed of a plurality of groups and individuals with different positions and interests. Consequently, the 'public' that is served by the development of public space may only be a fraction of the general public benefiting from urban transformation through rise in their property values or improvement in the quality of their living experience.

These differences also unpack the concept of sustainable development, which can be addressed through a technical or cultural framework, as exemplified by Antwerp. While a biological systemic view accepts that environmental assets can be relocated, a social and cultural view argues that environmental and cultural assets are unique and irreplaceable. The public spaces that are created in these different versions of sustainable development, therefore, are widely different in character and purpose. In the technical interpretation, public spaces are treated as ecological compensation areas, which can theoretically be placed anywhere to compensate for the loss of environmental assets elsewhere. In the cultural interpretation, however, public spaces are part of a specific cultural and historical social fabric, rather than objects in a void. As the Budapest case shows, sustainable development should include supporting local production and exchange of food, which the street and farmers markets exemplify. But when this localization of food comes into conflict with the property interests or the image of a well-ordered urban environment, it loses out. Meanwhile, when it is embraced by some local actors, it may be serving the experience economy, and its associated gentrification and tourism, rather than making a meaningful contribution to the local food production and exchange.

In developing a response to the identified challenges, the subdivision of public authorities into different departments seems to have been a longstanding answer, whereby each need is addressed by a different competence. However, these departments often enjoy different levels of power and influence, reflecting the way their subject matter is ranked in the list of priorities of the public authority and the public opinion. As Vienna shows, concentration on public space has allowed these different units, as well as different parties, an open space in which they can work together towards a common cause. Public space then becomes a sphere of learning that brings different political parties and administrative departments together. As the Vienna Charta shows, the potentials of public space are recognized not just in terms of singular policy fields, but for an innovative and antidiscriminatory approach to grassroots democracy. In the Swiss cases, in the context of increased social differentiation, competence and performance needed to be interlinked, and the politicians, professionals, and the publics needed to learn how to deal with one another in public spaces, with more knowledge and practice, and more competencies in everyday practices as well as professional practices.

The cases show that inclusive governance is a possibility, but apparently only after resorting to resistance, protest, and conflict, which has forced the others to listen and take into account the voices that had remained unheard. As Antwerp, Berlin, and Budapest show, environmental, cultural, and social activists forcefully brought important issues into focus for consideration, transforming the character of public spaces, even if to a limited extent. The former airfield in Berlin has offered a space of possibility, where different interests have clashed over the spacious field to fill it with meaning and use, whether in its social or built forms. Here, too, the idea of urban development had first relied on technocratic and economic concepts, hoping to control the outcome in a way that the investors and experts would have expected, but it was forced open by popular pressure and political campaigns. The opening of the field to the public shows the potential of the public space as a place that can link people together, either in action towards making it accessible or towards using it in very different ways. The case studies also show that gentrification is not an inevitable outcome of investment in the urban environment, if this investment is accompanied by support for the vulnerable, as the experiences of the earlier generations show. As the Viennese example displays, it is possible to soften the impact of the market operations on the more vulnerable population through continued support from the public authority.

# References

Action Committee Doel 2020. (2007). *Erfgoed, een mensenrecht ook in Doel.* Memorandum of the heritage-community of Doel, 9 February.

Agier, M. (2000). *Anthropologie du carnaval. La ville, la fête et l'Afrique à Bahia.* Marseille: Éditions Parenthèses.

Agier, M. (2009). *Esquisses d'une anthropologie de la ville. Lieux, situations, mouvements.* Paris: Academia-Bruylant.

Akkar, M. (2005). The changing 'publicness' of contemporary public spaces: a case study of the Grey's Monument Area, Newcastle upon Tyne. *Urban Design International, 10*(2), 95–113.

Akkar Ercan, M. (2007). Public Spaces of post-industrial cities and their changing roles. *METU JFA, 24*(1), 115–137.

Alexander, C. (2002.) *The nature of order: an essay on the art of building and the nature of the universe; Book two: The process of creating life.* Berkeley, CA: Center for Environmental Structure.

Alexander, C., Ishikawa, S., & Silverstein, M. (1977). *A pattern language: towns, buildings, construction.* New York: Oxford University Press.

Alexander, M. (2003). Local policies towards migrants as an expression of Host-Stranger relations: A proposed typology. *Journal of Ethnic and Migration Studies, 29*(3), 411–430.

Alkan, S. (2006). *Globalization, locality and struggle over a living space—The case of Karanfilkoy* (Master's thesis). Weimar, Germany: Institute for European Urban Studies, Bauhaus University Weimar.

Allen, J. (2006). Ambient power: Berlin's Potsdamer Platz and the seductive logic of public spaces. *Urban Studies, 43*(2), 441–455.

Allport, G. (1954). *The nature of prejudice.* Reading, MA: Addison-Wesley.

Allum, F. (2006). *Camorristi, politicians, and businessmen: The transformation of organized crime in post-war Naples.* Leeds, UK: Northestern University Press.

Allum, F. (2011). *Il crimine organizzato a Napoli.* Naples: L'Ancora del Mediterraneo.

Altas, N. E., & Ozsoy, A. (1998). Spatial adaptability and flexibility as parameters of user satisfaction for quality housing. *Building and Environment 33*(5), 315–323.

Amaturo, E. (Ed.). (2004). *Profili di povertà e politiche sociali a Napoli.* Naples: Guida.

Amin, A. (2002). Ethnicity and the multicultural city: Living with diversity. *Environment and Planning A, 34*(6), 959–980.

Amin, A. (2006). The good city. *Urban Studies, 43*(5), 1009–1023.

Amin, A. (2008). Collective culture and urban public space. *City, 12*(1), 5–24.

Amin, A. (2012). *Land of strangers.* London: Polity.

Amselle, J. L. (2001). *Branchements. Anthropologie de l'universalité des cultures.* Paris: Flammarion.

Anderson, B. (1991). *Imagined communities.* London: Verso.

Angotti, T. (2008). *New York for sale. Community planning confronts global real estate.* Cambridge, MA: MIT Press.

Arbaci, S. (2007). Ethnic segregation, housing systems and welfare regimes in Europe. *European Journal of Housing Policy, 7*(4), 401–433.

Arefi, M. (2011). Order in informal settlements: A case study of Pinar, Istanbul. *Built Environment, 37*(1), 42–56.

Arendt, H. (1995). *Qu'est-ce que la politique?* Paris: Seuil.

Arndt, A. (1961). *Demokratie als Bauherr.* Berlin: Akademie der Künste.

Arnstein, S. R. (1969). A ladder of citizen participation. *JAIP, 35*(4), 216–224.

Arslan, R. (1989). Gecekondulasmanin Evrimi. *Mimarlik 89*(6), 34–37.

Atkinson, R. (2003). Domestication by cappuccino or a revenge on urban space? Control and empowerment in the management of public spaces. *Urban Studies, 40*(9), 1829–1843.

Bachmann-Medick, D. (2010). *Cultural turns. Neuorientierung in den Kulturwissenschaften*. Hamburg: Rowohlt.

Bacqué, M.-H., & Fijalkow, Y. (2006). En attendant la gentrification : Discours et politiques à la Goutte d'Or (1982–2000). *Sociétés contemporaines, 3*, 63–83.

Baecker, D. (1994). Soziale Hilfe als Funktionssystem der Gesellschaft. *Zeitschrift für Soziologie 23*, 93–110.

Baharoglu, D., & Leitmann, J. (1998). Coping strategies for infrastructure: How Turkey's spontaneous settlements operate in the absence of formal rules. *Habitat International, 22*(2), 115–135.

Balducci, A., Fedeli, V., & Pasqui, G. (Eds.) (2011). *Strategic planning for contemporary urban regions. City of cities: A project for Milan*. Farnham, UK: Ashgate.

Balkin, S. (1989). *Self-employment for low-income people*. New York: Praeger.

Barbagallo, F. (1988). *Camorra e criminalità organizzata in Campania*. Naples: Liguori.

Barnett, C. (2008). Convening publics: The parasitical spaces of public action. In K. Cox, M. Low and J. Robinson (Eds.), *The Sage handbook of political geography* (pp. 403–426). London: Sage.

Barou, Y. (2012, July 24). Le modèle social européen, un atout face à la crise, *Le Monde*. Retrieved from http://www.lemonde.fr/idees/article/2012/07/24/le-modele-social-europeen-un-atout-face-a-la-crise_1737799_3232.html

Bartha, G. (2010). Rethinking the marketplace: A story of resistance and proactivity. In E. Steierhoffer and L. Polyák (Eds.), *Anatomy of a street* (pp. 29–34). London: Art Network Agency.

Bartoszewicz, D. (2010, August 20). Całkiem nowa ulica Chłodna. Wkrótce rusza remont [Chłodna is completely new: Renovations to start soon]. *Gazeta Wyborcza*. Retrieved from http://warszawa.gazeta.pl/warszawa/1,95194,8273460.html

Bartoszewicz, D. (2011, December 19). Będzie karuzela na Chłodnej? Marzenie projektanta ulicy [Will there be a carousel on Chłodna? A designer's dream]. *Gazeta Wyborcza*. Retrieved from http://warszawa.gazeta.pl/warszawa/1,34885,10461028.html

Baumeister, R. (1911). Bauordnung und Wohnungsfrage. Band IV. Heft III. Berlin: Ernst.

BBC. (2012, December 11). 2011 census: 45% of Londoners white British. Retrieved from http://www.bbc.co.uk/news/uk-england-london-20680565

Beckett, K., & Herbert, S. (2008). Dealing with disorder. Social control in the post-industrial city. *Theoretical Criminology 12*(1), 5–30.

Beguinot, C. (Ed.) (2009). *La Città. La crisi, le ragioni, i rimedi* (Vol. 30). Rome: Fondazione Della Rocca.

Beguinot, C., & Cardarelli, U. (1992). *Città cablata e nuova architettura*. Naples: DiPiST Università di Napoli Federico II, IPiGeT CNR.

Belanger, A. (2000). Sport venues and the spectacularisation of urban space in North America: The case of the Molson Centre in Montreal. *International Review for the Sociology of Sport, 35*(3), 378–397.

Belina, B. (2006). *Raum Überwachung Kontrolle. Vom staatlichen Zugriff auf städtische Bevölkerung*. Münster: Westfälisches Damfboot.

Belina, B., & Helms, G. (2003). Zero tolerance for the industrial past and other threats: Policing and urban entrepreneurialism in Britain and Germany. *Urban Studies, 40*(9), 1845–1867.

Belmessous, F., & Tapada-Berteli, T. (2011). *Public spaces developments in Lyon (France) and Barcelona (Spain): A successful strategy against social exclusion and urban poverty?* Paper presented at European Network for Housing Research 2011 conference. Retrieved from http://www.enhr2011.com/sites/default/files/Paper_Belmessous_TapadaBerteli_W14.pdf

Ben Joseph, E. (2005). *The code of the city. Standards and the hidden language of place making*. Cambridge, MA: MIT Press.

Ben Joseph, E., & Szold, T. S. (Eds.). (2005). *Regulating place: Standards and the shaping of urban America*. New York: Routledge.

The Berg (2012a). *The Berg*. Retrieved from http://www.facebook.com/thebergberlin

The Berg (2012b). *The Berg*. Retrieved from http://www.the-berg.de/press_release.html

Berker, T., Hartmann, M., Punie, Y., & Ward, K. (2006). *Domestication of media and technology*. Maidenhead: Open University Press.

Berman, M. (2006). *On the town: One hundred years of spectacle in times square.* New York: Random House.

Betker, F. (2005). Der öffentliche Raum in der "sozialistischen Stadt": Städtebau in der DDR zwischen Utopie und Alltag. In C. Bernhardt, G. Fehl, G. Kuhn, & U. von Petz (Eds.), *Geschichte der Planung des öffentlichen Raums* (Vol. 122, pp. 153–162). Dortmund: IRPUD.

Bewegung.taz. (2011). *1 qm Tempelhof.* Retrieved from http://bewegung.taz.de/aktionen/1qm-tempelhof/blogeintrag/ein-quadratmeter-tempelhof-fuer-jeden

Bhabha, H. K. (2004). *The location of culture.* London: Routledge.

Bianchetti, C. (2009). Quantità e quiete: Il discorso ideologico sull'abitare. *Archivio di Studi Urbani e regionali, 94,* 9–22.

Bierut, B. (1951). *The six-year plan for the reconstruction of Warsaw.* Warsaw: Książka i wiedza.

Bifulco, L. (Ed.). (2003). *Il genius loci del welfare. Strutture e processi della qualità sociale.* Rome: Officina Edizioni.

Bifulco, L., & Bricocoli, M. (2010). Organizing urban space. Tools, processes and public action. In C. Coletta, F. Gabbi, & G. Sonda (Eds.), *Urban Plots, Organizing Cities.* London: Ashgate.

Billig, N. (2009a). *Evaluation of open space form and use in an Istanbul squatter settlement.* Paper presented at 3rd International Conference on Landscape Architecture by ILA and ÖGLA. X-Larch III. LANDSCAPE—GREAT IDEA! Vienna, Austria.

Billig, N. (2009b). *The growth of unique urban forms and uses: Street use in informal verses planned residential areas in Istanbul.* Poster presented at International Urban Planning and Environment Association (IUPEA), 8th International Symposium: Parallel Patterns of Urban Growth and Decline, Kaiserslautern, Germany.

Billig, N. (2010). *The merging of infrastructure and public open space in a divided Istanbul squatter settlement.* Paper presented at Infrastrukturuurbanismus Symposium, Munich, Germany.

Bird, J. (1963). *The major seaports of the United Kingdom.* London: Hutchinson.

Bissell, D. (2010). Passenger mobilities: affective atmospheres and the sociality of public transport. *Environment and Planning D: Society and Space, 28,* 270–289.

Blomme, J. (2003). *History of the Port of Antwerp (1950–1975).* Unpublished document. Antwerp: Research Department of the Port of Antwerp.

Bloomfield, J., & Wood, P. (2011). *Intercultural spaces and centres.* Briefing paper of the Intercultural Cities joint action (EU and CoE).

Boaga, G. (1972). *Disegno, di strade: Fondamenti di metodologia metaprogettuale.* Rome: Officina Edizioni.

Boal, F. (2008). Territoriality on the Shankill-Falls Divide, Belfast. *Irish Geography, 41*(3), 349–366.

Boal, F., & Royle, S. (Eds.). (2006). *Enduring city, Belfast in the twentieth century.* London: Blackstaff.

Boarnet, M., Joh, K., Siembab, W., Fulton, W., & Nguyen, M. (2011). Retrofitting the suburbs to increase walking: Evidence from a land use–travel study. *Urban Studies, 48*(1), 129–159.

Boltanski, L., & Chiapello, E. (1999). *Le nouveau esprit du Capitalism.* Paris: Gallimard.

Boltanski, L., & Chiapello, E. (2005). *The new spirit of capitalism.* London: Verso.

Bonnes, M., Bonaiuto, M., Nenci, A., & Carrus, G. (Eds.). (2011). *Urban diversities—Environmental and social issues.* Göttingen: Hogrefe & Huber.

Bouly de Lesdain, S. (1999). Château Rouge, une centralité africaine à Paris. *Ethnologie Française, 29*(1), 86–99.

Bourdieu, P. (1983). Ökonomisches Kapital, kulturelles Kapital, soziales Kapital. In Reinhard Kreckel (Ed.), *Soziale ungleichheiten* (pp. 183–198). Göttingen: Schwarz.

Bourdieu, P. (1987). *Die feinen Unterschiede: Kritik der gesellschaftlichen Urteilskraft.* Frankfurt am Main: Suhrkamp.

Boyer, M. C. (2012). Collective memory under siege: The case of 'heritage tourism'. In C. G. Crysler, S. Cairns, & H. Heynen (Eds.), *The SAGE handbook of architectural theory* (pp. 325–339). London: Sage.

Bradley, W. (2010). The gentrification of Broadway Market. *Hackney History, 16,* 49–62.

Brand, S. (2005). Markets and the city, traditional spaces of commerce for a global society. In A. Siegel (Ed.), *Market hall. Expiration date: To be determined* (pp. 154–158). Budapest: Ernst Múzeum.

Bricocoli, M. (2009). Lo sguardo acquietato dell'urbanista sull'architettura dell'abitare. *Archivio di Studi Urbani e Regionali, 94,* 91–103.

Bricocoli, M., & Breckner, I. (2012). 'Geschlossene irrenanstalten' als ressourcen der stadterneuerung ['Prisons of madness' as sources of urban innovation]. In A. Eisinger, N. Brodowski, & J. Seifert (Eds.), *Freilegen immanenter potenziale städtischer räume* [*Urban reset. How to activate immanent potentials of urban spaces*] (pp. 146–155). Zurich: Birkhauser.

Bricocoli, M., & Cucca, R. (2012, August 1–4). *Local effects of a diffused and misleading rhetoric: Social mix and housing policies in Milan*. Paper presented at the Second International Sociological Association Forum of Sociology, Buenos Aires, Argentina.

Bricocoli, M., & Savoldi, P. (2010). *Milano downtown [Luoghi dell'abitare e azione pubblica]*. Milan: Et al. Edizioni.

Bricocoli, M., & Savoldi, P. (2012). Habiter par projets. In A. Berque, A. de Biase, & P. Bonnin (Eds.). *Donner lieu au monde: La poétique de l'habiter*. Paris: Editions donner lieu.

Bricocoli, M., de Leonardis, O., & Savoldi, P. (2011). *Open spaces, walls and housing. The aesthetics and politics of social order*. Paper presented at the 23rd Conference of the ENHR-European Network for Housing Research, Toulouse.

Bridge, G. (2005). *Reason in the city of difference: Pragmatism, communicative action and contemporary urbanism*. London: Routledge.

Brown, W. (2009). *Murs. Les murs de séparation et le déclin de la souveraineté étatique*. Paris: Les Prairies Ordinaires.

Bude, H., & Willisch, E. (Ed.). (2006). *Das Problem der Exklusion. Ausgegrenzte, Entbehrliche, Überflüssige*. Hamburg: Rowohlt.

Bushart, M. (1985). Bauplastik im Dritten Reich. In M. Bushart, B. Nicolai, & W. Schuster (Eds.), *Entmachtung der Kunst. Architektur, Bildhauerei und ihre Institutionalisierung von 1920 bis 1960* (pp. 104–113). Berlin: Fröhlich und Kaufmann.

Butler, J. (1993). *Bodies that matter*. New York: Routledge.

Butler, J. (1997). *Excitable speech. A politics of the performance*. London: Routledge.

Butler, T. (2003). Living in the bubble: Gentrification and its 'others' in North London. *Urban Studies, 40*(12), 2469–2486.

Butler, T., & Robson, G. (2003). *London calling: The middle classes and the re-making of inner London*. London: Berg Publishers.

Cagdas, G. (1995). Spatial organizations and functions in squatter dwellings: A case study in Istanbul. *Open House International, 20*(4), 40–45.

Calabi, D. (2004). *The market and the city: Square, street and architecture in early modern Europe*. Burlington: Ashgate.

Cameron, D. (2011, May 2). PM's speech at Munich security conference. Retrieved from http://www.number10.gov.uk/news/pms-speech-at-munich-security-conference

Carmona, M., Heath, T., Oc, T., & Tiesdell, S. (2010 [2003]). *Public places—urban spaces. The dimensions of urban design*. Oxford: Elsevier.

Carmona, M., de Magalhães, C., & Hammond, L. (2008). *Public space: The management dimension*, London: Routledge.

Cassidy, R., & Mullin, M. (2007). *Where the wild things are now: Domestication reconsidered*. London: Berg.

Castells, M. (1983). *The city and the grassroots: A cross-cultural theory of urban social movements*. London: Arnold.

Cavender, A. (2006). Gecekondu: Illusion and reality in one small project [online database]. Retrieved from http://www.onesmallproject.com/pagescontributors/contributorcavender.html

Center for Urban Pedagogy. (2011). Vendor power! Retrieved from http://welcometocup.org/Projects/MakingPolicyPublic/VendorPower

Charta Wien Online. (2012a). German version. Retrieved from https://charta.wien.gv.at/start/charta

Charta Wien Online. (2012b). English version. Retrieved from https://charta.wien.gv.at/start/charta/files/2012/12/20121206_charta_englisch.pdf

Chmielewska, E. (2008). Niepamięć w upamiętnianiu: Szczególność miejsc traumy a typowość pamięci w ikonosferze Warszawy [Remembering, commemorating and forgetting: The specificities of places of trauma and the ubiquity of memory in the iconosphere of Warsaw]. In K. Chudzimska-Uhera & B. Gutowski (Eds.), *Rzeźba w Polsce 1945–2008* (pp. 101–106). Orońsko: Centrum Rzeźby Polskiej.

Chmielewska, E. (2012). Vectors of looking: Reflections on the Luftwaffe's aerial survey of Warsaw, 1944. In M. Dorrian & F. Pousin (Eds.), *Seeing from above: The aerial view in visual culture*. London: I. B. Tauris.

Choay, F., & Merlin, P. (Eds.) (2000). *Dictionnaire de l'urbanisme et de l'aménagement*. Paris: Gallimard.

Choice cuts. Farmer's markets: Fresh food from the farmer is profitable and popular. (2003, August 2). *Economist*, Vol, 37.

Chomsky, N. (1965). *Aspects of the theory of syntax*. Cambridge, MA: MIT Press.

Chronopoulos, T. (2011). *Spatial regulation in New York City: From urban renewal to zero tolerance*. New York: Taylor and Francis.

Cities for Local Integration Policy Network (CLIP). (2010a). *Intercultural policies in European cities*. Dublin: European Foundation for the Improvement of Living and Working Conditions.

Cities for Local Integration Policy Network (CLIP) (2010b). *Intercultural policies in European cities: Best practice guide*. Dublin: European Foundation for the Improvement of Living and Working Conditions.

Cities of the night. (1991). *Economist, 321*, 15–17.

Clark, P. (2006). *The European city and green space: London, Stockholm, Helsinki and St Petersburg, 1850–2000*. Aldershot: Ashgate.

Clemente, M., & Esposito De Vita, G. (2008). *Città interetnica. Spazi, forme e funzioni per l'aggregazione e per l'integrazione*. Naples: Editoriale Scientifica.

Coeck, C., & Tessier, T. (2007). Project appraisal and decision-making in practice: Evidence from the Deurganckdock case in the Port of Antwerp. In E. Haezendonck (Ed.), *Transport evaluation project* (pp. 168–180). Antwerp: University of Antwerp.

Cohen, N. (2010, February, 27). Talk at Foodprint NYC, Studio-X, New York City. Retrieved from http://urbanomnibus.net/2010/08/foodprint-city

Coletta, C., Gabbi, F., & Sonda, G. (Eds). (2010). *Urban plots, organizing cities*. London: Ashgate.

Comedia. (2007). *Bringing people and communities together*. Whetherby: Commission on Integration and Cohesion.

Commission on Integration and Cohesion (CIC). (2007). *Our shared future—final report*. Whetherby: Author.

Costa, G., & Sabatinelli, S. (2012). City report: Milan, Wilco. *Publication n. 23, Welfare innovations at the local level in favour of cohesion*. WILCO Project. Bruxelles: European Commission.

Council of Europe (CoE). (2011). *Living together. Combining diversity with freedom in 21st century Europe*. Report of the Group of Eminent Persons of the Council of Europe. Strasbourg: Author.

Crang, M. (2000). Public space, urban space and electronic space: Would the real city please stand up? *Urban Studies, 37*(2), 301–317.

Crawford, M. (1992). The world in a shopping mall. In M. Sorkin (Ed), *Variations on a theme park: The new American city and the end of public space* (pp. 3–30). New York: Hill and Wang.

Crawford, M. (1999). Blurring the boundaries: Public space and private life. In J. Chase, M. Crawford, & J. Kaliski (Eds.), *Everyday urbanism*. New York: Monacelli.

Creed, G. W. (1998). *Domesticating revolution: From socialist reform to ambivalent transition in a Bulgarian village*. Philadelphia: Pennsylvania State University Press.

Cucca, R. (2012). The hidden unwanted. Patterns of immigrants' marginality in Copenhagen (Denmark) and Milan (Italy). In C. C. Yeakey (Ed.), *Living on the boundaries: Urban marginality in national and international context*. Bingley: Emerald Group Publishing.

Czakó, Á., & Sík, E. (1999). Characteristics and origins of the Comecon open air market in Hungary. *International Journal of Urban and Regional Research, 23*(4), 715–737.

Czarniawska, B. (1997). *Narrating the organization*. Chicago, IL: The University of Chicago Press.

Dangschat, J., & Hamedinger, A. (2009). Planning culture in Austria—The case of Vienna, the unlike city. In J. Knieling & F. Orthengrafen (Eds.), *Planning cultures in Europe. Decoding cultural phenomena in urban and regional planning* (pp. 95–112). London: Ashgate.

Dascher, K. (2007). Was stabilisiert der 'Stadtumbau Ost'? *Magazin Städte im Umbruch, 4*, 57–61.

Daval, J.-L. (2010a). L'affirmation de la sculpture. In G. Duby & J.-L. Daval (Eds.), *La sculpture. De la Renaissance au XXe siècle* (Vol. 2, pp. 1118–1133). Cologne: Taschen.

Daval, J.-L. (2010b). L'espace de la représentation. In G. Duby & J.-L. Daval (Eds.), *La sculpture. De la Renaissance au XXe siècle* (Vol. 2, pp. 1064–1091). Cologne: Taschen.

Daval, J.-L. (2010c). Monumentalité et nouvelles techniques. In G. Duby & J.-L. Daval (Eds.), *La sculpture. De la Renaissance au XXe siècle* (Vol. 2, pp. 1037–1063). Cologne: Taschen.

Davidson, R., & Entrikin, J. (2005). The Los Angeles coast as a public space. *Geographical Review, 95*(4), 578–593.

Davis, M. (1992). *City of quartz: Excavating the future of Los Angeles*. London: Vintage.

DCLG. (2008). *Guidance on meaningful interaction: How encouraging positive relationships between people can help build community cohesion*. London: Author.

de Biase, A., & Coralli, M., (2009). *Espaces en commun. Nouvelles formes de penser et habiter la ville*. Paris: L'Harmattan.

de Biase, A., & Rossi, C. (2006). *Chez nous. Identités et territoires dans les mondes contemporains*. Paris: Editions de La Villette.

deFonseca Feitosa, F., & Wissman, A. (2006). *Social mix policy approaches to urban segregation in Europe and the United States.* Unpublished manuscript, ZEF Universität Bonn.

De Frantz, M. (2005). From cultural regeneration to discursive governance: Constructing the flagship of the 'Museumsquartier Vienna' as a plural symbol of change. *International Journal of Urban and Regional Research, 29,* 50–66. doi: 10.1111/j.1468-2427.2005.00569.x

Degen, M., DeSilvey, C., & Rose, G. (2008). Experiencing visualities in designed urban environments: Learning from Milton Keynes. *Environment and Planning A, 40,* 1901–1920.

Delaney, C. (2011). *Investigating culture: An experiential introduction to anthropology* (2nd ed.). Oxford: Wiley-Blackwell.

de Leonardis, O. (2011). Dividing or combining citizens. The politics of active citizenship in Italy. In J. Newman & E. Tonkens (Eds.), *Participation, responsibility and choice. Summoning the active citizen in western Europe welfare states.* Amsterdam: Amsterdam University Press.

Demireva, N. (2011). *Immigration, briefing: Diversity and social cohesion.* Oxford: Oxford University Press.

Demps, L., & Paschke, C. L. (1998). *Flughafen Tempelhof—die Geschichte einer Legende.* Berlin: Ullstein.

De Souza, E., Silva, A., & Frith, J. (2012). *Mobile interfaces in public spaces: Locational privacy, control and urban sociability.* London: Routledge.

Deutsche, R. (1996). *Evictions: Art and spatial politics.* Cambridge, MA: MIT Press.

De Vriendt, J. (2009, 24 March). *Is it a good cause to swallow up a paradise as Doel for the sake of economic profit?* Paper presented at the International Conference Soin du patrimoine et citoyenneté active, Malines, Belgium.

Dewey, J. (1927). *The public and its problems.* Denver, CO: Alan Swallow.

Dewsbury, J. D., Harrison, P., Rose, M., & Wylie, J. (2002). Enacting geographies. *Geoforum, 33,* 437–440.

Dimitriou, O., & Koutrolikou, P. (2011), *Between public and private: 'Commons' and 'collective arenas'.* Paper presented at Creating Publics workshop, London, July 21–22.

Dines, N., Cattell, V., Gesler, W., & Curtis, S. (2006). *Public spaces, social relations and well-being in East London.* York: Policy Press for Joseph Rowntree Foundation.

Dixon, J. (2006). The ties that bind and those that don't: Toward reconciling group threat and contact theories of prejudice. *Social Forces, 84,* 2179–2804.

Domosh, M. (1998). Those 'gorgeous incongruities': Polite politics and public space on the streets of nineteenth-century New York City. *Annals of the Association of American Geographers, 88,* 209–226.

Donzelot, J. (1999). La nouvelle question urbaine. *Esprit, 258,* 87–114.

Donzelot, J., & Estebe, P. (1994). *L'État animateur: Essai sur la politique de la ville.* Paris: Esprit.

Donzelot, J., Mevel, C., & Wyvekens, A. (2003). *Faire société. La politique de la ville aux Etats-Unis et en France.* Paris: éd. du Seuil.

Dörre, K., Lessenich, S., & Rosa, H. (2009). *Soziologie Kapitalismus Kritik.* Frankfurt am Main: Suhrkamp.

Drache, D. (2008). *Defiant publics: The unprecedented reach of the global citizen.* Cambridge, UK: Polity.

Dündar, Ö. (2001). Models of urban transformation: Informal housing in Ankara. *Cities, 18*(6), 391–401.

Durth, W., Gutschow, N., & Düwel, J. (1998). *Architektur und Städtebau der DDR; Aufbau. Städte, Thesen, Dokumente. Band 2.* Frankfurt am Main: Campus.

EC. (1994). The Aalborg Charter, Brussels: European Commission. Retrieved from http://ec.europa.eu/environment/urban/pdf/aalborg_charter.pdf

EC. (2006). *Thematic strategy on the urban environment.* Brussels: European Commission.

EC. (2007). *The Leipzig charter on sustainable European cities.* Brussels: European Commission. Retrieved from http://ec.europa.eu/regional_policy/archive/themes/urban/leipzig_charter.pdf

EC. (2010a). *Europe 2020: A strategy for smart, sustainable and inclusive growth.* Brussels: European Commission.

EC. (2010b). *Making our cities attractive and sustainable.* Brussels: European Commission. Retrieved from http://ec.europa.eu/environment/urban/home_en.htm

EC. (2010c). *Green paper: Unlocking the potential of cultural and creative industries.* Brussels: European Commission. Retrieved from http://ec.europa.eu/culture/our-policy-development/doc/GreenPaper_creative_industries_en.pdf

EC. (2010d). *Why socio-economic inequalities increase?* Brussels: European Commission.

Eckardt, F., & Wildner, K. (2008). *Public Istanbul: Spaces and spheres of the urban.* Bielefeld: Transcript.

ECOTEC. (2007). *State of European cities report.* Brussels: European Commission.

EEA. (2009). *Ensuring quality of life in Europe's cities and towns.* Copenhagen: European Environment Agency. Retrieved from http://www.eea.europa.eu/publications/quality-of-life-in-Europes-cities-and-towns

Egercioğlu, Y., & Özdemir, S. (2007). *Changing dynamics of urban transformation process in Turkey: Izmir and Ankara cases.* Paper presented at Proceedings of the 47th International Congress of the European Regional Science Association, Paris, France, August 29–September 2.

El Khafif, M. (2009). *Inszenierter Urbanismus.* Stadtraum für Kunst, Kultur und Konsum im Zeitalter der Erlebnisgesellschaft. Saarbrücken: VDM.

Emerson, M. (Ed). (2011). *Interculturalism. Europe and its Muslims in search of sound societal models.* Brussels: Centre for European Policy Studies.

Emmenegger, B., & Litscher, M. (2011). *Perspektiven zu öffentlichen Räumen. Theoretische und praxisbezogene Beiträge aus der Stadtforschung.* Lucerne: interact.

Engelking, B., & Leociak, J. (2009). *The Warsaw ghetto: A guide to the perished city.* (Emma Harris, Trans.). New Haven, CT: Yale University Press.

Ergenoglu, A. S., Türkyçlmaz, C. C., Baytin, C. P., & Aytug, A. (2005). *Housing environment in the process of cultural change and transformation; Study in Istanbul/Armutlu squatter settlement.* Paper presented at Doing, Thinking, Feeling Home: The Mental Geography of Residential Environments, Delft University of Technology, Delft, The Netherlands, October 14–15.

Ergun, N. (1991). *Evaluation of upgrading plans as a proposal for the solution of squatter problems: The case of Talatpasa District.* Paper presented at Housing for the Urban Poor—European Network for Housing Research International Symposium, Istanbul, October 14–15.

Erman, T. (2001). The politics of squatter (gecekondu) studies in Turkey: The changing representations of rural migrants in the academic discourse. *Urban Studies, 38*(7), 983–1002.

Erste Group Immorent Online. (2013a). *Erste Campus. Quartier Belvedere.* Retrieved from http://www.erste-campus.at/en/context/quartier-belvedere.html

Erste Group Immorent Online. (2013b). *Wo Wien Welt Wird. Quartier Belvedere.* Retrieved from http://www.quartier-belvedere.at/home

Ertaş, H. (2010). The potential of Istanbul's unprogrammed public spaces. *Architectural Design, 80*(1), 52–57.

Esping-Andersen, G. (1999). *Social foundations of postindustrial economies.* Oxford: Oxford University Press.

Eurispes. (2008). *21° Rapporto Italia.* Rome: Koinè.

Fainstein, S. (2010). *The just city.* Ithaca, NY: Cornell University Press.

Fessler Vaz, L., Knierbein, S., & Welch Guerra, M. (2006). *Der öffentliche Raum in der Planungspolitik. Studien aus Rio de Janeiro und Berlin [Public space and planning policy. Research from Rio de Janeiro and Berlin].* Weimar: Bauhaus Verlag.

Fincher, R., & Jacobs, J. M. (1998). *Cities of difference.* New York: Guilford.

Fincher, R., & Iveson, K. (2008). *Planning and diversity in the city: Redistribution, recognition and encounter.* Basingstoke: Palgrave MacMillan.

Fischer, J. (2005). Die Prager Straße in Dresden. Zur Architektursoziologie eines utopischen Ensembles. *Ausdruck und Gebrauch—Dresdner wissenschaftliche Halbjahresheft. Architektur Wohnen Umwelt, 5,* 5–15.

Fleury, A. (2007). *Les espaces publics dans les politiques métropolitaines. Réflexions au croisement de trois expériences: De Paris aux quartiers centraux de Berlin et Istanbul* (Thesis). Université Panthéon-Sorbonne, Paris.

Flusty, S. (2001). The banality of interdiction: Surveillance control and the displacement of diversity. *International Journal of Urban and Regional Research, 25,* 658–664.

Foucault, M. (1967). Of other spaces: Utopias and heterotopias. (Jay Miskowiec, Trans.), *Diacritics,* Vol. 16, No. 1 (Spring, 1986), pp. 22–27.

Foucault, M. (1995). *Discipline & punish: The birth of the prison.* New York: Vintage.

Foucault, M. (2004). Geschichte der Gouvernementalität II. Die Geburt der Biopolitik. In M. Senellart (Ed.), *Vorlesungen am Collège der France (1975–1978)* (pp. 225–259). Frankfurt am Main: Suhrkamp.

Foucault, M. (2008). Geschichte der Gouvernementalität I. Sicherheit, Territorium, Bevölkerung. In M. Senellart (Ed.), *Vorlesungen am Collège der France (1975–1978)* (pp. 449–521). Frankfurt am Main: Suhrkamp.

Francis, M. (1989). Control as a dimension of public-space quality. In I. Altman & E. H. Zube (Eds.), *Public places and spaces* (pp. 147–172). New York: Plenum.

Franck, K., & Paxson, L. (2007). Transforming public space into sites of mourning and free expression. In K. Franck & Q. Stevens (Eds.), *Loose space: possibility and diversity in urban life* (pp. 132–153). New York: Routledge.

Franck, K. A., & Stevens, Q. (2007). *Loose space: Possibility and diversity in urban life.* London: Routledge.

Fraser, N. (1990). Rethinking the public sphere: A contribution to the critique of actually existing democracy. *Social Text, 25/26*, 56–80.

Fraser, N. (1992). Rethinking the public sphere: A contribution to the critique of actually existing democracy. In C. Calhoun (Ed.), *Habermas and the public sphere* (pp. 109–142). Cambridge, MA: MIT Press.

Fraser, N. (2008). *Scales of justice: Reimagining political space in a globalizing world*. Cambridge, UK: Polity.

Freeman, R. E. (2010). *Strategic management: A stakeholder approach*. Cambridge, UK: Cambridge University Press.

Fuchs, P. (2000). Systemtheorie und Soziale Arbeit. In P. Merten (Ed.), *Systemtheorie sozialer Arbeit. Neue Ansätze und veränderte Perspektiven* (pp. 157–175). Opladen: Leske + Budrich.

Fundacja Zmiana. (2009, October 29). Dewastacja ulicy Chłodnej pod hasłem rewitalizacji [Destruction of Chłodna Street under the guise of revitalization]. [Online petition]. Retrieved from http://www.petycje.pl/petycja/4588/dewastacja_ul._chlodnej_pod_haslem_rewitalizacji.html

Fyfe, N., Bannister, J., & Kearns, A. (2006). Respectable or respectful? (In)civility and the city. *Urban Studies, 43*, 919–937.

Fyfe, N. R. (Ed.). (1998). *Images of the street: Planning, identity, and control of public spaces*. London: Routledge.

Gaber, J., & Gaber, S. L. (2007). *Qualitative analysis for planning and policy: Beyond the numbers*. Chicago, IL: American Planning Association.

Gaffikin, F., McEldowney, M., & Sterrett, K. (2010). Creating shared public space in contested city: The role of urban design. *Journal of Urban Design, 15*(4), 493–513.

Gans, H. J. (2008). Involuntary segregation and the Ghetto: Disconnecting process and place, city and community. *International Journal of Urban and Regional Research, 7*(4), 353–357.

Gasser, K. (2004). *Kriminalpolitik oder City-Pflege?* Bedeutungsstrukturen polizeilicher Strategien im öffentlichen Raum der Stadt Bern. Bern. Neue Berner Beiträge zur Soziologie.

Gaus, H. J. (2002). The sociology of space: A use-centered view. *City and Community, 1*(4), 329–339.

GB* Online. (2013). *Gebietsbetreuung Stadterneuerung Wien Online Stadtteilbüro Sonnwendviertel*. Information und Austausch. Retrieved from http://www.gbstern.at/teams/gb10/stadtteilbuero-sonnwendviertel

Geddes, P. (1915). *Cities in evolution. An introduction to the town planning movement and to the study of civics*. London: Williams & Norgate.

Gehl, J. (1987). *Life between buildings: Using public space*. New York: Van Nostrand Reinhold.

Gehl, J. (2010). *Cities for people*. Washington, DC: Island.

Gerkan, M.v. (1990). *West-Östlicher Architektenworkshop zum Gesamtkunstwerk Dresden*. Hamburg: Christians.

Germain, A. (1997). L'étranger dans la ville. *Canadian Journal of Regional Science/Revue canadienne de sciences régionales, 20*(12), 237–254.

Gerő, A. (2003). Piac a csarnokban [Market in the hall]. In J. Rajk (Ed.), *Lehel: Tér-piac-vásár-csarnok* (pp. 39–42). Pécs: Jelenkor.

Ghorra-Gobin, C. (2001). *Réinventer le sens de la ville: Les espaces publics à l'heure globale*. Paris: L'Harmattan.

Giersig, N. (2008) *Multilevel urban governance and the 'European City': Discussing metropolitan reforms in Stockholm and Helsinki*. Wiesbaden: VS.

Gieryn, T. F. (2000). A space for place in sociology. *Annual Review of Sociology, 26*, 463–496.

Gonul, E., & Corut, I. (2007). From Almus to Kucukarmutlu: An ethnographic study of the rural and suburban space in relation to state and market intrusions. *Journal of Historical Studies, 5*, 33–67.

Gosewinkel, D. (Ed.). (2004). *Zivilgesellschaft – national und transnational*. Berlin: Sigma.

Goss, J. (1999). Once-upon-a-time in the commodity world: An unofficial guide to the mall of America. *Annals of the Association of American Geographers, 89*(1), 45–75.

Gottdiener, M. (1997). *Theming of America: Dreams, visions, and commercial spaces*. Oxford: Westview.

Gouba Craft Market. (2012). *About Gouba*. Retrieved from http://www.gouba.hu

Grillo, R. (2005). *Backlash against diversity? Identity and cultural politics in European cities* (Working Paper WP-05–14). Oxford: Centre on Migration, Policy and Society [COMPAS].

Gross, D. (2000). *Lost time: On remembering and forgetting in late modern culture*. Amherst: University of Massachusetts Press.

GrossMax. (2012). *Tempelhofer Feld*. Retrieved from http://www.grossmax.com/image.asp?x= 567

Guelf, F. M. (2010). *Die urbane Revolution*. Bielefeld: Transcript.

Gulersoy, N. Z. (1999). *I.T.U Ayazaga Kampusu Arazisinde Olusan Gecekondu Bolgesinin Planlamasina Yonelik Bir Arastirma*. Istanbul: Tübitak Konut Araştçrmalarç Ünitesi.

Guth, P. (1995). *Wände der Verheißung. Zur Geschichte der architekturbezogenen Kunst in der DDR*. Leipzig: Thom.

Habermas, J. (1989). *The structural transformation of the public sphere: An inquiry into a category of bourgeois society*. Cambridge, MA: MIT Press.

Hacihasanoglu, I., & Hacihasanoglu, O. (2006). Cultural processes and physical change in Sisli—Istanbul. *Habitat International, 30*(4), 902–915.

Hackenberg, K. (2010). *La communauté portuaire d'Anvers—L'identification des catégories analytiques servant à la description de son réseau informel* (Doctoral thesis). University of Paris VIII.

Hackney. (2003). *The future of Hackney. Hackney's community strategy discussion paper*. London: Borough of Hackney.

Hall, S. (1993). Culture, community, nation. *Cultural Studies, 7*, 349–363.

Hamilton-Baillie, B. (2008). Shared space: reconciling people, places and traffic. *Built Environment, 34*, 161–181.

Hamnett, C. (2003). *Unequal city: London in the global arena*. London: Routledge.

Handke, P. (1977). *Das Gewicht der Welt (The Weight of the World)*. Salzburg: Residenz.

Hann, C. (1992). Market principle, market-place and the transition in eastern Europe. In R. Dilley (Ed.), *Contesting markets*. Edinburgh: Edinburgh University Press.

Haraway, D. (1991). A cyborg manifesto. Science, technology and socialist-feminism in the late twentieth century. In D. Haraway (Ed.), *Simians, cyborgs and women: The reinvention of nature*. London: Routledge.

Hard, G. (2003). *Dimensionen geographischen Denkens*. Göttingen: V&R Unipress.

Harvey, D. (1990). *The condition of postmodernity: An enquiry into the origins of cultural change*. Oxford: Blackwell.

Harvey, D. (2000). *Spaces of hope*. Berkeley: University of California Press.

Harvey, D. (2011). *Le capitalisme contre le droit à la ville. Néoliberalisme, urbanisation, resistances*. Paris: Éditions Amsterdam.

Hauptbahnhof-Wien. (2012). *Facts & figures project Vienna main station*. Retrieved from http://www.hauptbahnhof-wien.at/de/Presse/Publikationen/Folder/FactsFigures.pdf

Healey, P. (1997). *Collaborative planning. Shaping places in fragmented societies*. London: Macmillan.

Healey, P. (2010). *Making better places. The planning project in the twenty-first century*. Basingstoke: Palgrave Macmillan.

Hegel, G. W. F. (1991). *Elements of the Philosophy of Right (Grundlinien der Philosophie des Rechts*. Naturrecht und Staatswissenschaft). Cambridge: Cambrige University Press.

Heiser, J. (2009, December 9). Postcards from Warsaw. [Web log post]. Retrieved from http://blog.frieze.com/postcard_from_warsaw

Helms, G., Atkinson, R., & MacLeod, G. (2007). Securing the city: Urban renaissance, policing and social regulation. *Urban Studies, 14*, 267–276.

Herbert, S. (2008). Contemporary geographies of exclusion I: Traversing Skid Road. *Progress in Human Geography, 32*, 1–8.

Herve, J. (2010). *Intercultural cities. A journey through 23 European cities*. Brussels: Eurocities.

Hessen Agentur GmbH & Studio UC/Klaus Overmeyer. (2008). *Suboptimale Nutzungen. Lieben lernen*. Wiesbaden: Hessisches Ministerium für Wirtschaft, Verkehr und Landesentwicklung.

Hobsbawm, E. J. (1990). *Nations and nationalism since 1780* (2nd ed.). Cambridge, UK: Cambridge University Press.

Holland, C., Clark, A., Katz, J., & Peace, S. (2007). *Social interactions in urban public places*. York: The Policy Press for the Joseph Rowntree Foundation.

Hooghe, M., Reeskens, T., & Stolle, D. (2007). Diversity, multiculturalism and social cohesion: Trust and ethnocentrism in European societies. In K. Banting, T. Courchene, & L. Seidle (Eds.), *Belonging? Diversity, recognition and shared citizenship in Canada* (Vol. III, pp. 387–410). Montreal: Institute for Research on Public Policy.

Hou, J. (2010). *Insurgent public space: Guerrilla urbanism and the remaking of contemporary cities*. London: Routledge.

Howard, E. (1902). *Garden cities of tomorrow*. London: Swan Sonnenschein.

Hubbard, P. (2008). Book review. [Review of *Publics and the city* by Kurt Iveson]. *Cultural Geographies, 15*(4), 524.

Hudson, M., Phillips, J., Ray, K., & Barnes, H. (2007). *Social cohesion in diverse communities*. York: Joseph Rowntree Foundation.

Huschke, W. J. (1998). *Die Luftbrücke nach Berlin 1948/49*. (Unpublished dissertation). TU Berlin.

Ingold, T. (2000). *The perception of the environment: Essays on livelihood, dwelling and skill*. London: Routledge.

Ireland, P. (2008). Comparing responses to ethnic segregation in urban Europe. *Urban Studies, 45*(7), 1333–1358.

Iveson, K. (2007). *Publics and the city*. Oxford: Wiley-Blackwell.

Jackson, P. (1980). *Ethnic groups and boundaries: 'Ordered segmentation' in urban neighbourhoods*. Oxford: Oxford Publishing.

Jackson, P. (1998). Domesticating the street. In N. Fyfe & J. Bannister (Eds.), *Images of the street: Planning, identity and control in public space* (pp. 176–191). London: Routledge.

Jackson, S. (2001). *Lines of activity: Performance, historiography, Hull-House domesticity*. Ann Arbor: University of Michigan Press.

Jacobs, J. (1961). *Death and life of great American cities*. New York: Random House.

Jacquier, C., Bienvenue, S., & Schlappa, H. (2007). *Regenera. Urban Regeneration of Deprived Areas across Europe. Sharing Experiences. Final Report*. The Regenera Cities (Coordination Greater Lyon), Saint Denis, France: URBACT.

Janecskó, K. (2010, April 23). A külvárosba űzné a pultozó zöldségárusokat a főpolgármester-helyettes [The deputy mayor would push vegetable stalls into the suburbs], *Origo*. Retrieved from http://www.origo.hu/itthon/20100423-a-fopolgarmesterhelyettes-megtiltana-a-zoldes-es-gyumolcs-arulast-budapest-belso.html

Janicka, E. (2011). *Festung Warschau [Fortress Warsaw]*. Warsaw: Wydawnictwo Krytyki Politycznej.

Jarzombek, M. (2001). Urban heterology: Dresden and the dialectics of post-traumatic history. In *Studies in theoretical and applied aesthetics* (Vol. 2). Lund: The School of Architecture at Lund University.

Jessop, B. (2003). Kapitalismus, Steuerung und Staat. In S. Buckel, R.-M. Dackweiler, & R. Noppe (Eds.), *Formen und Felder politischer Intervention* (pp. 30–49). Münster: Westfälisches Dampfboot.

Jimenez-Dominguez, B. (2007). Urban appropriation and loose spaces. In K. Franck & Q. Stevens (Eds.), *Loose space: Possibility and diversity in urban life* (pp. 96–112). New York: Routledge.

Jonker, G., & Amiraux, V. (2006). *Politics of visibility: Young Muslims in European public spaces*. Bielefeld: Transcript.

Kaiser, P., & Rehberg, K. S. (1999). *Enge und Vielfalt. Auftragskunst und Kunstförderung in der DDR—Analysen und Meinungen*. Hamburg: Junius.

Kalra, V., & Kapoor, N. (2008). *Interrogating segregation, integration and the community cohesion agenda* (CCSR Working Paper 2008–16). Manchester: The University of Manchester.

Kamleithner, C. (2008). Planung und Liberalismus. *Dérive, 30*, 5–8.

Kasson, J. (1978). *Amusing the million: Coney Island at the turn of the century*. New York: Hill and Wang.

Keff, B. (2011). Trup, Horror, Obczyzna [Corpse, Horror, Alienation]. Introduction to *Festung Warschau* by Elżbieta Janicka, 7–13. Warsaw: Wydawnictwo Krytyki Politycznej.

Keith, M., & Pile, S. (1993). *Place and the politics of Identity*. London: Routledge.

Keyder, C. (2005). Transformations in urban structure and the environment in Istanbul. In F. Adaman & M. Arsel (Eds.), *Environmentalism in Turkey: Between democracy and development?* England: Ashgate.

Kliems, A., & Dmitrieva, M. (2007). *The post-socialist city. Continuity and change in urban space and imagery*. Leipzig: Jovis.

Knierbein, S. (2010). *Die Produktion zentraler öffentlicher Räume in der Aufmerksamkeitsökonomie. Ästhetische, ökonomische und mediale Restrukturierungen durch gestaltwirksame Koalitionen am Beispiel Berlin seit 1980*. Wiesbaden: VS Verlag für Sozialwissenschaften.

Knierbein, S. (2011a). Aspern—Breathing life into an urban replica. On the role of conceived and lived public spaces in the future European city. In *Wien 3420 Aspern Citylab. Vision + Reality. The instruments of urban design* (pp. 71–73). Vienna: Aspern Development AG and Vienna City Administration (MA 18).

Knierbein, S. (2011b). Öffentliche Räume—Wissenschaftliches Minenfeld oder erkenntnistheoretische Chance? [Public spaces—Scientific minefields or epistemological opportunities?] In M. Litscher & B. Emmenegger (Eds.), *Perspektiven zu öffentlichen Räumen. Theoretische und praxisorientierte Beiträge aus der Stadtforschung* (pp. 127–151). Lucerne: interact.

Knierbein, S., Aigner, J., & Watson, S. (2012). Street markets in Vienna and Budapest economic (inter-) action spheres for migrants. In M. Dabringer & A. Trupp (eds.). *Wirtschaften mit Migrationshintergrund. Zur soziokulturellen Bedeutung ethnischer Ökonomien in urbanen Räumen* (pp. 93–106). Studien Vienna.

Koch, R., & Latham, A. (2013a). On the hard work of domesticating a public space. *Urban Studies*, 55(1), 6–21.

Koch, R., & Latham, A. (2013b). Rethinking urban public space: Accounts from a junction in West London. *Transaction of the Institute of British Geographers*, 37(4), 515–529.

Kohn, M. (2004). *Brave new neighborhoods: The privatization of public space*. New York: Routledge.

Konvitz, J. W. (1978). *Cities and the sea—Port-city planning in early modern Europe*. Baltimore, MD: John Hopkins University Press.

Koutrolikou, P. (2012). Spatialities of ethnocultural relations in multicultural East London: Discourses of interaction and social mix. *Urban Studies*, 49(10), 2049–2066.

Kraj, I., & Szczepaniuk, M. (2008, May 7). Chłodna będzie odnawiana, nie wiadomo, czy zwężana [Chłodna to be renovated but perhaps not narrowed]. *Życie Warszawy*. Retrieved from http://www.zw.com.pl/artykul/181,247306.html

Kunzru, H. (2006, January 5). A dispatch from Tony's café. *The Guardian*. Retrieved from http://www.guardian.co.uk

Laclau, E. (1990). *New reflections on the revolution of our time*. London: Verso.

Laclau, E., & Mouffe, C. (1991 [1985]). *Hegemonie und radikale Demokratie. Zur Dekonstruktion des Marxismus*. Wien: Passagen.

Lallement, E. (2010). *La ville marchande: Enquête à Barbès*. Paris: Editions Téraèdre.

Landeshauptstadt Dresden. (2000). *Städtebaulicher Ideen- und Realisierungswettbewerb Platzgestaltung Altmarkt Dresden. Auslobung. Vorabzug*. Dresden: Author.

Landeshauptstadt Dresden Dezernat für Stadtentwicklung. (1994). *Planungsleitbild Innenstadt Dresden*. Dresden: Landeshauptstadt Dresden.

Landeshauptstadt Dresden Dezernat für Stadtentwicklung & PP A/S Pesch Partner Architekten. (2007). *Lebendige Geschichte, Urbane Landschaft. Dresden Planungsleitbild Innenstadt 2007*. Dresden: Landeshauptstadt Dresden.

Landeshauptstadt Dresden & Goller, N. (2000). *Dresden, Europäische Stadt; Rückblick und Perspektiven der Stadtentwicklung*. Dresden: Landeshauptstadt Dresden.

Landeshauptstadt Dresden, Friedrich, A., & Lerm, M. (2000). *Platzgestaltung Altmarkt Dresden. Städtebaulicher Ideen- und Realisierungswettbewerb*. Dresden: Landeshauptstadt Dresden.

Lascoumes, P., & Le Gales, P. (2004). *Gouverner par les instruments*. Paris: Presses de la Fondation Nationale de Science politiques.

Latham, A., & McCormack, D. (2004). Moving cities: Rethinking the materialities of urban geographies. *Progress in Human Geography*, 28, 701–724.

Latour, B. (1991). Technology is society made durable. In J. Law (Ed.), *A sociology of monsters. Essays on power, technology and domination*. London: Routledge.

Laurier, E., & Philo, C. (2006). Cold shoulders and napkins handed: Gestures of responsibility. *Transactions of the Institute of British Geographers*, 31, 193–208.

Law, L. (2002). Defying disappearance: Cosmopolitan public spaces in Hong Kong. *Urban Studies*, 39, 1625–1645.

Le Corbusier. (1925). *Plan Voisin*. Paris: Esprit Nouveau.

Le Corbusier. (1994). *Urbanisme*. Paris: Flammarion.

Lecroart, P. (2007). From the plan to the city: Managing large-scale urban development projects in Europe. *Les Cahiers de l'Institut d'Aménagement et d'Urbanisme de la Région d'Île de France*, 146(June), 110–118.

Lees, L. (2003). The ambivalence of diversity and the politics of urban renaissance: The case of youth in downtown Portland, Maine. *International Journal of Urban and Regional Research*, 27, 613–634.

Lees, L. (2008). Gentrification and social mixing: Towards an inclusive urban renaissance? *Urban Studies*, 4(12), 2449–2470.

Lefebvre, H. (1968). *Le droit à la ville*. Paris: Anthropos.

Lefebvre, H. (1972). *Die Revolution der Städte*. Munich: Syndikat.

Lefebvre, H. (1974). *Kritik des Alltagslebens*. Band I. Munich: Hanser.

Lefebvre, H. (1975). *Kritik des Alltagslebens.* Band II. Munich: Hanser.

Lefebvre, H. (1991). *The Production of Space.* Oxford: Blackwell.

Lefebvre, H. (2000). *La production de l'espace [The production of space].* Paris: Anthropos.

Lefebvre, H. (2003). *The urban revolution.* Minneapolis: University of Minnesota Press.

Lefort, C. (1990). Die Frage der Demokratie. In Ulrich Rödel (Ed.), *Autonome Gesellschaft und libertäre Demokratie* (pp. 281–297). Frankfurt am Main: Suhrkamp.

Lefort, C., & Gauchet, M. (1990 [1967]). Über die Demokratie. In U. Rödel (Ed.), *Autonome Gesellschaft und libertäre Demokratie* (pp. 89–122). Frankfurt am Main: Suhrkamp.

Lehnerer, A. (2009). *Grand urban rules.* Rotterdam: 010 Publishers.

Lehtovuori, P. (2010). *Experience and conflict. The production of urban space.* Farnham: Ashgate.

Leitmann, J., & Baharoglu, D. (1999). Reaching Turkey's spontaneous settlements: The institutional dimension of infrastructure provision. *International Planning Studies, 4*(2), 195–212.

Lemiss, S. (2009). Mit dem Flughafen Tempelhof ist kein Gewinn zu machen. *Berliner Morgenpost.* 4 January 2009.

Lidwell, W., Holen, K., & Butler, J. (2011). *Universal principles of design.* Beverly, MA: Rockport.

Lippert, H. G., & Voisin, C. (2007). Die Wirklichkeit der Bilder. Visionen für Dresden nach 1990. *Dresdner Hefte, 92,* 78–95.

Litscher, M. (2011a). Die Wegweisung—eine unsichtbare Praxis in öffentlichen Stadträumen. *Dérive Zeitschrift für Stadtforschung, 45*(October), 37–41.

Litscher, M. (2011b). Starter-kit: Kompetenz für öffentliche Räume oder das Ertragen von Diversität in der Stadt. In B. Emmenegger & M. Litscher (Eds.), *Perspektiven zu öffentlichen Räumen. Theoretische und praxisbezogene Beiträge aus der Stadtforschung* (pp. 35–52). Lucerne: interact.

Litscher, M., Grossrieder, B., Mösch Payot, P., & Schmutz, M. (2012). *Wegweisung aus öffentlichen Stadträumen.* Lucerne: interact.

Lofland, L. (1973). *A world of strangers: Order and action in urban public space.* New York: Basic Books.

Loos, K. (2000). *Die Inszenierung der Stadt. Planen und Bauen im Nationalsozialismus in Weimar.* Doctoral thesis in engineering, Weimar: Bauhaus–Universität Weimar.

Löw, M. (2001). *Raumsoziologie.* Frankfurt am Main: Suhrkamp.

Low, S. (2006). The erosion of public space and the public realm: Paranoia, surveillance and privatization in New York City. *City and Society, 18*(1), 43–49.

Low, S., & Smith, N. (2006). *Politics of public space.* London: Routledge.

Lownsbrough, H., & Beunderman, J. (2007). *Equally spaced? Public space and interaction between diverse communities.* A Report for the Commission for Racial Equality. London: Demos.

Loyen, R. (2003). *Functieverschuivingen in de Antwerpse haven. Een macro-economische benadering (1901–2000).* Doctoral thesis, Leuven: Katholieke Universiteit Leuven.

Lussault, M. (2007). *L'homme spatial. La construction sociale de l'espace humain.* Paris: Seuil.

Lynch, K. (1960). *The image of the city.* Boston, MA: MIT Press.

MacKenzie, A. (2002). *Transductions: Bodies and machines at speed.* London: Continuum.

Madanipour, A. (1996). *Design of urban space: An inquiry into a socio-spatial process.* London: John Wiley & Sons.

Madanipour, A. (1999). Why are the design and development of public spaces significant for cities? *Environment and Planning B: Planning and Design, 26*(6), 879–891.

Madanipour, A. (2003a). *Cities actions against social exclusion.* Brussels: Eurocities.

Madanipour, A. (2003b). *Public and private spaces of the city.* London: Routledge.

Madanipour, A. (2004). Marginal public spaces in European cities. *Journal of Urban Design, 9*(3), 267–286.

Madanipour, A. (Ed.). (2010). *Whose public space? International case studies in urban development.* London: Routledge.

Madanipour, A. (2011a). *Knowledge economy and the city: Spaces of knowledge* London: Routledge.

Madanipour, A. (2011b). Living together or apart: Exclusion, gentrification and displacement. In T. Banerjee & A. Loukaitou-Sideris (Eds.), *Companion to urban design* (pp. 484–494). London: Routledge.

Madanipour, A. (2011c). Social exclusion and space. In R. T. LeGates & F. Stout (Eds.), *The city reader* (pp. 186–194). London: Routledge.

Madanipour, A. (2012). Ghetto. In S. J. Smith, M. Elsinga, L. F. O'Mahony, O. S. Eng, S. Wachter, & H. Lovell (Eds.), *International encyclopedia of housing and home* (Vol. 2, pp. 287–291). Oxford: Elsevier.

Madden, D. (2010). Revisiting the end of public space: Assembling the public in an urban park. *City & Community, 9,* 187–207.

Mäder, U. (2009). Draussen im Drinnen: Integration durch Ausschluss? In F. Kessl & H.-U. Otto (Eds.), *Soziale Arbeit ohne Wohlfahrtsstaat. Zeitdiagnosen, Problematisierungen und Perspektiven* (pp. 35–52). Munich: Juventa.

Mahmud, S., & Duyar-Kienast, U. (2001). Spontaneous settlements in Turkey and Bangladesh: Preconditions of emergence and environmental quality of gecekondu settlements and bustees. *Cities 18*(4), 271–280.

Mangin, D. (2004). *La ville franchisée—Formes et structures de la ville contemporaine.* Paris: Editions de la Villette.

Manley, D., van Ham, M., & Doherty, J. (2011). *Social mixing as a cure for negative neighbourhood effects: Evidence based policy or urban myth?* (Discussion Paper No. 5634). Bonn: Forschungsinstitut zur Zukunft der Arbeit.

Marchart, O. (2010). *Die politische Differenz.* Frankfurt am Main: Suhrkamp.

Marcuse, P. (2005). Enclaves yes, ghettos no. In D. Varady (Ed.), *Desegregating the city: Ghettos, enclaves, and inequality.* Albany: State University of New York Press.

Marcuse, P. (2009). From critical urban theory to the right to the city. *City, 13*(2–3), 185–197.

Margalit, G. (2002). Der Luftangriff auf Dresden. Seine Bedeutung für die Erinnerungspolitik der DDR und für die Herauskristallisierung einer Kriegserinnerung im Westen. In S. Düwell & M. Schmidt (Eds.), *Narrative der Shoah, Repräsentationen der Vergangenheit in Historiographie, Kunst und Politik* (pp. 189–207). Paderborn, Munich, Vienna, Zürich: Schöningh.

Massey, D. (1994). *Space, place, and gender.* Minneapolis: University of Minnesota Press.

Massey, D. (2007). *World city.* Cambridge, UK: Polity.

Massey, D., & Denton, N. (1993). *American apartheid: Segregation and the making of the underclass.* Cambridge, MA: Harvard University Press.

Massumi, B. (2002). *Parables for the virtual: Movement, affect, sensation.* Durham, NC: Duke University Press.

Mauss, M. (1950). Essai sur le don. Forme et raison de l'échange dans les sociétés archaïques. *Année sociologique, nouvelle série, I (1923–1924)*, pp. 30–186.

Mayer, M. (2008). To what end do we theorize socio-spatial relations? *Environment and Planning D: Society and Space, 26,* 414–419.

Mazza, L. (2007). *Redesigning citizenship.* Unpublished paper presented at the Isocarp Conference, Antwerpen, November.

Mazzoleni, D. (1990). City and the imaginary. *New Formations, 11,* 91–104.

McInroy, N. M. (2000). Urban regeneration and public space: The story of an urban park. *Space and Polity, 4*(1), 23–40.

McNeill, D. (2011). Fine grain, global city: Jan Gehl, public space and commercial culture in central Sidney. *Journal of Urban Design, 16*(2), 161–178.

MediaSpreeVersenken. (2011). Retrieved from http://www.ms-versenken.org

Meer, N., & Modood, T. (2011). How does interculturalism contrast with multiculturalism? *Journal of Intercultural Studies, 33*(2), 175–196.

Meng, M. (2011). *Shattered spaces: Encountering Jewish ruins in postwar Germany and Poland.* Cambridge, MA: Harvard University Press.

Menzl, M. (2010). Reurbanisierung? Zu-zugsmotive und lokale Bindungen der neuen Innenstadtbewohner. Das Beispiel der HafenCity Hamburg. In A. Dittrich-Wesbuer, W. Knapp, & F. Osterhage (Eds.), *Post-Suburbanisierung und die Renaissance der Innenstaedte—neue Entwicklungen in der Stadtregion.* Dortmund: Rohn-Verlag.

Merleau-Ponty, M. (1945). *Phénoménologie de la perception.* Paris: Gallimard.

Metrozones. (2008). *Saloon 1.* Retrieved from http://www.metrozones.info/mZ%20Saloons/ Saloons.htm#Saloon1

Metz, H. C. (1995). *Turkey: A country study.* Washington, DC: GPO for the Library of Congress.

Meyer, H. (1999). *City and port: Urban planning as a cultural venture in London, Barcelona, New York, and Rotterdam. Changing relations between public urban space and large scale infrastructure.* Utrecht: International Books.

Michel, B. (2005). *Stadt und Gouvernementalität.* Münster: Westfälisches Dampfboot.

Milgram, S. (2010). The familiar stranger: An aspect of urban anonymity. In S. Milgram & T. Blass (Eds.), *The individual in a social world: Essays and experiments* New York: McGraw-Hill.

Miller, K. (2007). *Designs on the public: The private lives of New York's public spaces.* Minneapolis: University of Minnesota Press.

Ministerium für Aufbau der Deutschen Demokratischen Republik. (1950). *Der Städtebau in der Deutschen Demokratischen Republik. Ein Beitrag zum deutschen Aufbau.* Berlin: Deutscher Zentralverlag.

Minton, A. (2009). *Ground control. Fear and happiness in the twenty-first century city.* London: Penguin.

Mitchell, D. (1995). The end of public space? People's park definitions of the public and democracy. *Annals of the Association of American Geographers, 85,* 108–133.

Mitchell, D. (2003). *The right to the city: Social justice and the fight for public space.* New York: Guilford.

Moniac, F. (2010). Das Rollfeld wird flügge: Tempelhofer Park. Retrieved from http://www.spreeblick.com/2010/05/28/das-rollfeld-wird-flugge-tempelhofer-park

Monnier, M. (1863). *La Camorra: Notizie storiche raccolte e documentate* (3rd ed.) Florence: G. Barbera.

Morales, A. (2009). Public markets as community development tools. *Journal of Planning Education and Research, 28,* 426–440.

Morgan, A., Dale, H., Le, W., & Edwards, P. (2010). Deaths of cyclists in London: Trends from 1992 to 2006. *BMC Public Health, 10*(1), article 699.

Morrisey, M., & Gaffikin, F. (2006). Planning for peace in contested space. *International Journal of Urban and Regional Research, 30*(4), 873–893.

Münk, D. (1993). *Die Organisation des Raumes im Nationalsozialismus. Eine soziologische Untersuchung ideologisch fundierter Leitbilder in Architektur, Städtebau und Raumplanung des Dritten Reich.* Bonn: Pahl-Rugenstein.

Munoz, F. (2003). Lock living: Urban sprawl in Mediterranean cities. *Cities, 20*(6), 381–385.

Museum of the History of Polish Jews. (2011). *Urban Space Project.* Retrieved from http://www.jewishmuseum.org.pl/en/cms/project-/

Musterd, S. (2003). Segregation and integration: A contested relationship. *Journal of Ethnic and Migration Studies, 29,* 623–641.

Musterd, S., & Ostendorf, W. (2007). Spatial segregation and Integration in the Netherlands. In K. Schönwälder (Ed.), *Residential segregation and the integration of immigrants: Britain, the Netherlands and Sweden* (pp. 7–40) (Discussion Paper No. SP IV 2007–602). Berlin: Wissenschaftszentrum Berlin für Sozialforschung (WZB).

Nasar, J. L. (1998). *The evaluative image of the city.* Thousand Oaks, CA: Sage.

National Association of British Markets Authorities (NABMA). (2005). *National retail markets survey.* Oswestry: Author.

Németh, J. (2009). Defining a public: The management of privately owned public space. *Urban Studies, 46*(11), 2463–2490.

Neuwirth, R. (2005). *Shadow cities: A billion squatters, a new urban world.* New York: Routledge.

Neuwirth, R. (2007). *Robert Neuwirth on our 'shadow cities'.* TED Talks. Retrieved from http://www.ted.com/talks/robert_neuwirth_on_our_shadow_cities.html

Novy, A., Redak, V., Jäger, J., & Hamedinger, A. (2001). The end of red Vienna. Recent ruptures and continuities in urban governance. *European Urban and Regional Studies, 8*(2), 131–144.

ODPM. (2006, March). *UK presidency, EU ministerial informal on sustainable communities, policy papers.* London: Office of the Deputy Prime Minister.

OEBB Online. (2010). *Vienna main station. More than just a train station.* Vienna: ÖBB-Infrastructure Corporation and the Vienna City Administration for Urban Planning and Development (MA 18). Retrieved from http://hauptbahnhof-wien.at/de/Presse/Publikationen/Folder/VIENNA_CENTRAL_STATION_Imagefolder_engl.pdf

OEBB Online. (2012). *Facts and figures.* Vienna: ÖBB-Infrastruktur AG. Retrieved from http://www.hauptbahnhof-wien.at/de/Presse/Publikationen/Folder/Faktenblatt_August_2012.pdf

OEBB Online. (2013). *The masterplan for the Vienna main station urban development project.* Vienna: ÖBB-Infrastruktur AG. Retrieved from http://hauptbahnhof-wien.at/de/Planungen/Stadtentwicklungsplan/Masterplan/index.jsp

OECD. (2008). *Growing unequal? Income distribution and poverty in OECD countries.* Paris: Author.

Oldenburg, R. (1989). *The great good place: Cafes, coffee shops, community centers, beauty parlors, general stores, bars, hangouts, and how they get you through the day.* New York: Paragon House.

Orum, A. M., & Zachary, N. (2010). *Common ground? Readings and reflections on public space.* London: Routledge.

Ossowski, S. (1967). Odbudowa Warszawy w świetle zagadnień społecznych [Rebuilding of Warsaw in light of societal concerns]. *Dzieła: Z zagadnień psychologii społecznej, 3,* 391–415. Warsaw: Państwowe Wydawnictwo Naukowe.

Ozdemir, I. M., & Gencosmanoglu, A. B. (2007). Metamorphism in culture and housing design: Turkey as an example. *Building and Environment, 42,* 1445–1452.

Ozsoy, A., Altas, N. E., Ok, V., & Pulat, G. (1996). Quality assessment model for housing: A case study on outdoor spaces in Istanbul. *Habitat International, 20*(2), 163–173.

Palermo, P. C., & Ponzini, D. (2010). *Spatial planning and urban development. Critical perspectives.* Dordrecht: Springer.

Palumbo, M. (2009a). Construire une autre goutte d'or? Histoire d'une rehabilitation par images, entre medias du passee et medias du futur. In A. De Biase & M. Coralli (Eds.), *Espaces en commun. Nouvelles formes de penser et habiter la ville.* Paris: L'Harmattan.

Palumbo, M. (2009b). *Figures de l'habiter, modes de négociation du pluralisme à Barbès ou de l'alterité comme condition quotidienne* (Lieux Communs Cahiers numéro 12). Nantes: ENSA.

Parkinson, J. (2011). *Democracy and public space: The physical sites of democratic performance.* Oxford: Oxford University Press.

Paul, J. (1992). Dresden: Suche nach der verlorenen Mitte. In K. von Beyme & H. Berger (Eds.), *Neue Städte aus Ruinen: deutscher Städtebau der Nachkriegszeit* (pp. 313–333). Munich: Prestel.

Peach, C. (1996). Does Britain have ghettos? *Transactions of the Institute of British Geographers,* New Series, 21, pp. 216–235.

Peach, C. (2007). Sleepwalking into ghettoisation? The British debate over segregation. In K. Schönwälder (Ed.), *Residential segregation and the integration of immigrants: Britain, the Netherlands and Sweden* (pp. 7–40) (Discussion Paper No. SP IV 2007–602). Berlin: Wissenschaftszentrum Berlin für Sozialforschung (WZB).

Pettigrew, T. (1998). Intergroup contact theory. *Annual Review of Psychology, 49,* 65–85.

Pfaller, R. (2008). *Das schmutzige Heilige und die reine Vernunft. Symptome der Gegenwartskultur.* Frankfurt am Main: Fischer Taschenbuch.

Pfaller, R. (2011). *Wofür es sich zu leben lohnt. Elemente materialistischer Philosophie.* Frankfurt am Main: Fischer.

Piotrowski, I. (2007). *Chłodna: Wielkość i zapomnienie warszawskiej ulicy w świetle literatury pięknej, wspomnień i fotografii [Chłodna: The grandeur and obscurity of a Warsaw street in light of literature, memoirs and photography].* Warsaw: TRIO.

Pirhofer, G., & Stimmer, K. (2007). Pläne für Wien—Theorie und Praxis der Wiener Stadtplanung 1945 bis 2005. *Perspektiven-Heft 1–2/2007.* Retrieved from http://www.wien.gv.at/stadtentwicklung/grundlagen/pdf/planungsgeschichte.pdf

Plachta, E. (2003). *Census 2001—Key findings.* London: Borough of Hackney.

Planning Aid for London (PAL). (2005). *Cohesive housing report.* London: Planning Aid for London.

Pressman, J. L., & Wildavsky, A. (1973). *Implementation. How great expectations in Washington are dashed in Oakland or, why it's amazing that federal programs work at all?* Berkeley: University of California Press.

Putnam, R. D. (2007). E pluribus unum: Diversity and community in the twenty-first century. The 2006 Johan Skytte Prize Lecture. *Scandinavian Political Studies, 30,* 137–174.

Raco, M. (2003). Remaking place and securitising space: Urban regeneration and the strategies, tactics and practices of policing in the UK. *Urban Studies, 40,* 1869–1887.

Rajk, L. (2011). *Regulations and the market.* Lecture at the A Market for Every District: Food, Consumption, Urbanism Conference, Budapest, March 19.

Ranci, C. (2011). Competitiveness and social cohesion in western European cities. *Urban Studies, 48*(13), 2789–2804.

Rancière, J. (2011). The thinking of dissensus: Politics and aesthetics. In P. Bowman & R. Stamp (Eds.), *Reading Rancière.* New York: Continuum.

Rath, J. (2011, January 6). Debating multiculturalism: Europe's reaction in context. *Harvard International Review.* Retrieved from http://hir.harvard.edu

Rehberg, K. S. (2002). Das Canaletto-Syndrom; Dresden, als imaginäre Stadt. *Ausdruck und Gebrauch— Dresdner wissenschaftliche Halbjahresheft. Architektur Wohnen Umwelt, 1,* 78–88.

Rehberg, K. S. (2004). Vor-Bilder für ein Gesellschaftsprojekt. In R. Lindner, C. Mennicke, & S. Wagler (Eds.), *Kunst im Stadtraum—Hegemonie und Öffentlichkeit* (pp. 43–69). Dresden: DRESDENPostplatz.

Reiners, D., Malli, G., & Reckinger, G. (2006). *Bürgerschreck Punk. Lebenswelten einer unerwünschten Randgruppe.* Vienna: Löcker.

Ricœur, P. (1984). *Time and narrative.* Chicago: University of Chicago Press.

Riis, J. (1890). *How the other half lives: Studies among the tenements of New York.* New York: Scribner.

Rogers, P., & Coaffee, J. (2005). Moral panics and urban renaissance. *City, 9,* 321–340.

Rolshoven, J. (2003). Von der Kulturraum- zur Raumkulturforschung. Theoretische Herausforderungen an eine Kultur- und Sozialwissenschaft des Alltags. *Zeitschrift für Volkskunde, 99,* 189–213.

Rolshoven, J. (2010, March). Cultural studies in architecture. *Newsletter, 2*(2), 2–3. Retrieved from http://www.iacsa.eu

Rose, N. (2008). Governing cities, govering citizens. *Zeitschrift für Stadtforschung, 31*, 13–20.

Roskamm, N. (2011). *Dichte: Eine transdisziplinäre Dekonstruktion. Diskurse zu Stadt und Raum*. Bielefeld: Transcript.

Roskamm, N. (2012). Das Reden vom Raum. *Peripherie, 125/126*, 171–189.

Rossberg, I., & Tiedt, H.-G. (1990). Leitideen für die Stadtentwicklung Dresdens. *Bauwelt, 48*, 2426–2428.

RWI, DIFU, NEA, & PRAC. (2010). *Second state of European cities report*. Brussels: European Commission.

Sadeh, E. (2010). *Politics of public space: A survey*. London: Routledge.

Salamon, L. (2002). *The tools of government*. New York: Oxford University Press.

Sales, I., & Ravveduto, M. (2006). *Le strade della violenza. Malviventi e bande di camorra a Napoli*. Naples: L'Ancora del Mediterraneo.

Sampieri, A. (2011). *L'abitare collettivo*. Milan: FrancoAngeli.

Sandercock, L. (1998). *Towards cosmopolis: Planning for multicultural cities*. London: John Wiley.

Sandercock, L. (2000). Cities of (in)difference and the challenge for planning. *disP — The Planning Review, 36*(140), 7–15.

Sansot, P. (2009). *Variations Paysagères*. Paris: Payot & Rivages.

Sassen, S. (1991). *The global city: New York, London, Tokyo*. Princeton, NJ: Princeton University Press.

Saviano, R. (2006). *Gomorra. Viaggio nell'impero economico e nel sogno di dominio della Camorra*. Milan: Arnoldo Mondadori.

Schmid, C. (2010). *Stadt, Raum und Gesellschaft*. Stuttgart: Franz Steiner.

Schmidt-Tomczak, S. (2010). War *alles nur* Schau. *Die Inszenierung von Warschaus Stadtlandschaft [War-Saw: Staging the Urban Landscape]*. Paper presented at the International Symposium Gewalt und Theatralität, Heinrich Heine Universität, Düsseldorf, April 15–17.

Schmitz, F. (1997). *Flughafen Tempelhof*. Berlin: be.bra.

Schönwälder, K. (Ed.). (2007). *Residential segregation and the integration of immigrants: Britain, the Netherlands and Sweden* (Discussion Paper Nr. SP IV 2007–602). Berlin: Wissenschaftszentrum Berlin für Sozialforschung (WZB).

Schreiber, V. (2005). Regionalisierung von Unsicherheit in der kommunalen Kriminalprävention. In G. Glasze, R. Pütz, & M. Rolfes (Eds.), *Diskurs—Stadt – Kriminalität. Städtische (Un)Sicherheiten aus der Perspektive von Stadtforschung und Kritischer Kriminalgeographie* (pp. 74–79). Bielefeld: transcript, pp. 59–103.

Seiß, R. (2010, December 3.). Urbanistische Ödnis. Die neue rot-grüne Regierung Wiens ringt um eine städtebauliche Wende. *Neue Zürcher Zeitung Online*. Retrieved from http://www.nzz.ch/aktuell/feuilleton/uebersicht/urbanistische-oednis-1.8545733

Seiß, R. (2013). *Wer baut Wien? Hintergründe und Motive der Stadtentwicklung Wiens seit 1989* (4th ed.). Salzburg: Pustet.

Sennett, R. (1994). *Flesh and stone*. New York: Norton.

Sennett, R. (2008). *Verfall und Ende des öffentlichen Lebens. Die Tyrannei der Intimität*. Berlin: Berliner Taschenbuch.

Sennett, R. (2006a). *The culture of the new capitalism*. New Haven, CT: Yale University Press.

Sennett, R. (2006b). *The open city: The closed system and the brittle city*. London: Urban Age.

Sennett, R. (2010). The public realm. In G. Bridge & S. Watson (Eds.), *The Blackwell city reader* (pp. 261–272). Chichester: Blackwell.

SenStadt. (2008). Ergebnis Volksentscheid: Keine Mehrheit für die Offenhaltung THF—Nachnutzung kann beginnen. Retrieved from http://www.berlin.de/flughafen-tempelhof/discoursemachine.php?page=detail&id_item=9843

SenStadt. (2010). Parklandschaft Tempelhof. Berlin: Senatsverwaltung für Stadtentwicklung. Auslobung.

Senyapili, T. (1978). *Bütünleşmemiş Kentli Nüfus Sorunu*. Ankara, Turkey: ODTÜ, Mimarlęk Fakültesi.

Senyapili, T. (2004). Charting the 'voyage' of squatter housing in urban spatial 'quadruped'. *European Journal of Turkish Studies, 1*, 1–19.

Sewing, W. (2002). Berlin—vom Mythos zur Metropole? In H. Berking & R. H. Faber (Eds.), *Städte im Globalisierungsdiskurs* (pp. 97–111). Würzburg: Königshausen und Neumann.

Shaftoe, H. (2008). *Convivial urban spaces. Creating effective public places*. London: Earthscan.

Siebel, W. (2004). *Die europäische Stadt [The European city]*. Frankfurt am Main: Suhrkamp.

Siebel, W. (2010). Die Zukunft der städte. *Aus Politik und Zeitgeschichte, Das Parlament, 17*, 3–9.

Siebolt, S. (2010, October 10). Merkel says German multiculturalism has failed. *REUTERS.* Retrieved from http://www.reuters.com

Siegel, A. (2005) Introduction. In A. Siegel (Ed.), *Market hall. Expiration date: To be determined* (pp. 105–107). Budapest: Ernst Múzeum.

Siegel, A. (2011). *Consumption and Open-Air Food Markets.* Lecture at the 'A market for every district: Food, consumption, urbanism' conference, Hungarian Contemporary Architecture Centre, Budapest, March 19.

Sienkiewicz, K. (2010). *Agnieszka Kurant. Culture.* (Trans. Katarzyna Różańska). Last updated by Agnieszka Le Nart, April 2012. Retrieved from http://www.culture.pl/web/english/resources-visual-arts-full-page/-/eo_event_asset_publisher/eAN5/content/agnieszka-kurant

Sík, E., & Wallace, C. (1999). The development of open-air markets in east-central Europe. *International Journal of Urban and Regional Research, 23*(4), 697–714.

Silk, M., & Amis, J. (2006). Bursting the tourist bubble: Sport and the spectacularisation of urban space. In H. Gibson (Ed.), *Sport Tourism: Paradigms and Theories.* London: Frank Cass.

Silverstone, R., & Hirsch, E. (1992). *Consuming technologies: Media and information in domestic spaces.* London: Routledge.

Simmel, G. (1984). Die Grossstädte und das Geistesleben. In Wagenbach-Verlag (Eds.), *Das Individuum und die Freiheit. Essais* (pp. 192–204). Berlin: Wagenbach.

Simmel, G. (1990). Digression sur l'étranger. In Y. Grafmeyer, & I. Joseph, (Eds.), *L'école de Chicago—naissance de l'écologie urbaine.* Paris: Aubier

Simmel, G. (1997). The sociology of space. In D. Frisby & M. Featherstone (Eds.), *Simmel on culture: Selected writings* (pp. 137–174). London: Sage.

Simon, P. (1998). L'intégration au quartier à l'epreuve de la rénovation. In N. Haumont, J.-P. Lévy, & M.-H. Bacqué (Eds.), *La ville éclatée: quartiers et peuplement* (pp. 193–208). Paris: L'Harmattan.

Simpson, P. (2011). Street performance and the city: Public space, sociality, and intervening in the everyday. *Space and Culture, 14*(4), 415–430.

Smith, N. (1996). *The new urban frontier: Gentrification and the revanchist city.* London: Routledge.

Smithsimon, G. (2008). Dispersing the crowd: Bonus plazas and the creation of public space. *Urban Affairs Review, 43*(3), 325–351.

Somma, P. (1991). *Spazio e razzismo.* Milan: Francoangeli.

Sorkin, M. (1992). *Variations on a theme park: The new American city and the end of public space.* New York: Hill and Wang.

Steiner, T. (2009). *Best-practice im öffentlichen Raum.* Lucerne: interact.

Stengers, I. (2005). The Cosmopolitical Proposal. In B. Latour & P. Weibel (Eds.), *Making things public: Atmospheres of democracy* (pp. 994–1003). Cambridge, MA: MIT Press.

Stenning, A., Smith, A., Rochovská, A., & Święek, D. (2010). *Domesticating neo-liberalism.* Oxford: Wiley.

Stevens, Q. T. (2007). *The ludic city: Exploring the potential of urban spaces.* London: Routledge.

Sutcliffe, T. (2001). Ditch pickings. *Time Out,* Issue 1611, July 4–11 2001.

Suykens, F. (1988). Op weg naar een Europese havenpolitiek? In L. Tricot (Ed.), *Liber Amicorum Lionel Tricot* (pp. 493–501). Antwerp: Kluwer Rechtswetenschappen.

Suykens, F., Asert, G., De Vos, A., Thijs, A., & Veraghtert, K. (1986). *Antwerp—a port for all seasons.* Antwerp: Ortelius.

Szalai, A. (2005). The changing world of the market and market hall. In A. Siegel (Ed.), *Market hall. Expiration date: To be determined* (pp. 145–153). Budapest: Ernst Múzeum.

Szimpla. (2012). Retrieved from http://www.szimpla.hu

Tajfel, H. (1982). Social psychology of intergroup relations. *Annual Review of Psychology, 33,* 1–29.

Tas, H. I., & Lightfoot, D. R. (2005). Gecekondu settlements in Turkey: Rural—urban migration in the developing European periphery. *Journal of Geography, 104*(6), 263–271.

Tatar, E. M. (2008, May 9). Fantomowe czucie miasta. Kilka słów o wspólnym projekcie Anny Baumgart i Agnieszki Kurant [Phantoms of the city: A few words about Anna Baumgart's and Angieszka Kurant's joint project]. *Obieg.* Retrieved from http://www.obieg.pl/teksty/7840#1

Terzi, F., & Fulin, B. (2005). *Does the upgrading plan help to improve squatter settlements? Case study: Kagithane, Istanbul.* Paper presented at The Dream of a Greater Europe—Association of European Schools of Planning (AESOP) Congress, Vienna, Austria, July 13–17.

THF. (2012). 100%Tempelhof. Retrieved from http://thf100.de

Thomas de la Pena, C. (2003). *The body electric: How strange machines built the modern American.* New York: New York University Press.

Thrift, N. (2005). But malice aforethought: Cities and the natural history of hatred. *Transactions of the Institute of British Geographers, 30*, 133–150.

Tibaijuka, A. (2005). *Keynote speech.* Paper presented at 22nd World Congress of the International Union of Architects—Cities: Grand Bazaar of Architectures, Istanbul, July 4–8.

Tolra, J. (2011). *Promoting markets: The Barcelona model.* Lecture at A Market for Every District: Food, Consumption, Urbanism Conference, Budapest, March 19.

Tonkiss, F. (2006), *Space, the city and social theory: Social relations and urban forms.* Cambridge, UK: Polity.

Toubon, J.-C., & Messamah, K. (1990). *Centralité immigrée. Le quartier de la Goutte d'Or, Paris.* Paris: Ciemi-L'Harmattan.

Trouillot, M.-R. (1995). *Silencing the past: Power and the production of history.* Boston, MA: Beacon.

Turgut, H. (2001). Culture, continuity and change: Structural analysis of the housing pattern in squatter settlement. *Global Built Environment Review, 1*(1), 17–25.

Turgut, H., Aksoy, M., Paker, N., Inceoglu, A., & Saglamer, G. (1995). *Home and street, relationship of home-street in squatter settlements and urbanization.* Paper presented at VII. International Building and Life Conference, Turkey.

Turgut-Yildiz, H., & Inalhan, G. (2007). *Cultural and spatial dynamics of Istanbul: New housing trends.* Paper presented at ENHR 2007 International Conference—Sustainable Urban Areas, Rotterdam, June 25–28.

Türker-Devecigil, P. (2005). Urban transformation projects as a model to transform gecekondu areas in Turkey: The example of Dikmen Valley—Ankara. *European Journal of Housing Policy, 5*(2), 211–229.

Türkoglu, H. (1997). Residents' satisfaction of housing environments: The case of Istanbul, Turkey. *Landscape and Urban Planning, 39*(1), 55–67.

Turner, V. (1964). Betwixt and between: The liminal period in rites de passage. In M. E. Spiro (Chair), *Symposium on New Approaches to the Study of Religion.* Seattle: American Ethnological Society.

Uitermark, J. (2003). Social mixing and the management of disadvantaged neighbourhood: The Dutch policy of urban restructuring revisited. *Urban Studies, 40*(3), 531–549.

United Nations Human Settlements Programme. (2012). *State of the world cities 2012/2013. Prosperity of cities.* Retrieved from http://www.unhabitat.org/pmss/listItemDetails.aspx?publicationID = 3387

Urban, T. (2010, January 8). Gedächtnislücke, ausgestellt [Memorial omission exhibited]. *Suddeutsche Zeitung.*

Urban Justice Center. (2011). Street vendor project. Retrieved from http://streetvendor.org

Urząd Dzielnicy Wola. (2010). Podsumowanie Konferencji—Prezentacja zrewitalizowanej ulicy Chłodnej [Conference summary—A presentation of revitalized Chłodna]. Retrieved from http://www.wola.waw.pl/page/index.php?str = 1371

Urząd Dzielnicy Wola. (2011a, September 15). Kercelak—otwarcie ulicy Chłodnej [Kercelak—Chłodna street opening]. Retrieved from

Urząd Dzielnicy Wola. (2011b). Mapa ulicy Chłodnej [Map of Chłodna Street]. Retrieved from http://www.przewodnik.wola.waw.pl/page/index.php?str = 1439

Urząd Dzielnicy Wola. (2011c). *Nasza Chlodna [Our Chłodna].* Bydgoszcz: Pomorska Oficyna Wydawniczo-Reklamowa.

Urzykowski, T. (2009, December 30). Gigantyczny wielokropek pamięci już wisi nad Chłodną [A gigantic ellipsis of memory hangs over Chłodna]. *Gazeta Wyborcza.* Retrieved from http://warszawa.gazeta.pl/warszawa/1,34880,7410198.html

Vadas, F. (2005). A surviving building type. In A. Siegel (Ed.), *Market hall. Expiration date: To be determined* (pp. 145–153). Budapest: Ernst Múzeum.

Vaiou, D., & Kalandides, A. (2009). Cities of 'others': Public space and everyday practices. *Geografica Helvetica, 1/2009*, 11–20.

Valentine, G. (2008). Living with difference: Reflections on geographies of encounter. *Progress in Human Geography, 32*(3), 323–337.

Van Acker, J. (1975). *Antwerpen—van Romeins veer tot wereldhaven.* Antwerp: Mercurius.

Vanderbilt, T. (2008). *Traffic: Why we drive the way we do.* New York: Vintage.

Van Hooydonk, E. (1996a). *Beginselen van havenbestuursrecht. Onderzoek naar de grondlagen en de draagwijdte van de havenbestuurlijke autonomie.* Brugge: Die Keure.

Van Hooydonk, E. (1996b). The legal aspects of the Hanseatic tradition. In L. Bekemans & S. Beckwith (Eds.), *Ports for Europe—Europe's maritime future in a changing environment* (pp. 347–378). Brugge: European Interuniversity Press.

VCA. (1994). Step 94, Stadtentwicklungsplan für Wien 1994. Beiträge zur Stadtforschung, Stadtentwicklung und Stadtgestaltung (Nummer 53), Stadt Wien, Magistratsabteilung 18 - Stadtentwicklung und Stadtplanung, Vienna: City of Vienna.

VCA. (2005). *StEP 05, Urban development plan Vienna 2005* (extended version in German). Vienna: Magistrat Department for Urban Development and Urban Planning (MA 18).

VCA. (2006). *Integration im öffentlichen Raum.* Vienna: Magistrat Department for Urban Development and Urban Planning (MA 18) in cooperation with Kon-Text and the Department of Spatial Development, Infrastructural and Environmental Planning, Vienna University of Technology.

VCA. (2008a). *Aspern airfield master plan. Executive summary.* Vienna: Magistrat Department for District Planning and Land Use (MA 21b) under the auspices of Aspern Airfield Project Team.

VCA. (2008b). *Neuinterpretation öffentlicher Raum. Eine Studienreihe für die Wiener Bezirke.* Vienna: Magistrat Department for Urban Development and Urban Planning (MA 18) under the auspices of Magistrat Department for Architecture and Urban Design (MA 19) in cooperation with Schwarzundschwarz Architekten.

VCA. (2009a). *FreiraumStadtraumWien. Vorsorge. Gestaltung. Management. Der Weg zum Leitbild für den öffentlichen Raum.* Vienna: Magistrat Department for Urban Development and Urban Planning (MA 18) under the auspices of Magistrat Department for Architecture and Urban Design (MA 19).

VCA. (2009b). *Öffentlicher Raum in Stadtentwicklungsgebieten.* Study elaborated by Raum2. Contracted by the Municipal Direction for Planning (MD-BD). Retrieved from http://www.raum2.at/projekte.php?id = 57

VCA. (2009c). *Partitur des öffentlichen Raumes. Planungshandbuch.* Vienna: Wien 3420 Aspern Development AG in cooperation with the Magistrat Department for Urban Development and Urban Planning (MA 18) and Gehl Architects ApS.

VCA. (2010). *Free Space Vienna Public Space. Provision, design, management. Mission statement for Vienna's public space.* Vienna: Magistrat Department for Urban Development and Urban Planning (MA 18).

VCA. (2011). *Stadtentwicklung Hauptbahnhof Wien Untersuchung des Stadtentwicklungsgebietes "Sonnwendviertel" im Hinblick auf seine Einbettung in die bestehende Stadtstruktur.* Study elaborated by Raum2. Contracted by the Municipal Department MA21B. Retrieved from http://www.raum2.at/projekte.php?id = 50

VCA. (forthcoming, 2013). *Werkstattbericht Wissensplattform Stadtentwicklung.* Study by the Institute for Local Planning, Vienna University of Technology. Vienna: The Magistrat Department for Urban Development and Urban Planning (MA 18).

VCA Online. (2011). *Statistical yearbook 2011* (in German). Retrieved from http://www.wien.gv.at/statistik/publikationen/jahrbuch-2011.html

VCA Online. (2012a). *Download summary of panel debate Schwedenplatz redesign from 19th June 2012* (in German). Retrieved from https://schwedenplatz.wien.gv.at/ppr19/schwedenplatz/files/2012/08/120619_Protokoll_Podiumsdiskussion_Zukunft_Schwedenplatz.pdf

VCA Online. (2012b). *Vienna central station.* Retrieved from http://www.wien.gv.at/english/transportation-urbanplanning/central-station.html

VCA Online. (2013a). *Neuer Stadtteil im Sonnwendviertel.* Retrieved from http://www.wien.gv.at/bauen-wohnen/sonnwendviertel.html

VCA Online. (2013b). Projekt Hauptbahnhof Wien. Retrieved from http://www.wien.gv.at/verkehr-stadtentwicklung/hauptbahnhof.html

VCA Online. (2013c). *UN-study: Vienna is the most prosperous city in the world.* Retrieved from http://www.wien.gv.at/english/politics-administration/un-study.html

VCA Online. (2013d) *Vienna charter. Shaping the future together.* Retrieved from http://www.wien.gv.at/english/living-working/vienna-charter.html

VCA Online. (2013e). *Zukunft Schwedenplatz.* Mischen Sie mit. Retrieved from https://schwedenplatz.wien.gv.at/ppr19/schwedenplatz

Vertovec, S., & Wessendorf, S. (Eds.). (2010). *The multiculturalism backlash. European discourses, policies and practices.* London: Routledge.

Vertovec, S. (2007a). *New complexities of cohesion in Britain: Super-diversity, transnationalism and civil-integration.* London: Commission on Integration and Cohesion.

Vertovec, S. (2007b). Super-diversity and its implications. *Ethnic and racial studies, 30*(6), 1024–1054.

Vitcbsky, P. (2006). *The reindeer people: Living with animals and spirits in Siberia.* London: Harper Collins.

Voisin, C. (2007). Le centre, la mémoire, l'identité. Des usages de l'histoire dans la (re)-construction du Nouveau marché de Dresde. *Espaces et sociétés, 130*(3), 87–101.

Voisin, C. (2008). Continuité? Rupture? Le difficile choix de la forme de la construction du centre-ville Dresde, Chemnitz, Magdeburg. In C. Vallat & F. Dufaux (Eds.), *Pérennité urbaine, ou la ville par-delà ses métamorphoses* (Vol. 1). Paris: L'Harmattan.

Voisin, C. (2011). *A Dresde, le rêve se conjugue au passé. La difficulté de Dresde pour redéfinir son identité lue à travers l'art public.* Bordeaux: Doc Géo.

Voisin, C. (2013). *La création de nouveaux espaces publics au centre de Dresde et de Chemnitz: Quels espaces pour quelle société?* (Dissertation). Université de Lyon/Technische Universität, Dresden.

Wark, M. (2011). *The beach beneath the street.* London: Verso.

Wasilkowska, A. (2010). Marketmeter. Retrieved from http://www.olawasilkowska.com/en-75-marketmeter.html

Watson, S. (2006). *City publics. The (dis)enchantments of public encounters.* London: Routledge.

Watson, S. (2009). The magic of the marketplace: Sociality in a neglected public space. *Urban Studies, 46*(80), 1577–1591.

Watson, S., & Studdert, D. (2006). *Markets as sites for social interaction.* Bristol: Policy Press/Joseph Rowntree Foundation.

Wehrheim, J. (2006). *Die überwachte Stadt – Sicherheit, Segregation und Ausgrenzung. 2. Auflage.* Opladen: Barbara Budrich.

Werlen, B. (2010). *Gesellschaftliche Räumlichkeit 2.* Stuttgart: Steiner.

Wessendorf, S. (2011). *Commonplace diversity and the 'ethos of mixing': Perceptions of difference in a London neighbourhood* (Working paper 91). Oxford: Centre on Migration, Policy and Society.

White, W. H. (1988). *City. Rediscovering the centre.* New York: Doubleday.

Whyte, W. H. (1980). *The social life of small urban spaces.* Washington, DC: The Conservation Foundation.

Wien 3420. (2012). *The project. Aspern. Vienna's urban lakeside* (4th ed.). Retrieved from http://www.aspern-seestadt.at/resources/files/2013/1/2/2851/bp12-das-projekt-en-final-web.pdf

Wien International Homepage. (2011). *Aspern urban lakeside: General public creates a city.* Retrieved from http://www.wieninternational.at/en/aktuell/vienna-charter-seven-points-for-vienna-en

Wien International Homepage. (2012). *Vienna charter: Seven points for Vienna.* Retrieved from http://www.wieninternational.at/en/aktuell/vienna-charter-seven-points-for-vienna-en

Will, T., & Schmidt, E. (2002). Vom Trugbild eines historischen Neumarktes. *Sächsische Zeitung,*(17 November), 16.

Wilson, E. (1992). *Sphinx in the city.* Berkeley: University of California Press.

Winter, E. (2011). Speech by city of Vienna representative for the Main Station Project. Retrieved from http://www.rosenstein-stuttgart.de/index.php?id=45

Wirth, L. (1938). Urbanism as a way of life. *The American Journal of Sociology, 44*(1), 1–24.

Wolf, C. (1999). *Gauforen. Zentren der Macht. Zur nationalsozialistischen Architektur und Stadtplanug.* Berlin: Berlin Verlag Bauwesen.

Wood, P. (Ed.). (2009). *Intercultural cities towards a model for intercultural integration.* Brussels: Council of Europe and European Commission.

Yalcintan, M., & Erbas, A. (2003). Impacts of 'gecekondu' on the electoral geography of Istanbul. *International Labor and Working-Class History, 64,* 91–111.

Yin, R. (2003). *Case study research: Design and methods* (3rd ed.). Thousand Oaks, CA: Sage.

Young, I. M. (1990). *Justice and the politics of difference.* Princeton, NJ: Princeton University Press.

Young, J. E. (1989). The biography of a memorial icon: Nathan Rapoport's Warsaw ghetto monument. *Representations, 26,* 69–106.

Young, J. E. (2000). *At memory's edge: After-images of the Holocaust in contemporary art and architecture.* New Haven, CT: Yale University Press.

Zanini, P. (1997). *Il significato dei confini* (4th ed.). Milan: Bruno Mondadori.

Zukin, S. (1991). *Landscapes of power. From Detroit to Disneyworld.* Berkeley: University of California Press.

Zukin, S. (1995). *The cultures of cities.* Oxford: Blackwell.

Zukin, S. (2008). Consuming authenticity. *Cultural Studies, 22*(5), 724–748.

Zukin, S. (2009). *Naked city: The death and life of authentic urban places.* Oxford: Oxford University Press.

Zyśk, D. (2005, February 11). Nowa inicjatywa na Woli [A new initiative in the Wola District]. *Życie Warszawy.* Retrieved from http://www.zyciewarszawy.pl/artykul/135419.html

# Index

Note: page numbers in italic type refer to figures; those in bold type refer to tables.